I remember writing in a grade school composition that I wanted to be a wizard when I grew up. Being a manga artist now, I do feel a little like a wizard. Joy!

– Yoshiyuki Nishi

Yoshiyuki Nishi was born in Tokyo. Two of his favorite manga series are *Dragon Ball* and the robot-cat comedy *Doraemon*. His latest series, *Muhyo & Roji's Bureau of Supernatural Investigation*, debuted in Japan's *Akamaru Jump* magazine in 2004 and went on to be serialized in *Weekly Shonen Jump*.

MUHYO & ROJI'S

BUREAU OF SUPERNATURAL INVESTIGATION

VOL. 8

The SHONEN JUMP Manga Edition

STORY AND ART BY
YOSHIYUKI NISHI

Translation & Adaptation/Alexander O. Smith
Touch-up Art & Lettering/Brian Bilter
Cover Design/Izumi Hirayama
Interior Design/Yukiko Whitley
Editor/Amy Yu

Editor in Chief, Books/Alvin Lu
Editor in Chief, Magazines/Marc Weidenbaum
VP, Publishing Licensing/Rika Inouye
VP, Sales and Product Marketing/Gonzalo Ferreyra
VP, Creative/Linda Espinosa
Publisher/Hyoe Narita

Printed in the U.S.A.

Published by VIZ Media, LLC
P.O. Box 77010
San Francisco, CA 94107

SHONEN JUMP Manga Edition
10 9 8 7 6 5 4 3 2 1
First printing, December 2008

THE WORLD'S
MOST POPULAR MANGA

www.viz.com

www.shonenjump.com

SHONEN JUMP MANGA EDITION

Muhyo & Roji's Bureau of Supernatural Investigation BSI

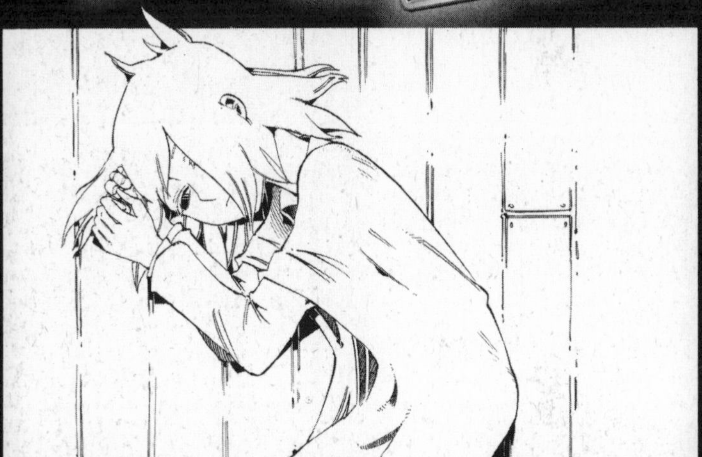

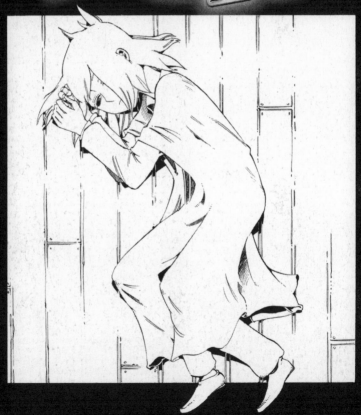

Vol. 8 Bonds

Story & Art by **Yoshiyuki Nishi**

Dramatis Personae

Jiro Kusano (Roji)

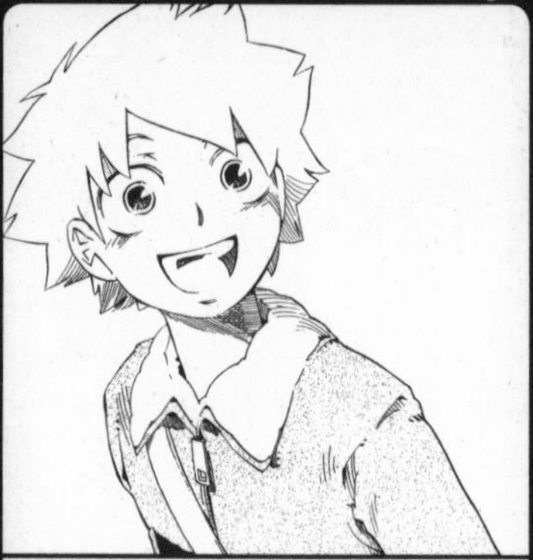

Assistant at Muhyo's office, recently promoted from the lowest rank of "Second Clerk" to that of (provisional) "First Clerk." Roji has a gentle heart and has been known to freak out in the presence of spirits. Lately, he has been devoting himself to the study of magic law so that he can pull his own weight someday.

Toru Muhyo (Muhyo)

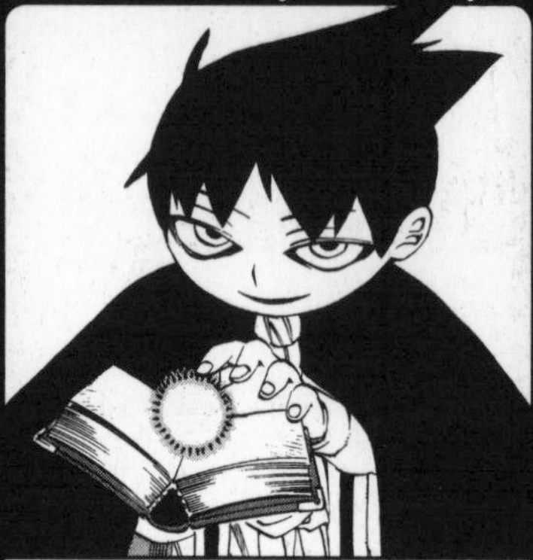

Young, genius magic law practitioner with the highest rank of "Executor." Always calm and collected (though sometimes considered cold), Muhyo possesses a strong sense of justice and even has a kind side. Sleeps a lot to recover from the exhaustion caused by his practice.

Yu Abiko (Biko)

Muhyo's classmate and an Artificer. Makes seals, pens, magic law books, and other accoutrements of magic law.

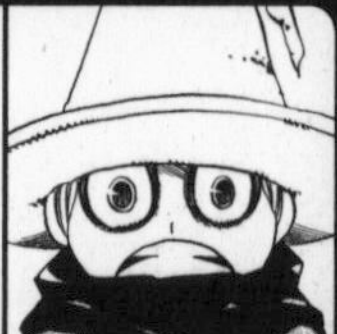

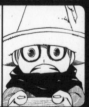

Yoichi Himukai (Yoichi)

Judge and Muhyo's former classmate. Expert practitioner of all magic law except execution.

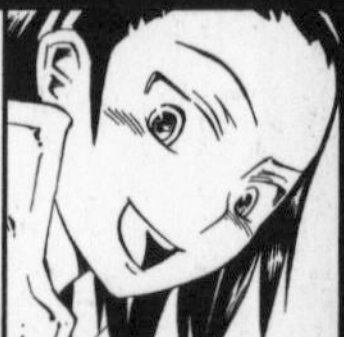

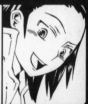

Rio Kurotori (Rio)

Charismatic Artificer who turned traitor when the Magic Law Association stood by and let her mother die.

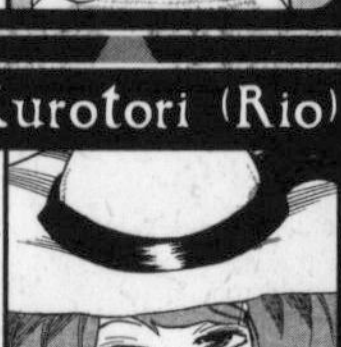

Soratsugu Madoka (Enchu)

Muhyo's former classmate and Executor-hopeful until one event turned him onto the traitor's path.

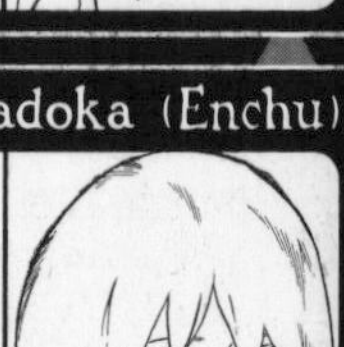

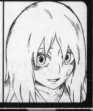

Hanao Ebisu (Ebisu)

Judge and Goryo's former underling, fired after his failure during the showdown against Muhyo at the haunted apartments.

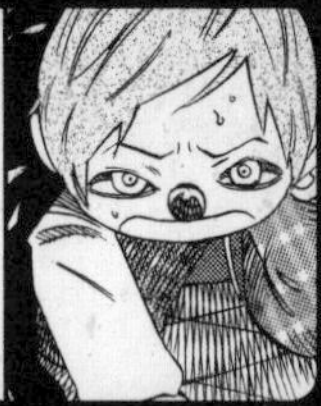

Daranimaru Goryo (Goryo)

An Executor and gifted strategist who considers Muhyo his rival. Head of the Goryo Group syndicate.

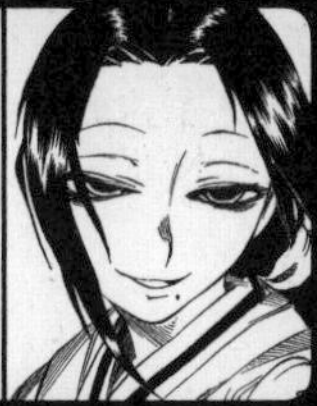

Reiko Imai

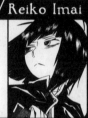

Brave judge who joined Muhyo and gang during the fight against Face-Ripper Sophie.

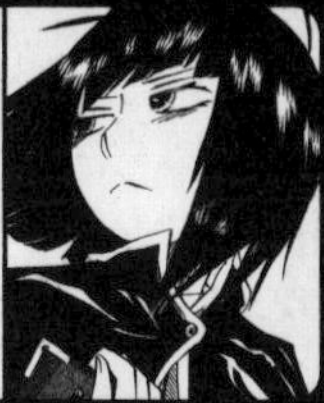

Tomas

Member of the forbidden magic law group "Ark." He has a twisted appreciation for beauty.

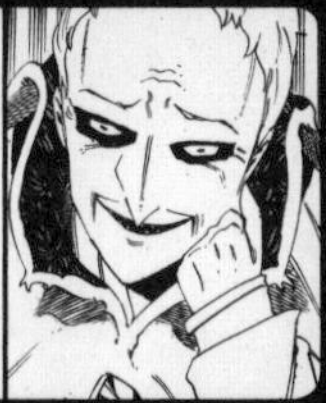

The Story

Magic law is a newly established practice for judging and punishing the increasing crimes committed by spirits; those who use it are called "practitioners."
After Muhyo forces him to go on leave, Roji participates in a Magic Law Academy retreat. The retreat turns into mayhem when powerful ghosts attack, but Roji prevails. Meanwhile, Muhyo seeks to form a contract with one of the lords of the underworld, Pluto, for which he must impress Pluto with his worth and power. Muhyo succeeds, but it wasn't easy. Muhyo and Roji are reunited, both surer of their own abilities than before. They'll need all they can muster to face the looming shadow of forbidden magic law.

Nana Takenouchi (Nana)

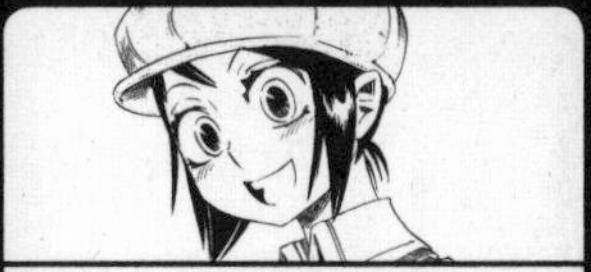

High school student, spirit medium and aspiring photographer. Working as an assistant photographic investigator.

Kiriko

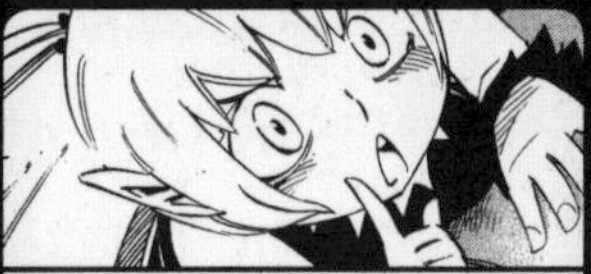

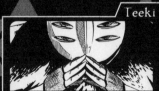

Envoy summoned to break Muhyo's contract with Pluto (which didn't end up happening).

Teeki

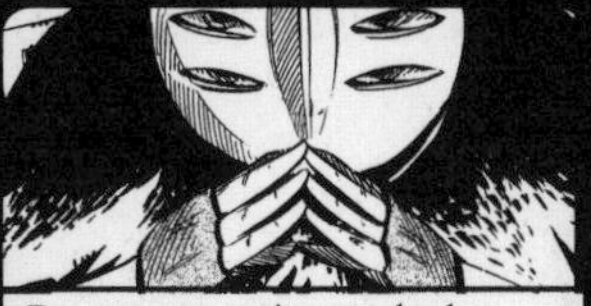

Dangerous entity marked as a traitor to the Magic Law Association for 800 years.

Muhyo & Roji's Bureau of Supernatural Investigation BSI

CONTENTS

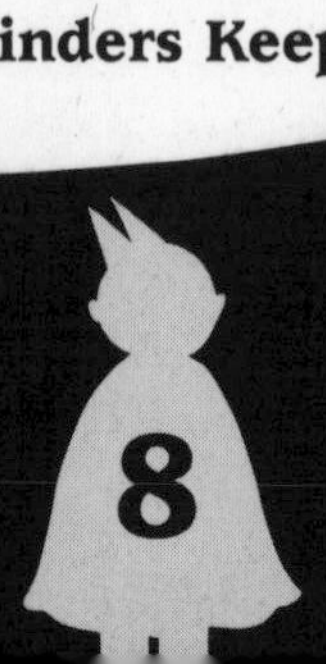

8

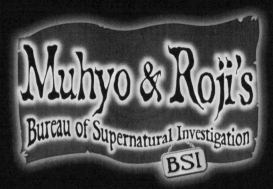

ARTICLE 60
TOMAS

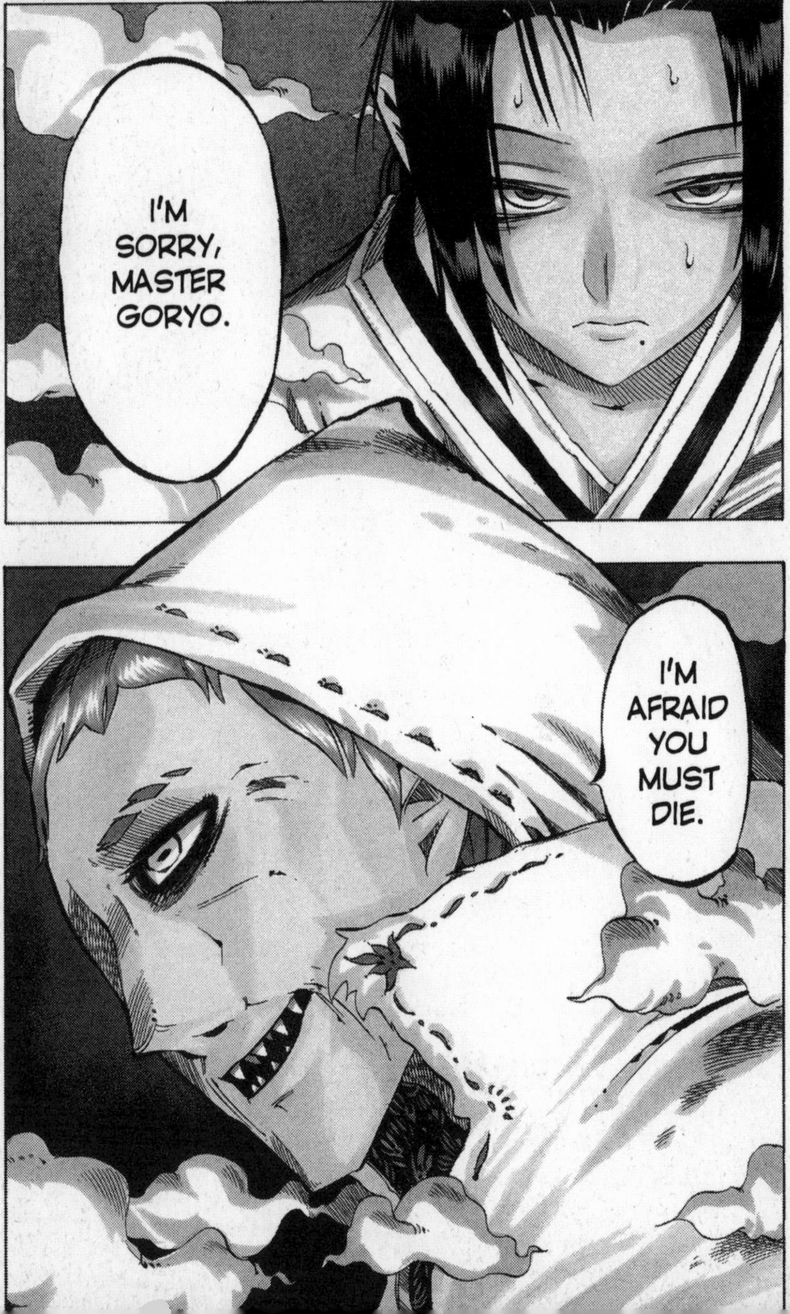
I'M SORRY, MASTER GORYO.
I'M AFRAID YOU MUST DIE.

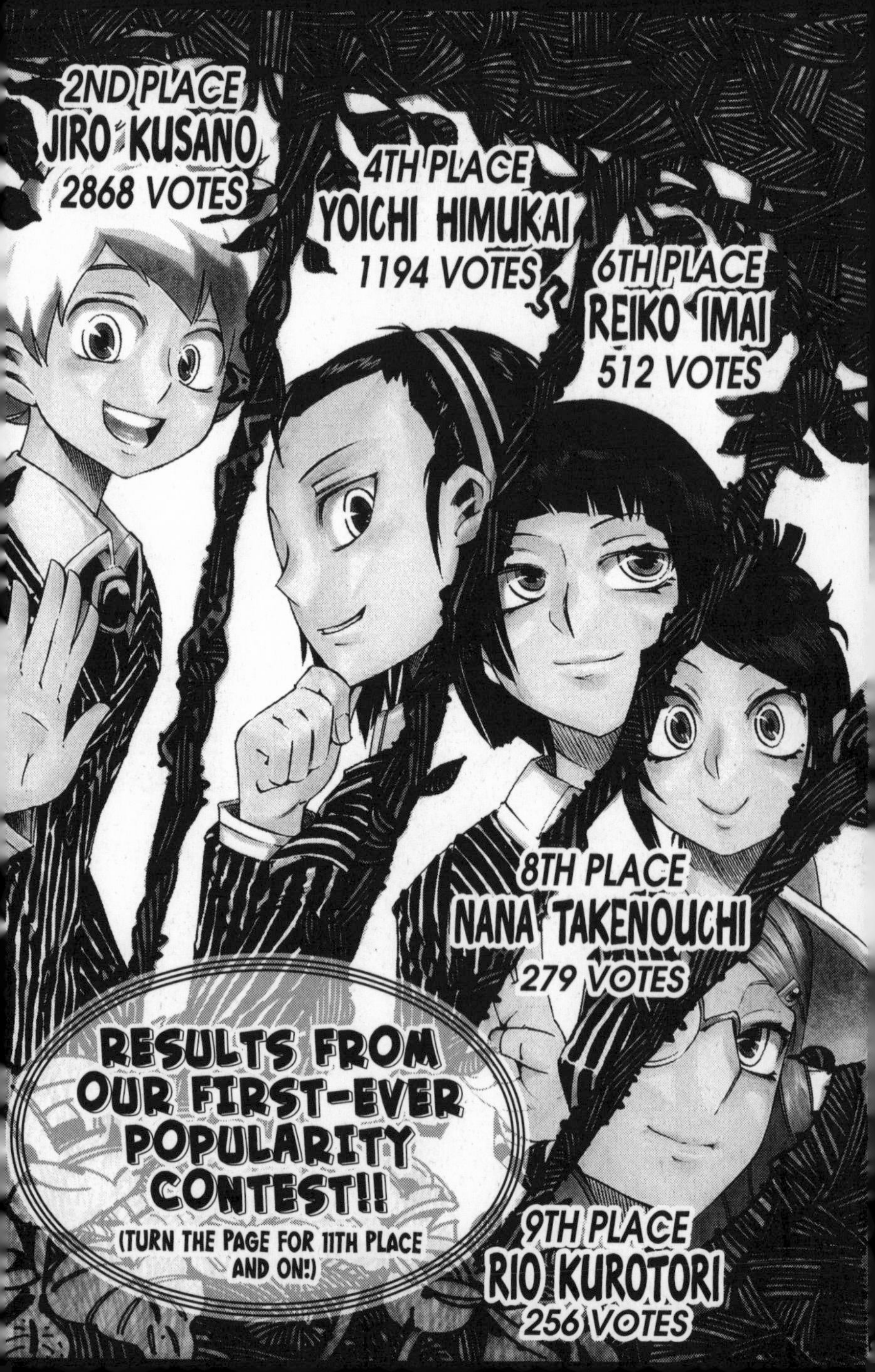
2ND PLACE
JIRO KUSANO
2868 VOTES
4TH PLACE
YOICHI HIMUKAI
1194 VOTES
6TH PLACE
REIKO IMAI
512 VOTES
8TH PLACE
NANA TAKENOUCHI
279 VOTES
RESULTS FROM OUR FIRST-EVER POPULARITY CONTEST!!
(TURN THE PAGE FOR 11TH PLACE AND ON!)
9TH PLACE
RIO KUROTORI
256 VOTES

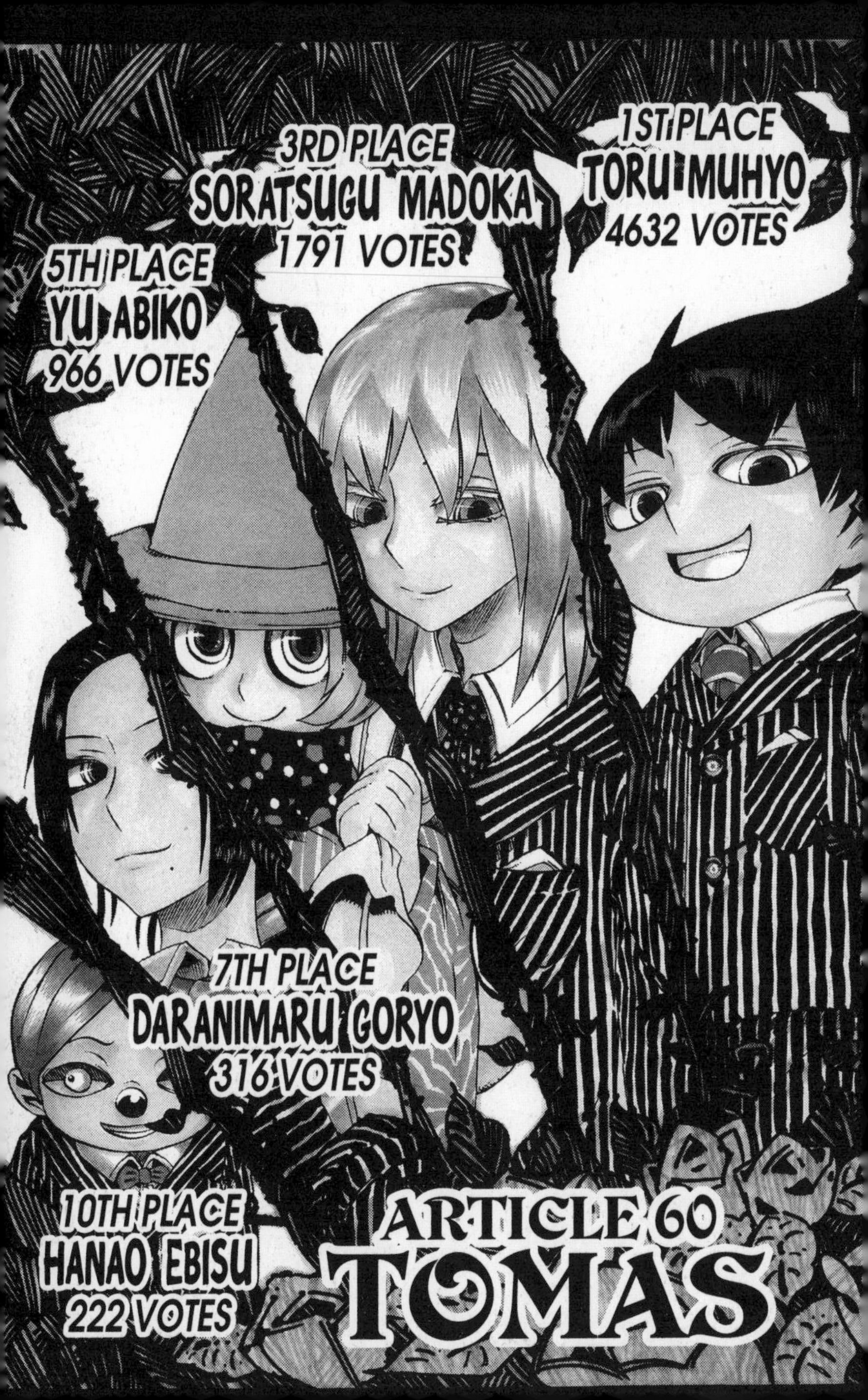
1ST PLACE
TORU MUHYO
4632 VOTES
3RD PLACE
SORATSUGU MADOKA
1791 VOTES
5TH PLACE
YU ABIKO
966 VOTES
7TH PLACE
DARANIMARU GORYO
316 VOTES
ARTICLE 60
TOMAS
10TH PLACE
HANAO EBISU
222 VOTES

1ST CHARACTER POPULARITY CONTEST RESULTS!!

11TH TO 46TH PLACE

21ST		GHOST-HAND STRIKE	**11TH**		PAGE KLAUS
22ND		TAEKO OKAZAKI	**12TH**		PLUTO LUALALIE
23RD		NEURO NOGAMI	**13TH**		LILI
24TH		RIE INOUE	**14TH**		YOSHIYUKI NISHI
25TH		KENJI SATO	**15TH**		SOPHIE
26TH		THE GIRL AT BIKO'S OFFICE	**16TH**		MARIL
27TH		THE OWL OF NO RETURN	**17TH**		ZANSETSU HIRATA
28TH		ASSISTANT JUDGE FUJIWARA	**18TH**		YUURI
29TH		MAGIRON MEN	**19TH**		TEEKI
30TH		ABEYUKI YONTANI	**20TH**		THE ADMIRAL BELOW

39TH The Hat-Shaped Haunt (Grudge)

40TH The Ghost on the Bridge

41ST Mr. Maeda

42ND Rikopin Man

43RD Sosei Okochi

44TH Goryo's Older Brother (?)

45TH The Ship Captain

46TH The Nightmare-Sucking Elephant (?!)

31ST The Curry Lady

32ND The Chair that Tried to Eat Roji

33RD Moto-Kyu

34TH Sophie's Sister

35TH Little Tomato

36TH Nana's Papa

37TH Nozomi

38TH Lurker in the Leaves

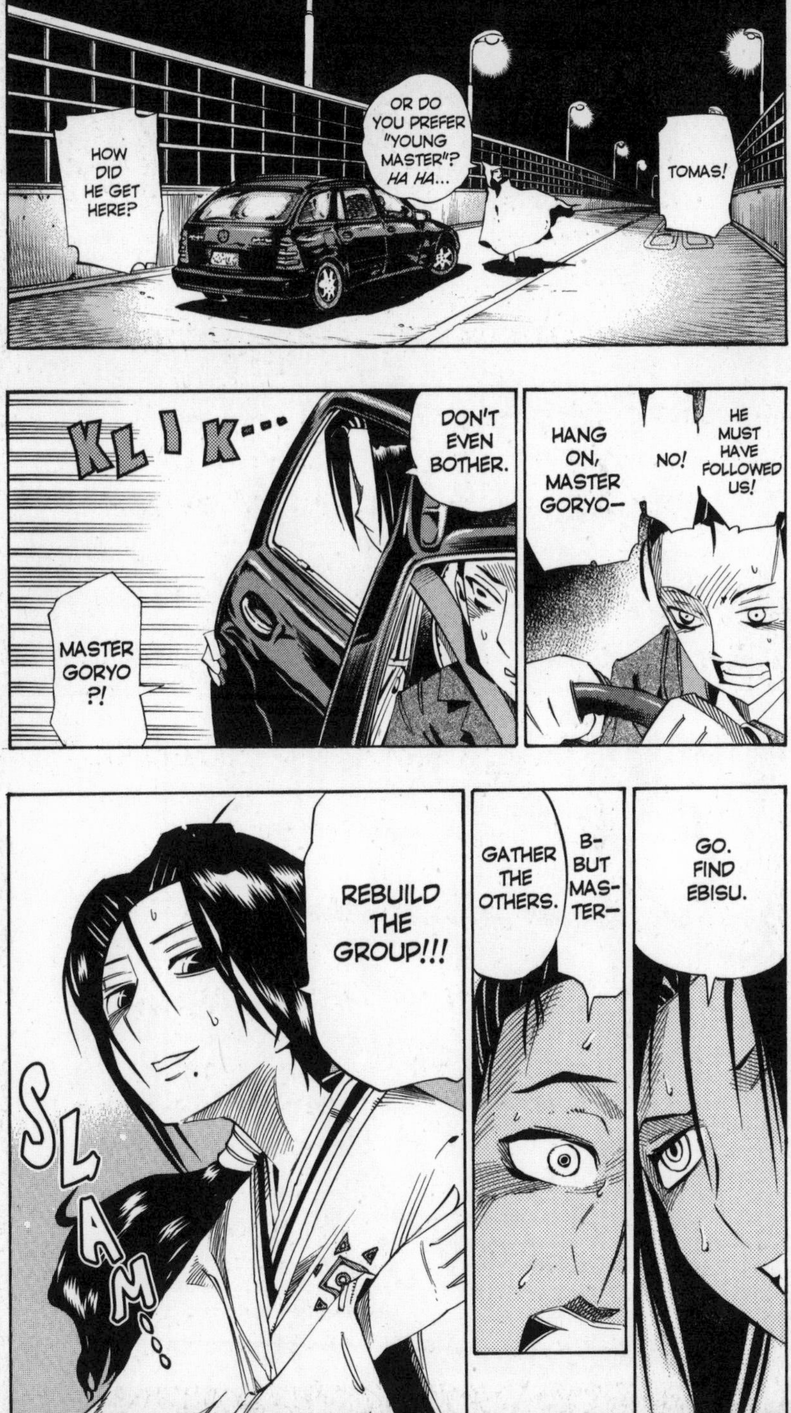
TOMAS!
OR DO YOU PREFER "YOUNG MASTER"? HA HA...
HOW DID HE GET HERE?
HE MUST HAVE FOLLOWED US!
NO!
HANG ON, MASTER GORYO—
DON'T EVEN BOTHER.
KLIK...
MASTER GORYO ?!
GO. FIND EBISU.
B-BUT MAS-TER—
GATHER THE OTHERS.
REBUILD THE GROUP!!!
SLAM...

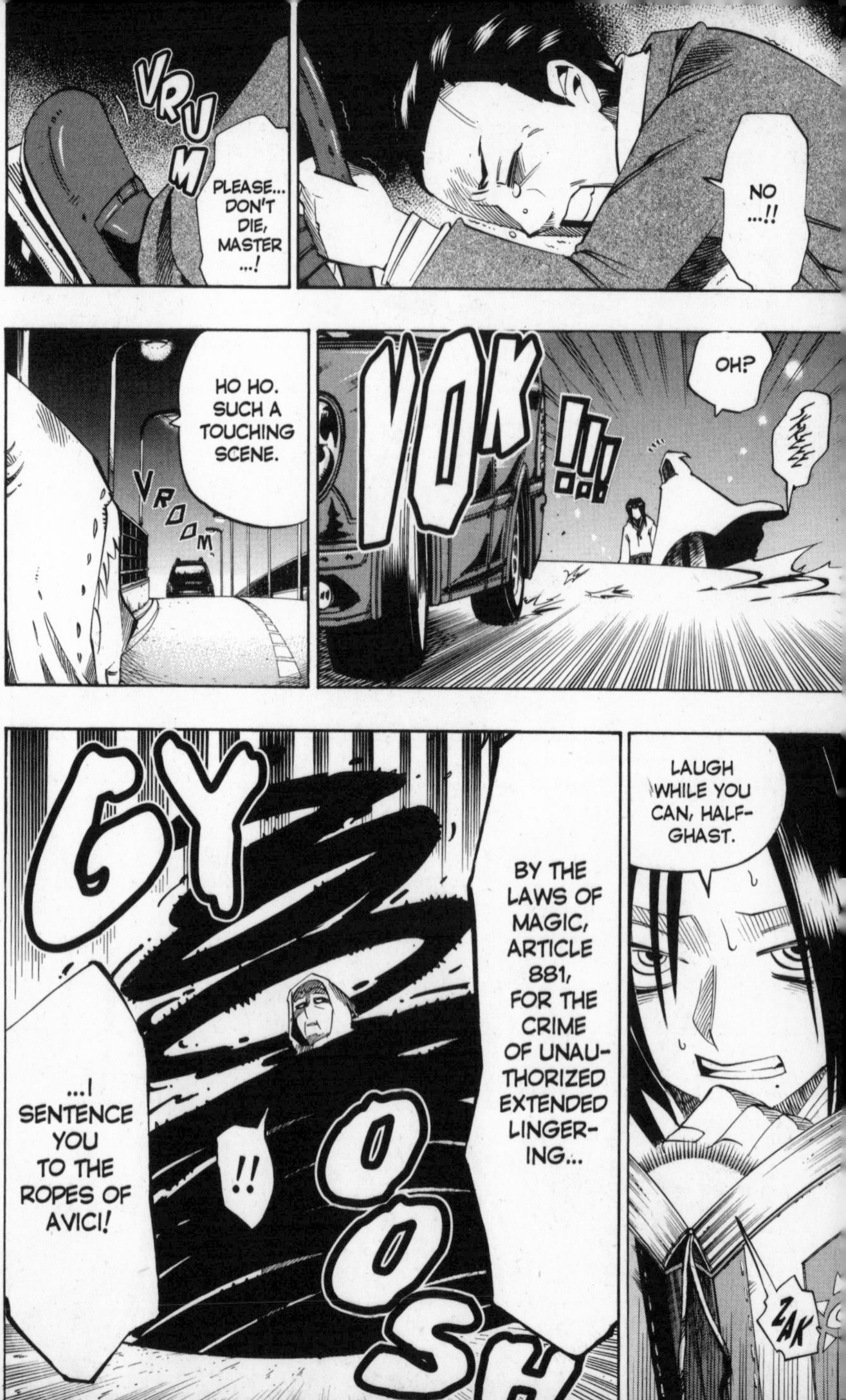
NO ...!!
VRUM
PLEASE... DON'T DIE, MASTER ...!
OH?
VOK !!!
HO HO. SUCH A TOUCHING SCENE.
VROOM
LAUGH WHILE YOU CAN, HALF-GHAST.
ZAK
BY THE LAWS OF MAGIC, ARTICLE 881, FOR THE CRIME OF UNAUTHORIZED EXTENDED LINGERING...
...I SENTENCE YOU TO THE ROPES OF AVICI!
!!
GYOOOSH

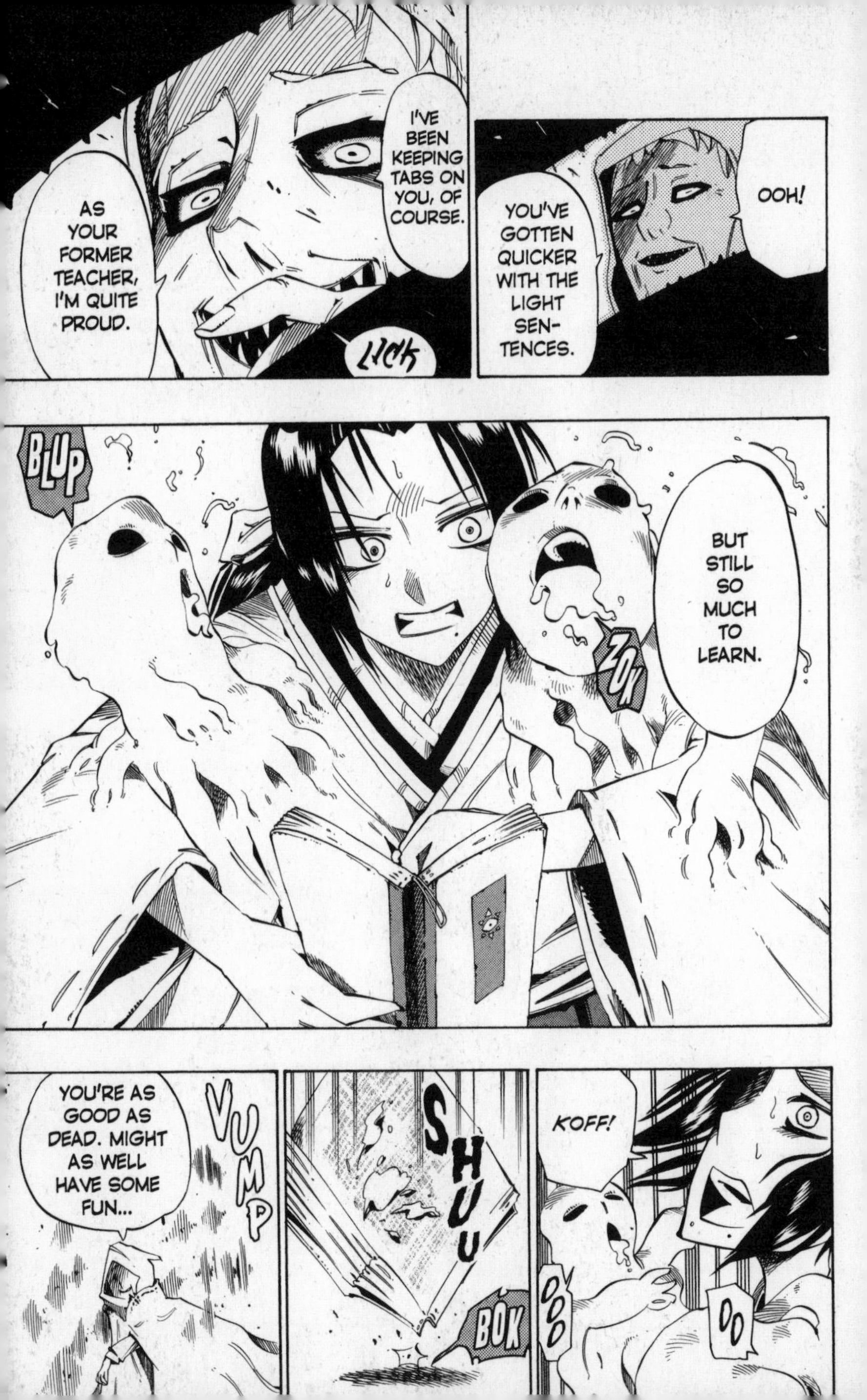
OOH!
YOU'VE GOTTEN QUICKER WITH THE LIGHT SEN-TENCES.
I'VE BEEN KEEPING TABS ON YOU, OF COURSE.
AS YOUR FORMER TEACHER, I'M QUITE PROUD.
LICK
BUT STILL SO MUCH TO LEARN.
ZOK
BLUP
KOFF!
OO
OOO
SHUUU
BOK
VUMP
YOU'RE AS GOOD AS DEAD. MIGHT AS WELL HAVE SOME FUN...

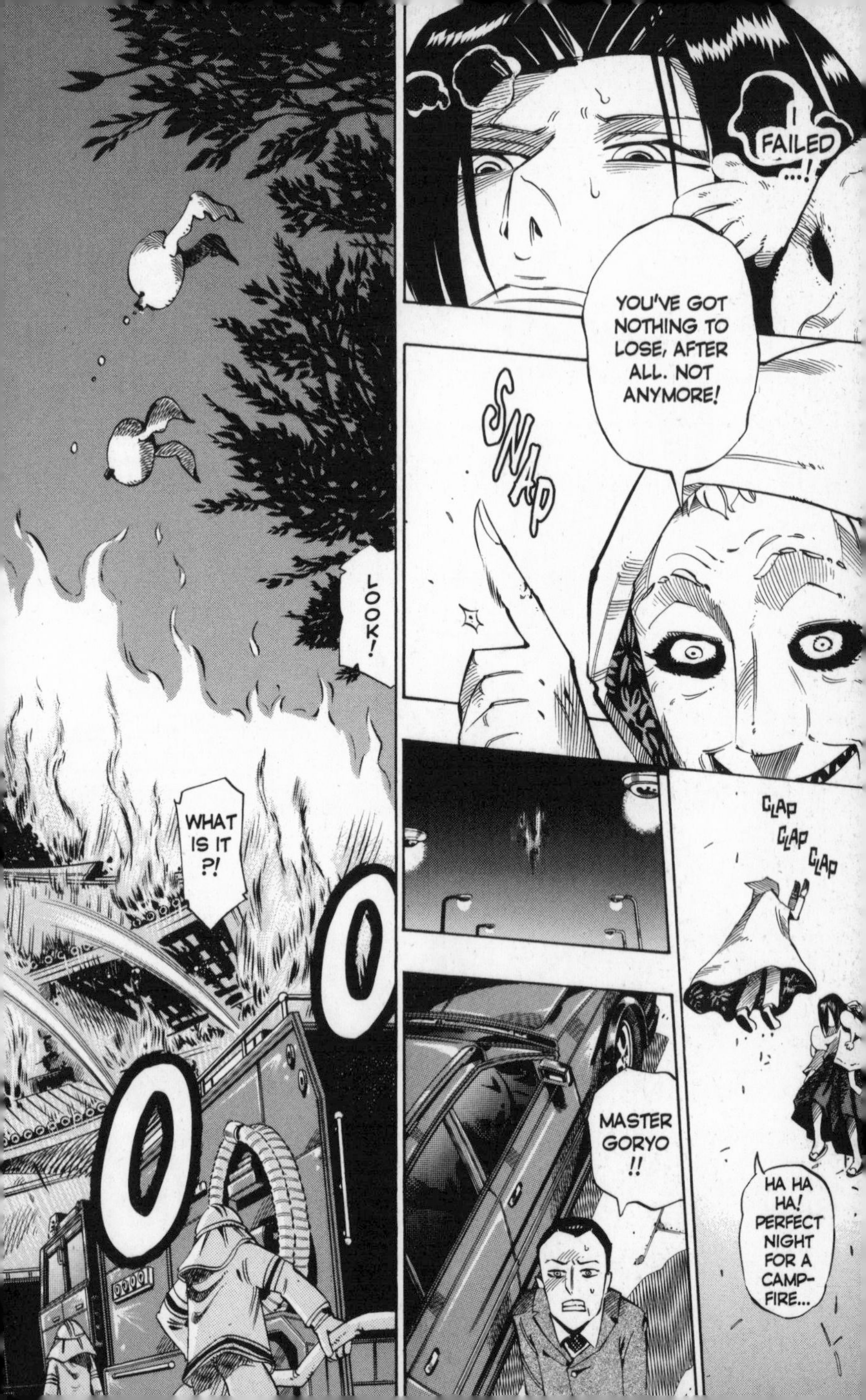
I FAILED ...!
YOU'VE GOT NOTHING TO LOSE, AFTER ALL. NOT ANYMORE!
SNAP
CLAP CLAP CLAP
HA HA HA! PERFECT NIGHT FOR A CAMP-FIRE...
MASTER GORYO !!
LOOK!
WHAT IS IT ?!

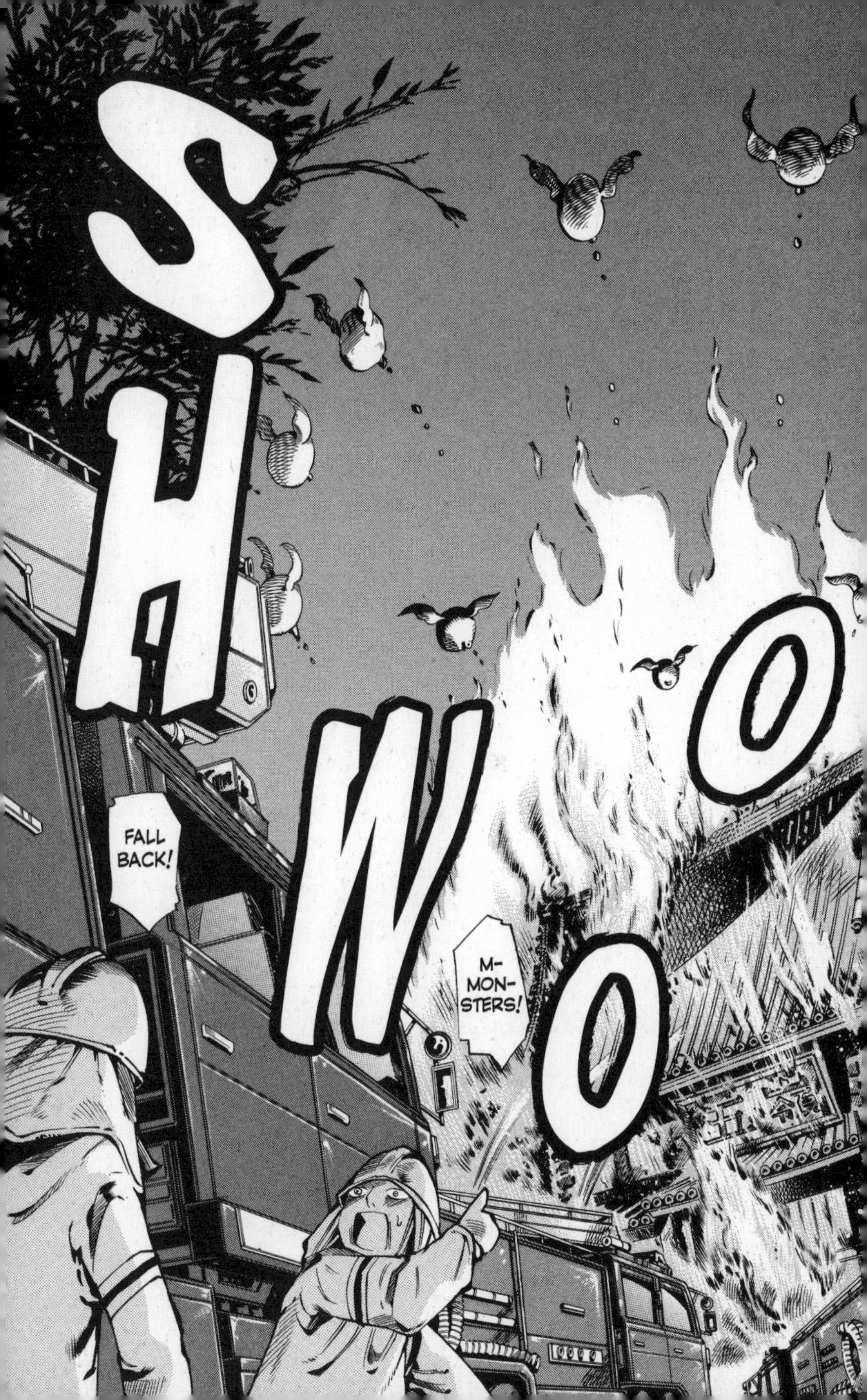
SHWOOO
M- MON- STERS!
FALL BACK!

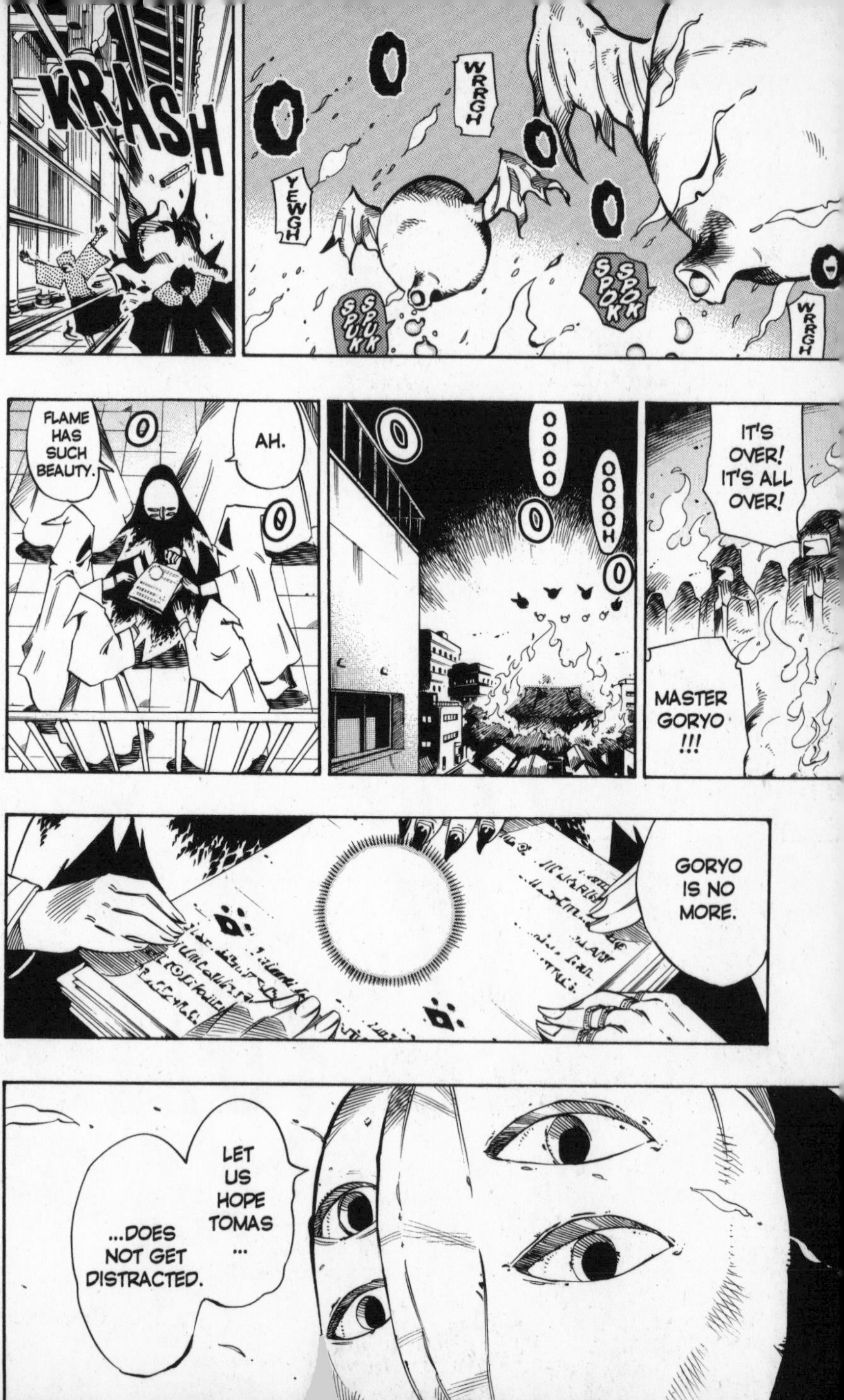
WRRGH
SPOK SPOK
WRRGH
YEWGH
SPUK SPUK
KRASH
IT'S OVER! IT'S ALL OVER!
MASTER GORYO!!!
OOOOH
OOOO
AH.
FLAME HAS SUCH BEAUTY.
GORYO IS NO MORE.
LET US HOPE TOMAS...
...DOES NOT GET DISTRACTED.

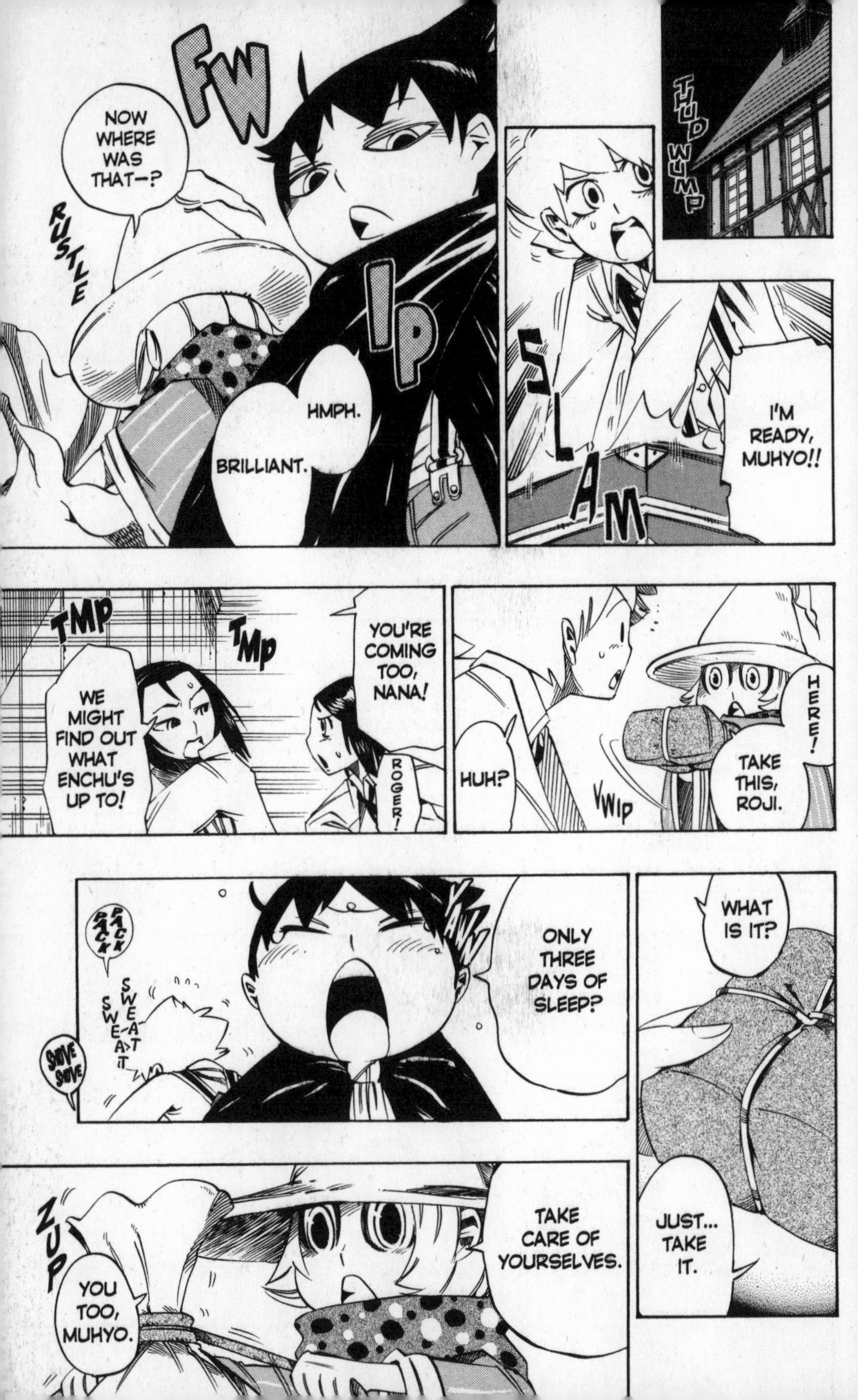
THUD WUMP
I'M READY, MUHYO!!
SLAM
FWIP
NOW WHERE WAS THAT—?
RUSTLE
HMPH.
BRILLIANT.
HERE!
TAKE THIS, ROJI.
VWIP
HUH?
YOU'RE COMING TOO, NANA!
ROGER!
TMP
TMP
WE MIGHT FIND OUT WHAT ENCHU'S UP TO!
WHAT IS IT?
JUST... TAKE IT.
YAWN
ONLY THREE DAYS OF SLEEP?
PACK PACK
SWEAT SWEAT
SHOVE SHOVE
TAKE CARE OF YOURSELVES.
ZUP
YOU TOO, MUHYO.

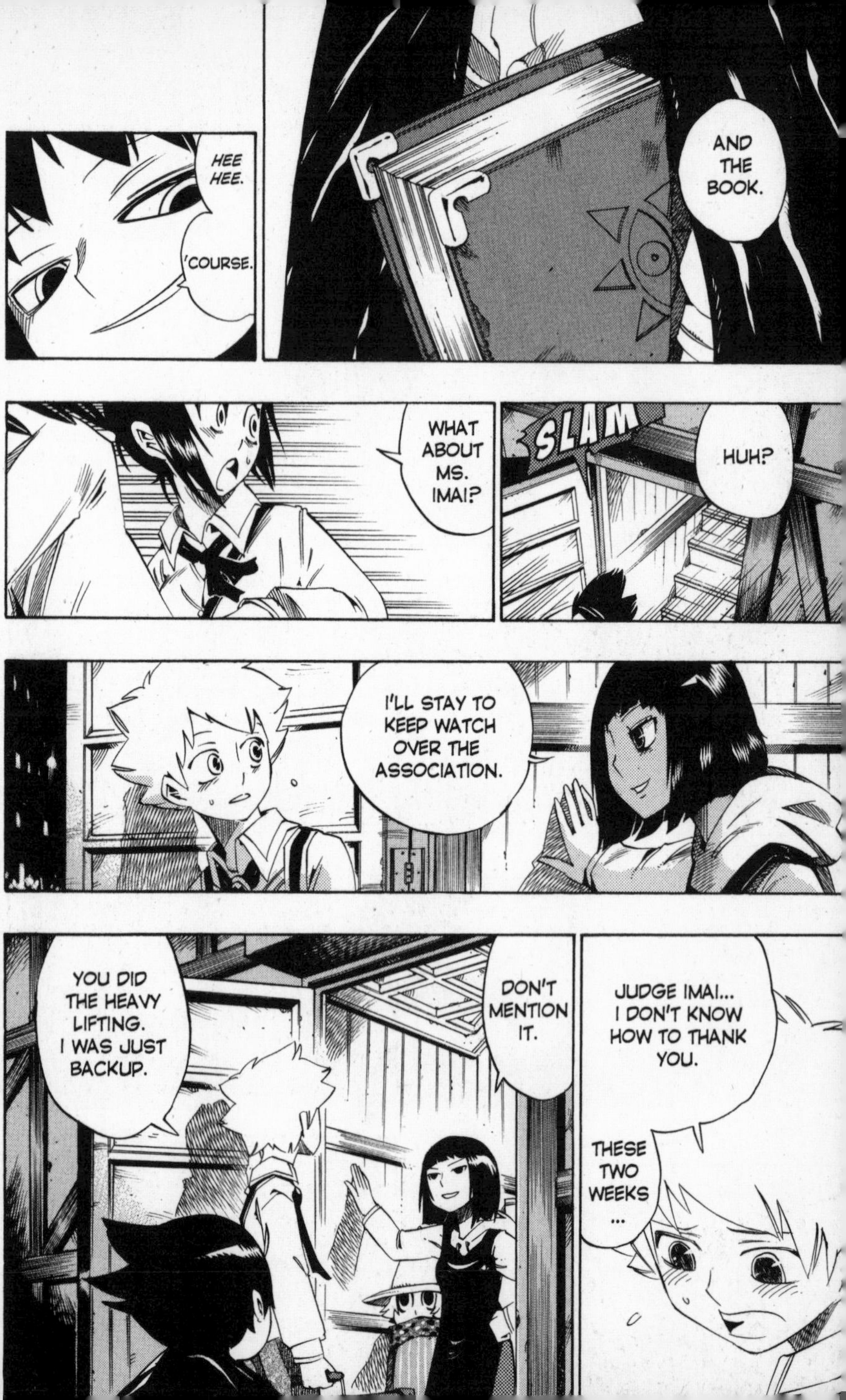
AND THE BOOK.
HEE HEE.
'COURSE.
SLAM
HUH?
WHAT ABOUT MS. IMAI?
I'LL STAY TO KEEP WATCH OVER THE ASSOCIATION.
JUDGE IMAI... I DON'T KNOW HOW TO THANK YOU.
THESE TWO WEEKS ...
DON'T MENTION IT.
YOU DID THE HEAVY LIFTING. I WAS JUST BACKUP.

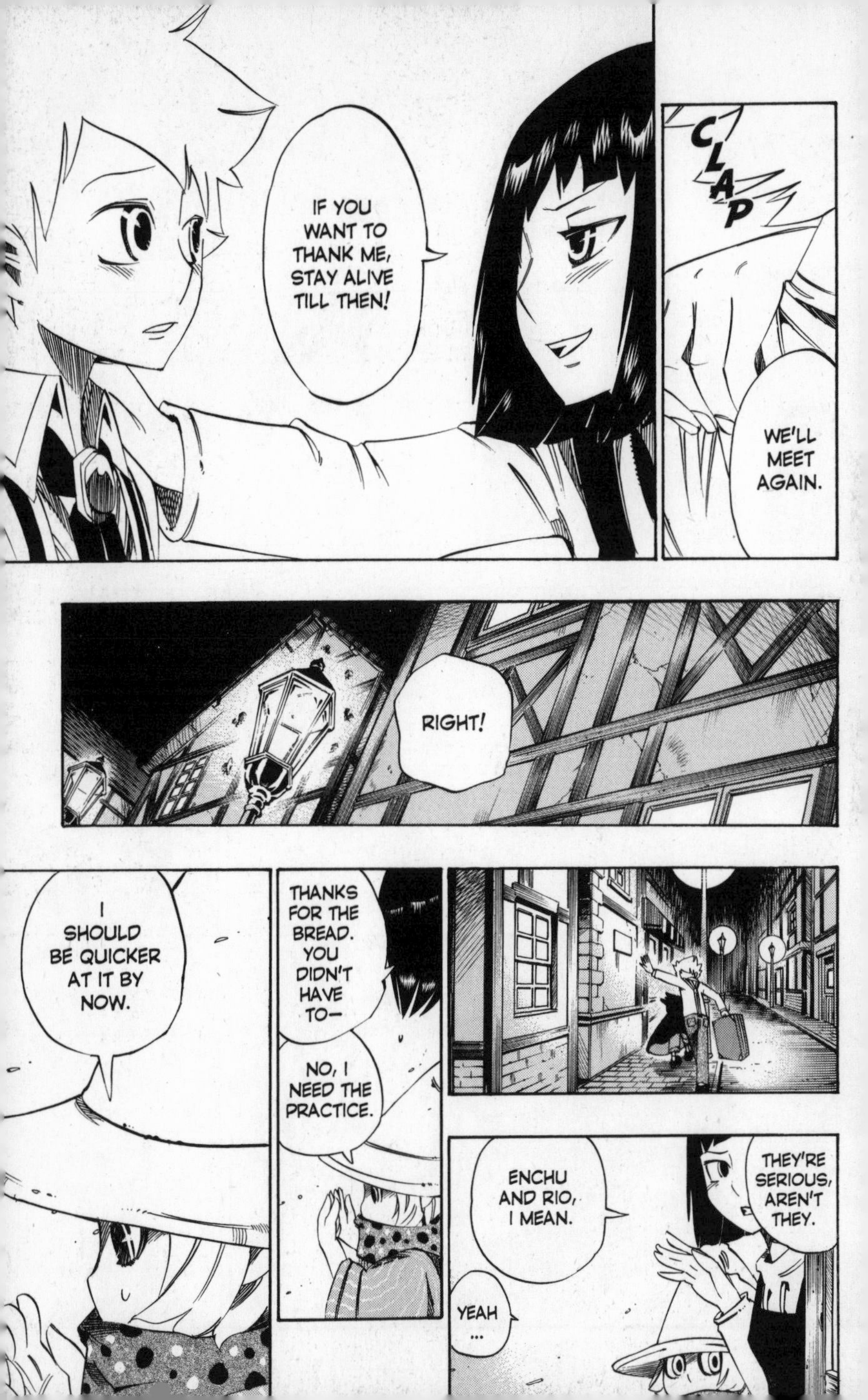
CLAP
WE'LL MEET AGAIN.
IF YOU WANT TO THANK ME, STAY ALIVE TILL THEN!
RIGHT!
THEY'RE SERIOUS, AREN'T THEY.
ENCHU AND RIO, I MEAN.
YEAH ...
THANKS FOR THE BREAD. YOU DIDN'T HAVE TO—
NO, I NEED THE PRACTICE.
I SHOULD BE QUICKER AT IT BY NOW.

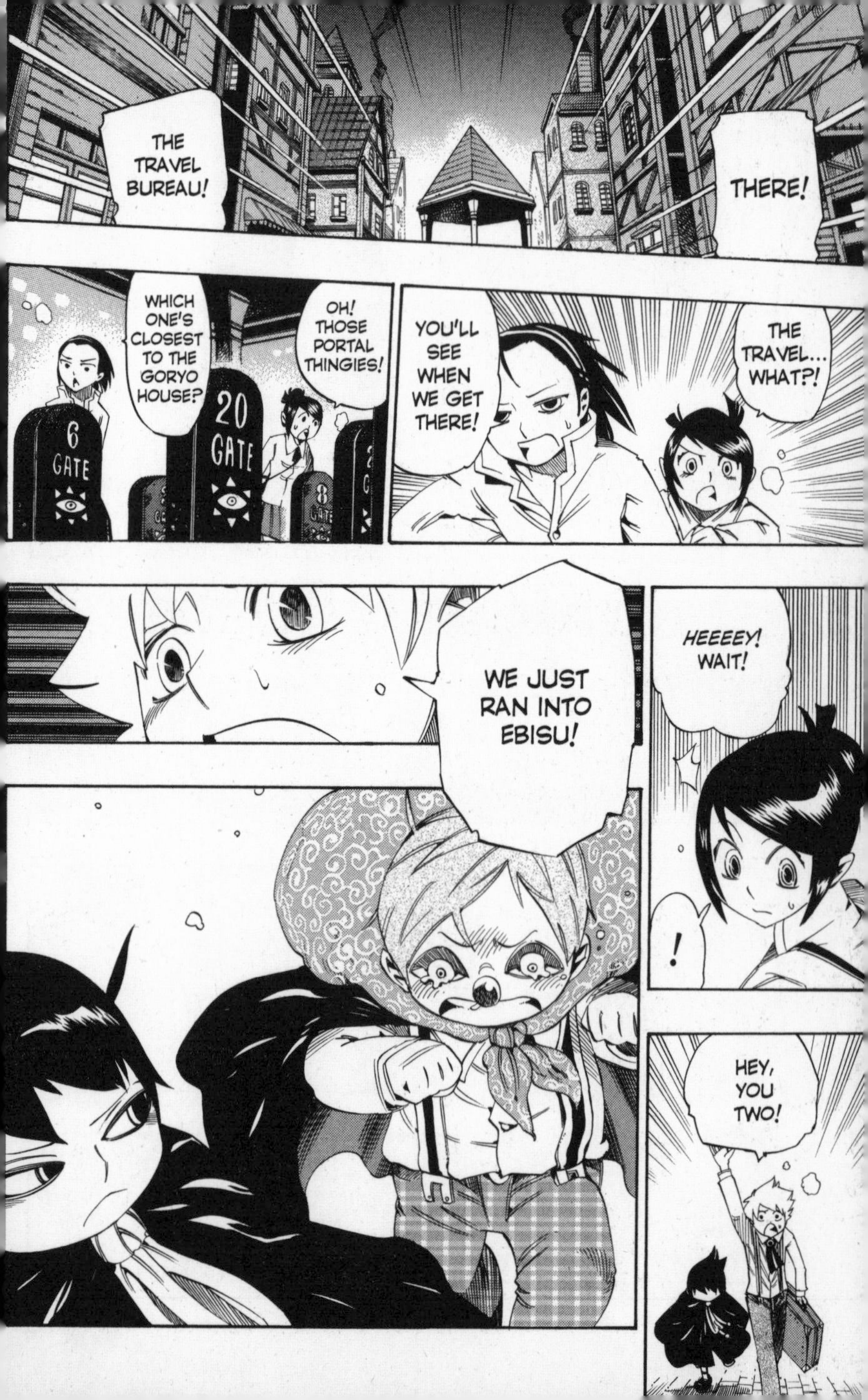
THERE!
THE TRAVEL BUREAU!
THE TRAVEL... WHAT?!
YOU'LL SEE WHEN WE GET THERE!
OH! THOSE PORTAL THINGIES!
WHICH ONE'S CLOSEST TO THE GORYO HOUSE?
20 GATE
8 GATE
6 GATE
HEEEEY! WAIT!
!
HEY, YOU TWO!
WE JUST RAN INTO EBISU!

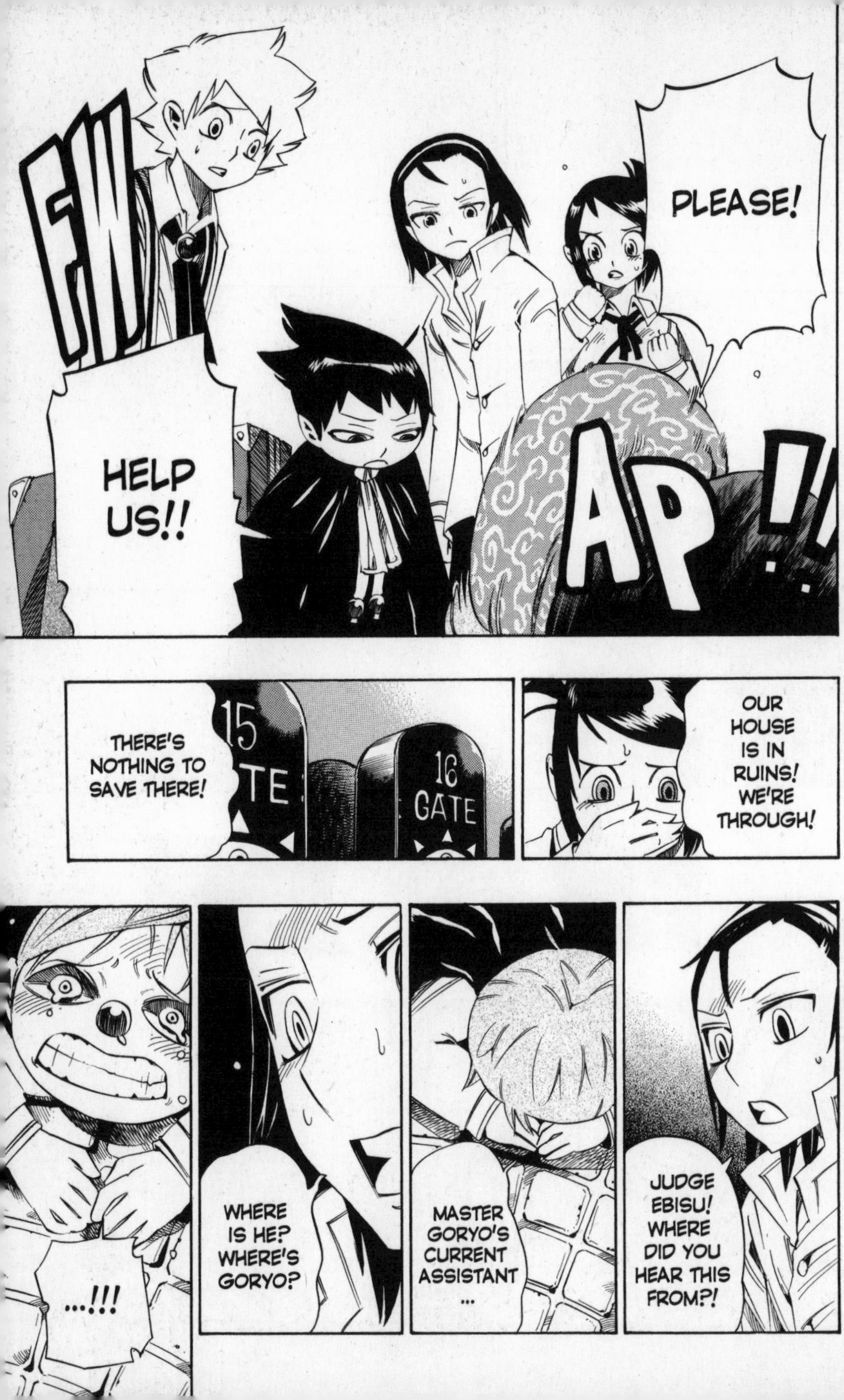
PLEASE!
AP!!
HELP US!!
OUR HOUSE IS IN RUINS! WE'RE THROUGH!
16 GATE
THERE'S NOTHING TO SAVE THERE!
JUDGE EBISU! WHERE DID YOU HEAR THIS FROM?!
MASTER GORYO'S CURRENT ASSISTANT ...
WHERE IS HE? WHERE'S GORYO?
...!!!

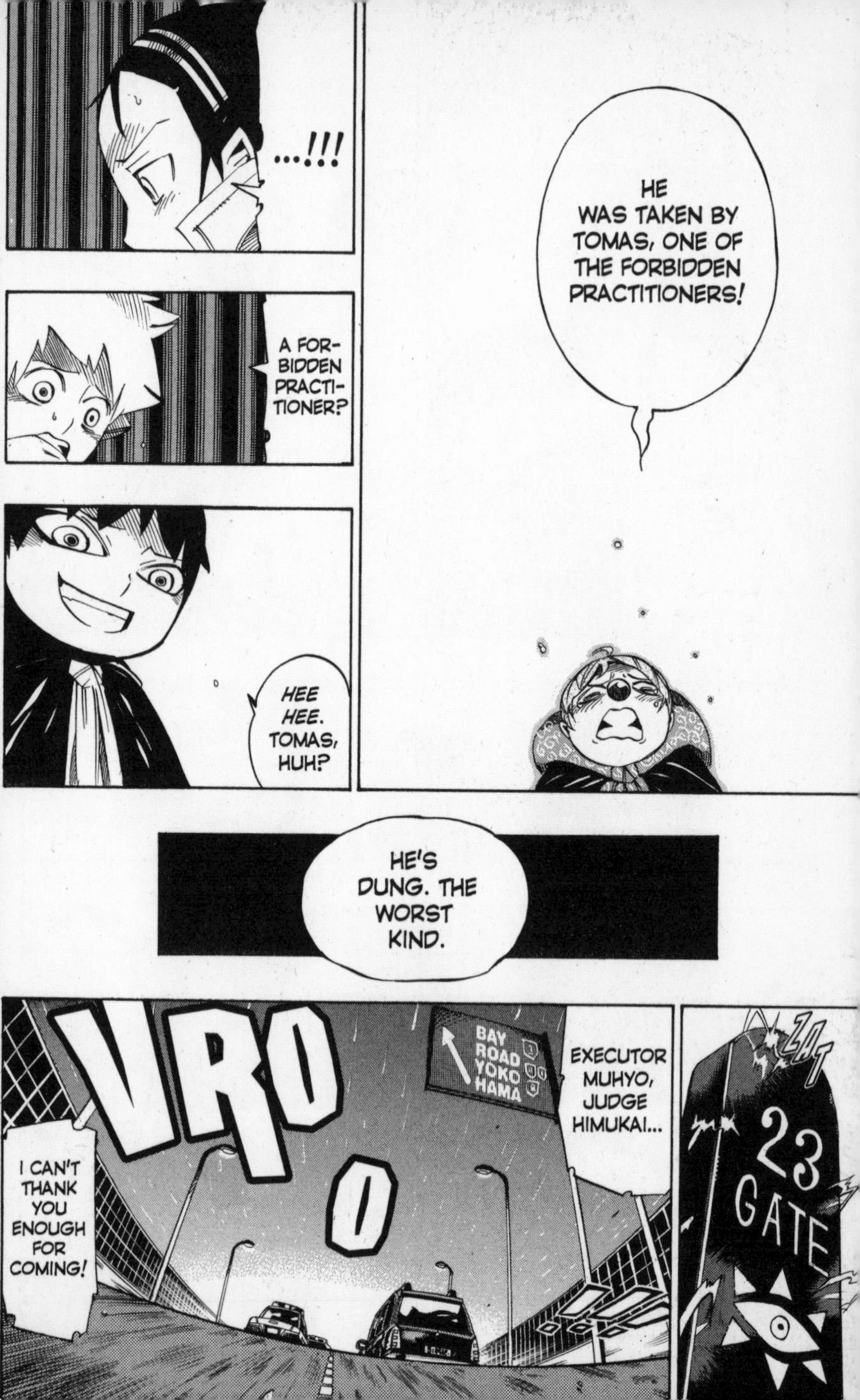
HE WAS TAKEN BY TOMAS, ONE OF THE FORBIDDEN PRACTITIONERS!
...!!!
A FOR-BIDDEN PRACTI-TIONER?
HEE HEE. TOMAS, HUH?
HE'S DUNG. THE WORST KIND.
ZAT
23 GATE
EXECUTOR MUHYO, JUDGE HIMUKAI...
BAY ROAD YOKO HAMA
VRO
O
I CAN'T THANK YOU ENOUGH FOR COMING!

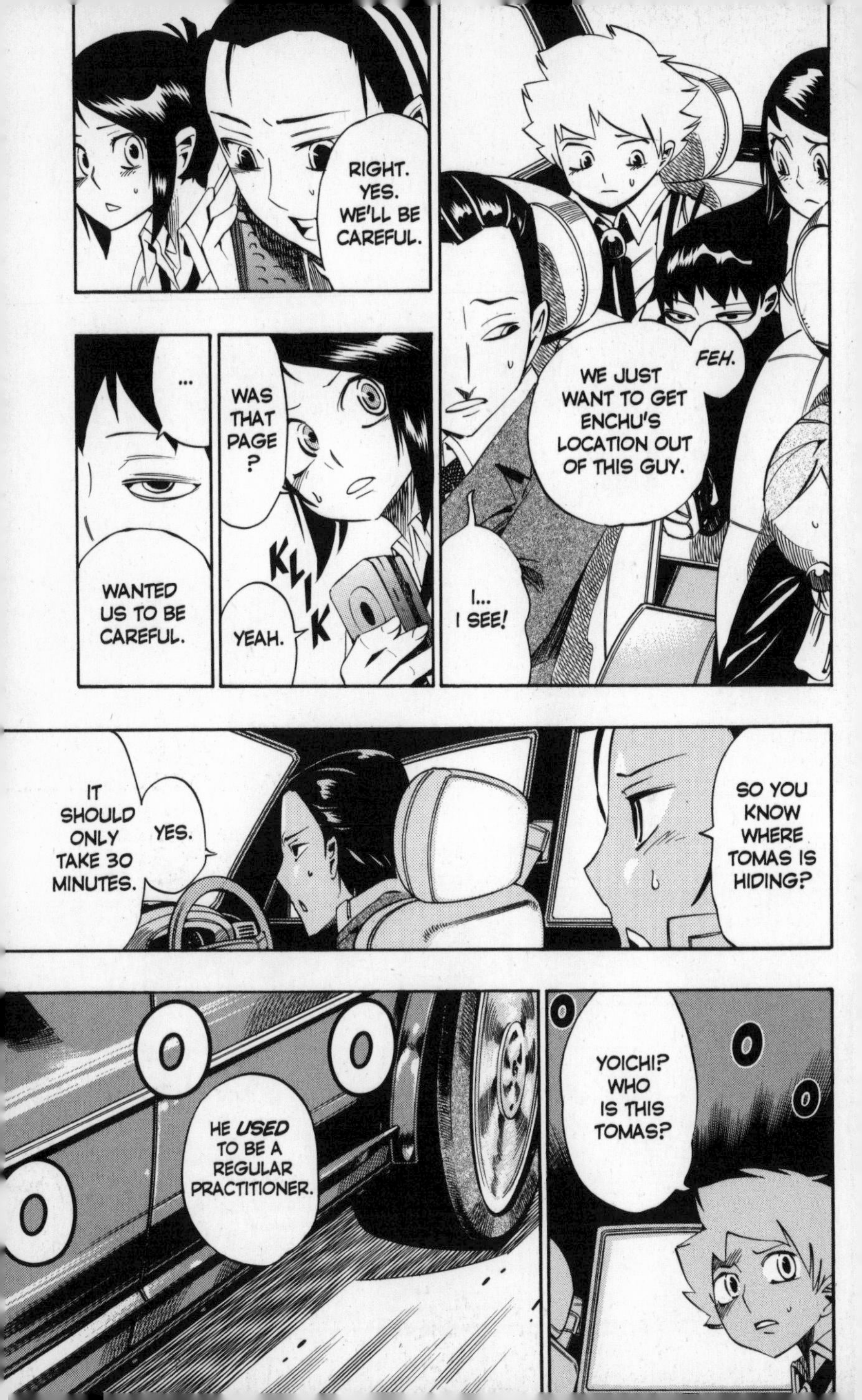
FEH.
WE JUST WANT TO GET ENCHU'S LOCATION OUT OF THIS GUY.
I... I SEE!
RIGHT. YES. WE'LL BE CAREFUL.
WAS THAT PAGE?
KLIK
YEAH.
...
WANTED US TO BE CAREFUL.
SO YOU KNOW WHERE TOMAS IS HIDING?
YES.
IT SHOULD ONLY TAKE 30 MINUTES.
YOICHI? WHO IS THIS TOMAS?
HE *USED* TO BE A REGULAR PRACTITIONER.

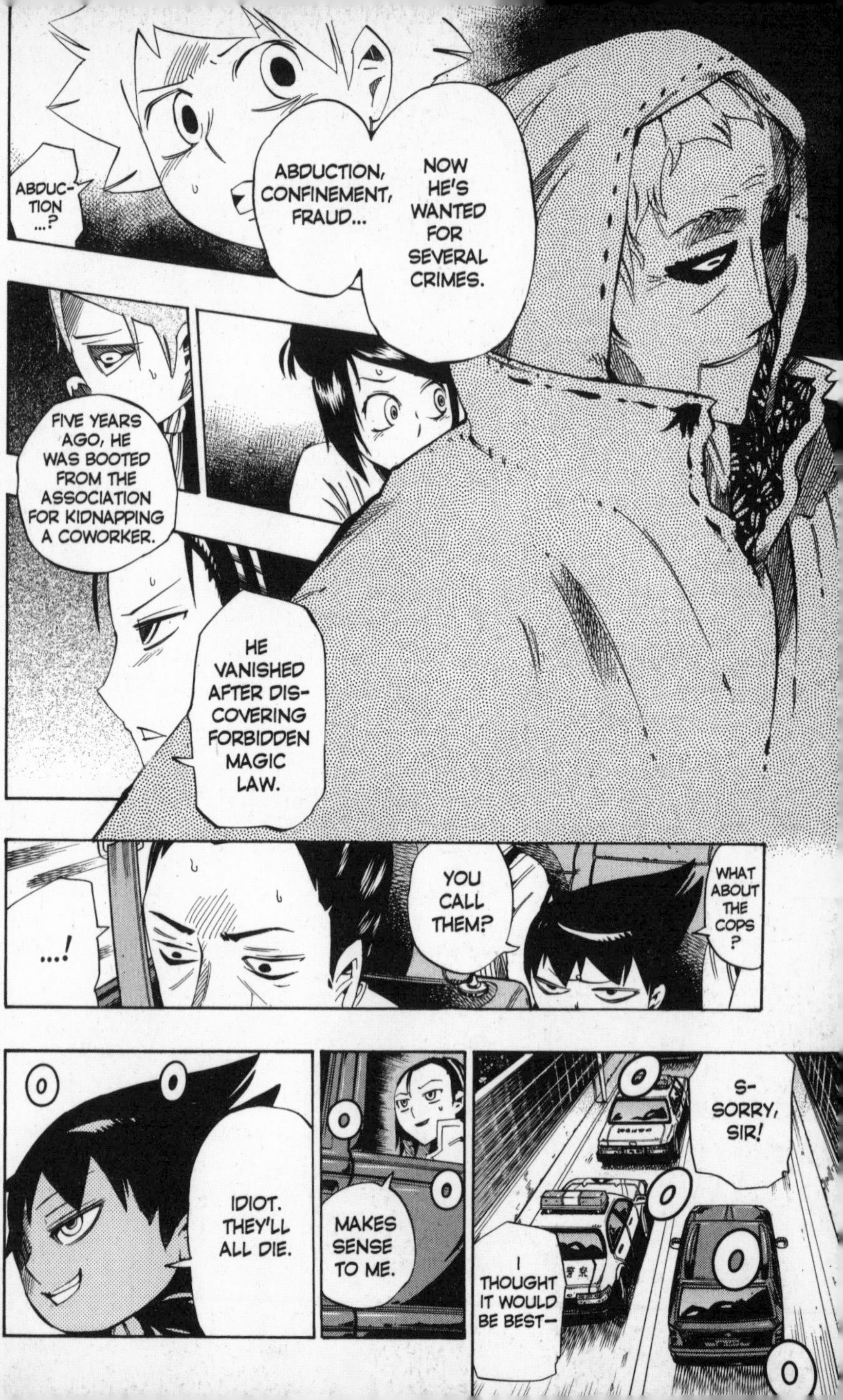
ABDUCTION, CONFINEMENT, FRAUD... NOW HE'S WANTED FOR SEVERAL CRIMES.
ABDUCTION...?
FIVE YEARS AGO, HE WAS BOOTED FROM THE ASSOCIATION FOR KIDNAPPING A COWORKER.
HE VANISHED AFTER DIS-COVERING FORBIDDEN MAGIC LAW.
WHAT ABOUT THE COPS?
YOU CALL THEM?
...!
S-SORRY, SIR!
I THOUGHT IT WOULD BE BEST—
MAKES SENSE TO ME.
IDIOT. THEY'LL ALL DIE.

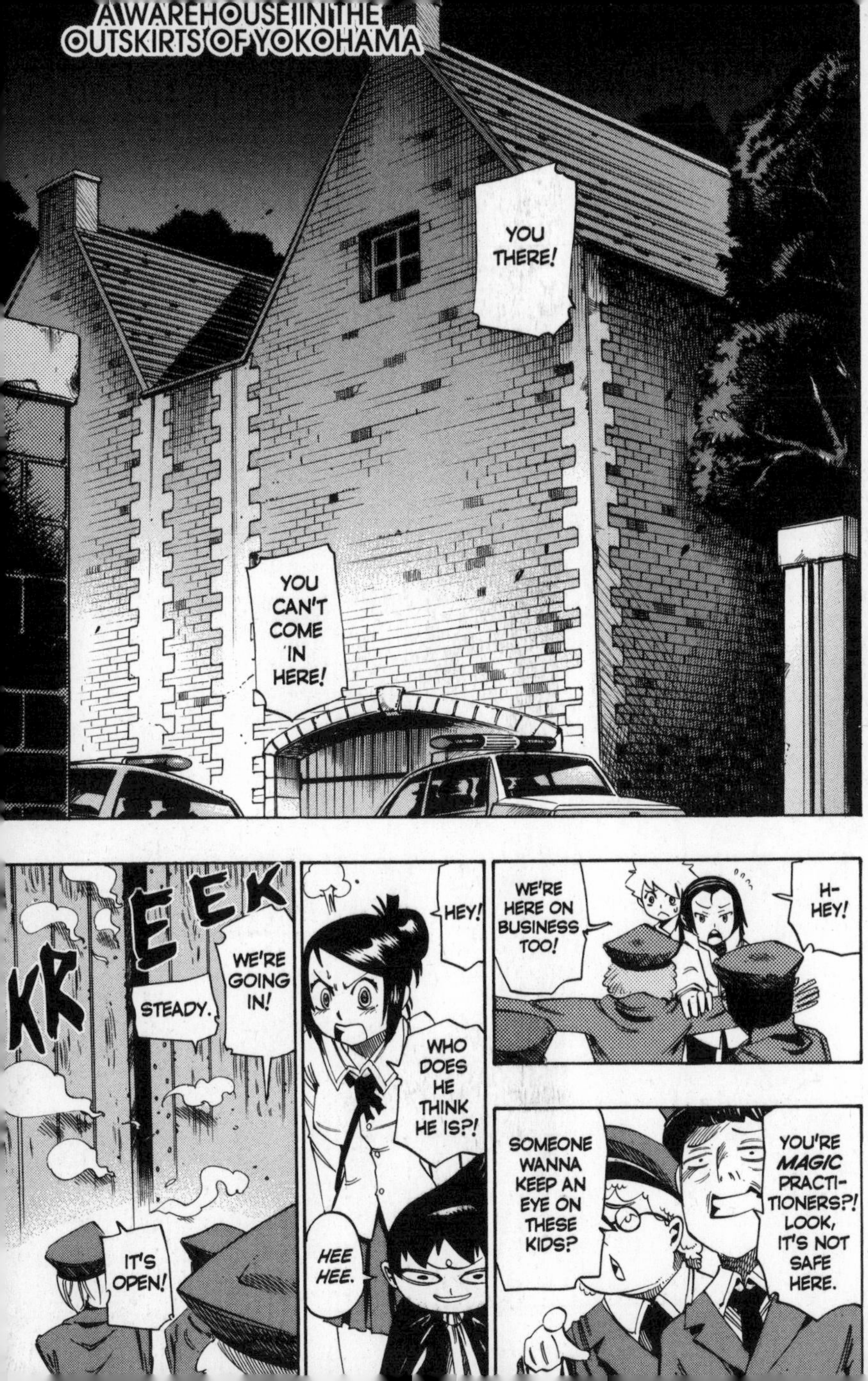
A WAREHOUSE IN THE OUTSKIRTS OF YOKOHAMA
YOU THERE!
YOU CAN'T COME IN HERE!
H-HEY!
WE'RE HERE ON BUSINESS TOO!
YOU'RE *MAGIC* PRACTITIONERS?! LOOK, IT'S NOT SAFE HERE.
SOMEONE WANNA KEEP AN EYE ON THESE KIDS?
HEY!
WHO DOES HE THINK HE IS?!
HEE HEE.
KREEK
WE'RE GOING IN!
STEADY.
IT'S OPEN!

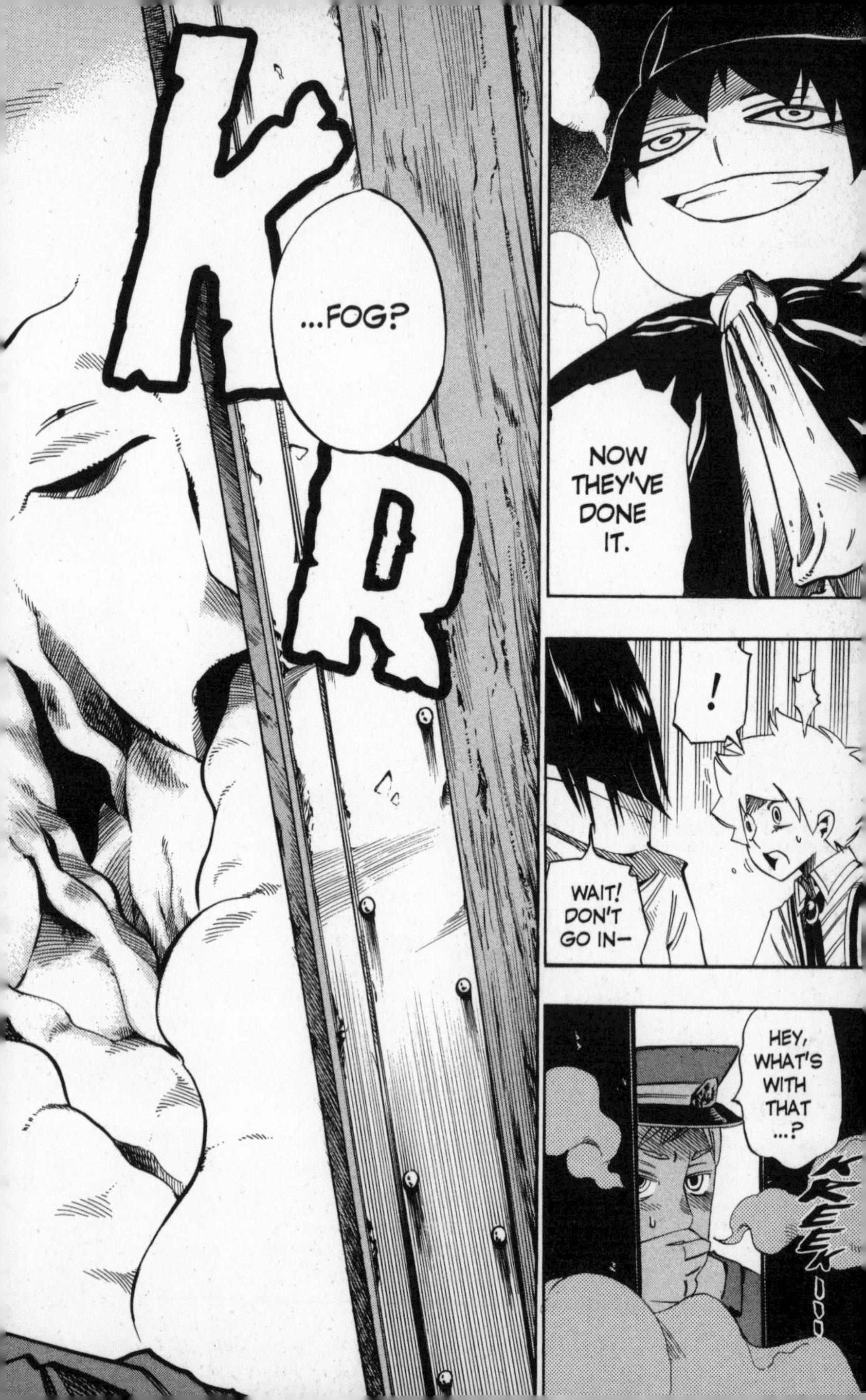
NOW THEY'VE DONE IT.
!
WAIT! DON'T GO IN–
HEY, WHAT'S WITH THAT ...?
...FOG?

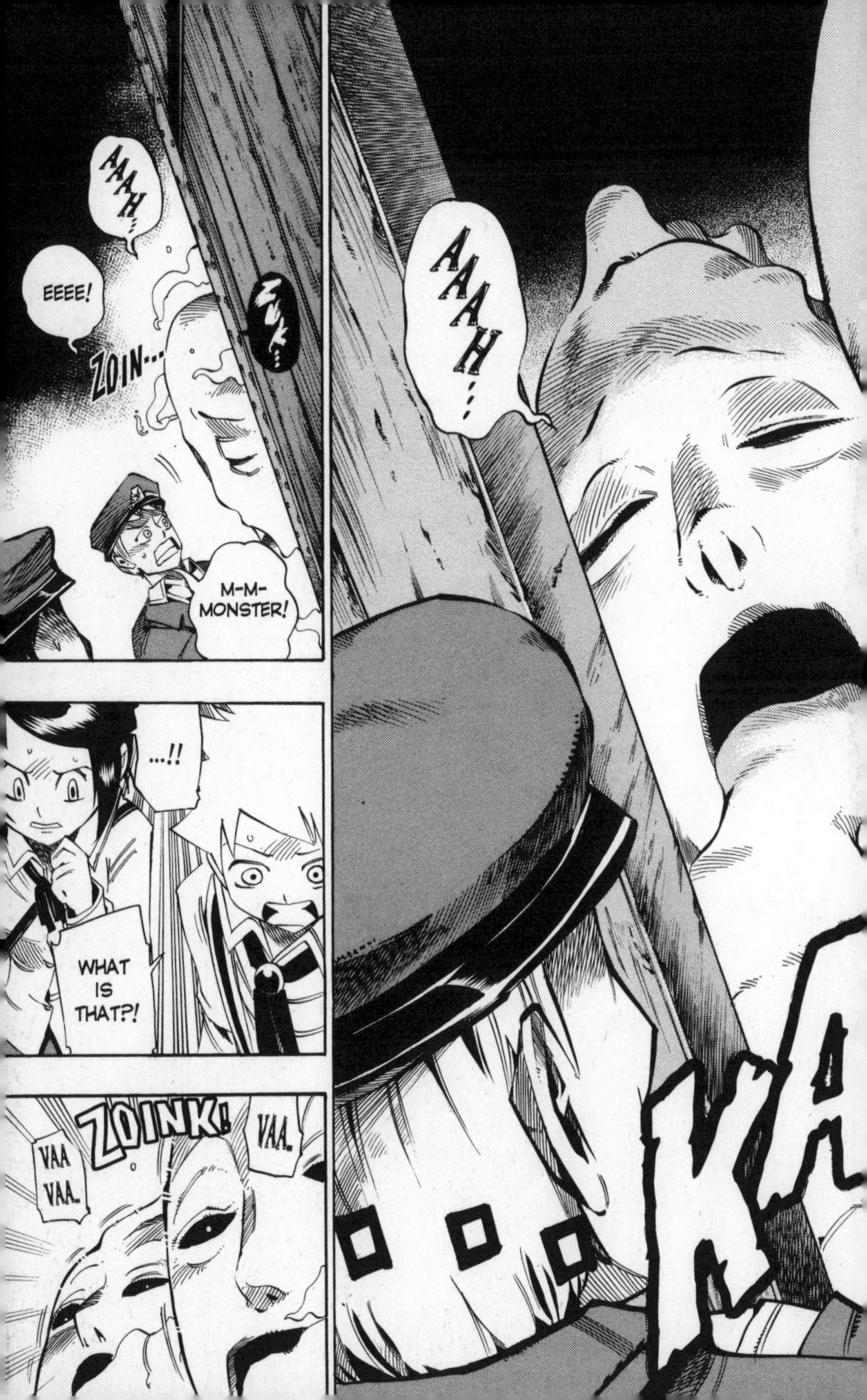
AAAH...
KA
AAAH...
EEEE!
ZOIN...
M-M-MONSTER!
...!!
WHAT IS THAT?!
VAA...
ZOINK!
VAA VAA...

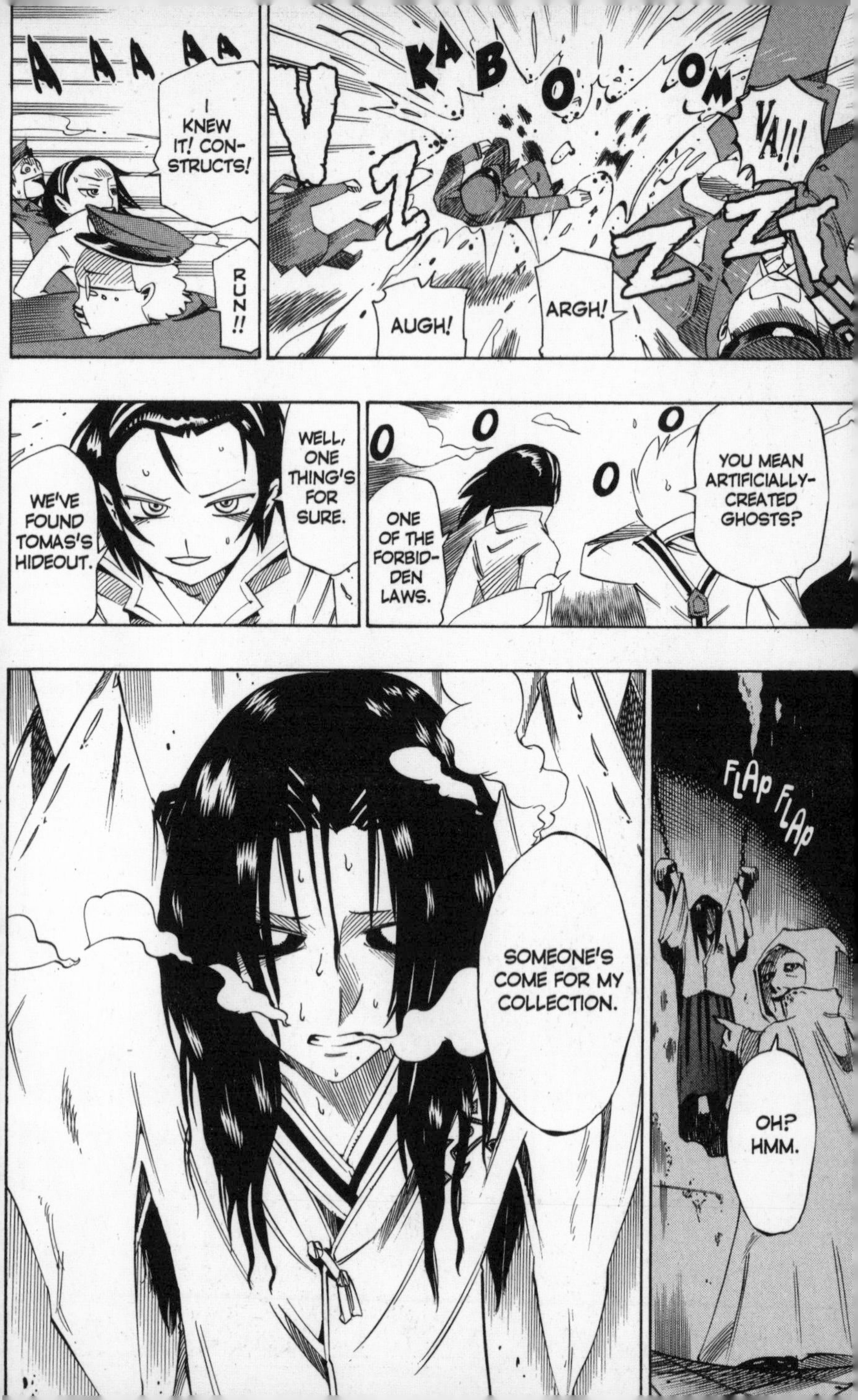
VA!!!
KABOOM
VZZZT
ARGH!
AUGH!
AAAAA
I KNEW IT! CONSTRUCTS!
RUN!!
YOU MEAN ARTIFICIALLY-CREATED GHOSTS?
OOOO
ONE OF THE FORBIDDEN LAWS.
WELL, ONE THING'S FOR SURE.
WE'VE FOUND TOMAS'S HIDEOUT.
FLAP FLAP
OH? HMM.
SOMEONE'S COME FOR MY COLLECTION.

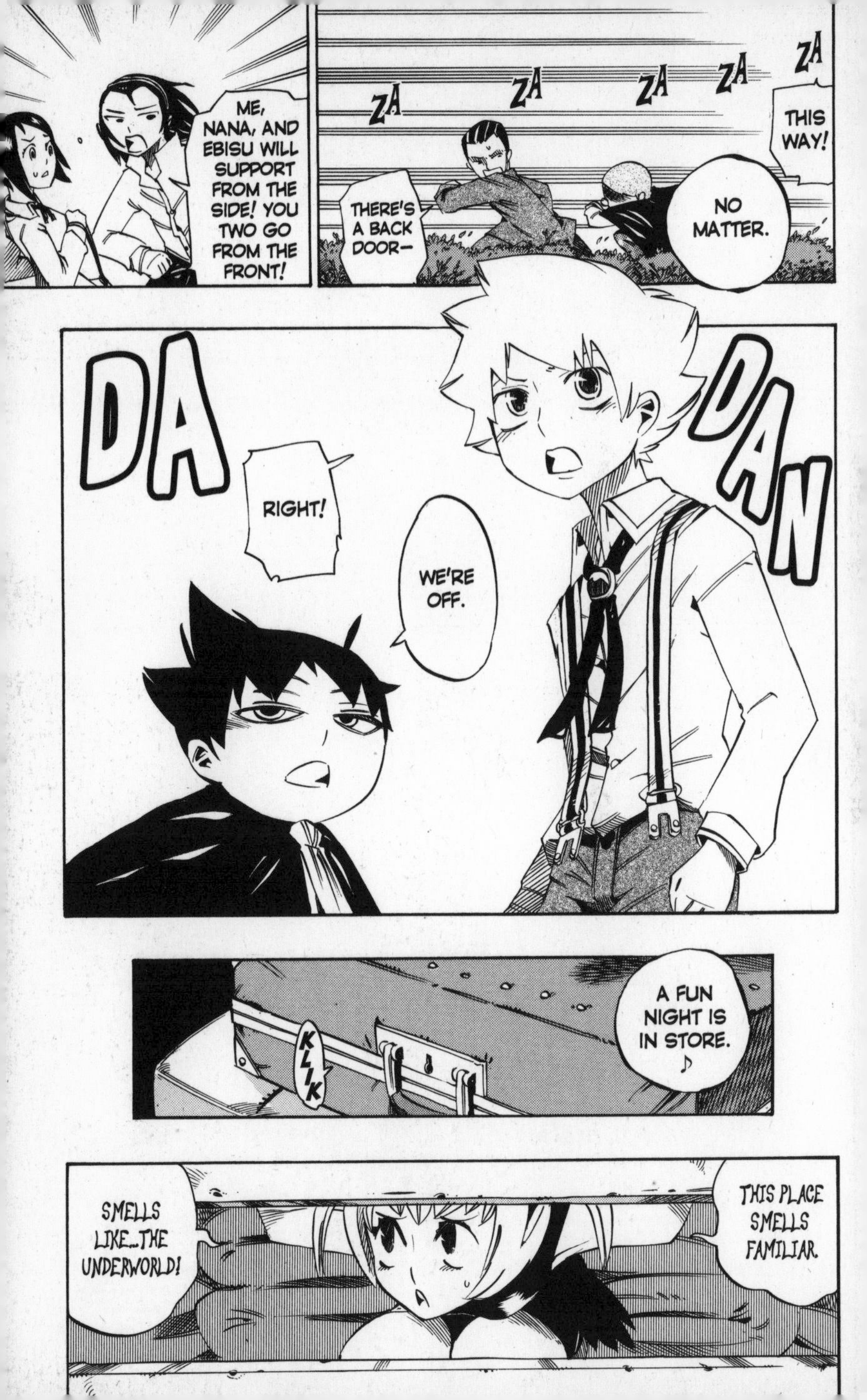
ZA
ZA
ZA
ZA
ZA
THIS WAY!
NO MATTER.
THERE'S A BACK DOOR—
ME, NANA, AND EBISU WILL SUPPORT FROM THE SIDE! YOU TWO GO FROM THE FRONT!
DA
DAN
RIGHT!
WE'RE OFF.
A FUN NIGHT IS IN STORE. ♪
KLIK
THIS PLACE SMELLS FAMILIAR.
SMELLS LIKE...THE UNDERWORLD!

KIRIKO IN ROJI'S BAG

A FAITHFULL READER.

...

JABIN

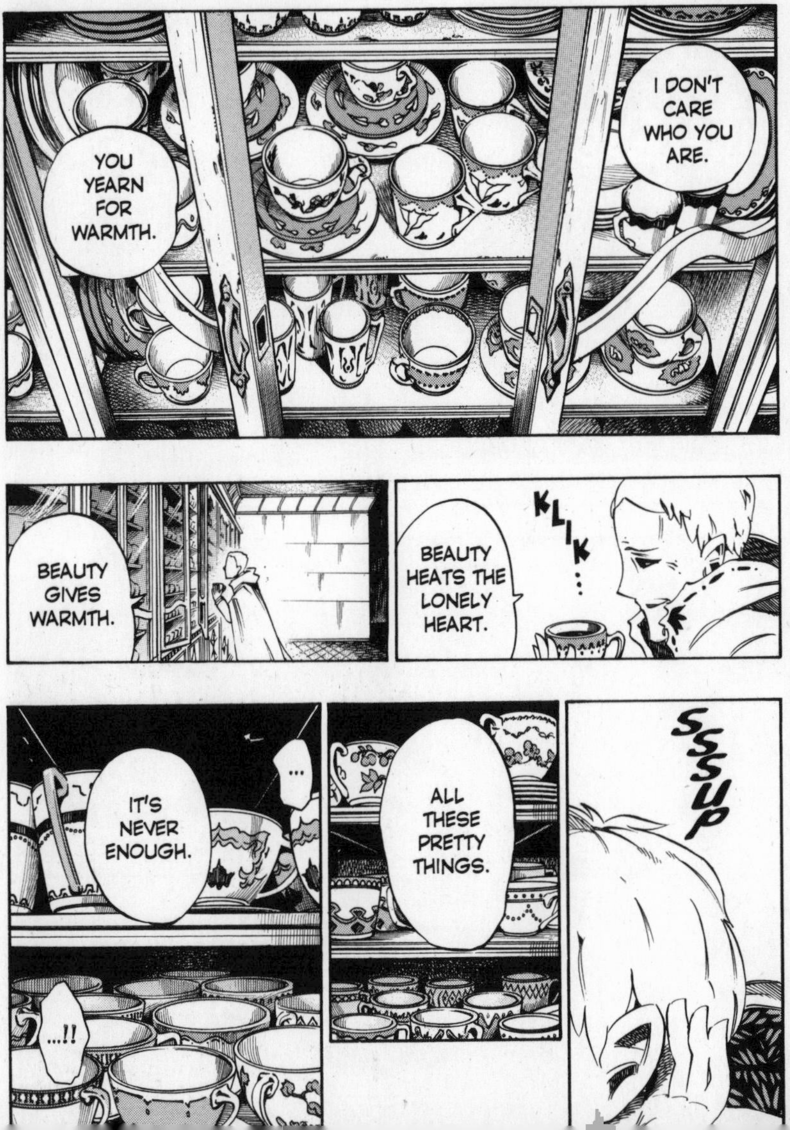
I DON'T CARE WHO YOU ARE.
YOU YEARN FOR WARMTH.
KLIK...
BEAUTY HEATS THE LONELY HEART.
BEAUTY GIVES WARMTH.
SSSUP
ALL THESE PRETTY THINGS.
...
IT'S NEVER ENOUGH.
...!!

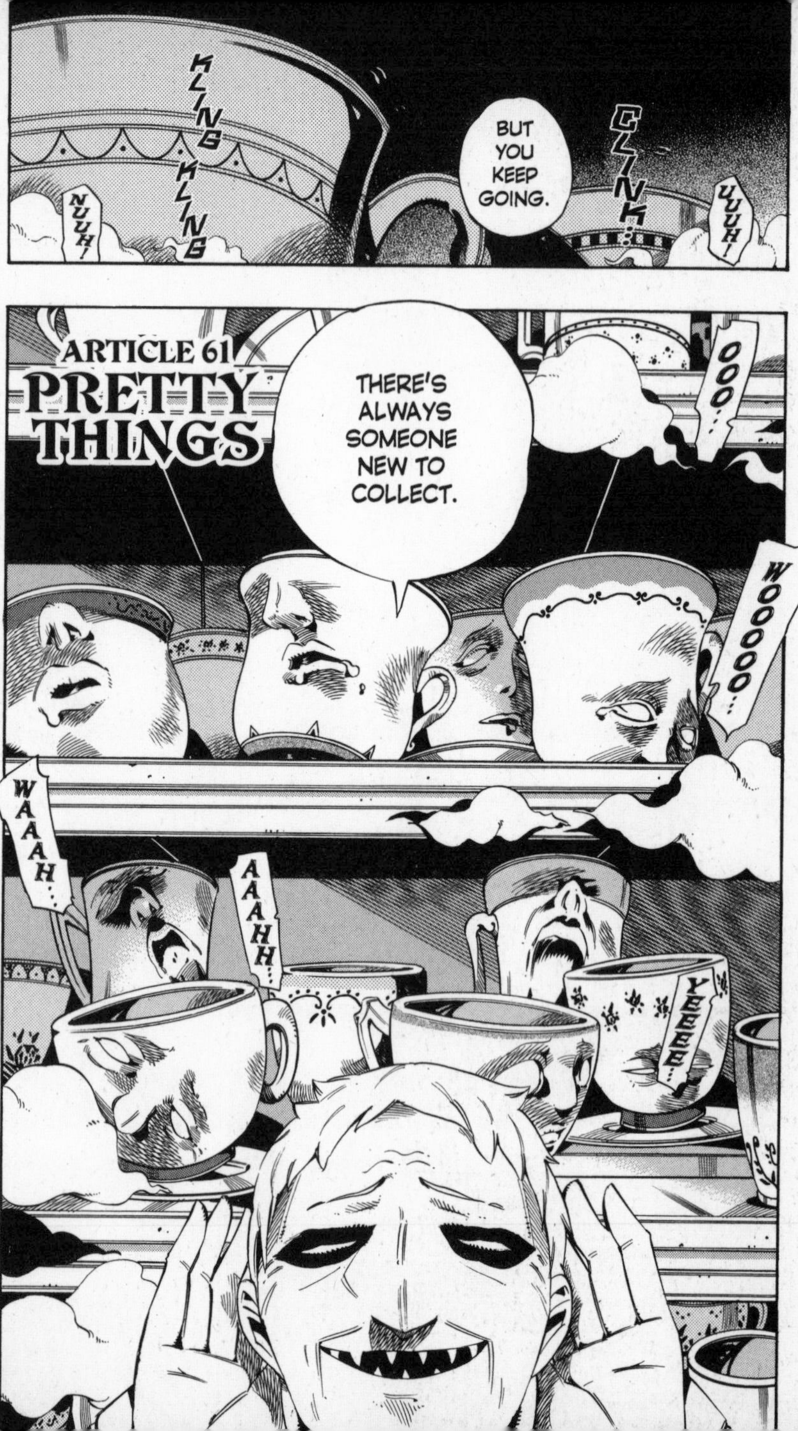
UUUH!
CLINK...
BUT YOU KEEP GOING.
KLING KLING
NUUH!
ARTICLE 61
PRETTY THINGS
OOO...
THERE'S ALWAYS SOMEONE NEW TO COLLECT.
WOOOOOO...
YEEEE...
AAAAHH...
WAAAAH...

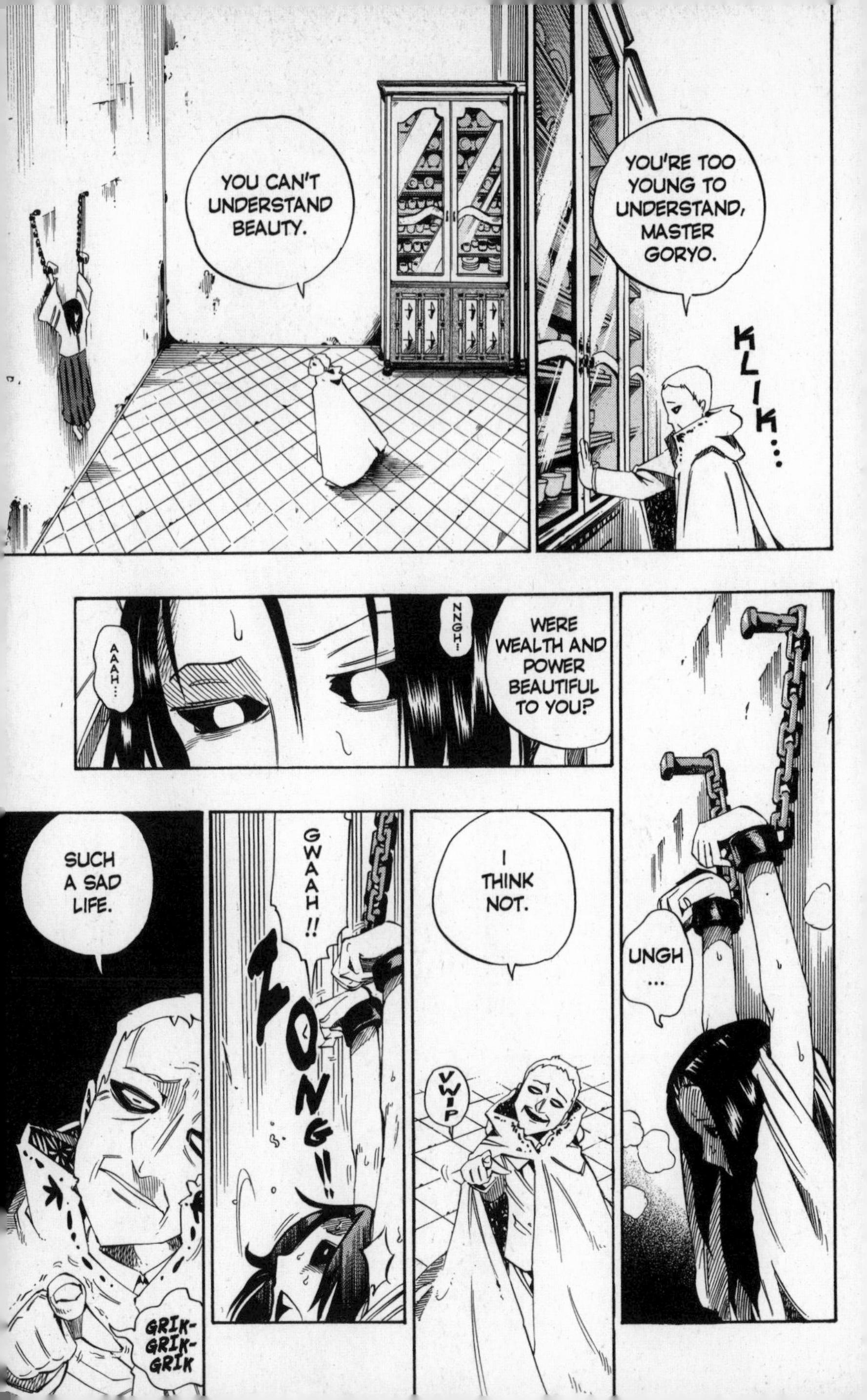
YOU'RE TOO YOUNG TO UNDERSTAND, MASTER GORYO.
KLIK...
YOU CAN'T UNDERSTAND BEAUTY.
UNGH ...
WERE WEALTH AND POWER BEAUTIFUL TO YOU?
NNGH...
AAAH...
I THINK NOT.
VWIP
GWAAH!!
ZONG!!
SUCH A SAD LIFE.
GRIK-GRIK-GRIK

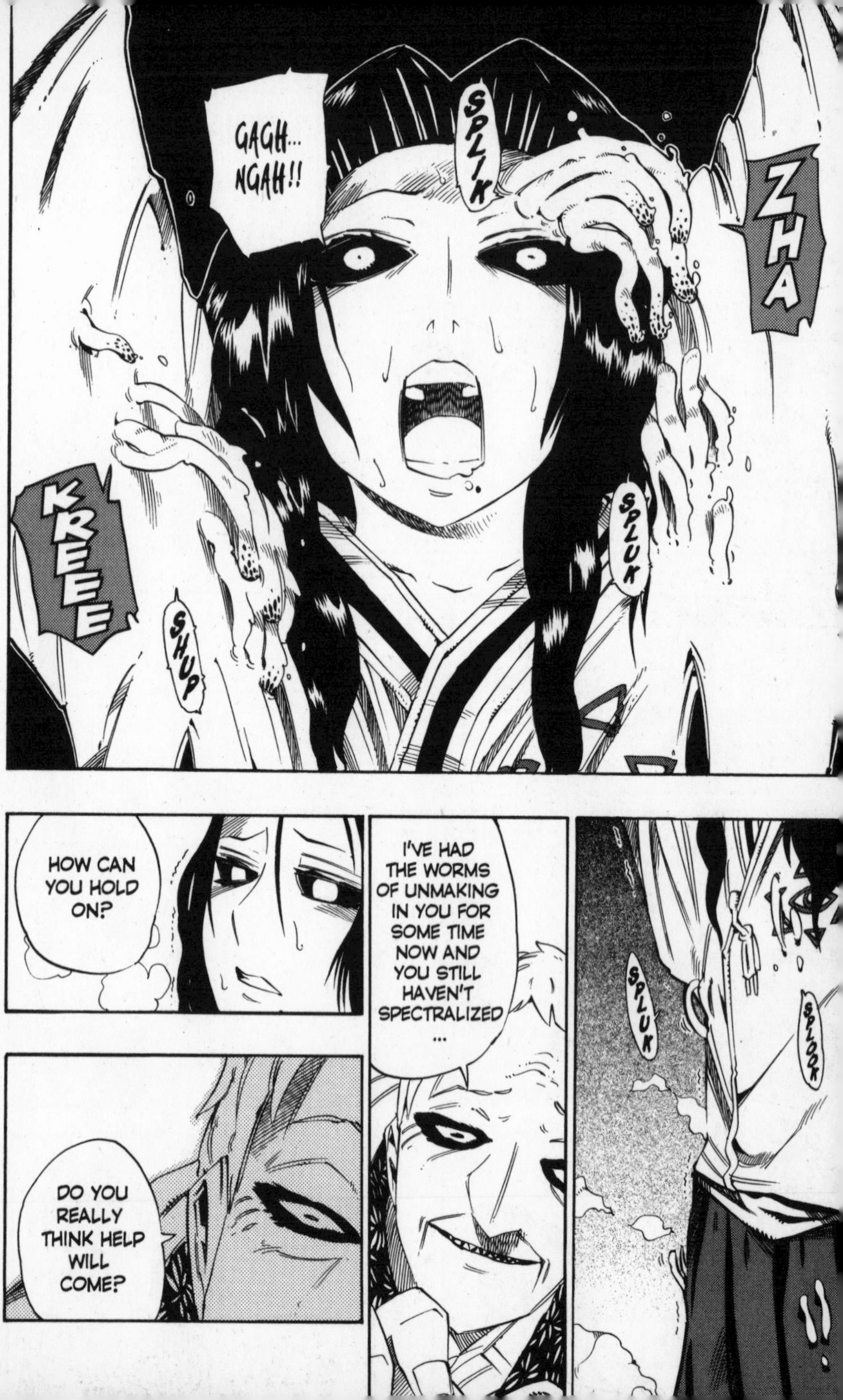
ZHA
SPLIK
GAGH... NGAH!!
SPLUK
KREEE
SHUP
SPLOOK
SPLUK
!!
I'VE HAD THE WORMS OF UNMAKING IN YOU FOR SOME TIME NOW AND YOU STILL HAVEN'T SPECTRALIZED ...
HOW CAN YOU HOLD ON?
DO YOU REALLY THINK HELP WILL COME?

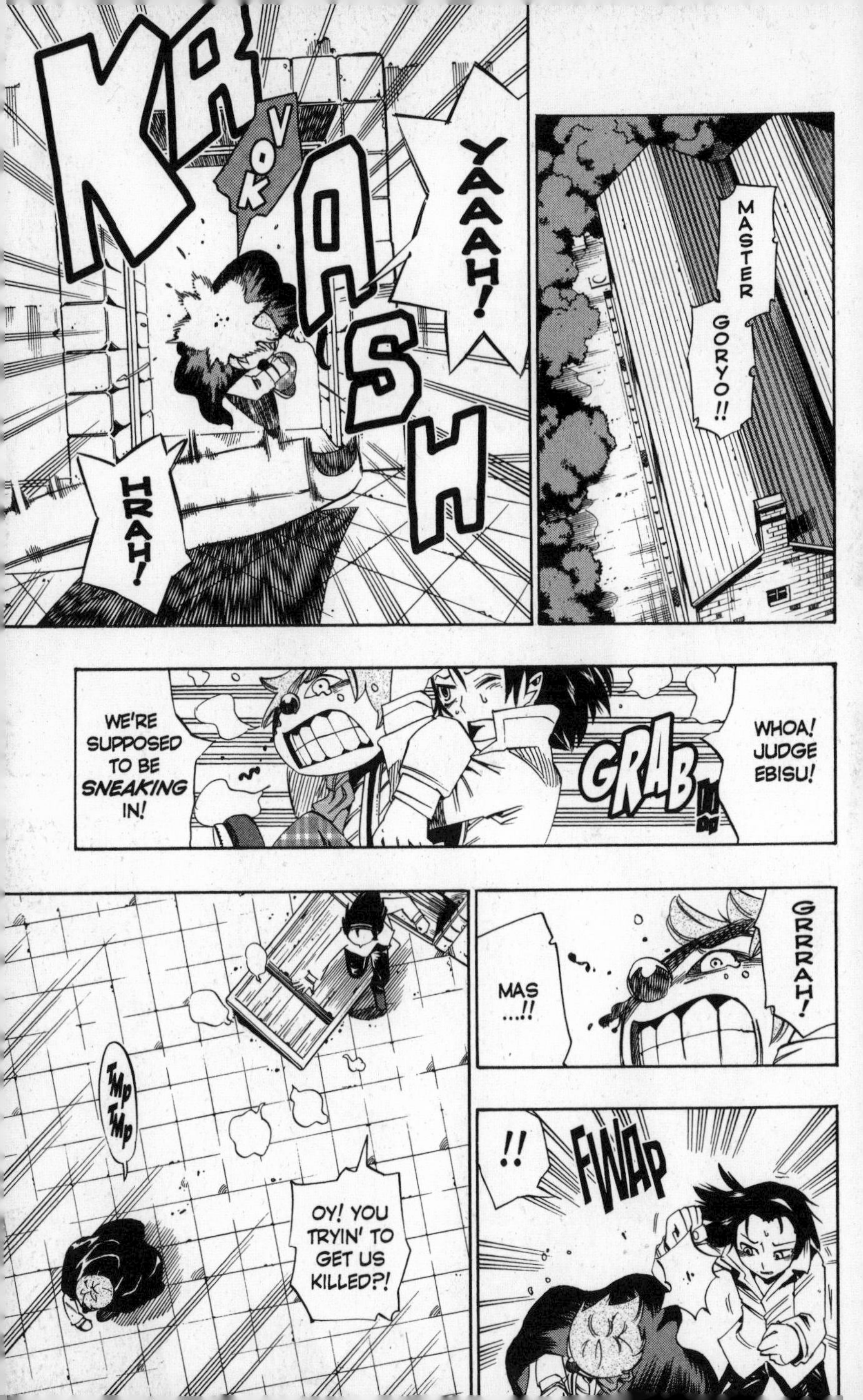
MASTER GORYO!!
YAAAH!
KRASH
VOK
HRAH!
WHOA! JUDGE EBISU!
GRAB
WE'RE SUPPOSED TO BE SNEAKING IN!
GRRRAH!
MAS ...!!
FWAP
!!
TMP TMP
OY! YOU TRYIN' TO GET US KILLED?!

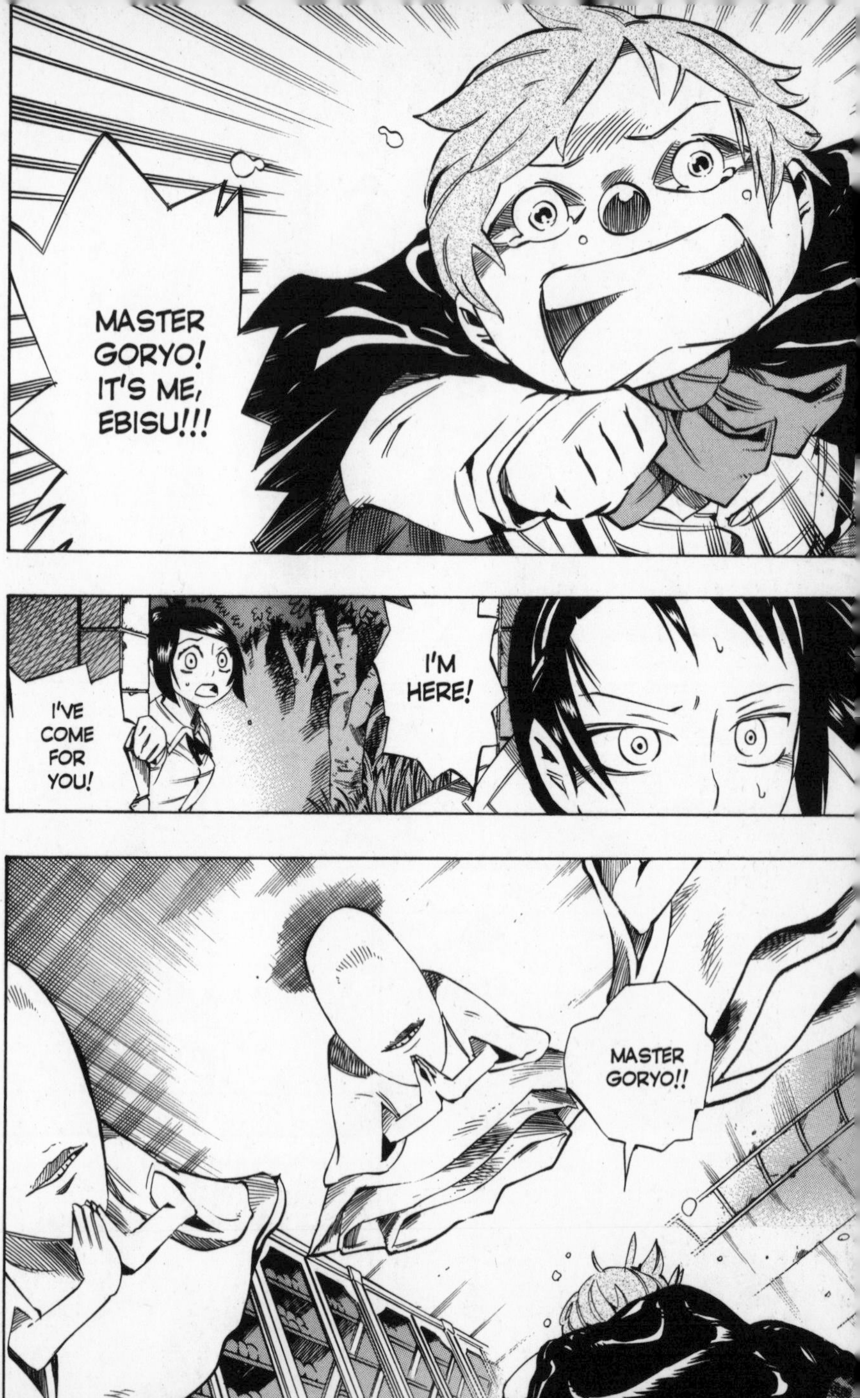
MASTER GORYO! IT'S ME, EBISU!!!
I'M HERE!
I'VE COME FOR YOU!
MASTER GORYO!!

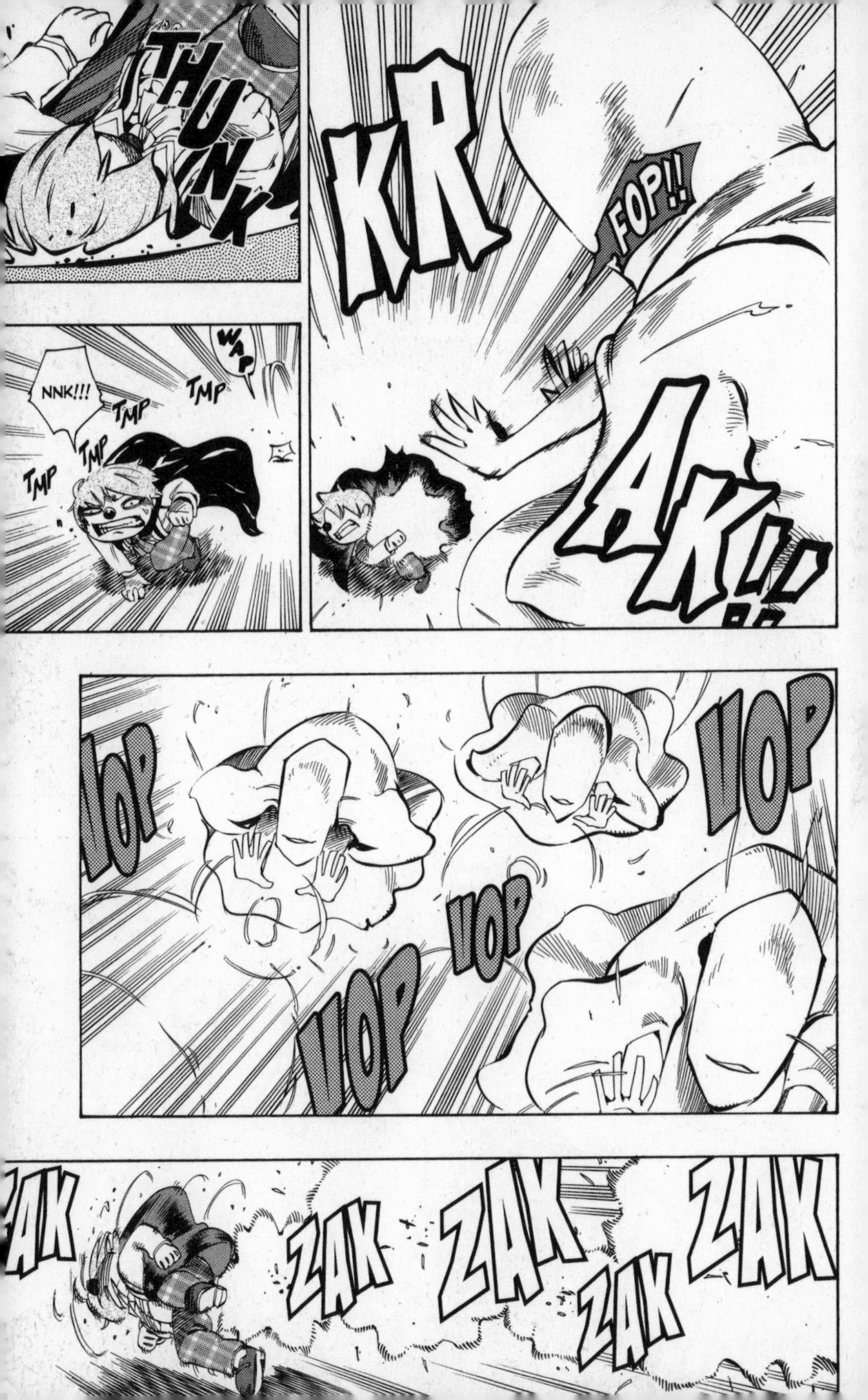
KR
FOP!!
AK!!
THUNK
WAP
TMP
NNK!!!
TMP
TMP
TMP
VOP
VOP
VOP
VOP
ZAK
ZAK
ZAK
ZAK

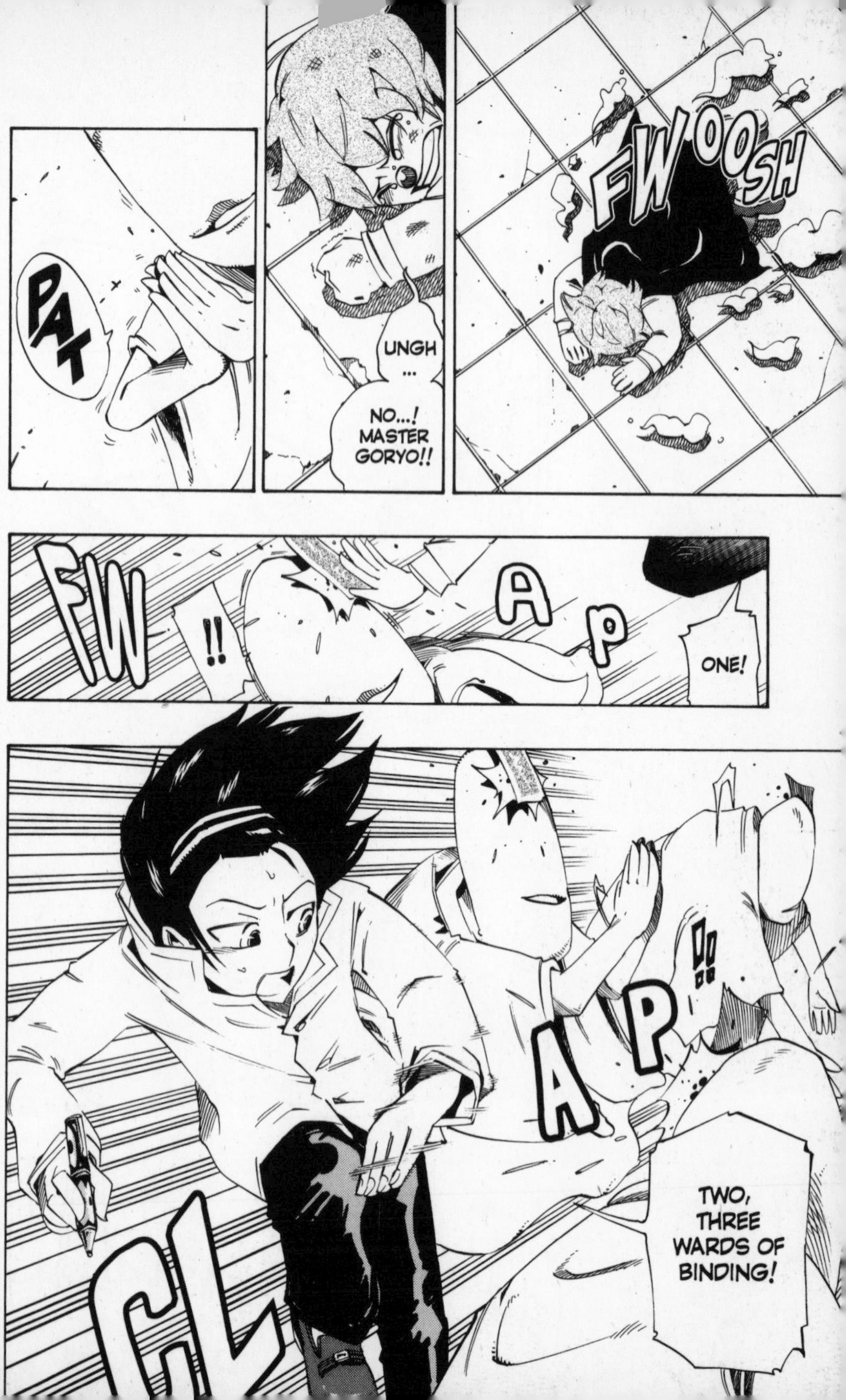
FWOOSH
UNGH ...
NO...! MASTER GORYO!!
PAT
ONE!
A p
FW !!
!!
A P
TWO, THREE WARDS OF BINDING!
CL

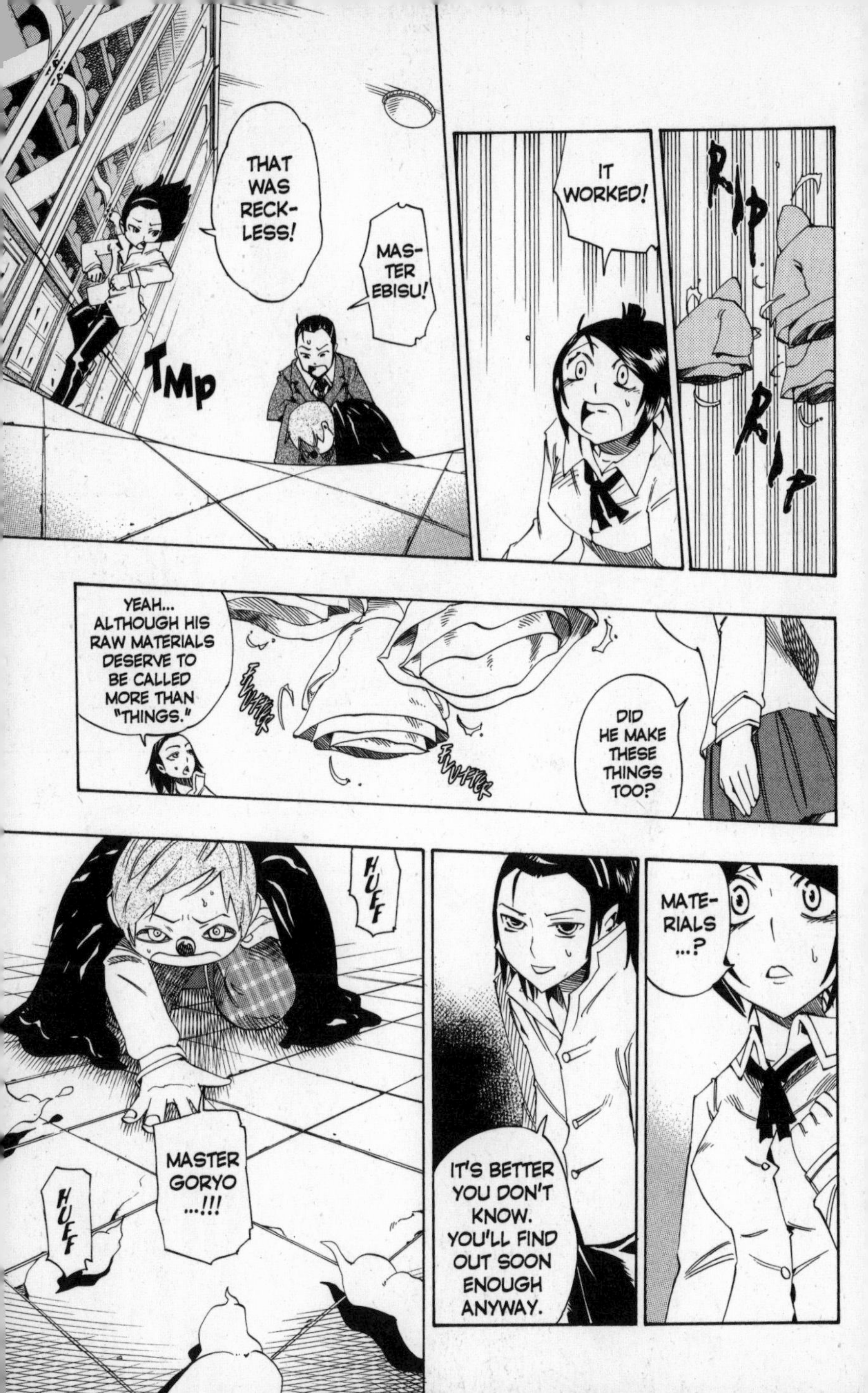
RIP
RIP
IT WORKED!
MAS-TER EBISU!
THAT WAS RECK-LESS!
TMP
DID HE MAKE THESE THINGS TOO?
YEAH... ALTHOUGH HIS RAW MATERIALS DESERVE TO BE CALLED MORE THAN "THINGS."
MATE-RIALS ...?
IT'S BETTER YOU DON'T KNOW. YOU'LL FIND OUT SOON ENOUGH ANYWAY.
HUFF
MASTER GORYO ...!!!
HUFF

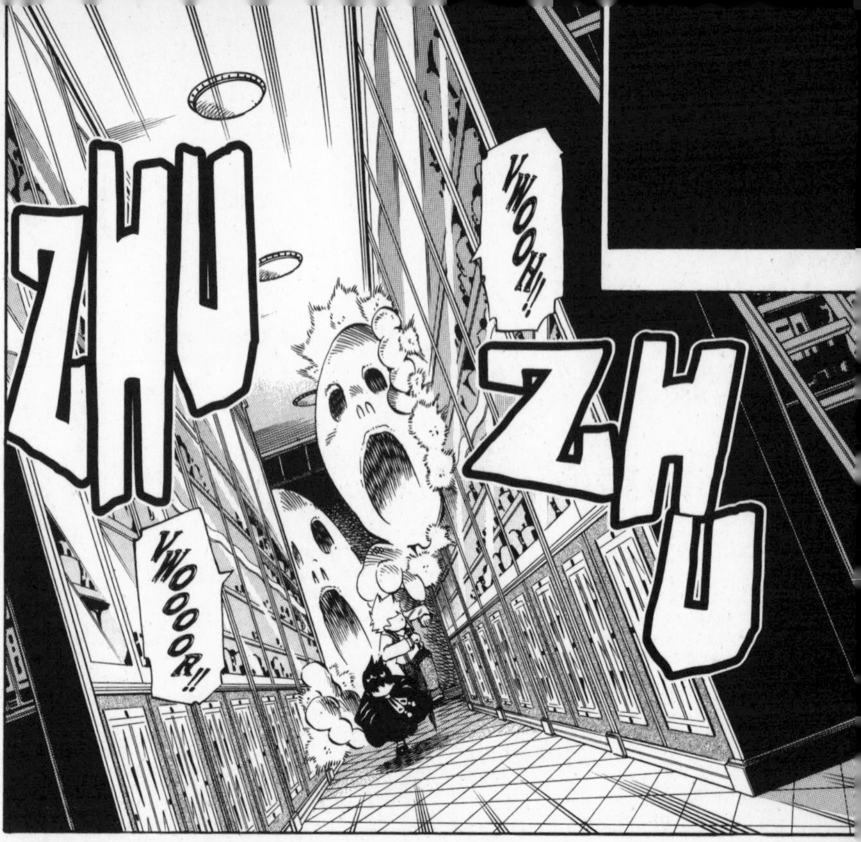
VWOOOH!!
ZHU
ZHU
VWOOOOOR!!

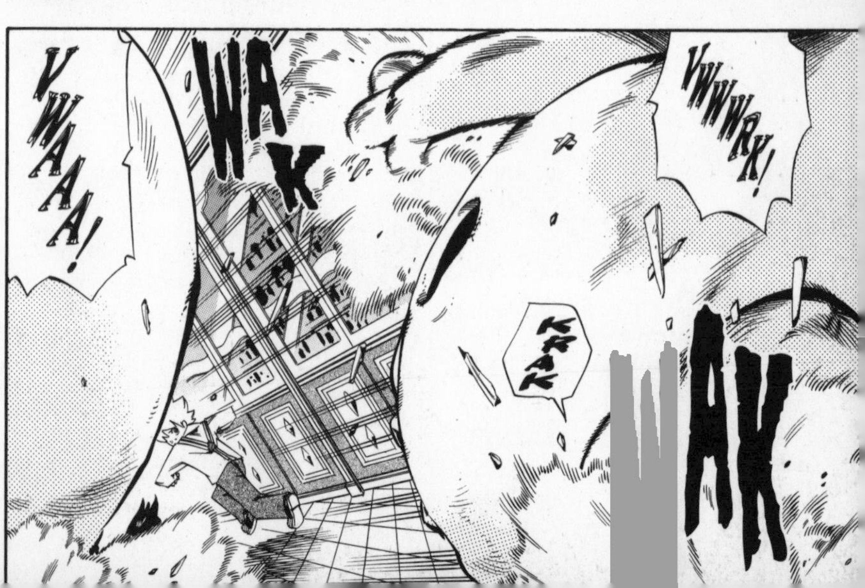
VWWWRK!
WAK
KRAK
WAK
VWAAAA!

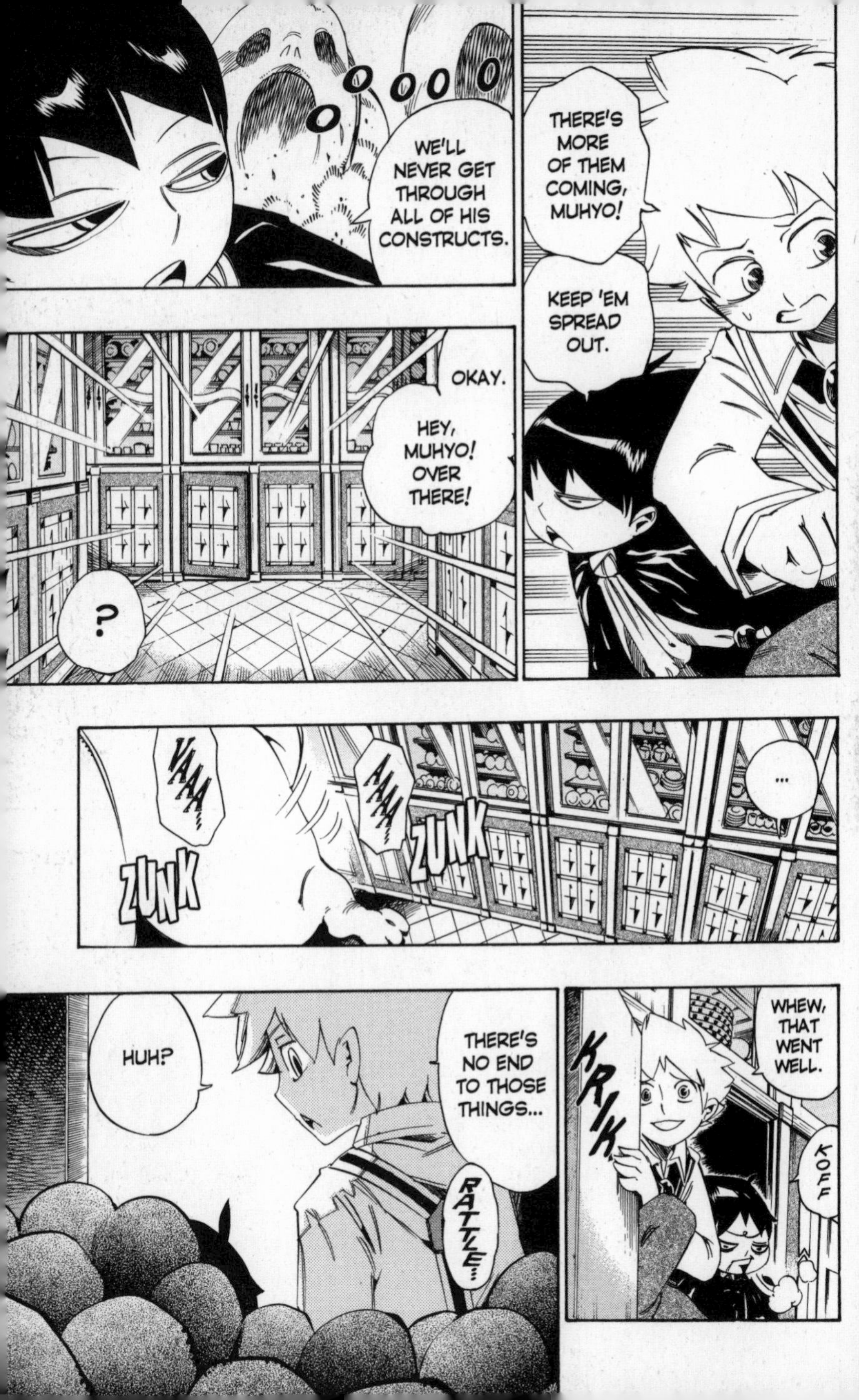
THERE'S MORE OF THEM COMING, MUHYO!
KEEP 'EM SPREAD OUT.
OOOOOO
WE'LL NEVER GET THROUGH ALL OF HIS CONSTRUCTS.
OKAY.
HEY, MUHYO! OVER THERE!
?
...
ZUNK
AAAA
ZUNK
VAAA
WHEW, THAT WENT WELL.
KRIK
KOFF
THERE'S NO END TO THOSE THINGS...
RATTLE...
HUH?

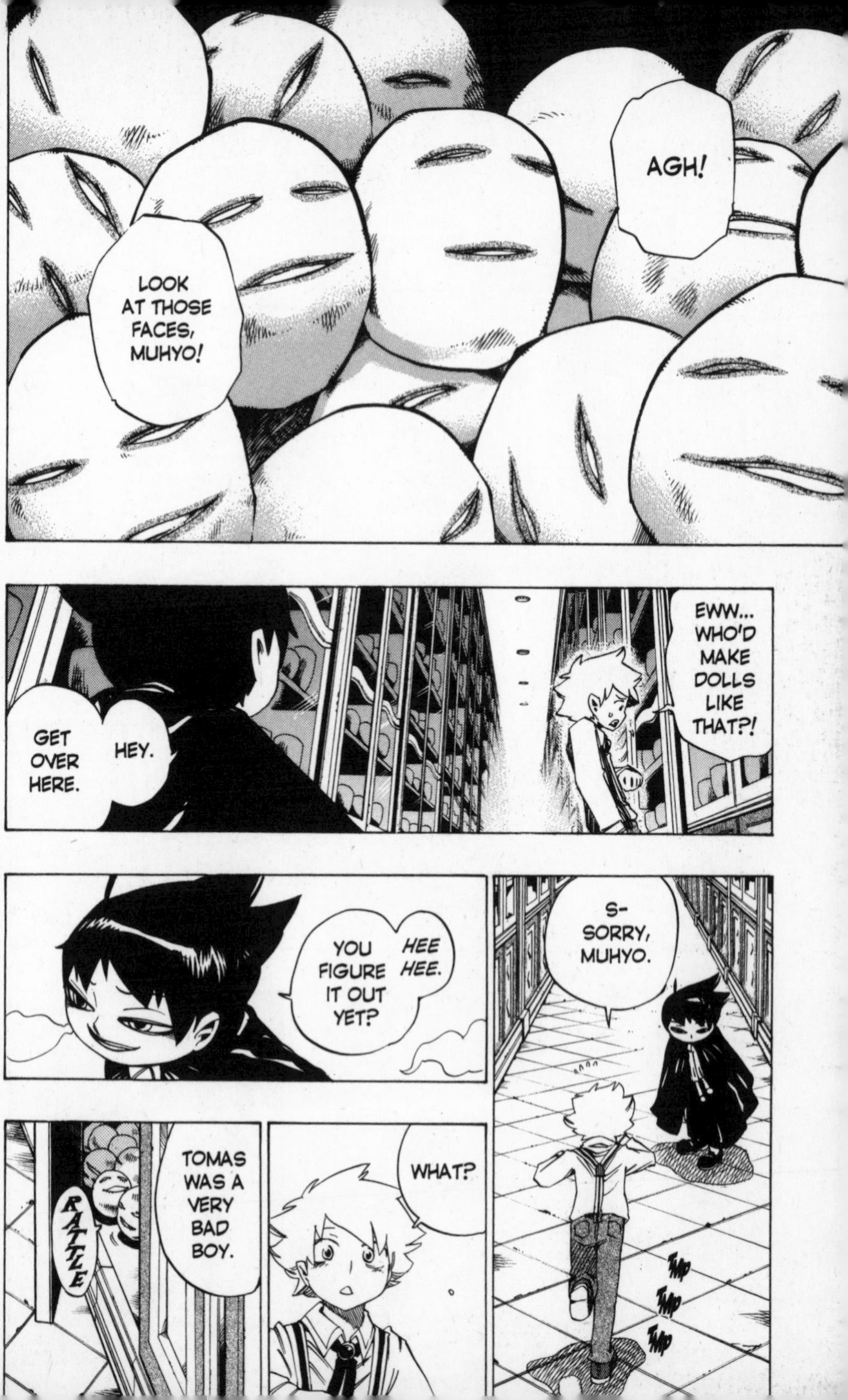
AGH!
LOOK AT THOSE FACES, MUHYO!
EWW... WHO'D MAKE DOLLS LIKE THAT?!
HEY.
GET OVER HERE.
S-SORRY, MUHYO.
TMP
TMP
TMP
HEE HEE.
YOU FIGURE IT OUT YET?
WHAT?
TOMAS WAS A VERY BAD BOY.
RATTLE

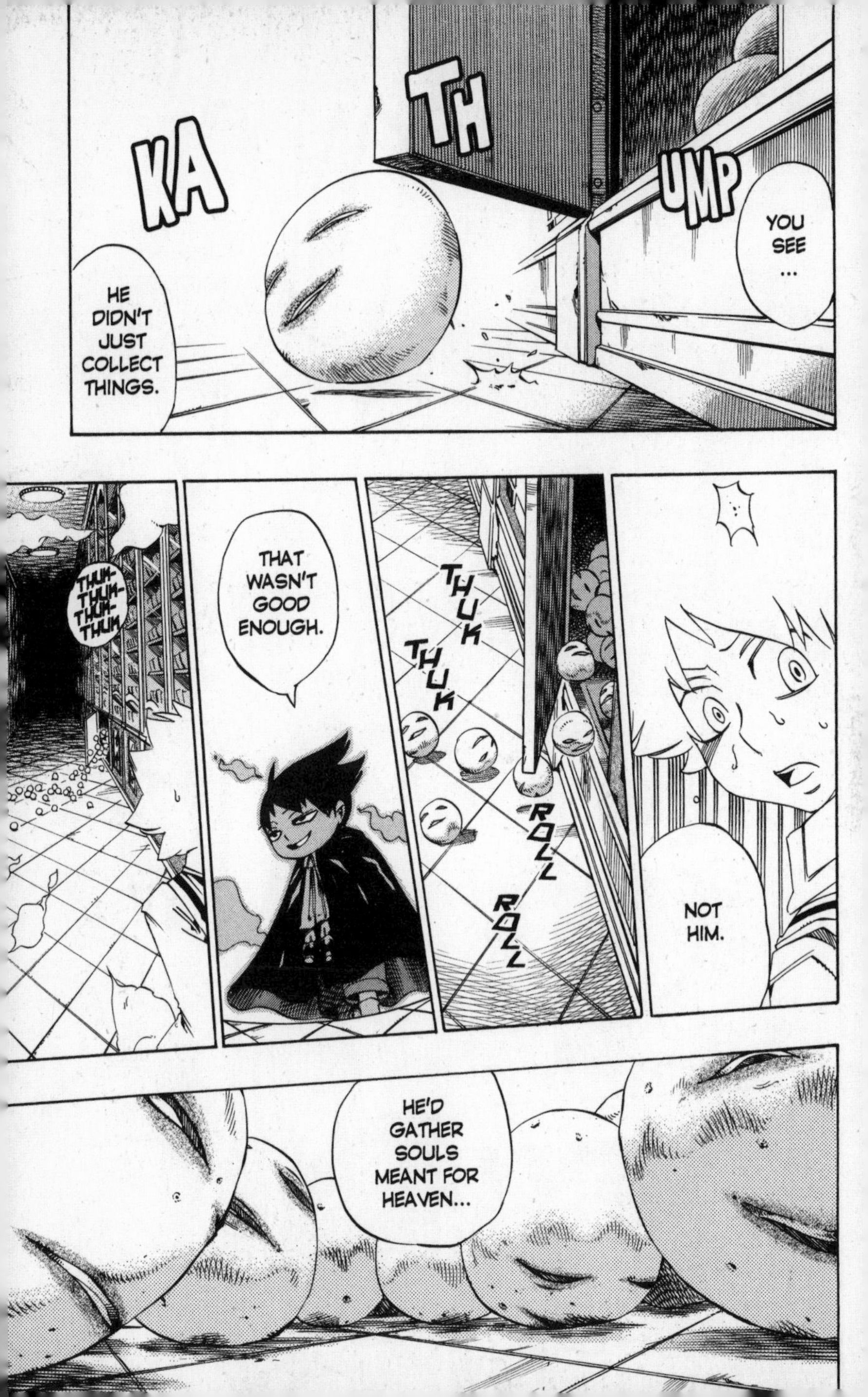
YOU SEE ...
KA TH UMP
HE DIDN'T JUST COLLECT THINGS.
NOT HIM.
THUK
THUK
ROLL
ROLL
THAT WASN'T GOOD ENOUGH.
THUM-THUM-THUM-THUM
HE'D GATHER SOULS MEANT FOR HEAVEN...

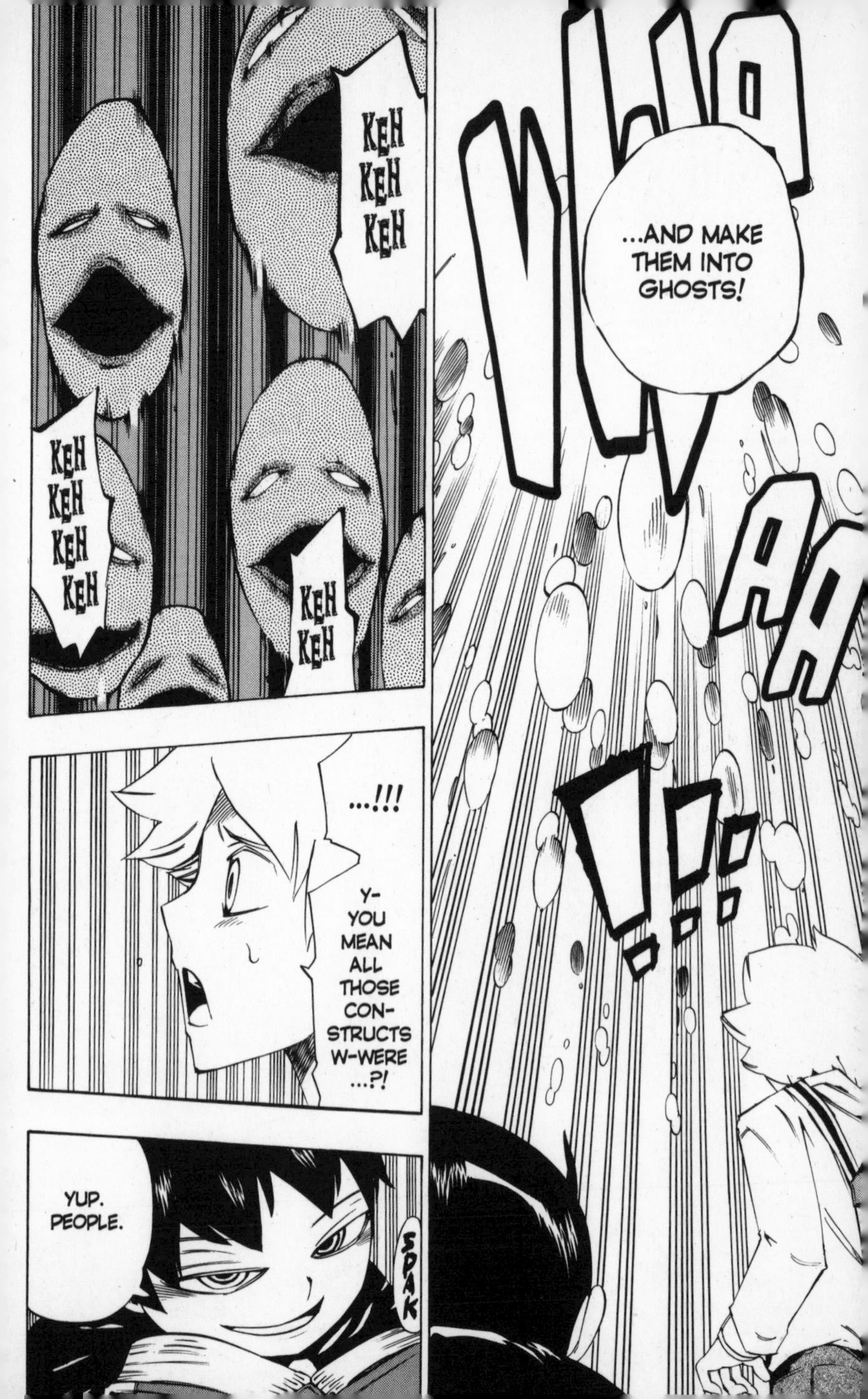
WHOAA!!
...AND MAKE THEM INTO GHOSTS!
KEH KEH KEH
KEH KEH KEH KEH
KEH KEH
...!!!
Y-YOU MEAN ALL THOSE CON-STRUCTS W-WERE ...?!
YUP. PEOPLE.
SPAK

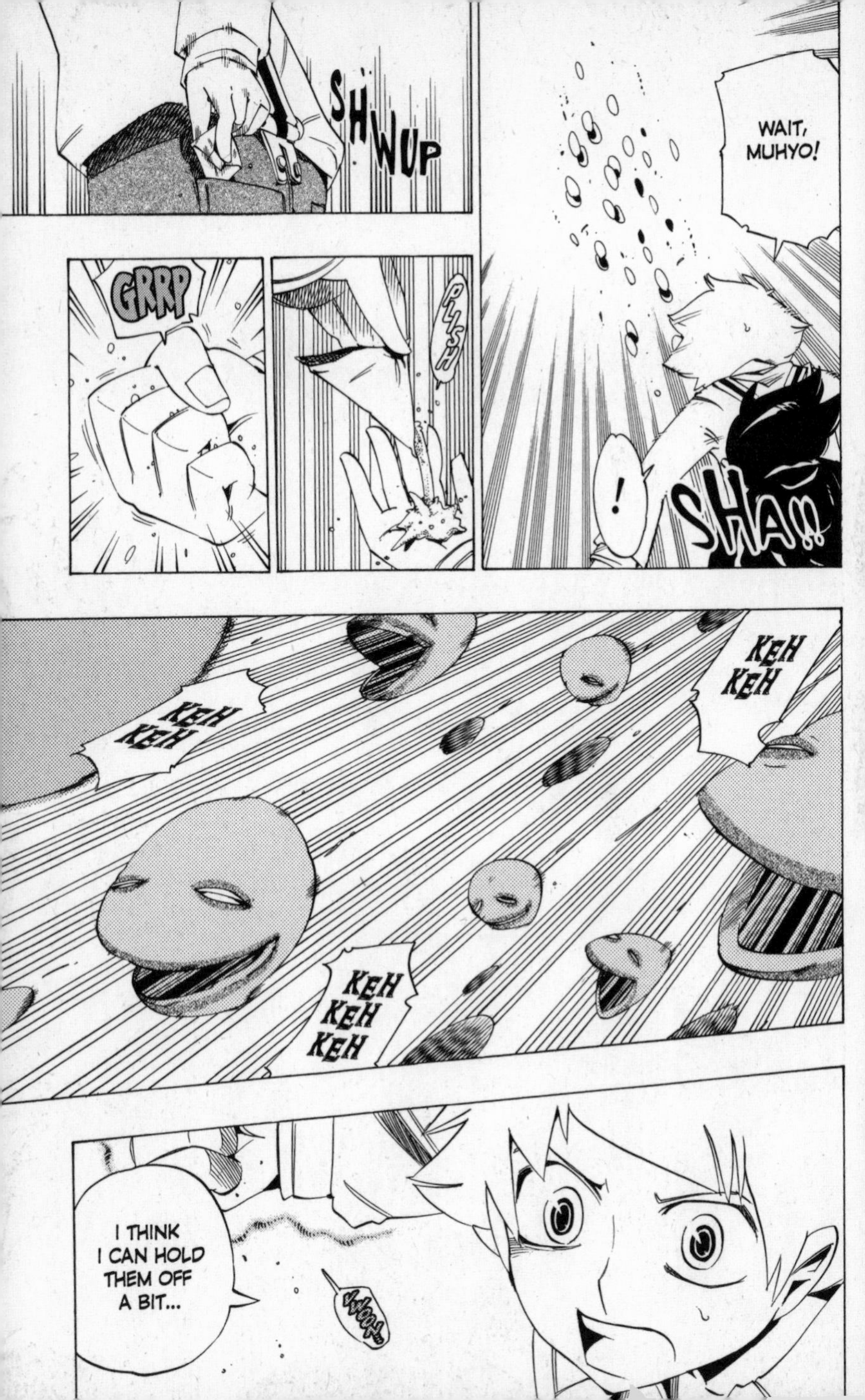
WAIT, MUHYO!
!
SHA!!
SHWUP
PLISH
GRRP
KEH KEH
KEH KEH
KEH KEH KEH
I THINK I CAN HOLD THEM OFF A BIT...

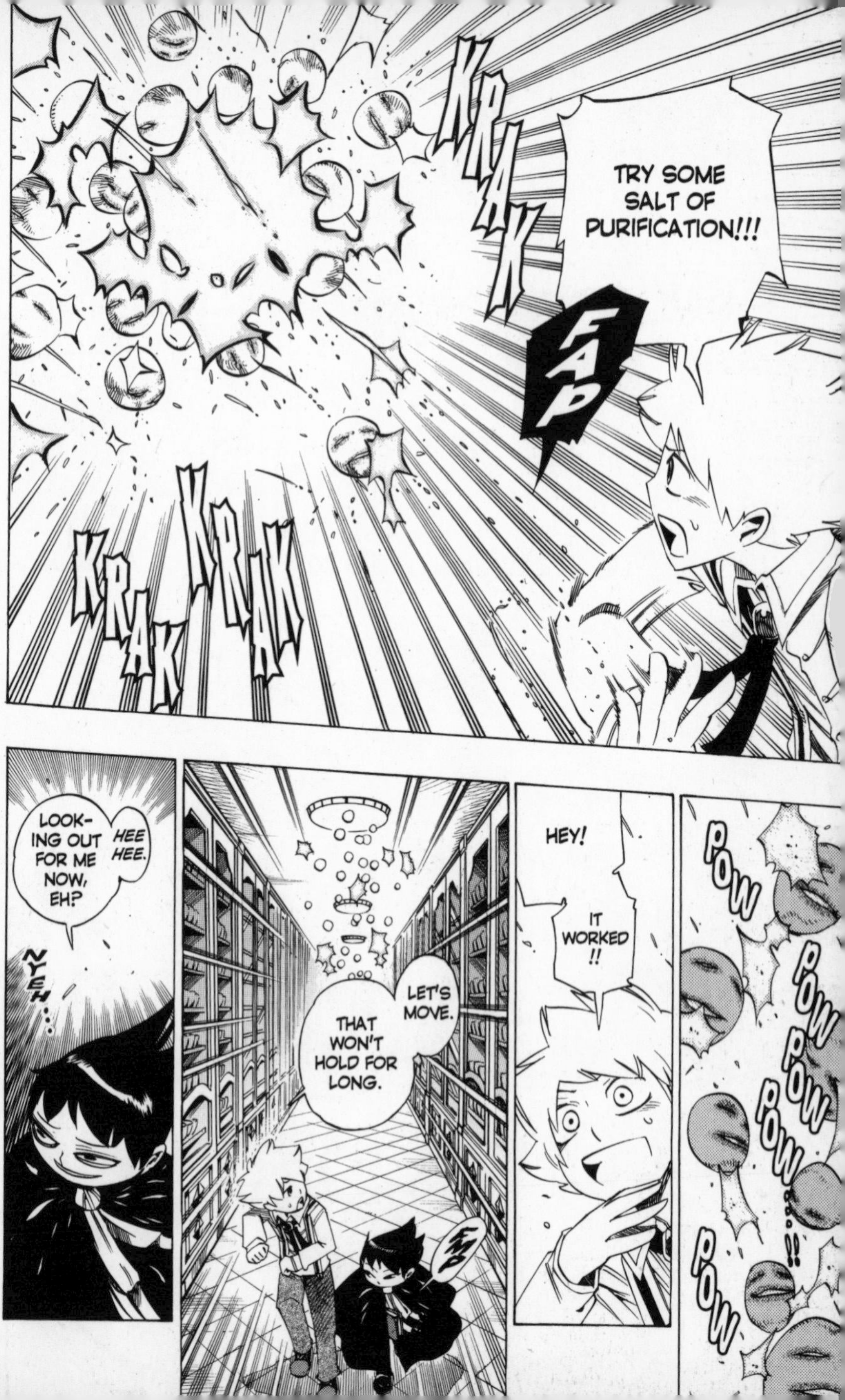
KRAK
TRY SOME SALT OF PURIFICATION!!!
FAP
KRAK
KRAK
POW
POW
POW
POW
POW...!!
POW
POW
HEY!
IT WORKED!!
LET'S MOVE.
THAT WON'T HOLD FOR LONG.
EMP
LOOKING OUT FOR ME NOW, EH?
HEE HEE.
NYEH...

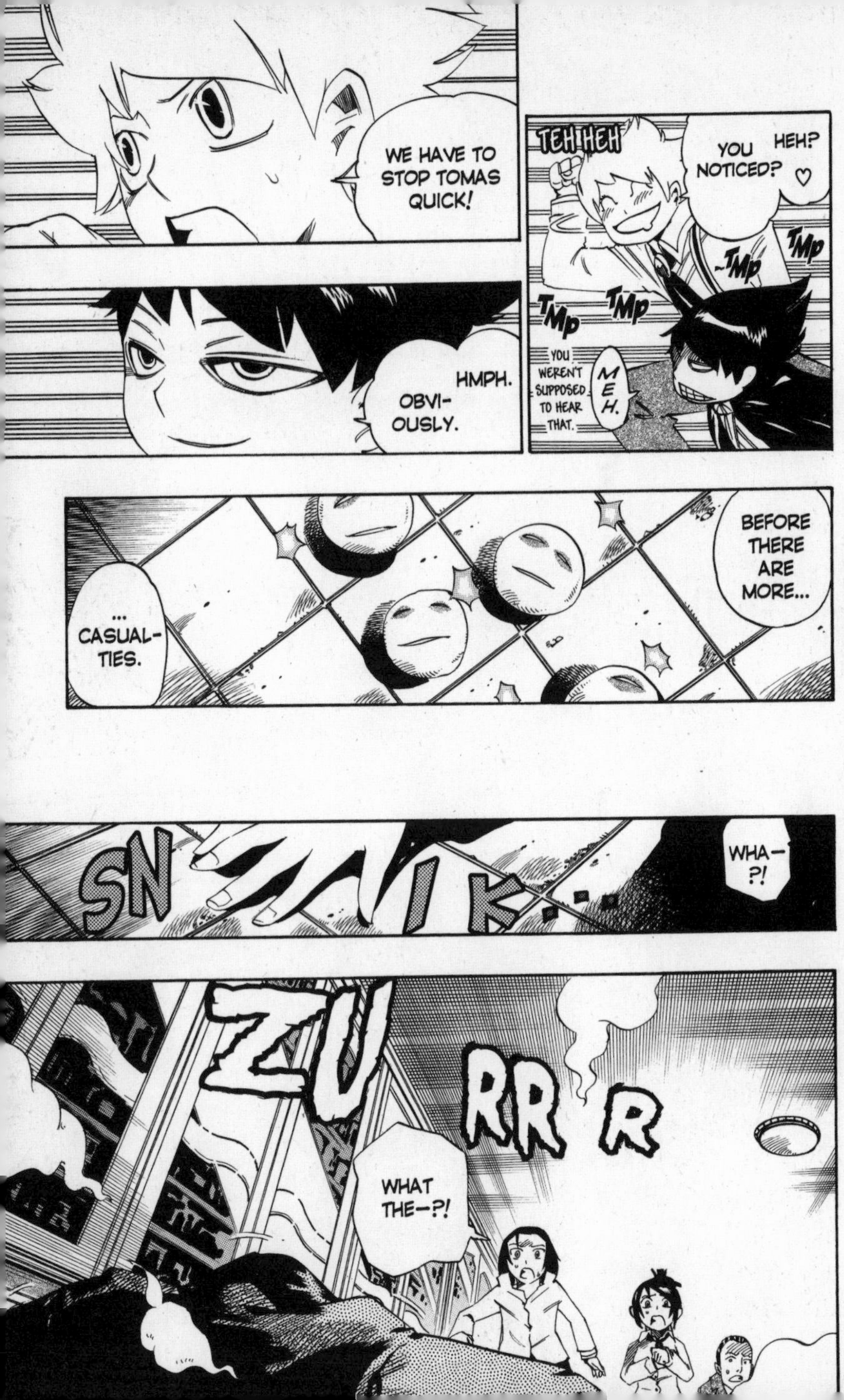
HEH? YOU NOTICED? ♥
TEH HEH
TMP TMP TMP TMP
MEH.
YOU WEREN'T SUPPOSED TO HEAR THAT.
WE HAVE TO STOP TOMAS QUICK!
HMPH. OBVIOUSLY.
BEFORE THERE ARE MORE...
... CASUALTIES.
WHA-?!
SNIK...
ZURRR
WHAT THE-?!

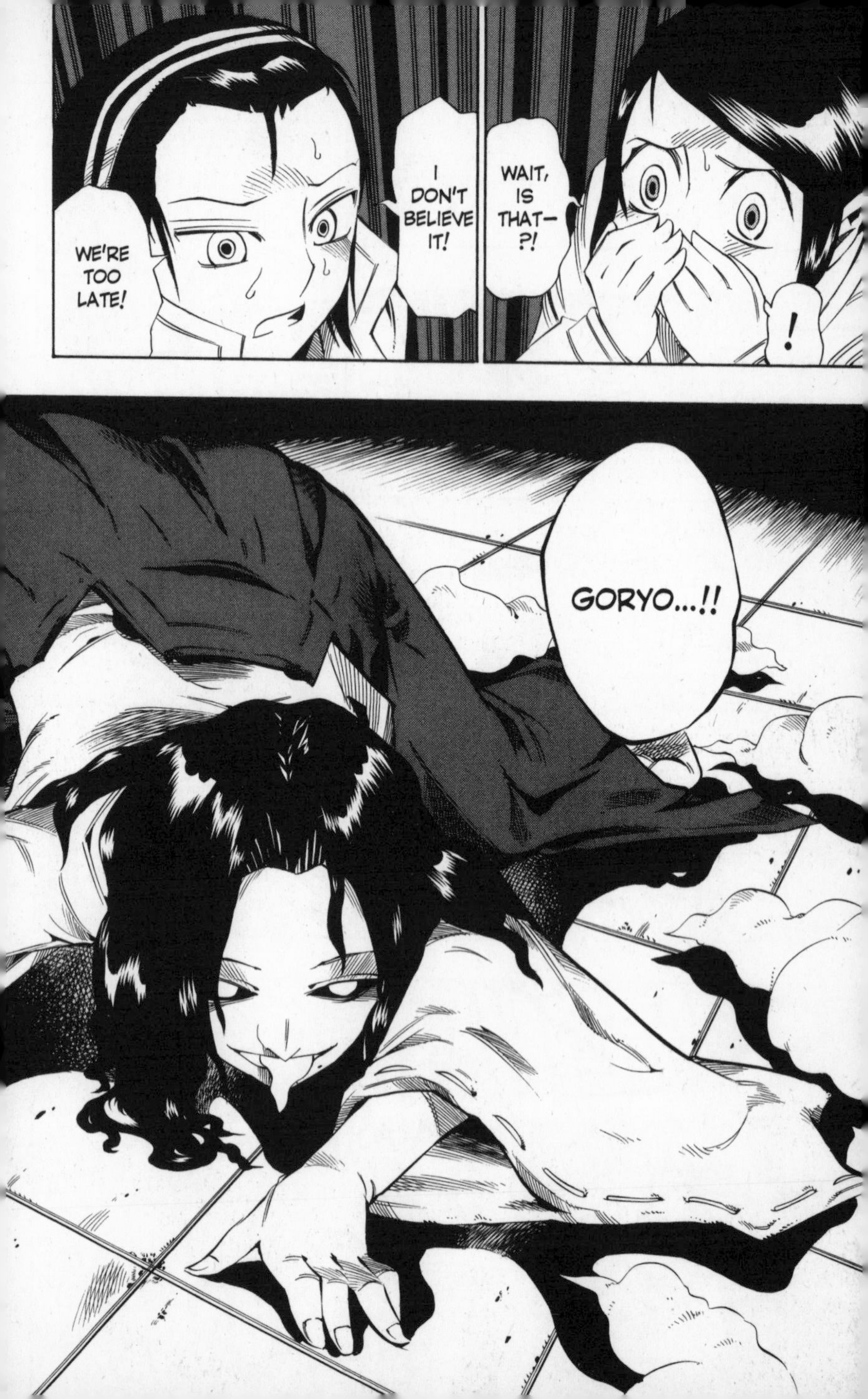
WAIT, IS THAT—?!
!
I DON'T BELIEVE IT!
WE'RE TOO LATE!
GORYO...!!

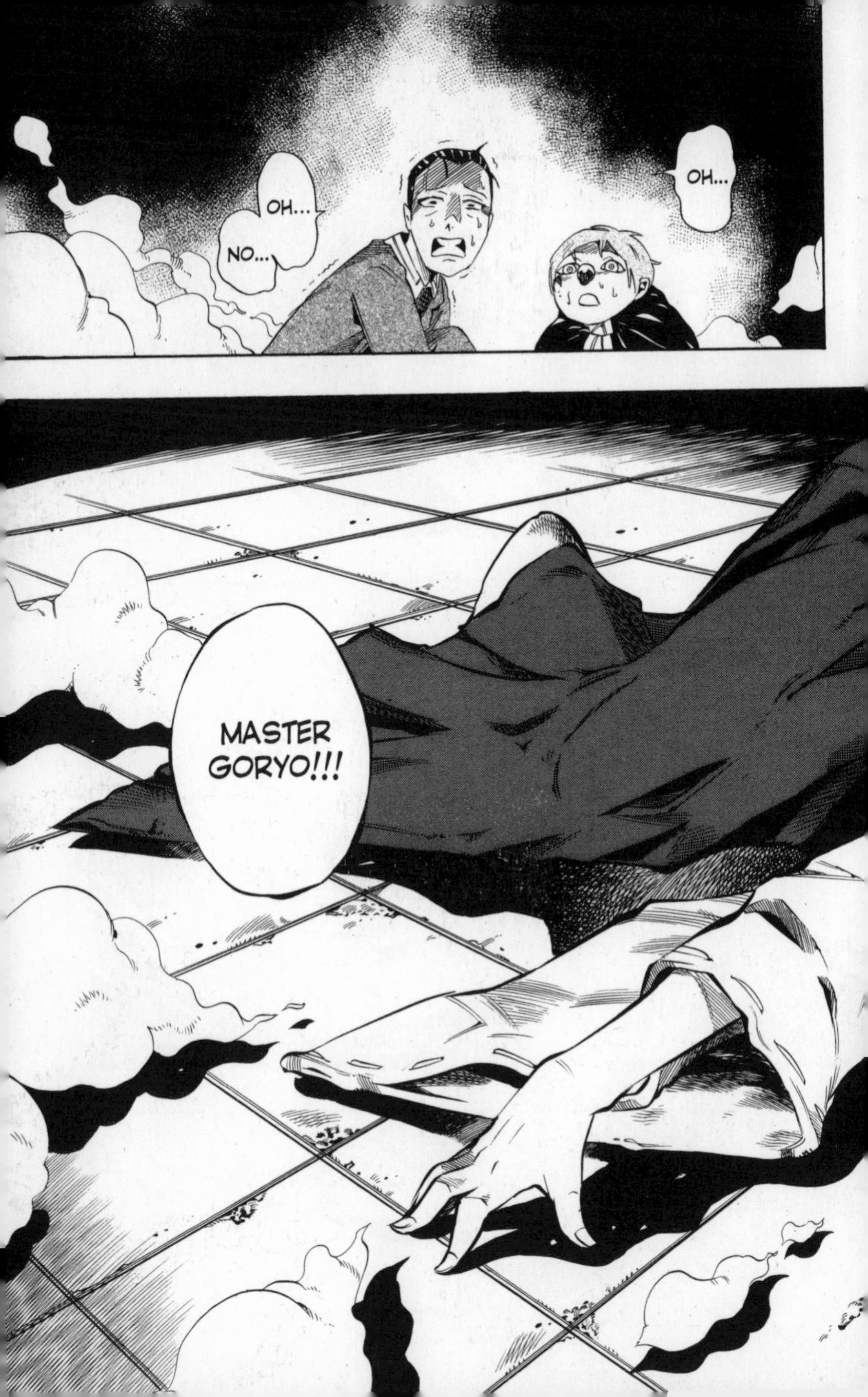
OH...
OH... NO...
MASTER GORYO!!!

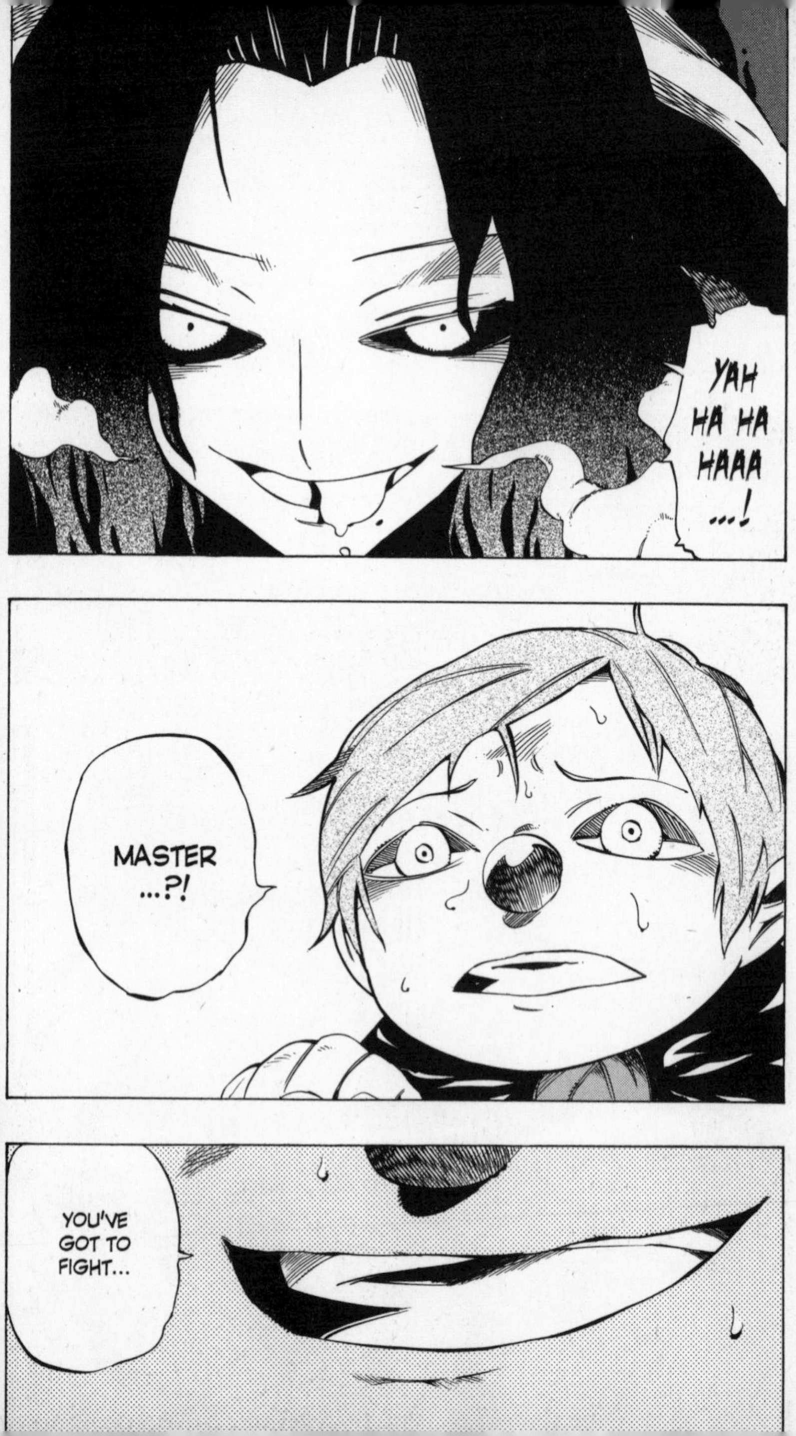
YAH HA HA HAAA ...!
MASTER ...?!
YOU'VE GOT TO FIGHT...

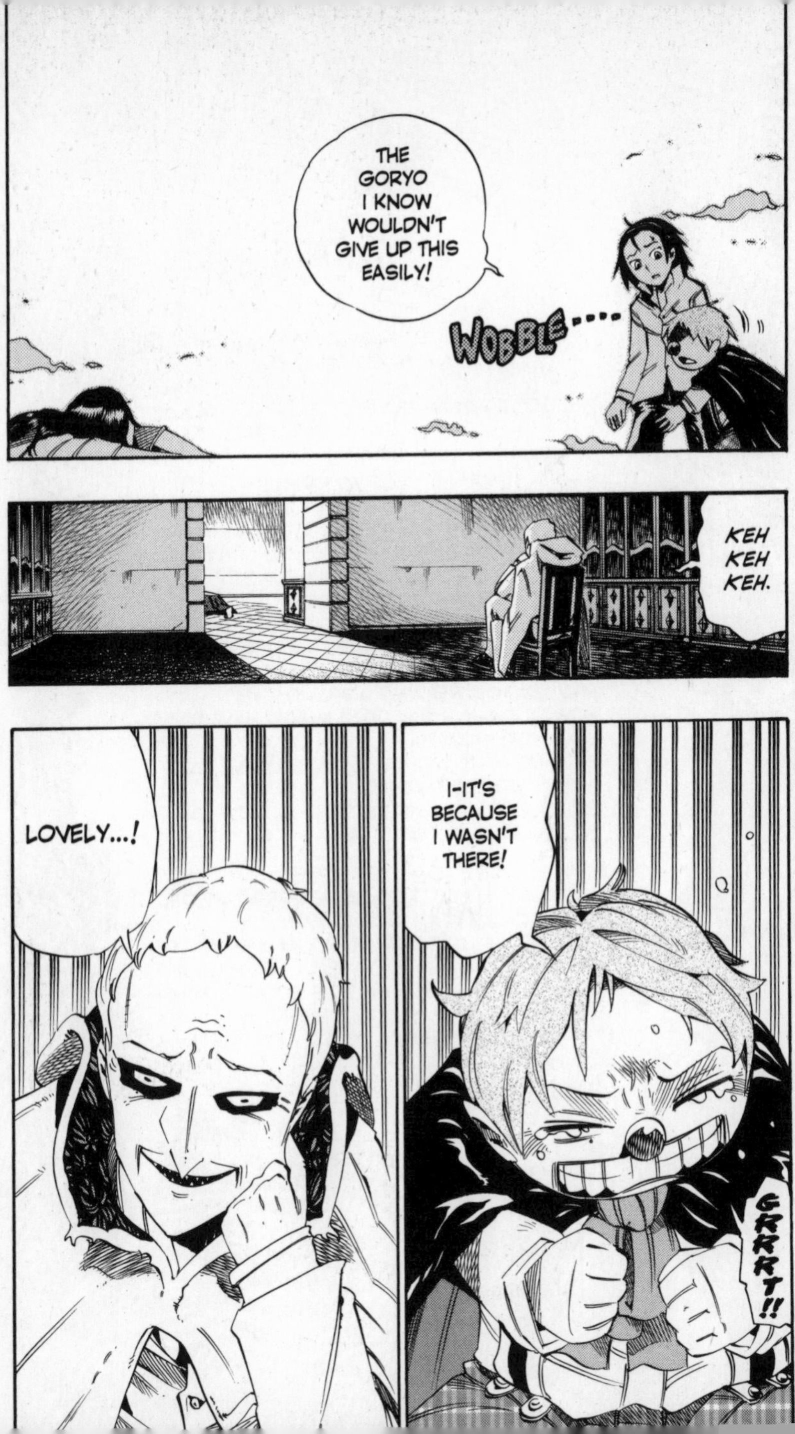
THE GORYO I KNOW WOULDN'T GIVE UP THIS EASILY!
WOBBLE....
KEH KEH KEH.
I-IT'S BECAUSE I WASN'T THERE!
GRRRT!!
LOVELY...!

HEY, IT'S ME, BACK TO ANSWER MORE QUESTIONS!
WHAM, SOCK, POWWEE!

Q: I'VE GOT A LOT OF QUESTIONS. SORRY. m(_ _)m
                                    -K.S., GIFU PREFECTURE

(1) WHY IS YOICHI SO COLD TO KIRIKO?
     BECAUSE SHE'S HIS ENVOY?
(2) WHAT ABOUT THIS "AROERO" BUSINESS MUHYO
     KEEPS GOING ON ABOUT? DID YOU JUST
     MAKE THAT UP? AND WHAT LANGUAGE
     IS "AROERO" SUPPOSED TO BE?
(3) WHY IS ROJI SUCH A LITTLE GIRL?!
(4) SPEAKING OF GIRLS, GORYO'S A GIRL TOO,
     ISN'T HE?
(5) AND YOICHI'S WEARING A WIG, RIGHT?
(6) HOW MUCH HAIR GEL DOES MUHYO HAVE TO
     USE EVERY MORNING?
(7) LILI AND MARIL AREN'T JAPANESE NAMES...SO
     WHERE ARE THEY FROM?
(8) BELLOCENT IS ALWAYS GIGGLING. HOW CAN
     WE MAKE HIM STOP?

A: YOW! SO MANY! ERM... LET'S SEE...
    (1) REALLY? IS HE? (2) IT SEEMED RIGHT AT THE
    TIME. HE CALLS IT AN INCANTATION. THE
    LANGUAGE IS UNDERSPEAK. YOU KNOW, WHAT
    THEY SAY DOWN THERE. (3) YEAH, I WONDER THAT
    MYSELF. (4) YOUR GUESS IS AS GOOD AS MINE.
    (5) HAH! (6) HE SLEEPS ON IT WEIRD, THAT'S ALL.
    (7) THEY'RE BRITISH. (8) I COULD HAVE HIM
    SCREAM, LIKE YOICHI. "AAAAAUGH!"

         WOW, THAT WAS TOUGH...

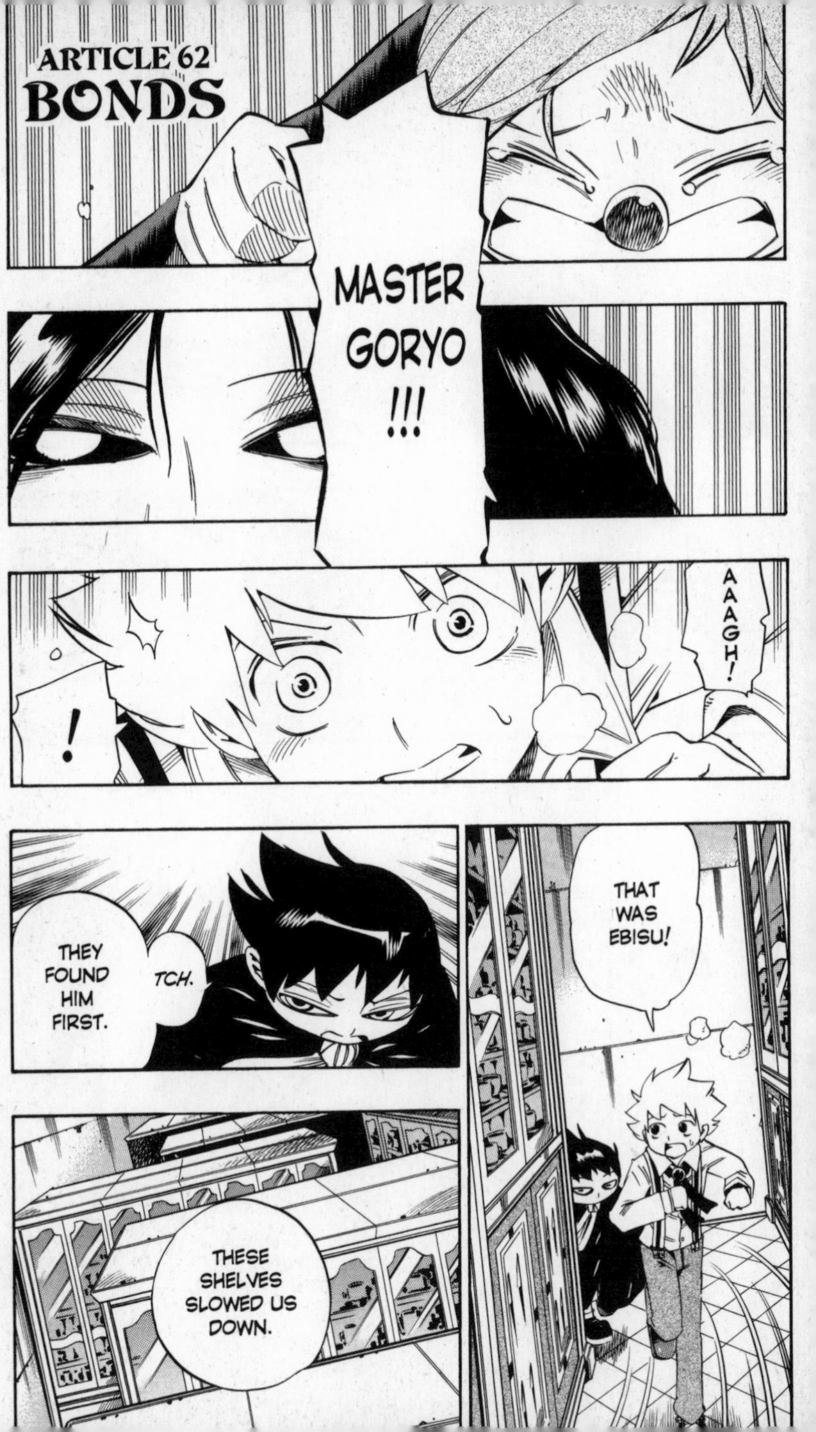
ARTICLE 62
BONDS
MASTER GORYO!!!
AAAGH!
!
THAT WAS EBISU!
TCH.
THEY FOUND HIM FIRST.
THESE SHELVES SLOWED US DOWN.

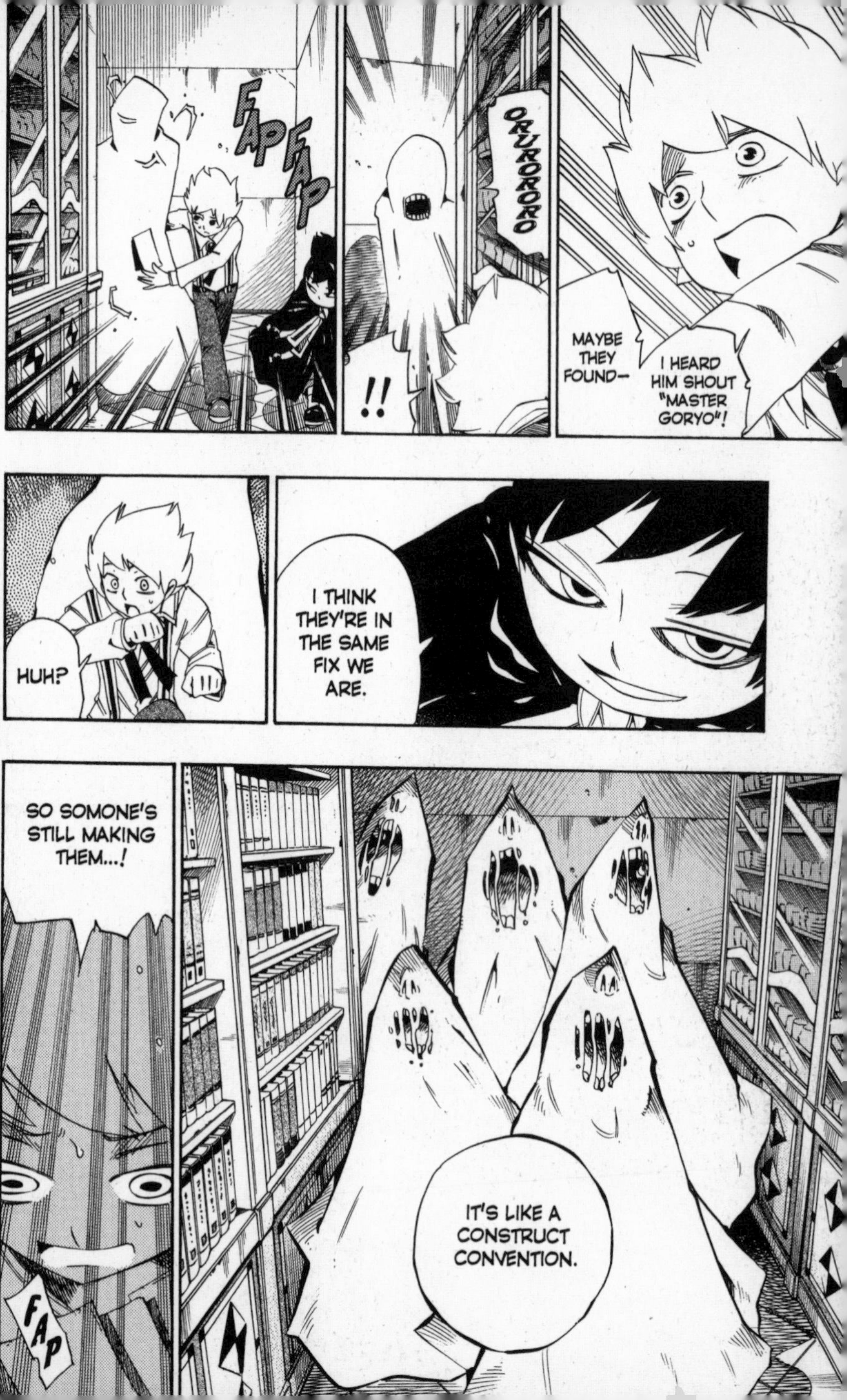

I HEARD HIM SHOUT "MASTER GORYO"!
MAYBE THEY FOUND—
ORURORORO
!!
FAP FAP FAP
I THINK THEY'RE IN THE SAME FIX WE ARE.
HUH?
IT'S LIKE A CONSTRUCT CONVENTION.
SO SOMONE'S STILL MAKING THEM...!
FAP

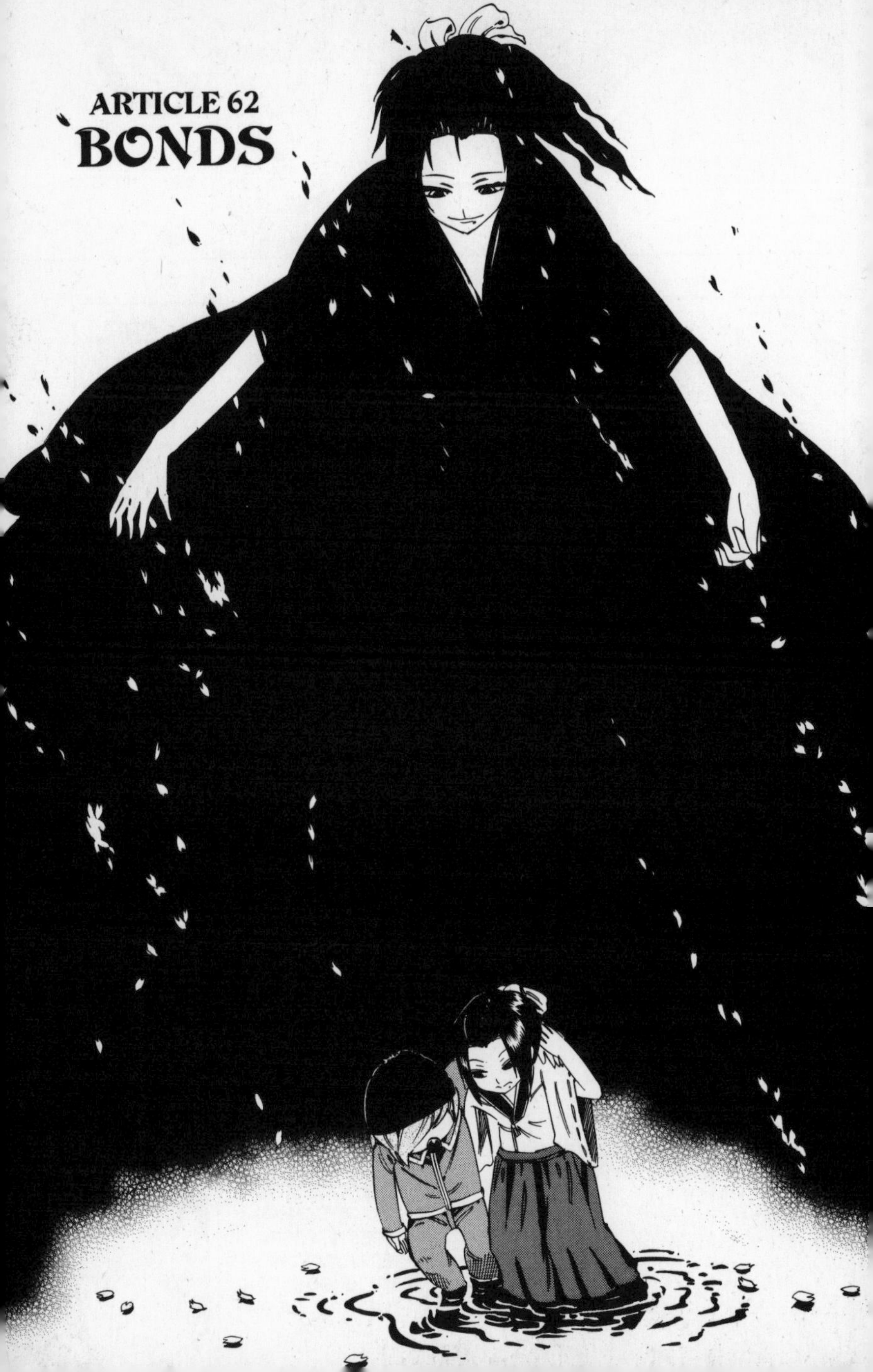
ARTICLE 62
BONDS

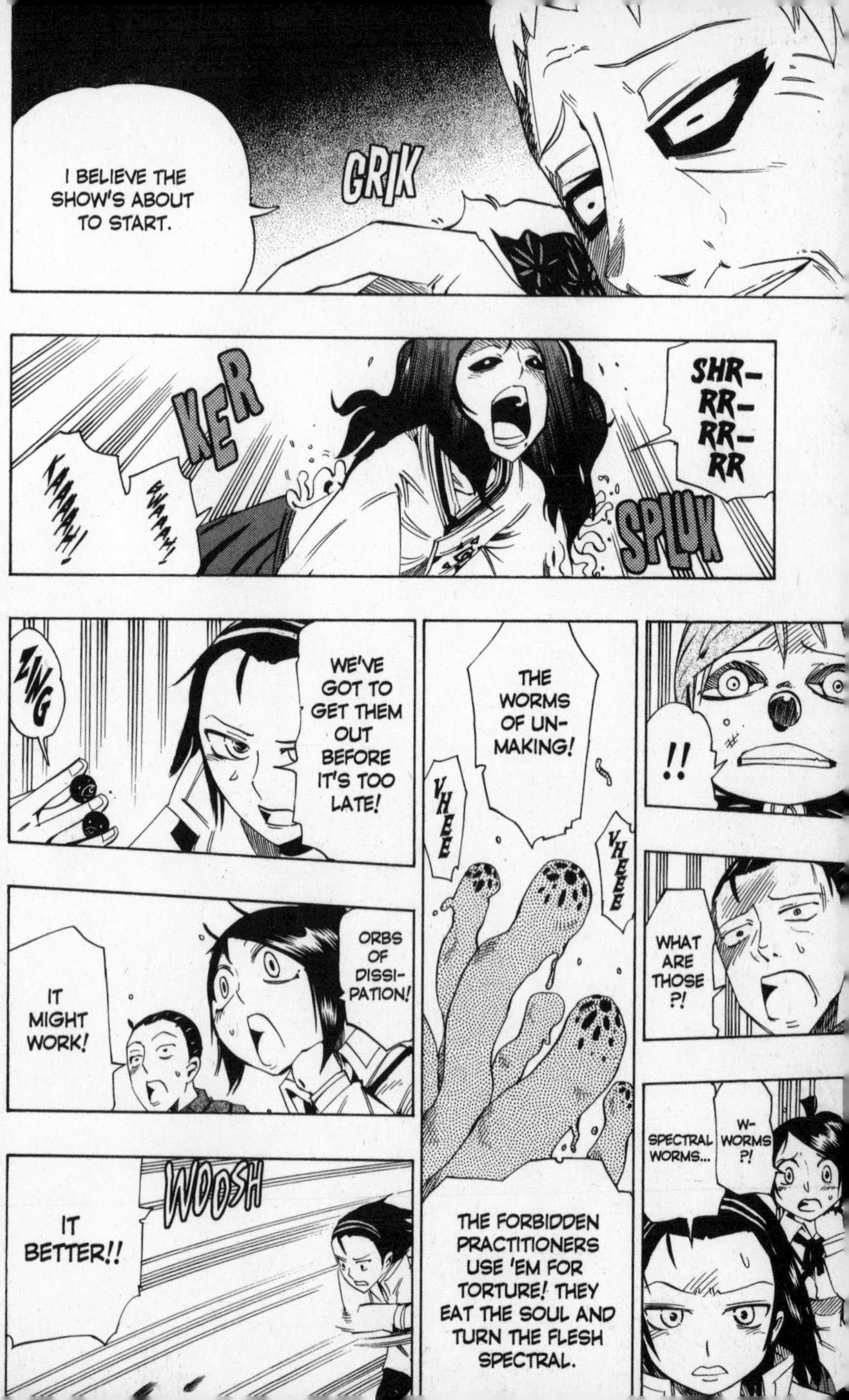

I BELIEVE THE SHOW'S ABOUT TO START.
GRIK
SHR-RR-RR-RR
SPLUK
KER
!!
WHAT ARE THOSE?!
W-WORMS?!
SPECTRAL WORMS...
THE WORMS OF UN-MAKING!
VHEEE
VHEE
THE FORBIDDEN PRACTITIONERS USE 'EM FOR TORTURE! THEY EAT THE SOUL AND TURN THE FLESH SPECTRAL.
WE'VE GOT TO GET THEM OUT BEFORE IT'S TOO LATE!
ZING
ORBS OF DISSIPATION!
IT MIGHT WORK!
WOOSH
IT BETTER!!

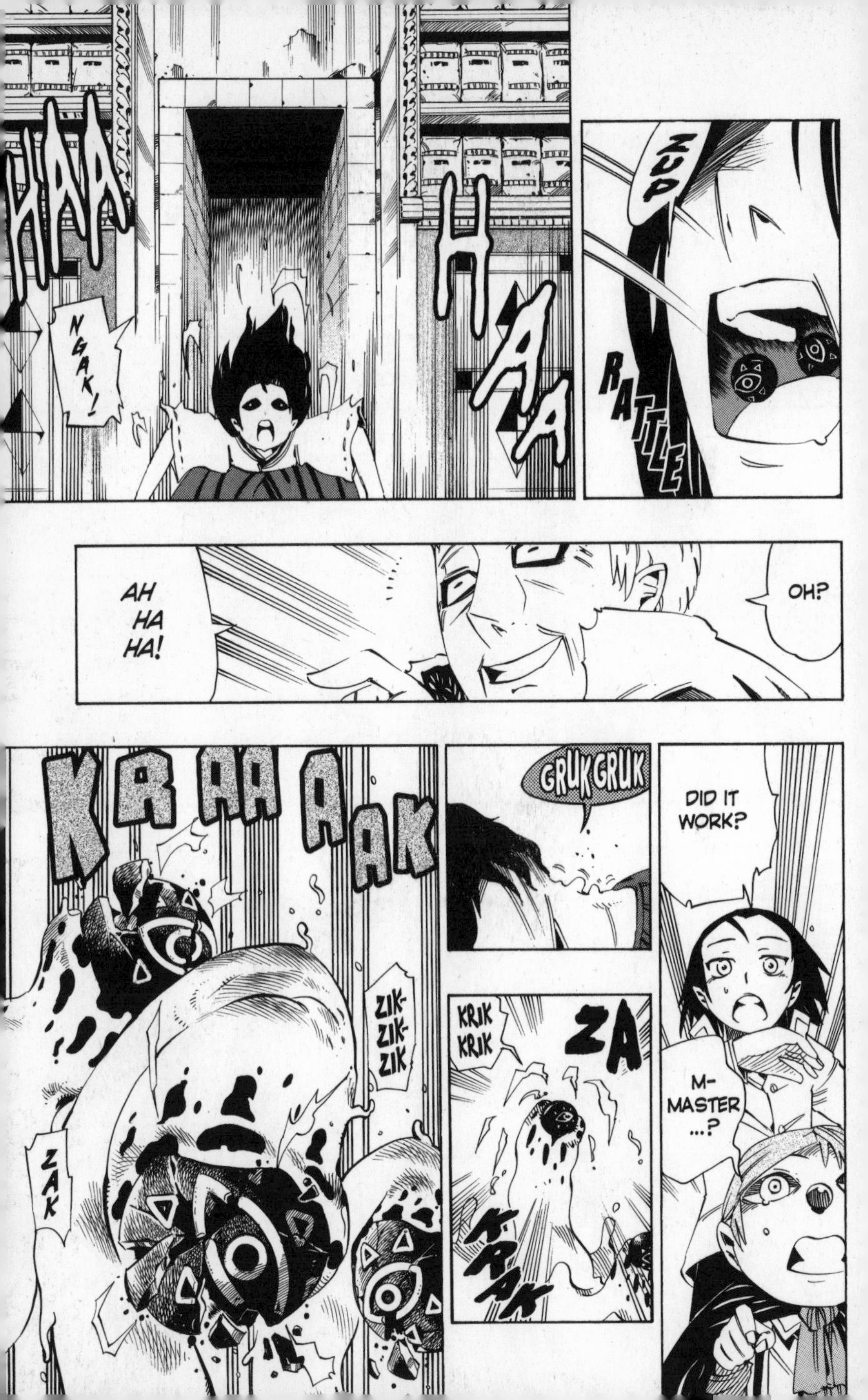
ZUP
RATTLE
HAA
HAA
NGAK!
OH?
AH HA HA!
DID IT WORK?
M-MASTER ...?
GRUKGRUK
ZA
KRIK KRIK
KRAK
KRAAAAK
ZIK-ZIK-ZIK
ZAK

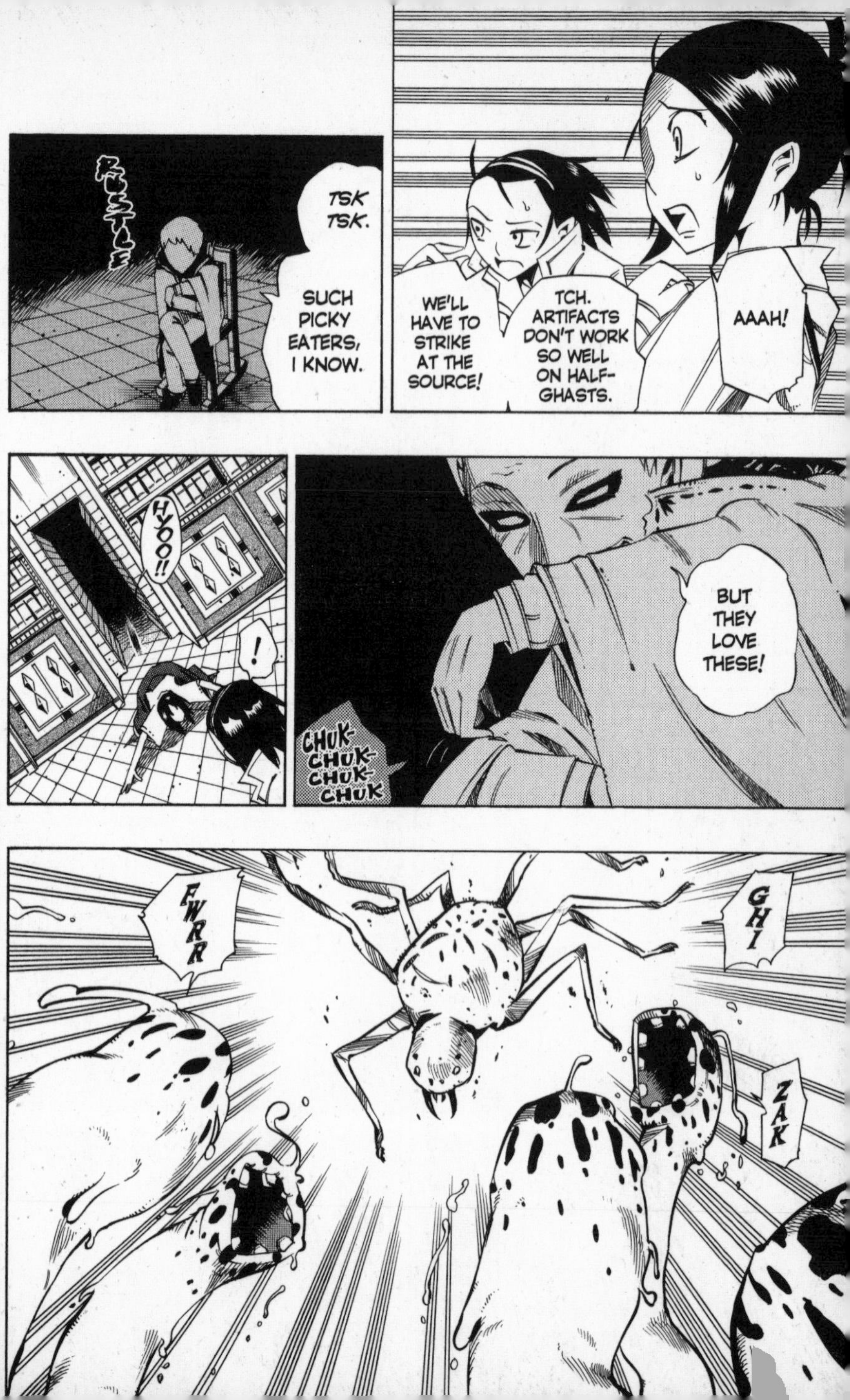
AAAH!
TCH. ARTIFACTS DON'T WORK SO WELL ON HALF-GHASTS.
WE'LL HAVE TO STRIKE AT THE SOURCE!
TSK TSK.
SUCH PICKY EATERS, I KNOW.
RUSTLE
BUT THEY LOVE THESE!
CHUK-CHUK-CHUK-CHUK
HYOO!!
!
GHI
ZAK
FWRR

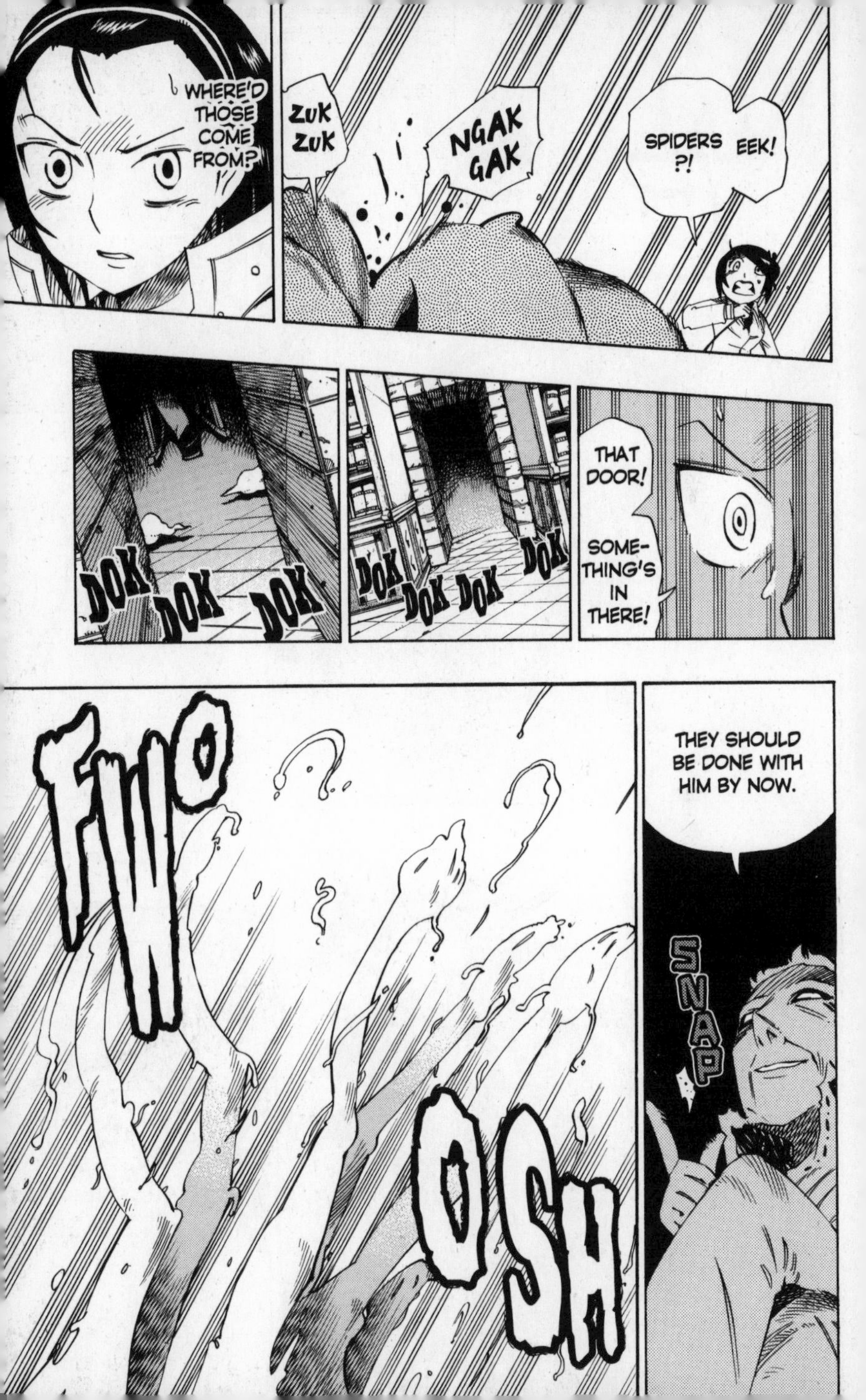
EEK!
SPIDERS ?!
NGAK GAK
ZUK ZUK
WHERE'D THOSE COME FROM?
THAT DOOR!
SOME-THING'S IN THERE!
DOK DOK DOK DOK
DOK DOK DOK
THEY SHOULD BE DONE WITH HIM BY NOW.
SNAP
FWOOSH

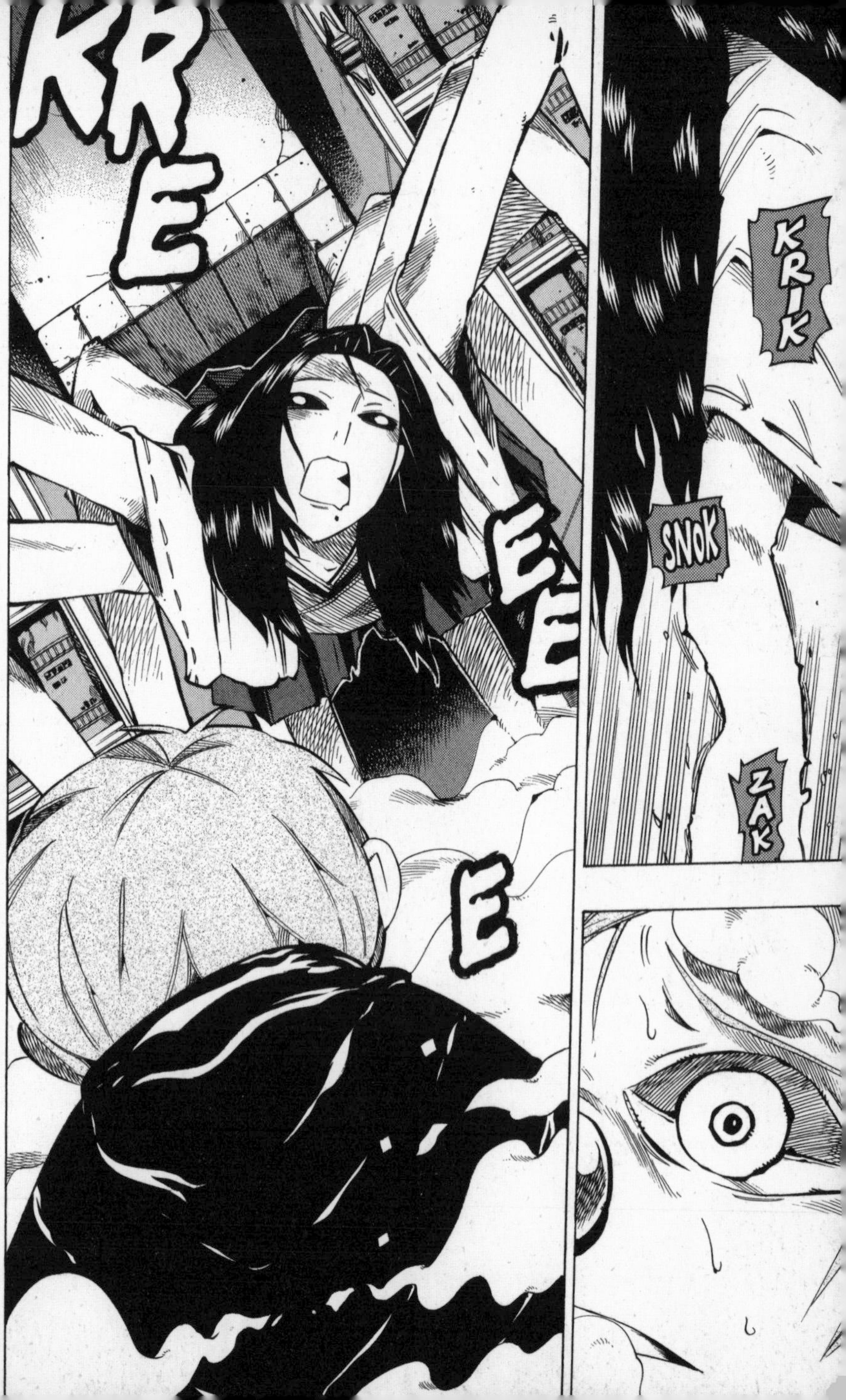
KRIK
SNOK
ZAK
KREEEE

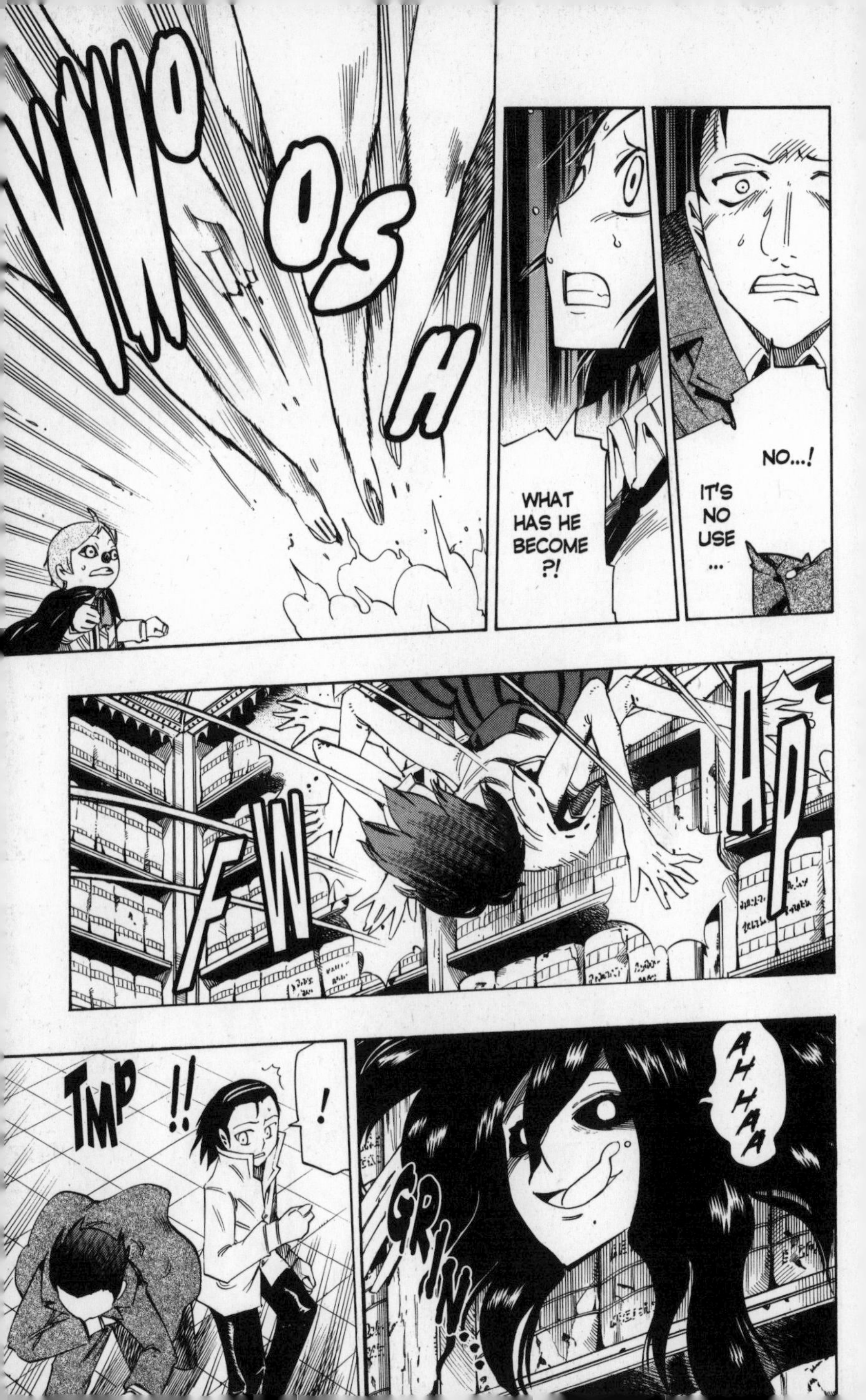
NO...!
IT'S NO USE ...
WHAT HAS HE BECOME ?!
WHOOSH
FWAP
AHHAA
GRIN
!
TMP !!

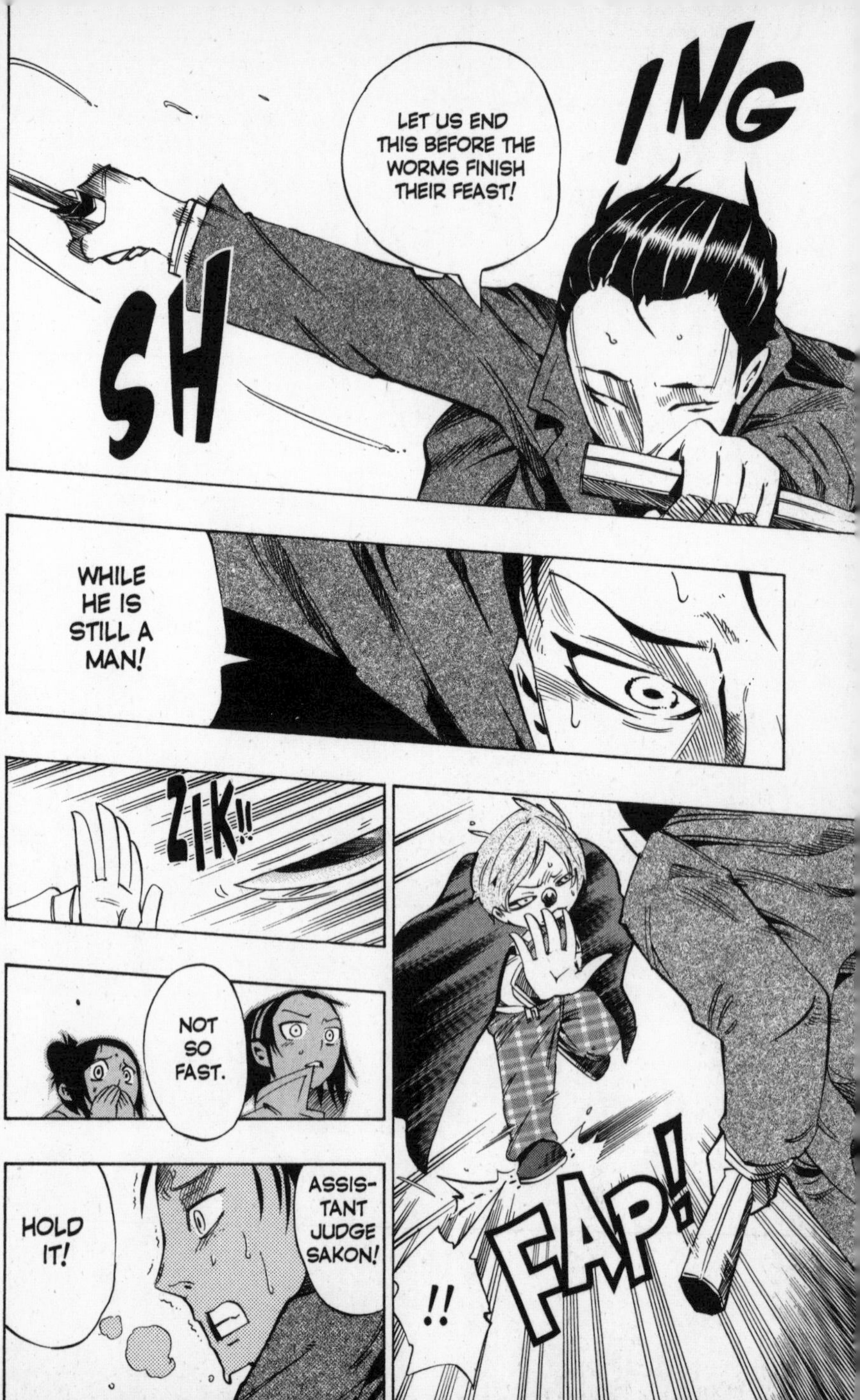
ING
LET US END THIS BEFORE THE WORMS FINISH THEIR FEAST!
SH
WHILE HE IS STILL A MAN!
FAP!
!!
ZIK!!
NOT SO FAST.
ASSIS-TANT JUDGE SAKON!
HOLD IT!

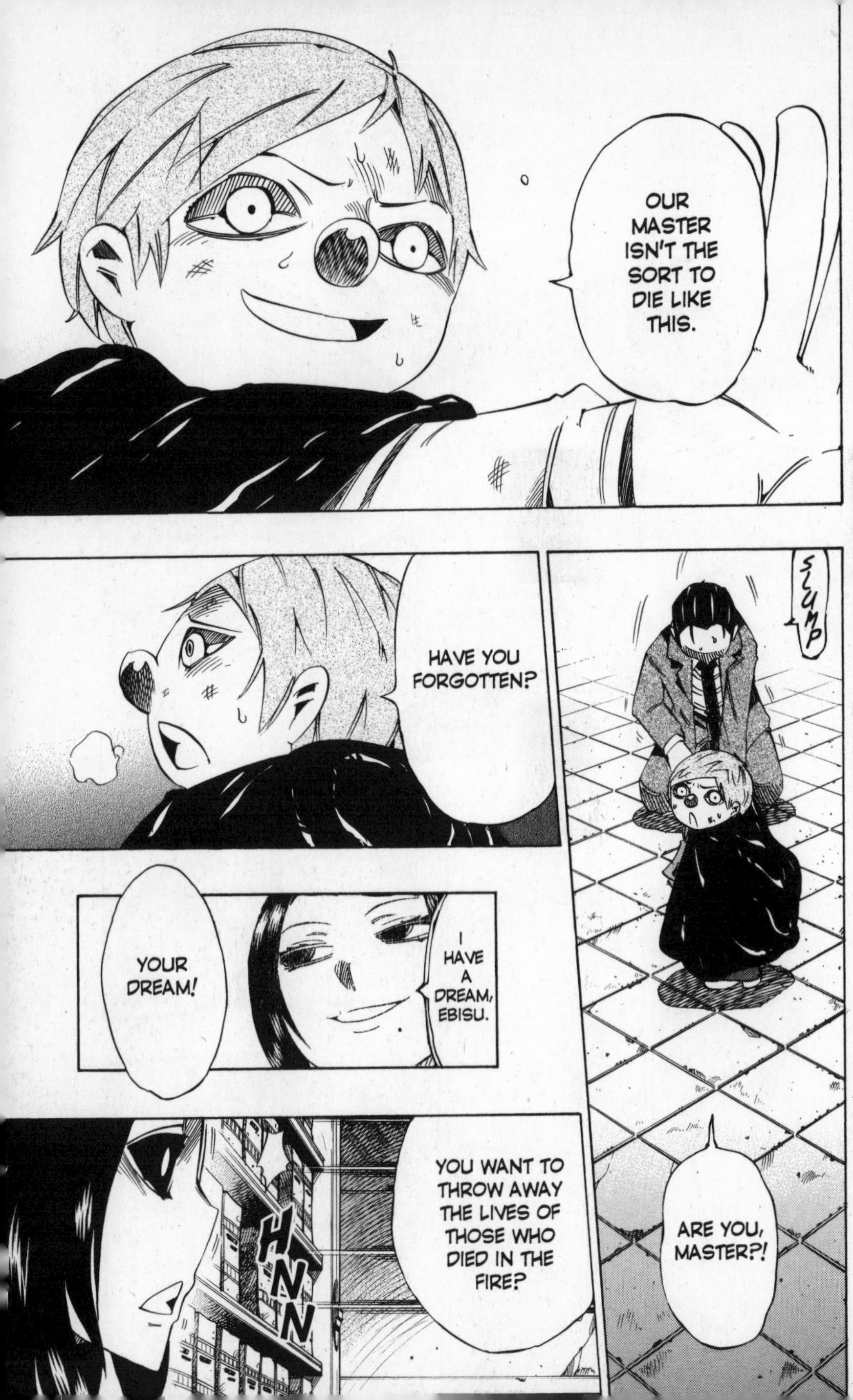
OUR MASTER ISN'T THE SORT TO DIE LIKE THIS.
SLUMP
ARE YOU, MASTER?!
HAVE YOU FORGOTTEN?
I HAVE A DREAM, EBISU.
YOUR DREAM!
HNN
YOU WANT TO THROW AWAY THE LIVES OF THOSE WHO DIED IN THE FIRE?

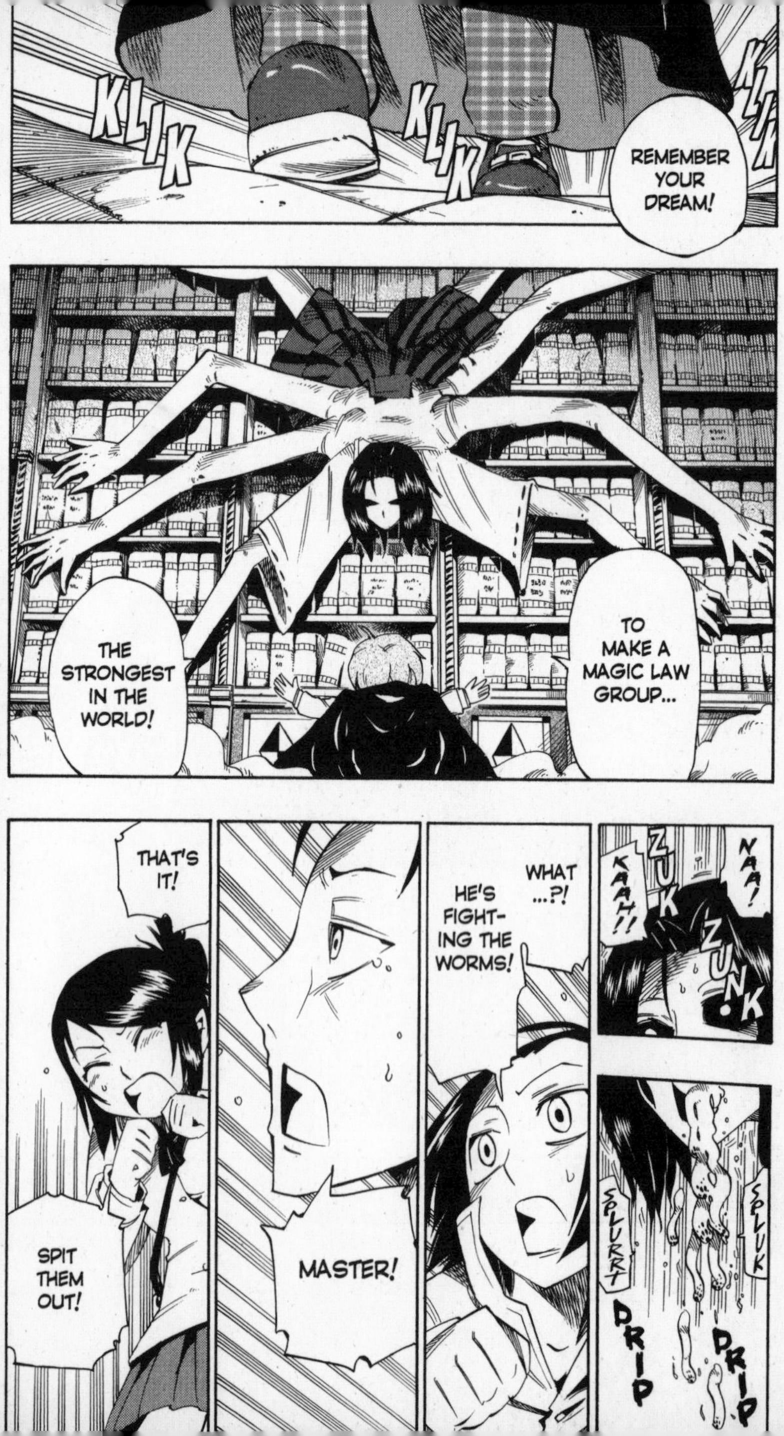
KLIK
REMEMBER YOUR DREAM!
KLIK
KLIK
TO MAKE A MAGIC LAW GROUP...
THE STRONGEST IN THE WORLD!
NAAA!
ZUK
KAAAH!!
ZUNK
SPLUK
SPLURRT
DRIP
DRIP
WHAT ...?!
HE'S FIGHT-ING THE WORMS!
MASTER!
THAT'S IT!
SPIT THEM OUT!

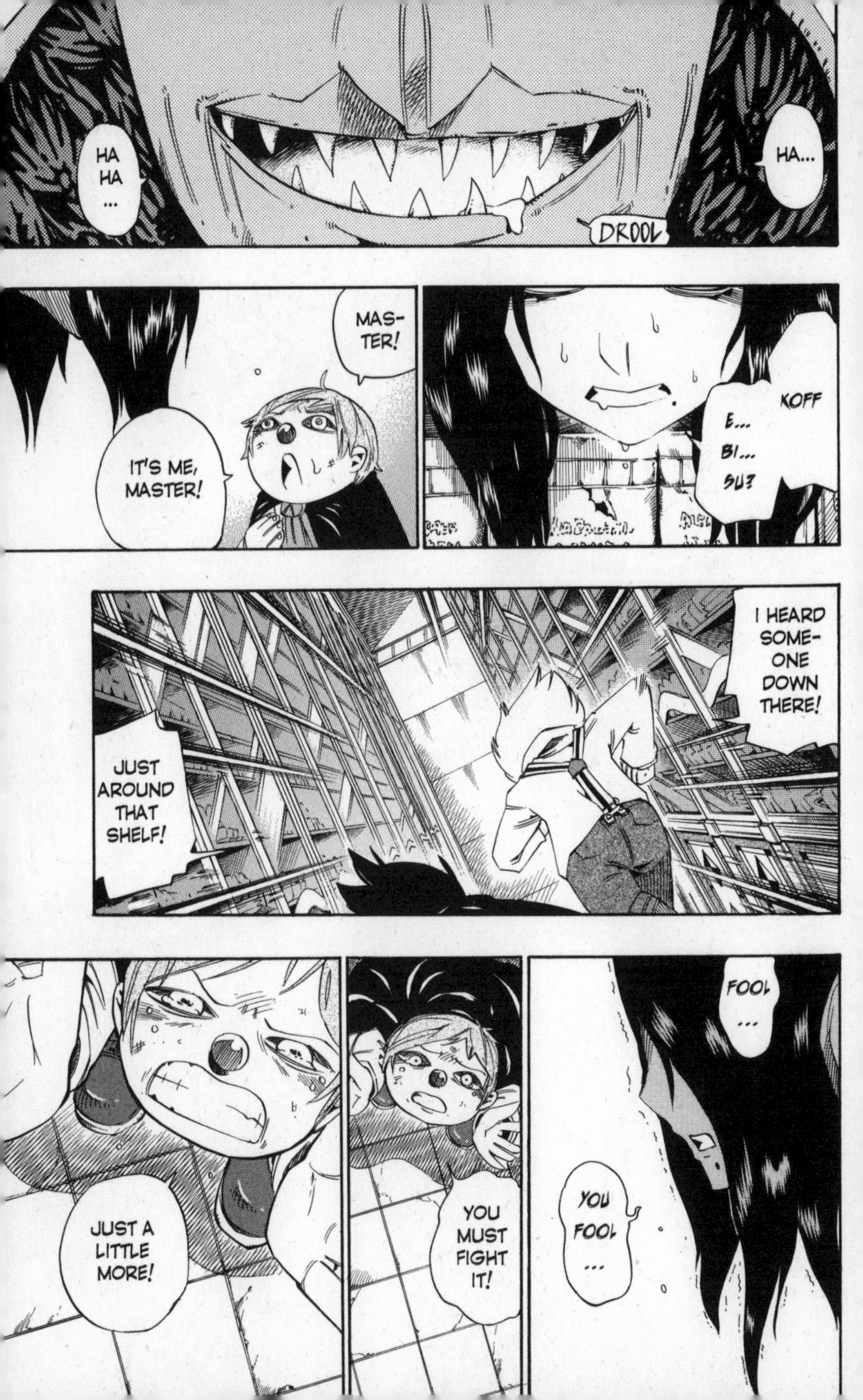
HA...
HA HA ...
DROOL
KOFF
E... BI... SU?
MASTER!
IT'S ME, MASTER!
I HEARD SOMEONE DOWN THERE!
JUST AROUND THAT SHELF!
FOOL ...
YOU FOOL ...
YOU MUST FIGHT IT!
JUST A LITTLE MORE!

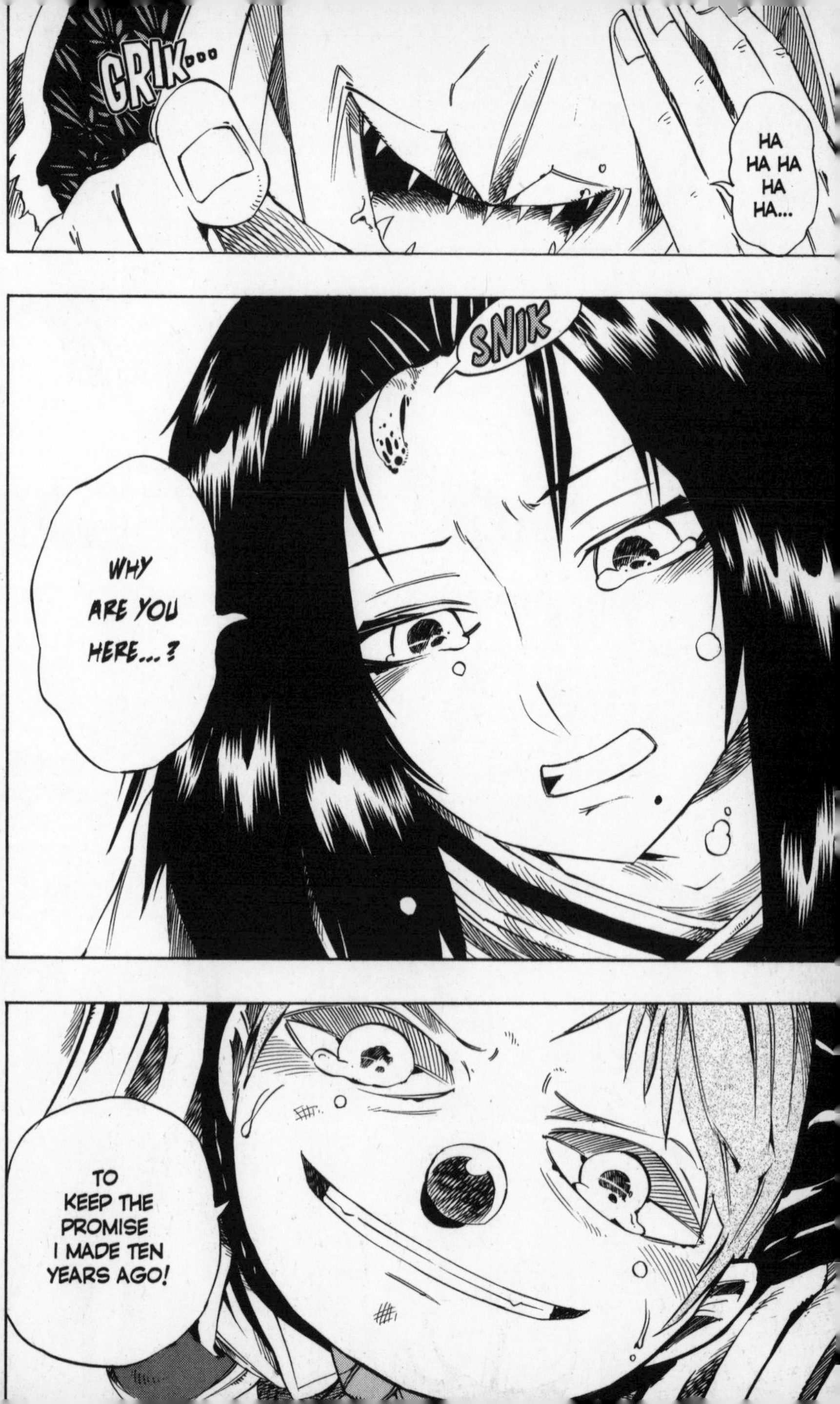
HA HA HA HA HA...
GRIK...
SNIK
WHY ARE YOU HERE...?
TO KEEP THE PROMISE I MADE TEN YEARS AGO!

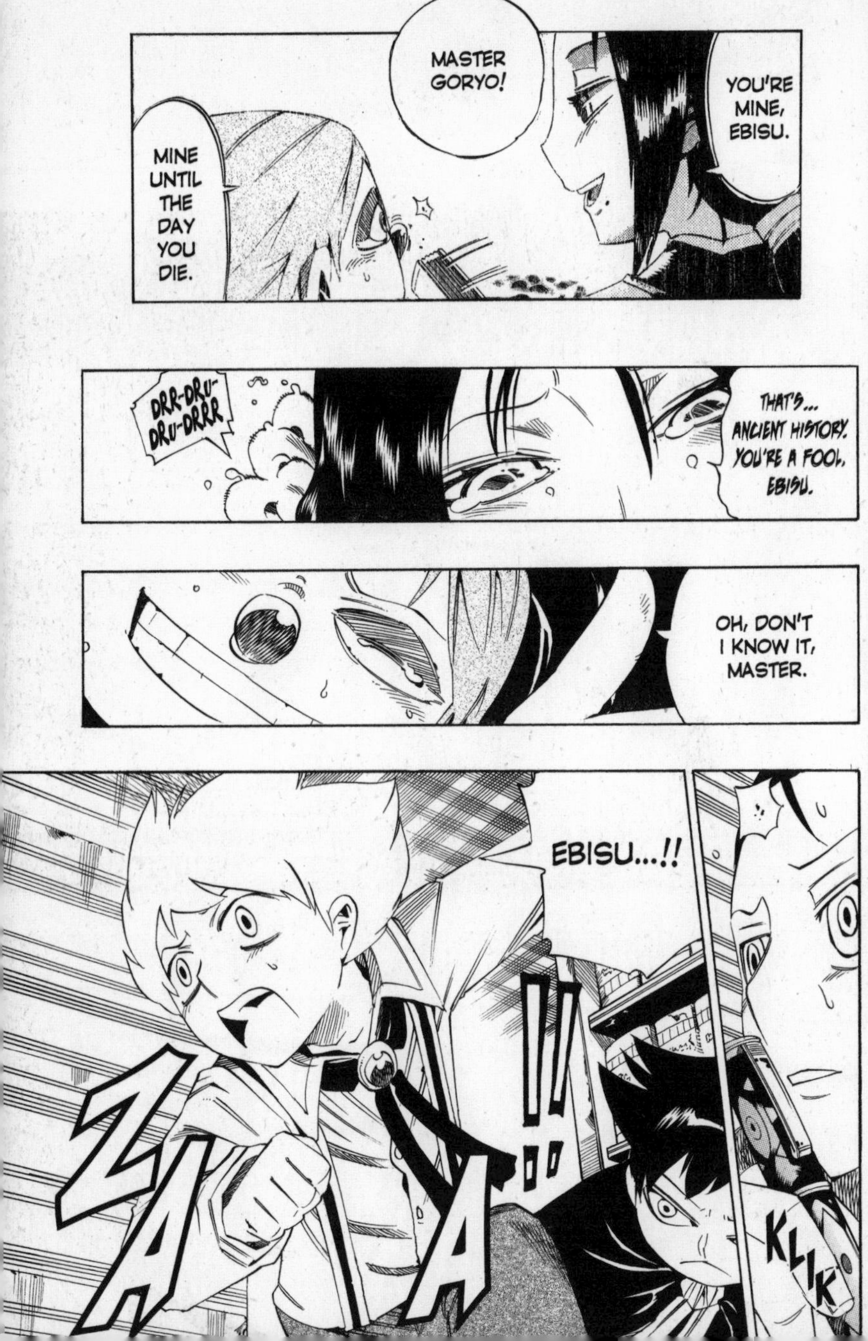
YOU'RE MINE, EBISU.
MASTER GORYO!
MINE UNTIL THE DAY YOU DIE.
THAT'S... ANCIENT HISTORY. YOU'RE A FOOL, EBISU.
DRR-DRU-DRU-DRRR
OH, DON'T I KNOW IT, MASTER.
EBISU...!!
KLIK
ZAA!!

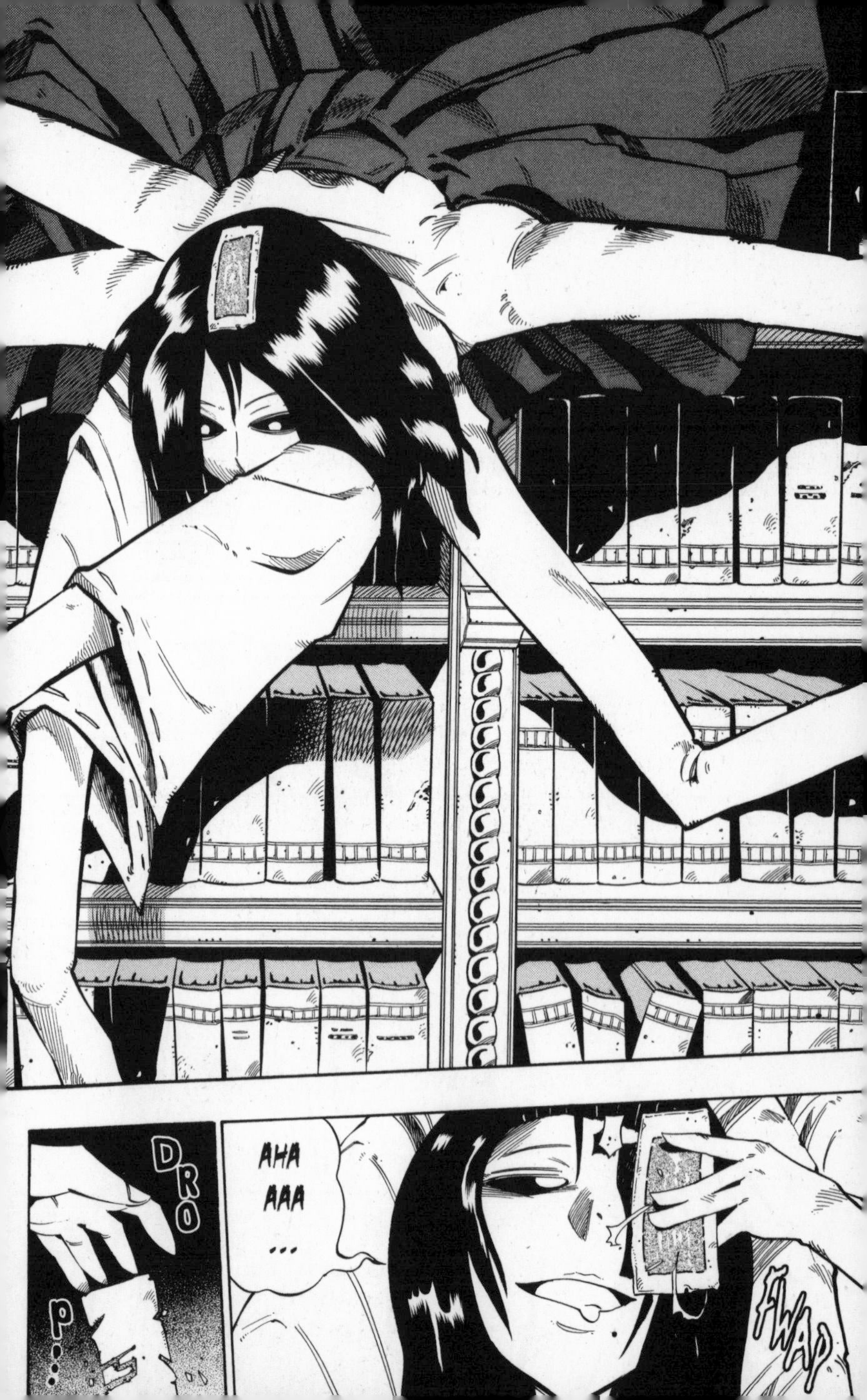
AHA AAA ...
FWAP
DROP...

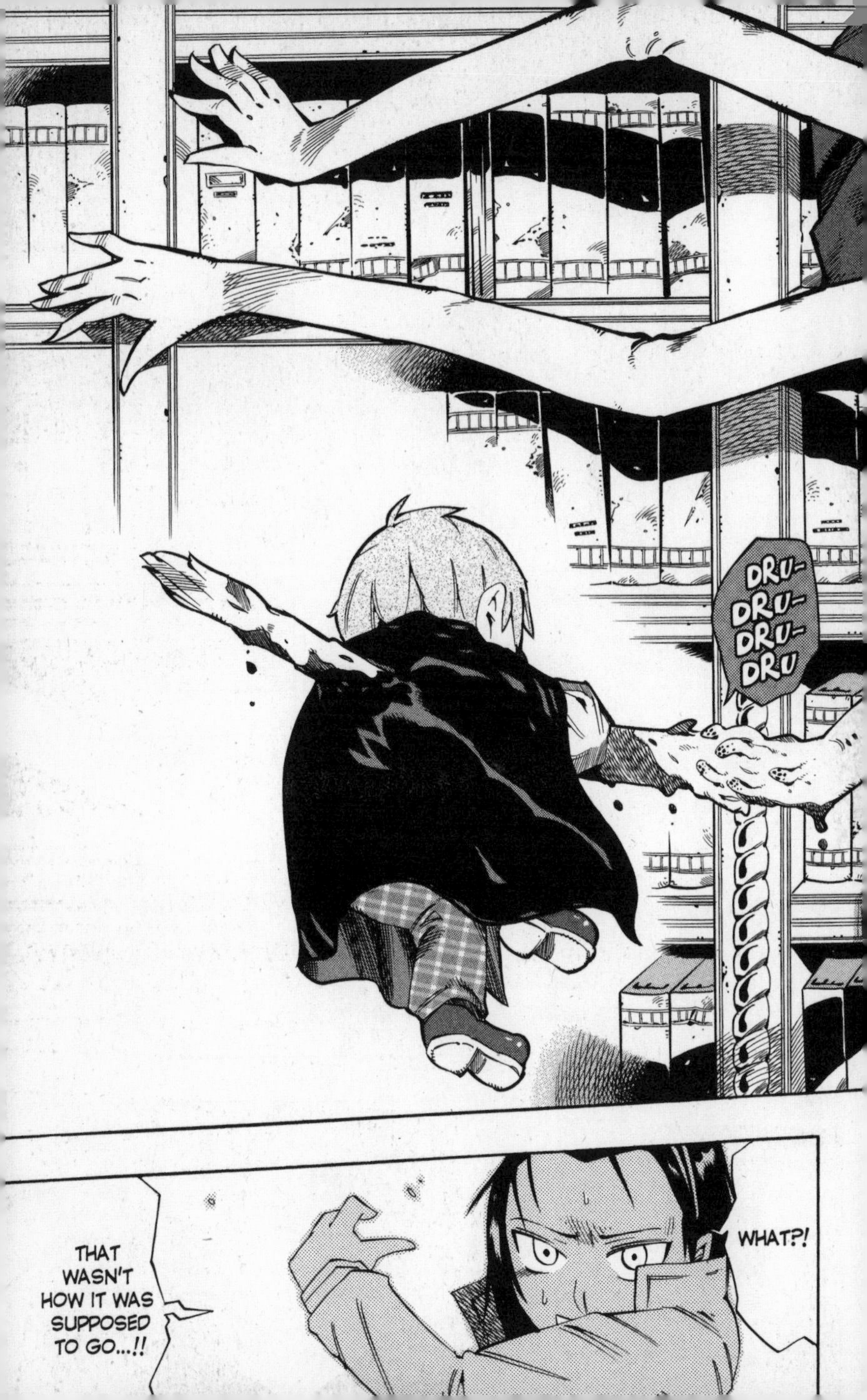
DRU-DRU-DRU-DRU
WHAT?!
THAT WASN'T HOW IT WAS SUPPOSED TO GO...!!

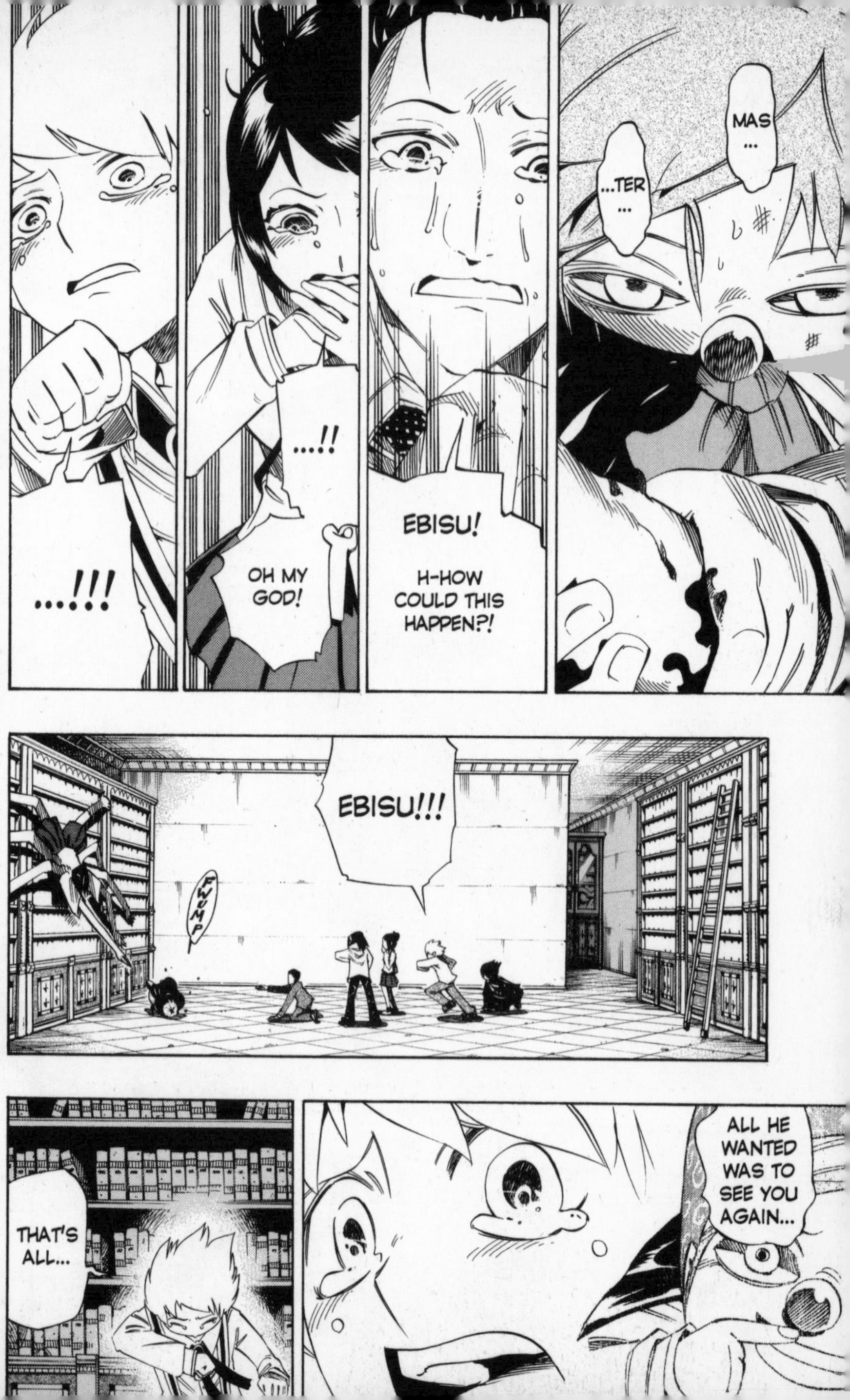
MAS...
...TER...
EBISU!
H-HOW COULD THIS HAPPEN?!
...!!
OH MY GOD!
...!!!
EBISU!!!
FWUMP
ALL HE WANTED WAS TO SEE YOU AGAIN...
THAT'S ALL...

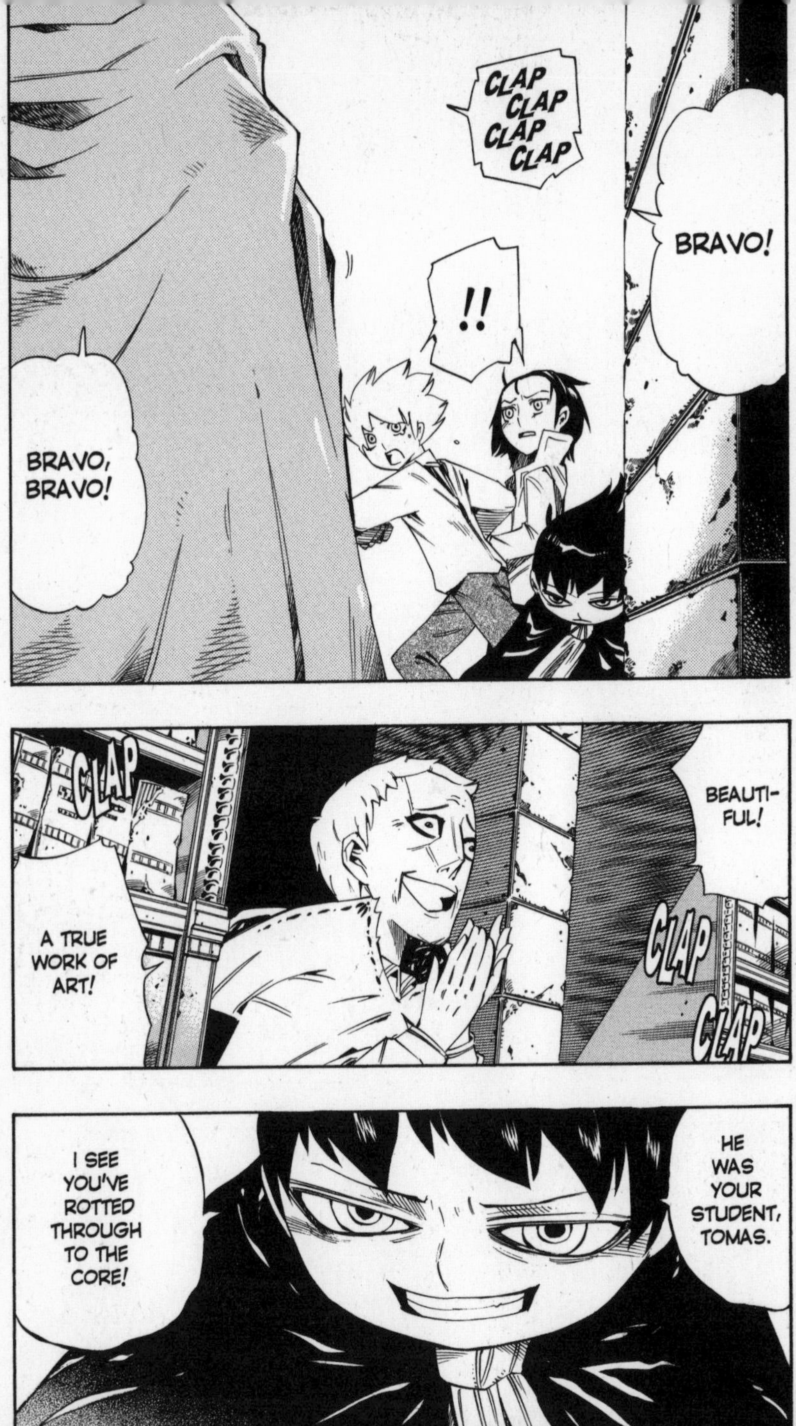
BRAVO!
CLAP CLAP CLAP CLAP
!!
BRAVO, BRAVO!
BEAUTI-FUL!
CLAP CLAP
A TRUE WORK OF ART!
CLAP
HE WAS YOUR STUDENT, TOMAS.
I SEE YOU'VE ROTTED THROUGH TO THE CORE!

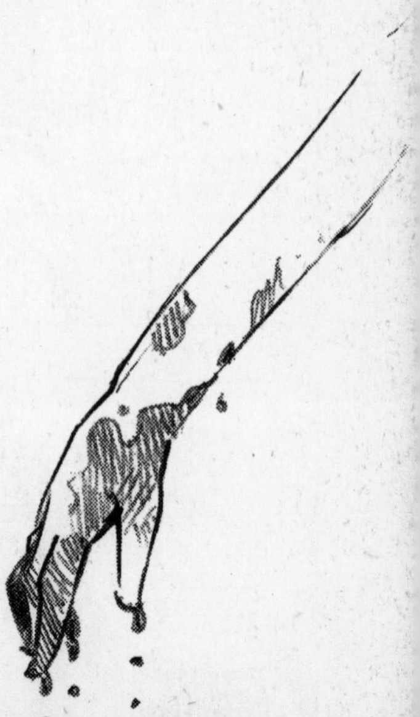

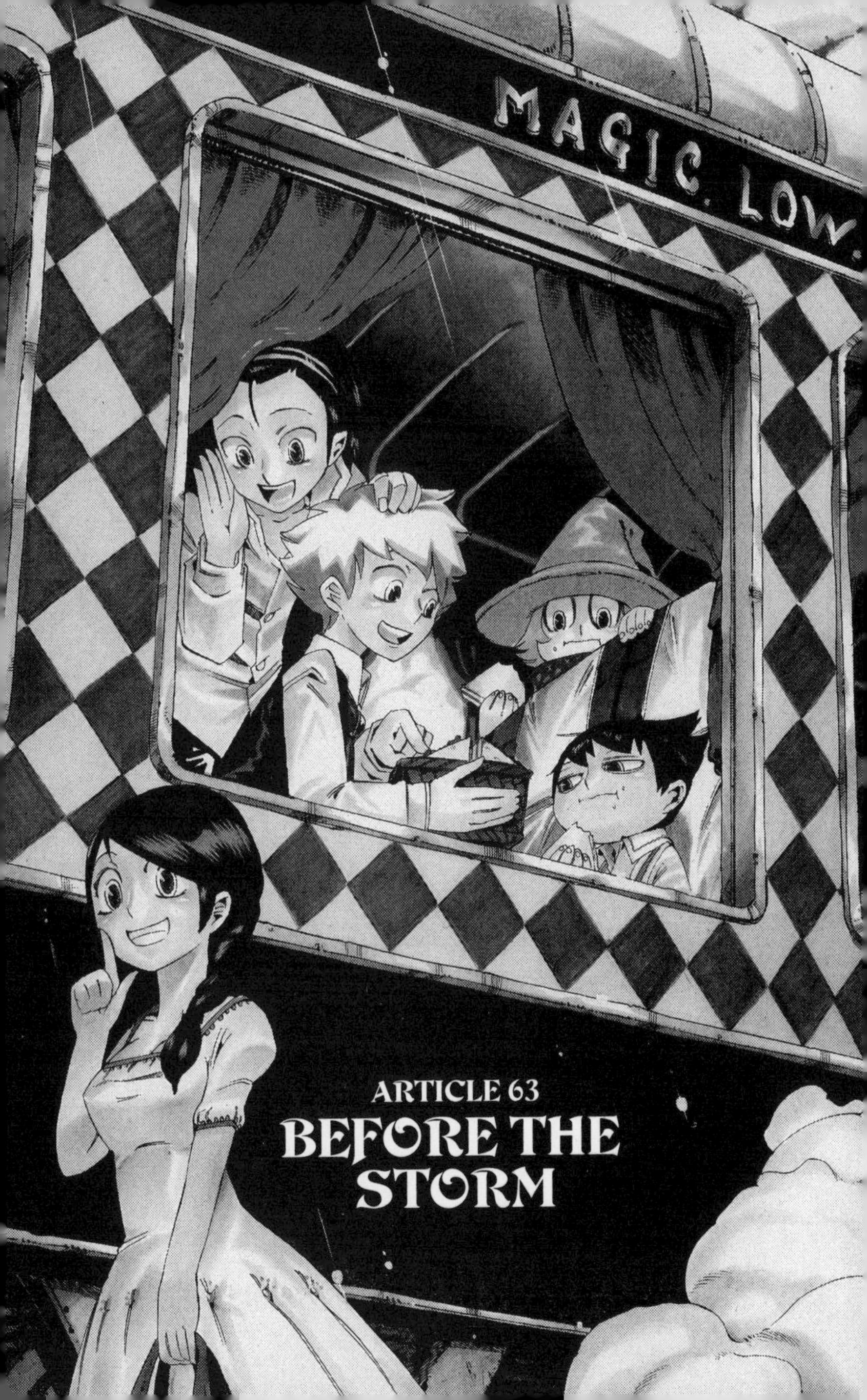
MAGIC. LOW.
ARTICLE 63
BEFORE THE STORM

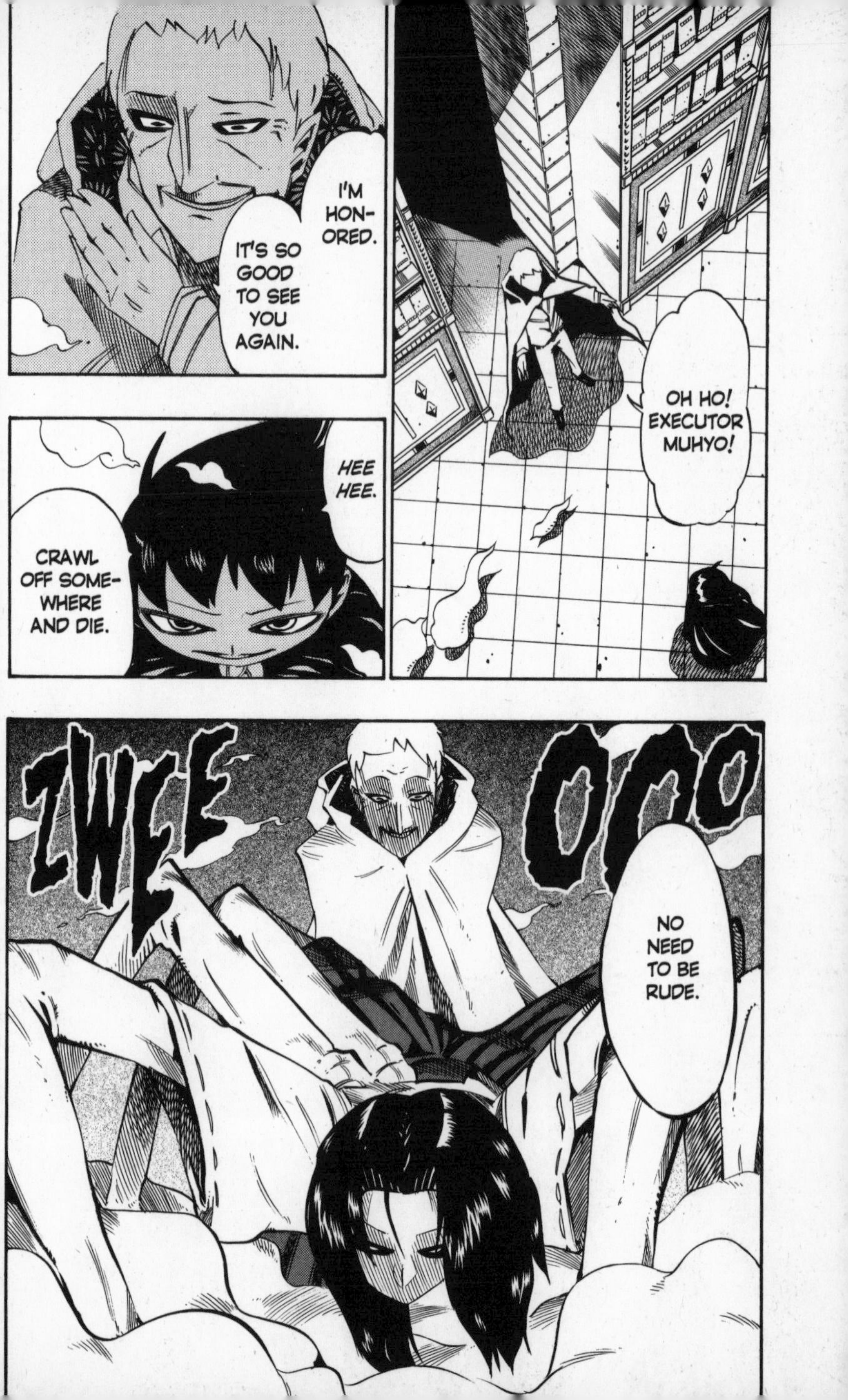
OH HO! EXECUTOR MUHYO!
I'M HONORED.
IT'S SO GOOD TO SEE YOU AGAIN.
HEE HEE.
CRAWL OFF SOMEWHERE AND DIE.
ZWEE OOO
NO NEED TO BE RUDE.

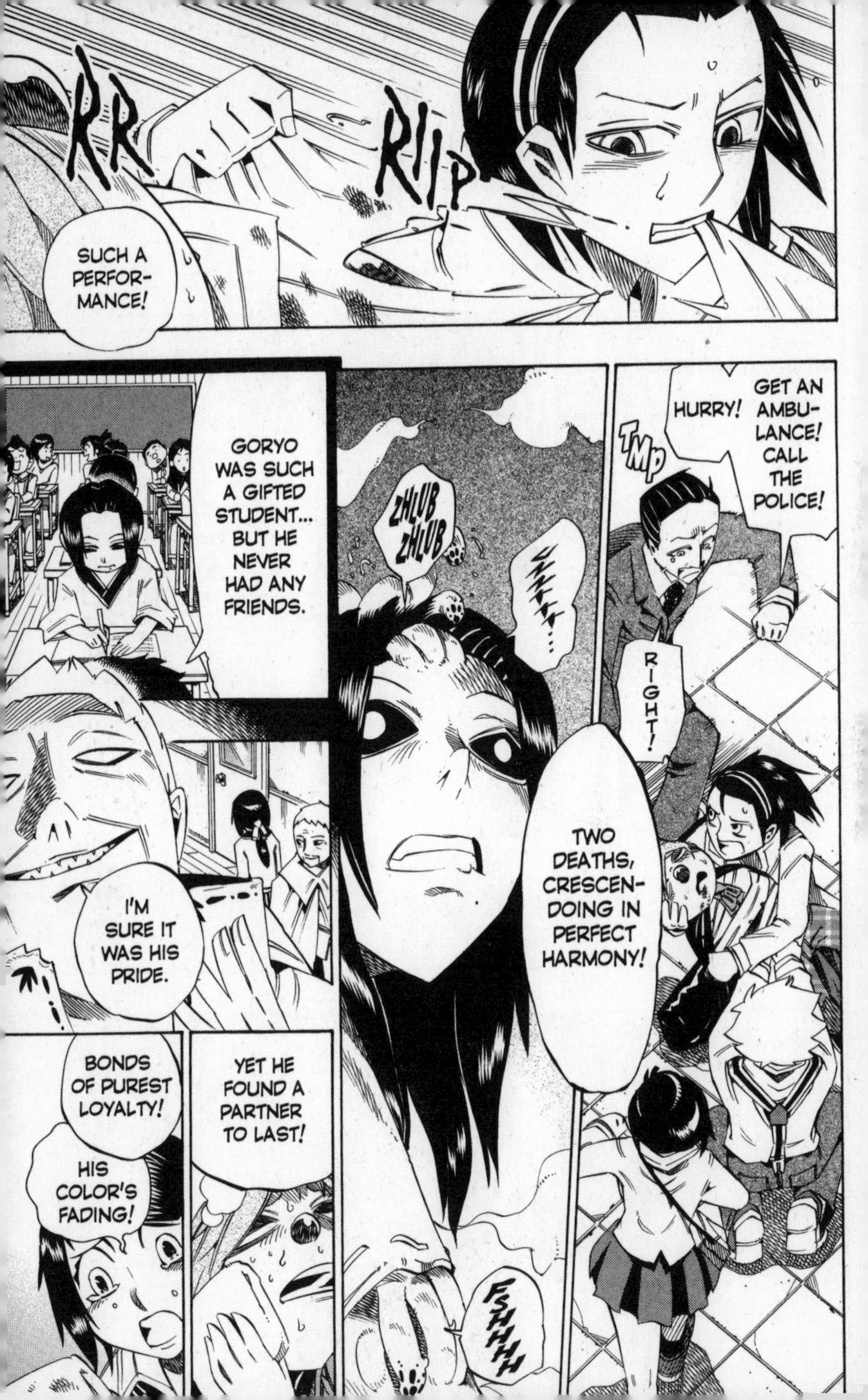

RR RIIP
SUCH A PERFORMANCE!
GET AN AMBULANCE! CALL THE POLICE!
HURRY!
TMP
RIGHT!
ZHLUB ZHLUB
TWO DEATHS, CRESCENDOING IN PERFECT HARMONY!
FSHHHH
GORYO WAS SUCH A GIFTED STUDENT... BUT HE NEVER HAD ANY FRIENDS.
I'M SURE IT WAS HIS PRIDE.
YET HE FOUND A PARTNER TO LAST!
BONDS OF PUREST LOYALTY!
HIS COLOR'S FADING!

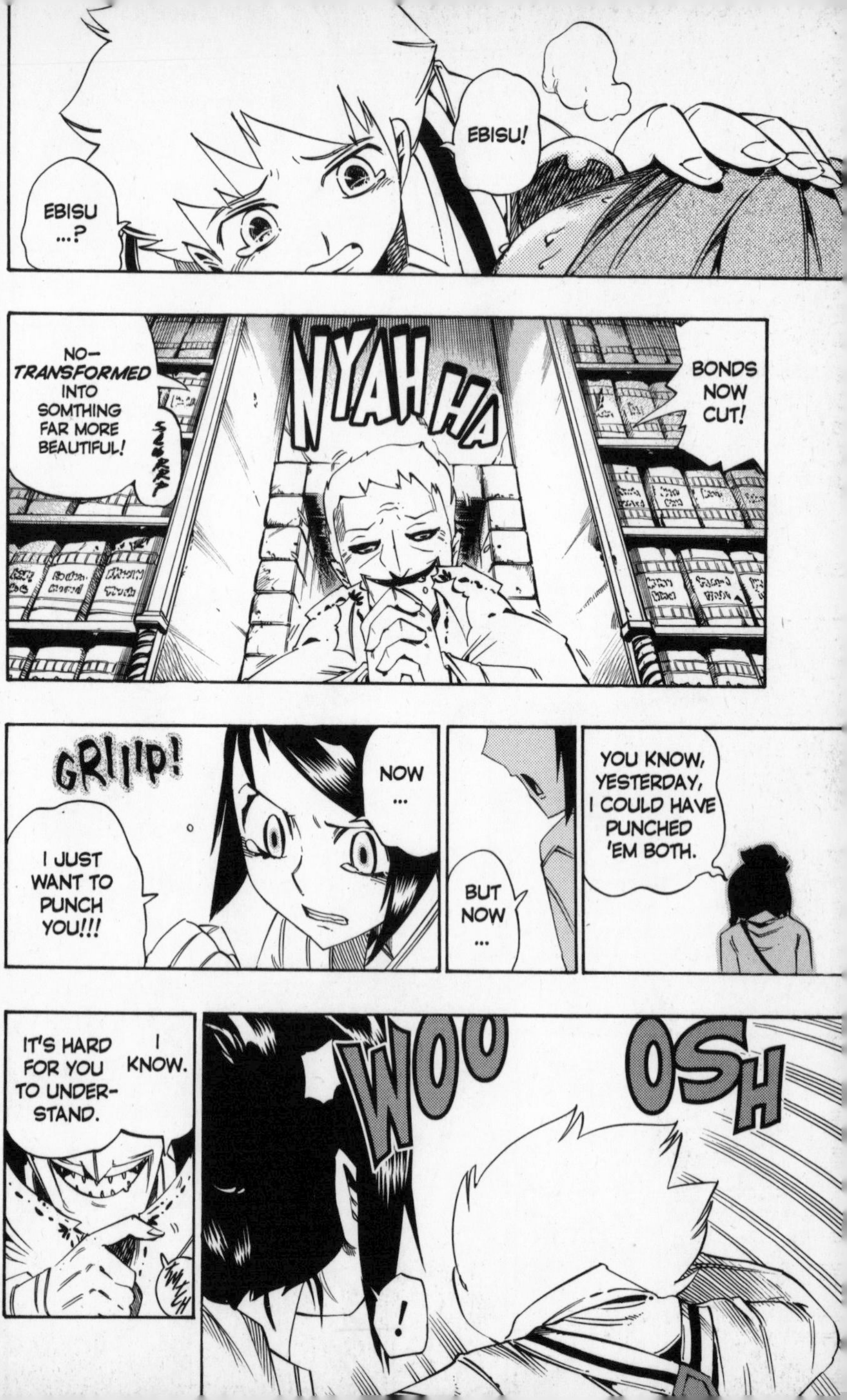
EBISU!
EBISU ...?
BONDS NOW CUT!
NYAH HA
NO—*TRANSFORMED* INTO SOMTHING FAR MORE BEAUTIFUL!
YOU KNOW, YESTERDAY, I COULD HAVE PUNCHED 'EM BOTH.
BUT NOW ...
NOW ...
GRIIIP!
I JUST WANT TO PUNCH YOU!!!
WOOOSH
!
I KNOW.
IT'S HARD FOR YOU TO UNDER-STAND.

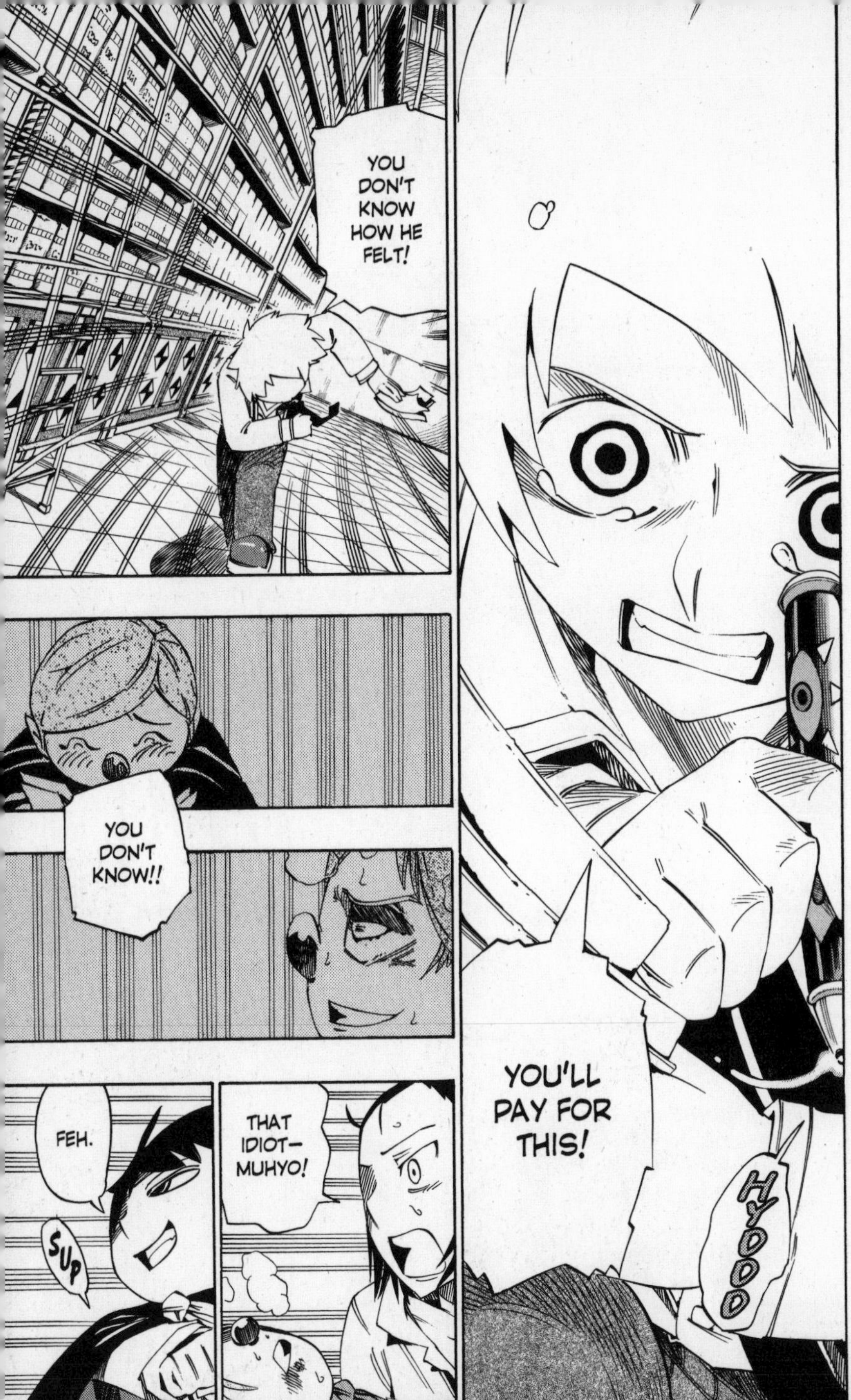
YOU'LL PAY FOR THIS!
HYDDD
YOU DON'T KNOW HOW HE FELT!
YOU DON'T KNOW!!
THAT IDIOT— MUHYO!
FEH.
SUP

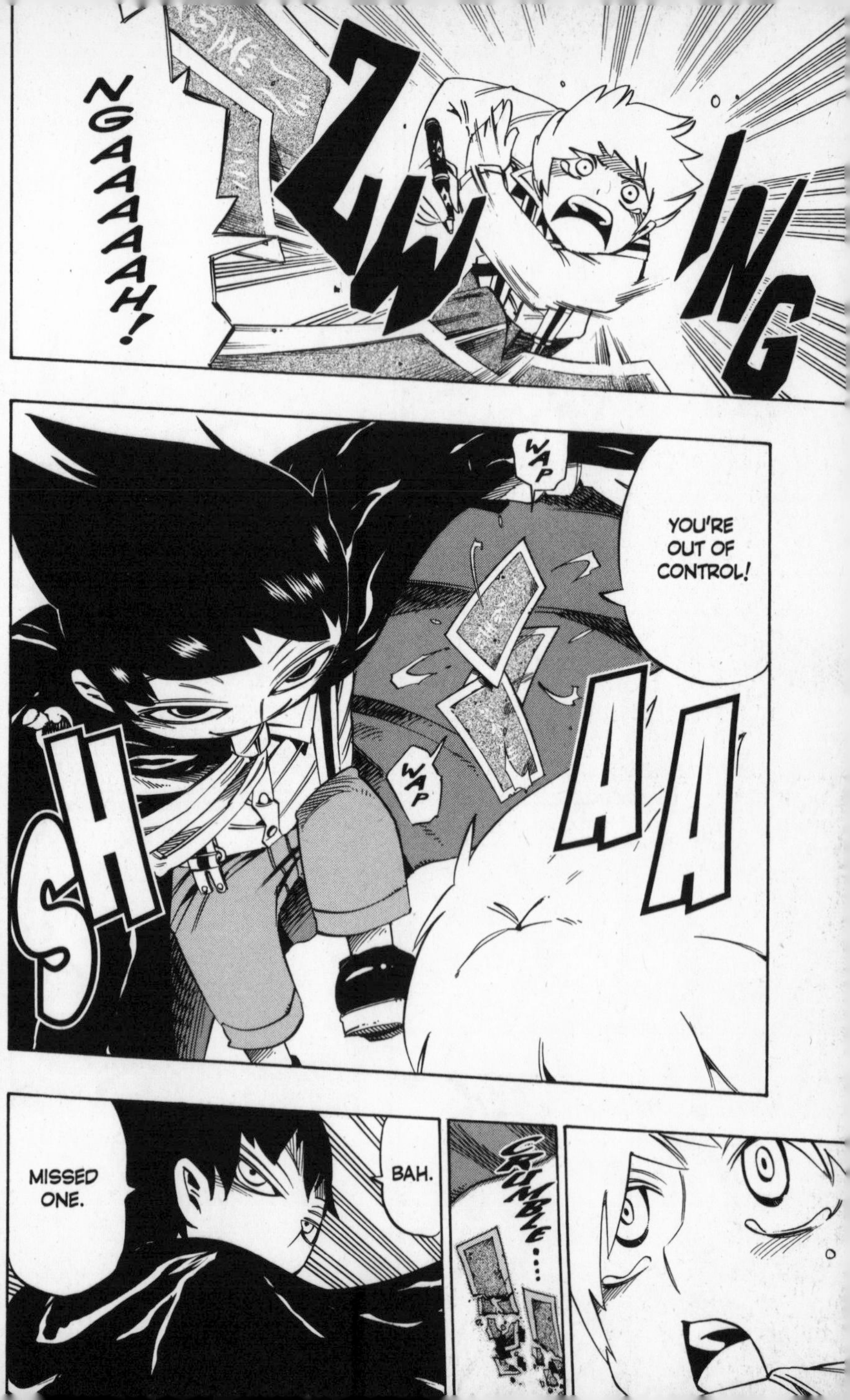
ZWING
NGAAAAAAH!
WAP
YOU'RE OUT OF CONTROL!
WAP
SHAA
CRUMBLE....
BAH.
MISSED ONE.

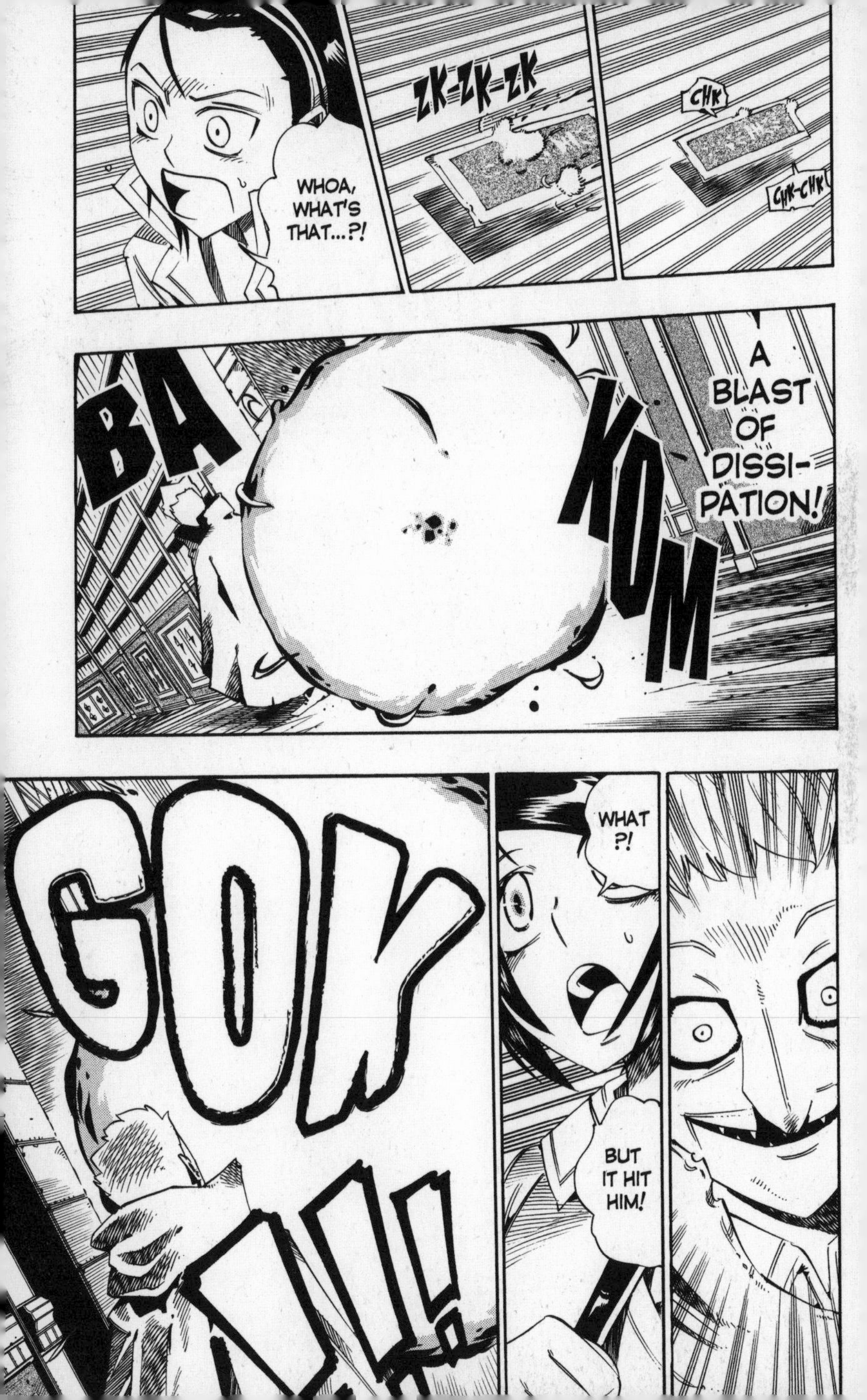
CHK
CHK-CHK
ZK-ZK-ZK
WHOA, WHAT'S THAT...?!
A BLAST OF DISSIPATION!
BA KOM
WHAT ?!
BUT IT HIT HIM!
GOK

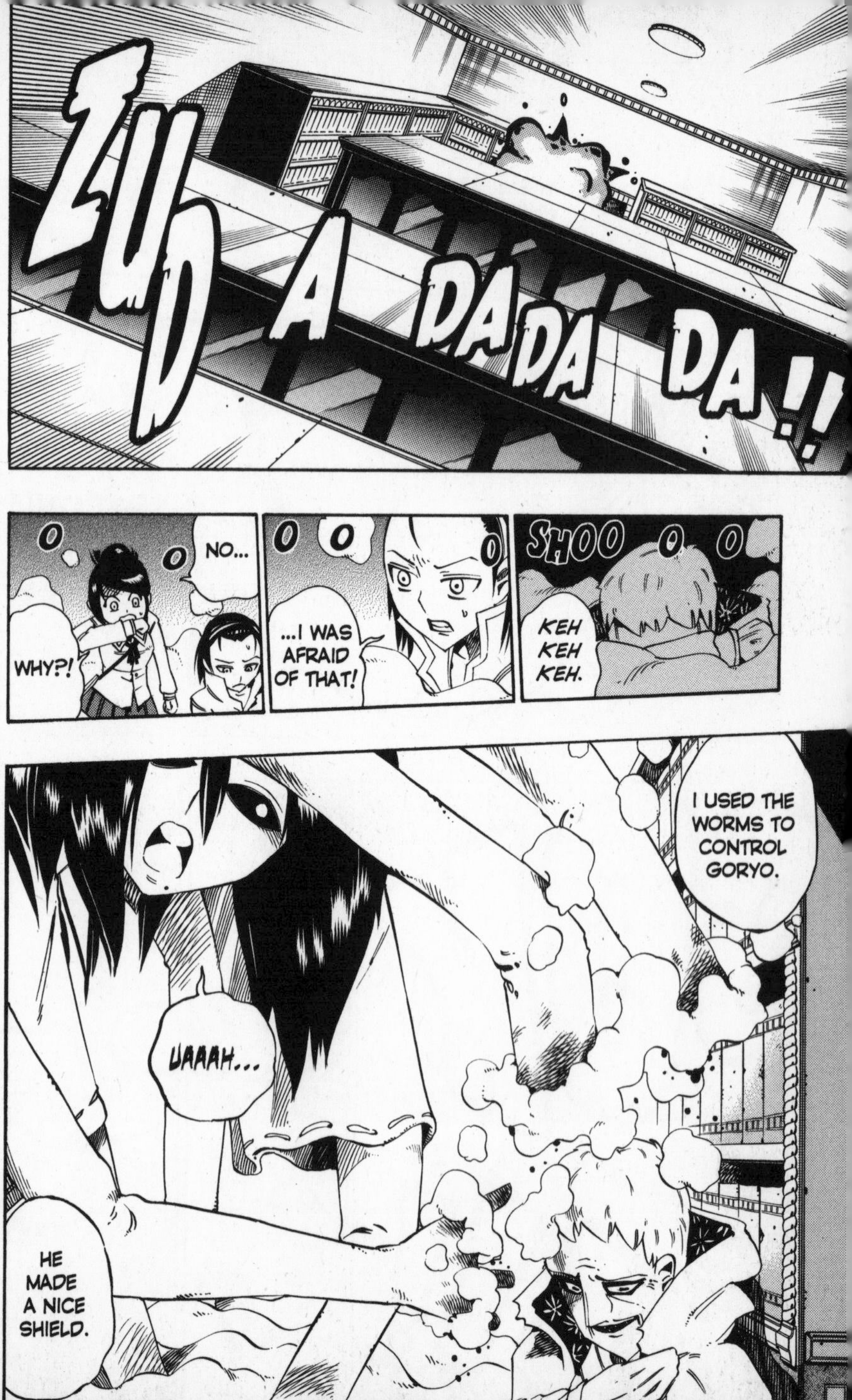
ZUD A DADADA DA!!
SHOO O O
KEH KEH KEH.
O O
...I WAS AFRAID OF THAT!
NO...
O O O
WHY?!
I USED THE WORMS TO CONTROL GORYO.
UAAAH...
HE MADE A NICE SHIELD.

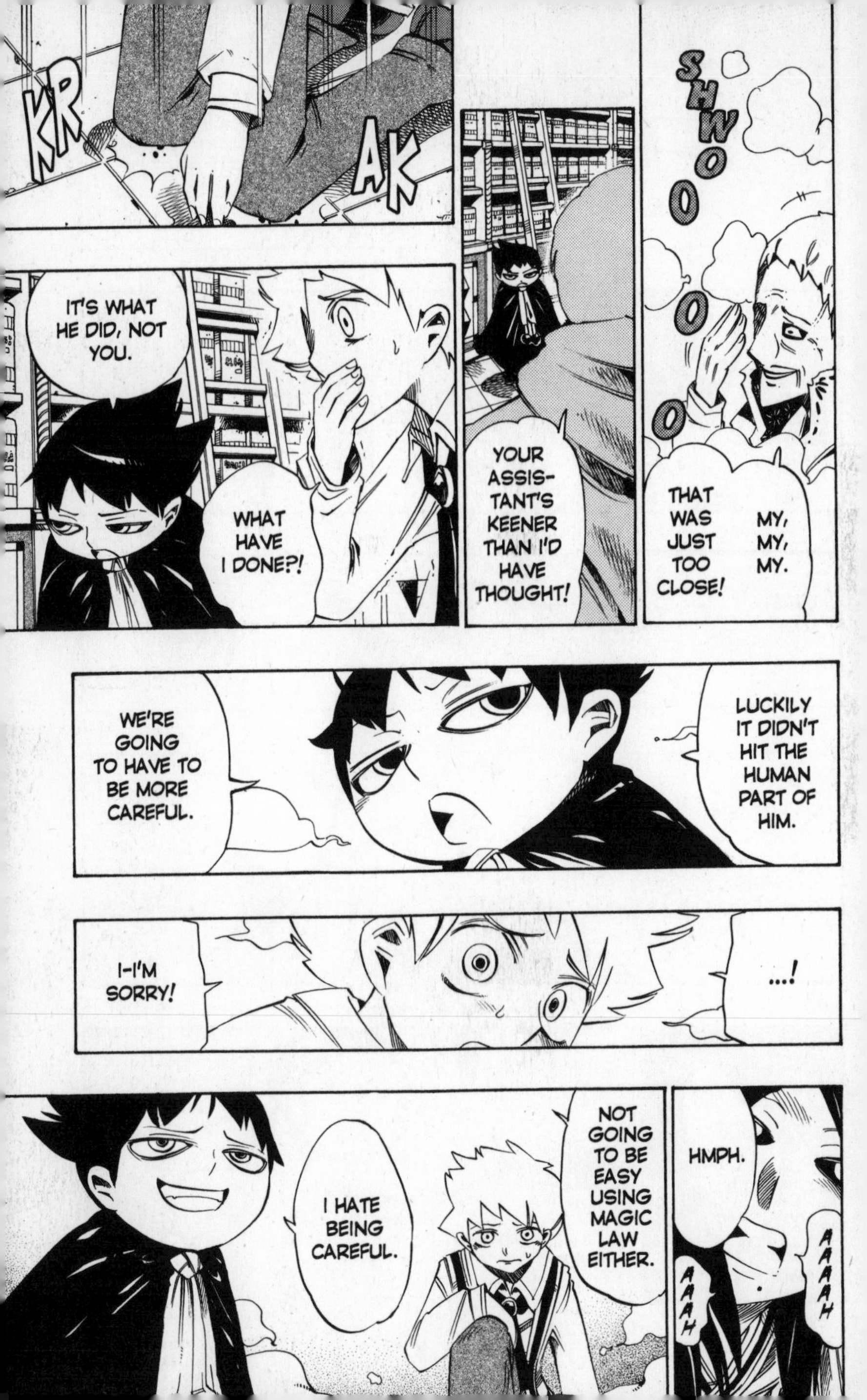
SHWOOOOOO
MY, MY, MY.
THAT WAS JUST TOO CLOSE!
YOUR ASSISTANT'S KEENER THAN I'D HAVE THOUGHT!
KRAK
WHAT HAVE I DONE?!
IT'S WHAT HE DID, NOT YOU.
LUCKILY IT DIDN'T HIT THE HUMAN PART OF HIM.
WE'RE GOING TO HAVE TO BE MORE CAREFUL.
...!
I-I'M SORRY!
HMPH.
AAAAH
AAAAH
NOT GOING TO BE EASY USING MAGIC LAW EITHER.
I HATE BEING CAREFUL.

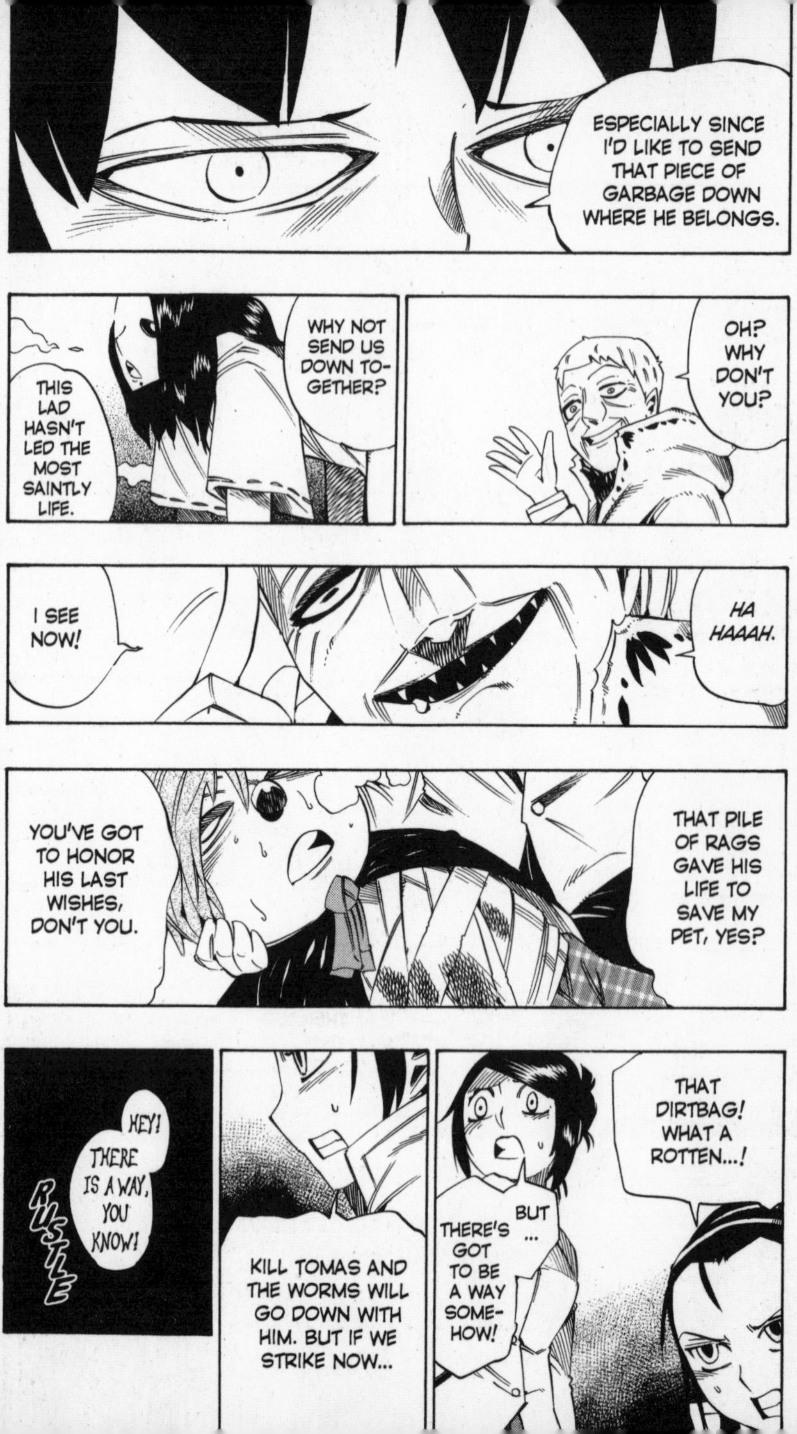
ESPECIALLY SINCE I'D LIKE TO SEND THAT PIECE OF GARBAGE DOWN WHERE HE BELONGS.
OH? WHY DON'T YOU?
WHY NOT SEND US DOWN TO-GETHER?
THIS LAD HASN'T LED THE MOST SAINTLY LIFE.
HA HAAAH.
I SEE NOW!
THAT PILE OF RAGS GAVE HIS LIFE TO SAVE MY PET, YES?
YOU'VE GOT TO HONOR HIS LAST WISHES, DON'T YOU.
THAT DIRTBAG! WHAT A ROTTEN...!
BUT ... THERE'S GOT TO BE A WAY SOME-HOW!
KILL TOMAS AND THE WORMS WILL GO DOWN WITH HIM. BUT IF WE STRIKE NOW...
HEY! THERE IS A WAY, YOU KNOW!
RUSTLE

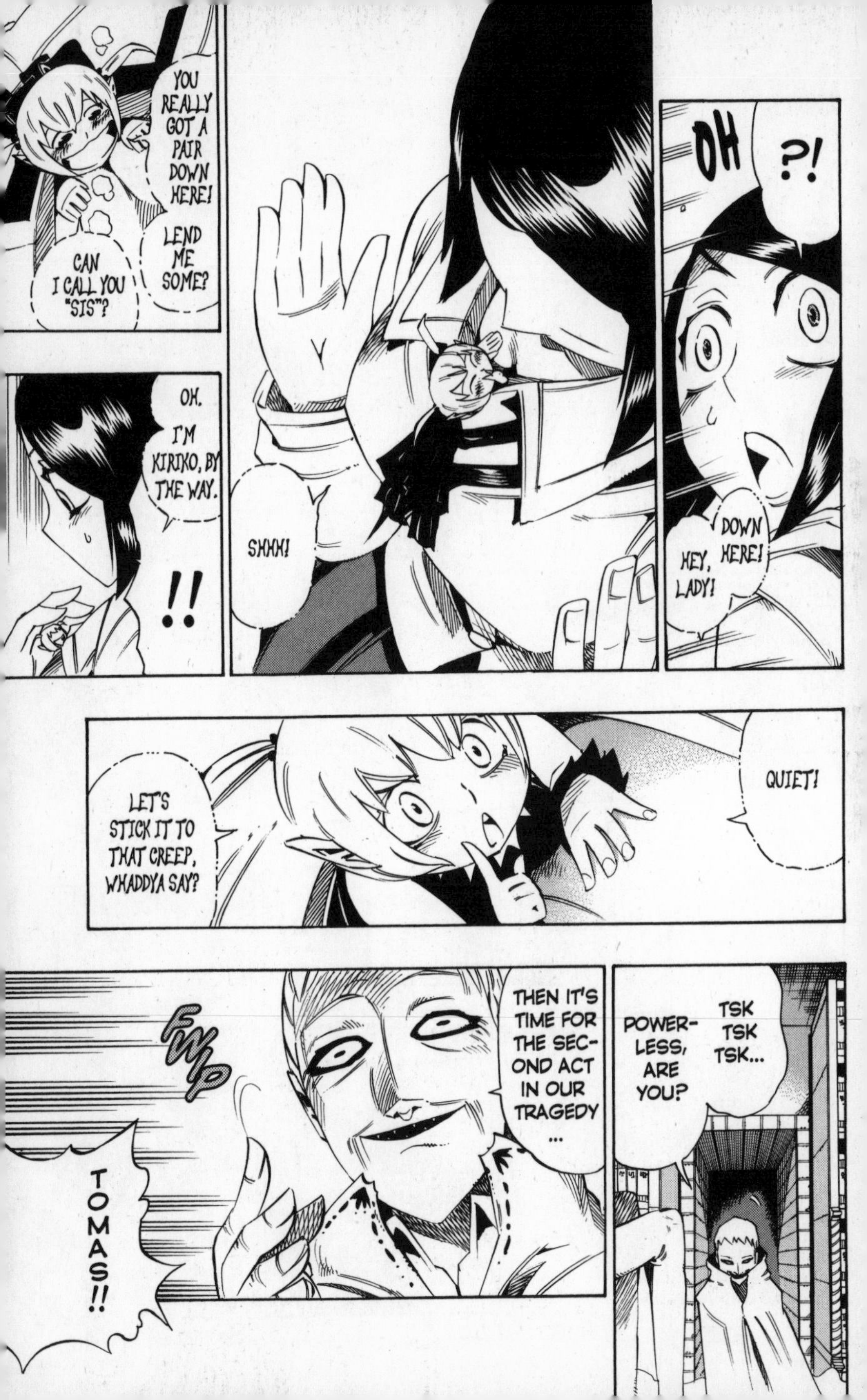
OH
?!
HEY, LADY! DOWN HERE!
SHHH!
YOU REALLY GOT A PAIR DOWN HERE!
LEND ME SOME?
CAN I CALL YOU "SIS"?
OH. I'M KIRIKO, BY THE WAY.
!!
QUIET!
LET'S STICK IT TO THAT CREEP, WHADDYA SAY?
TSK TSK TSK...
POWER-LESS, ARE YOU?
THEN IT'S TIME FOR THE SEC-OND ACT IN OUR TRAGEDY ...
FWIP
TOMAS!!

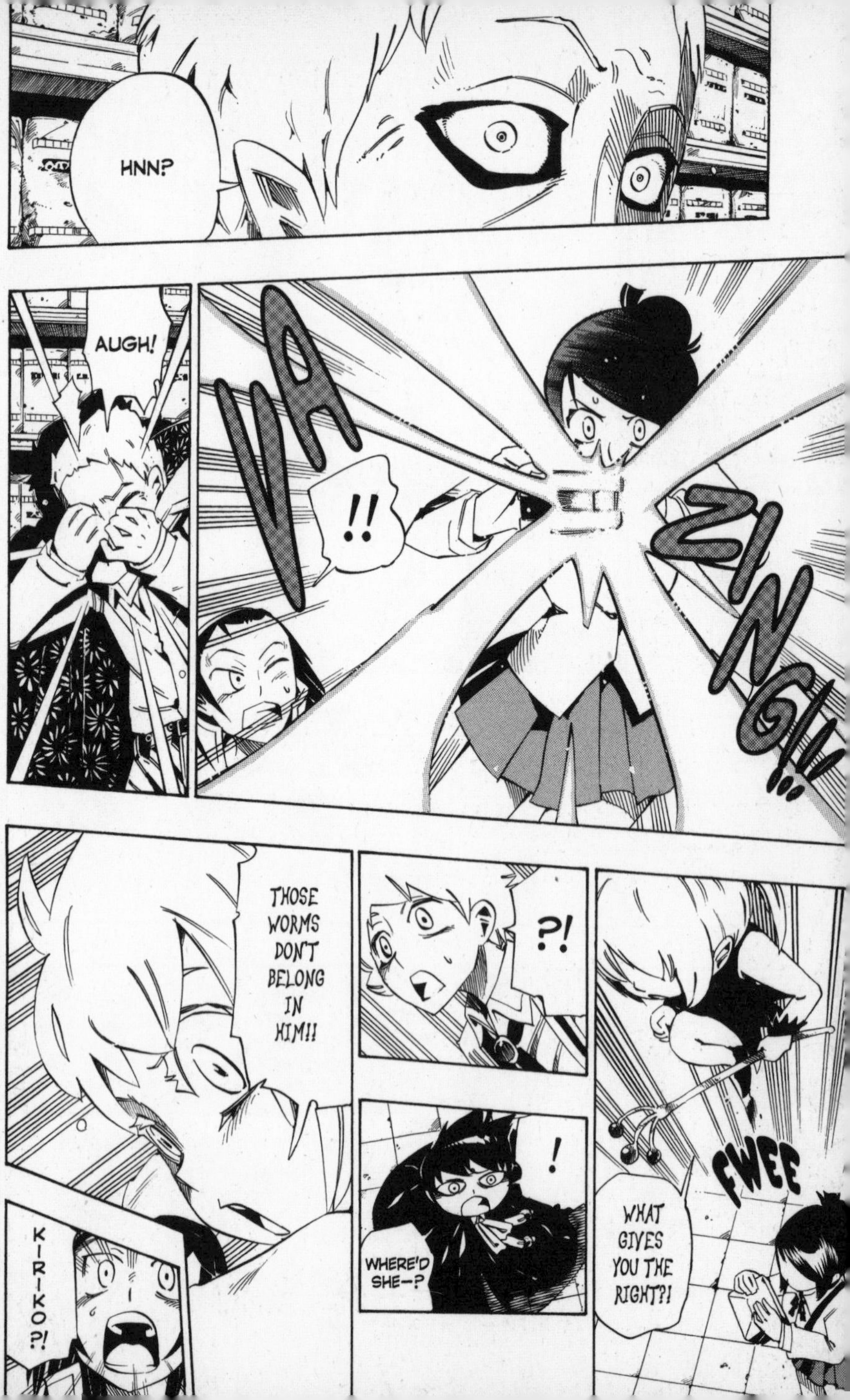
HNN?
VA
!!
ZING!!!
AUGH!
FWEE
WHAT GIVES YOU THE RIGHT?!
?!
!
WHERE'D SHE—?
THOSE WORMS DON'T BELONG IN HIM!!
KIRIKO?!

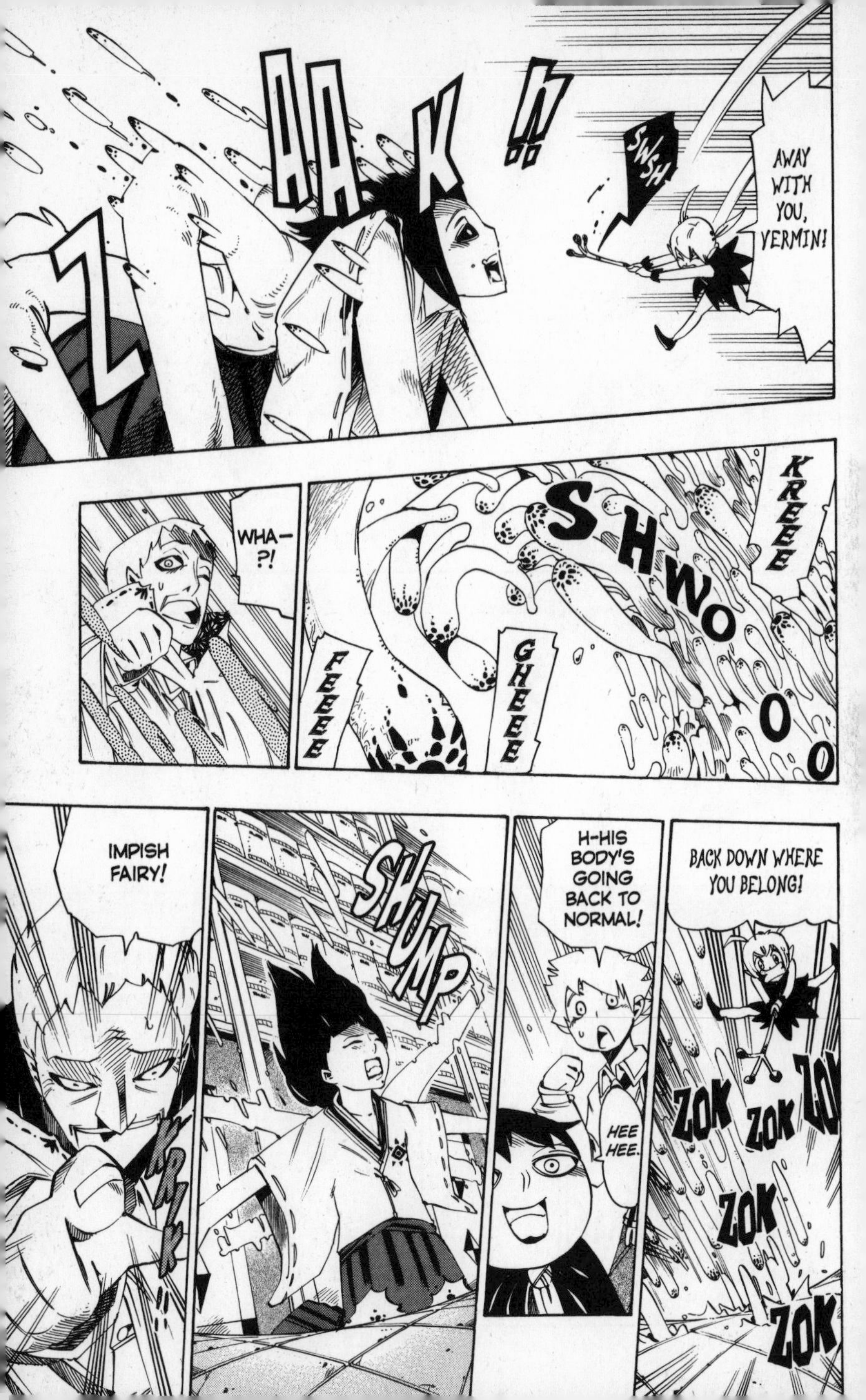
AWAY WITH YOU, VERMIN!
SWSH
ZAAK!!
KREEE
SHWOOOO
GHEEEE
FEEEE
WHA-?!
BACK DOWN WHERE YOU BELONG!
ZOK ZOK ZOK
ZOK
ZOK
H-HIS BODY'S GOING BACK TO NORMAL!
HEE HEE.
SHUMP
IMPISH FAIRY!

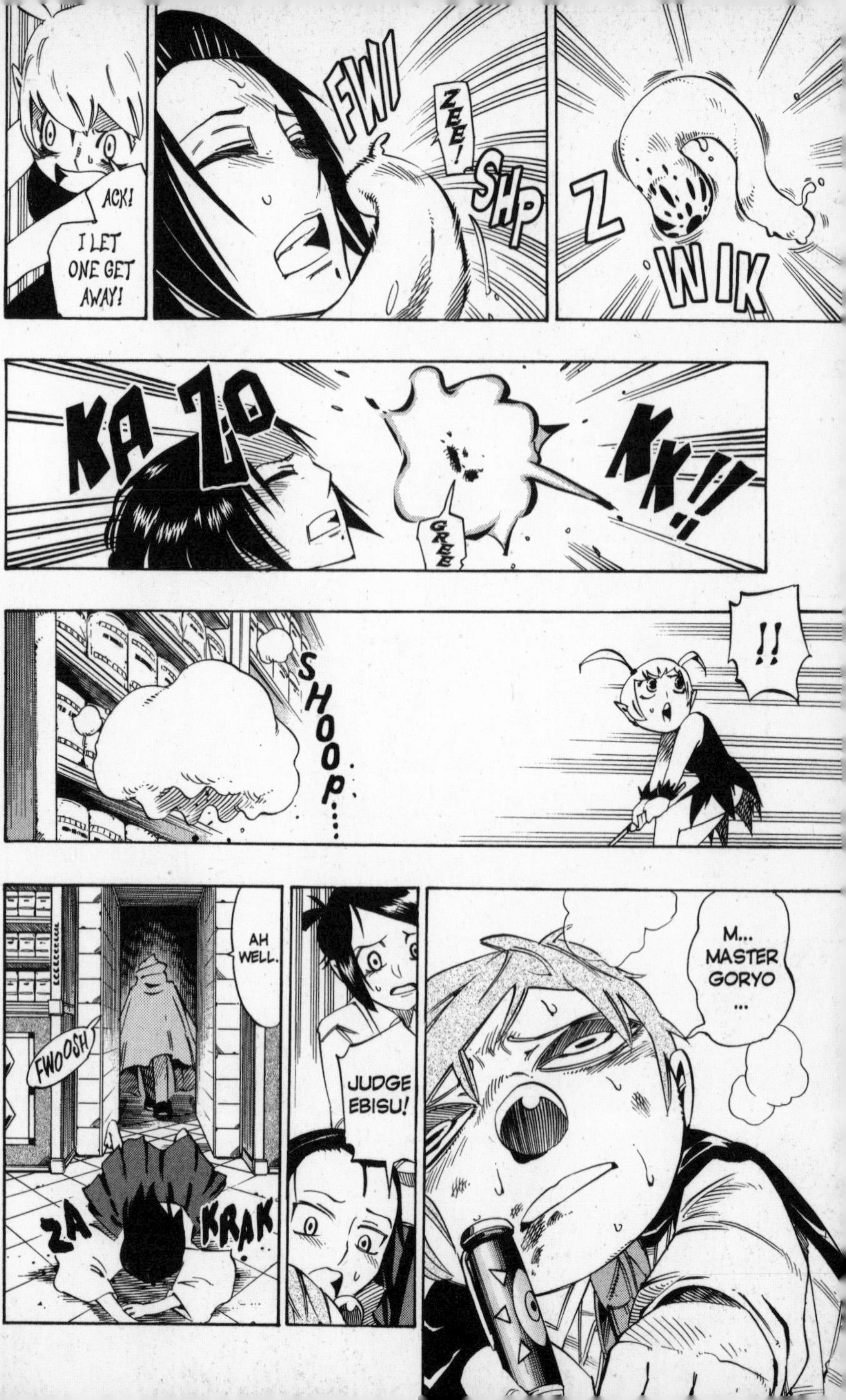
Z
WIK
ZEE!
FWI
SHP
ACK!
I LET ONE GET AWAY!
KA ZO KK!!
GREE
!!
SHOOP....
M... MASTER GORYO ...
AH WELL.
JUDGE EBISU!
FWOOSH
ZA KRAK

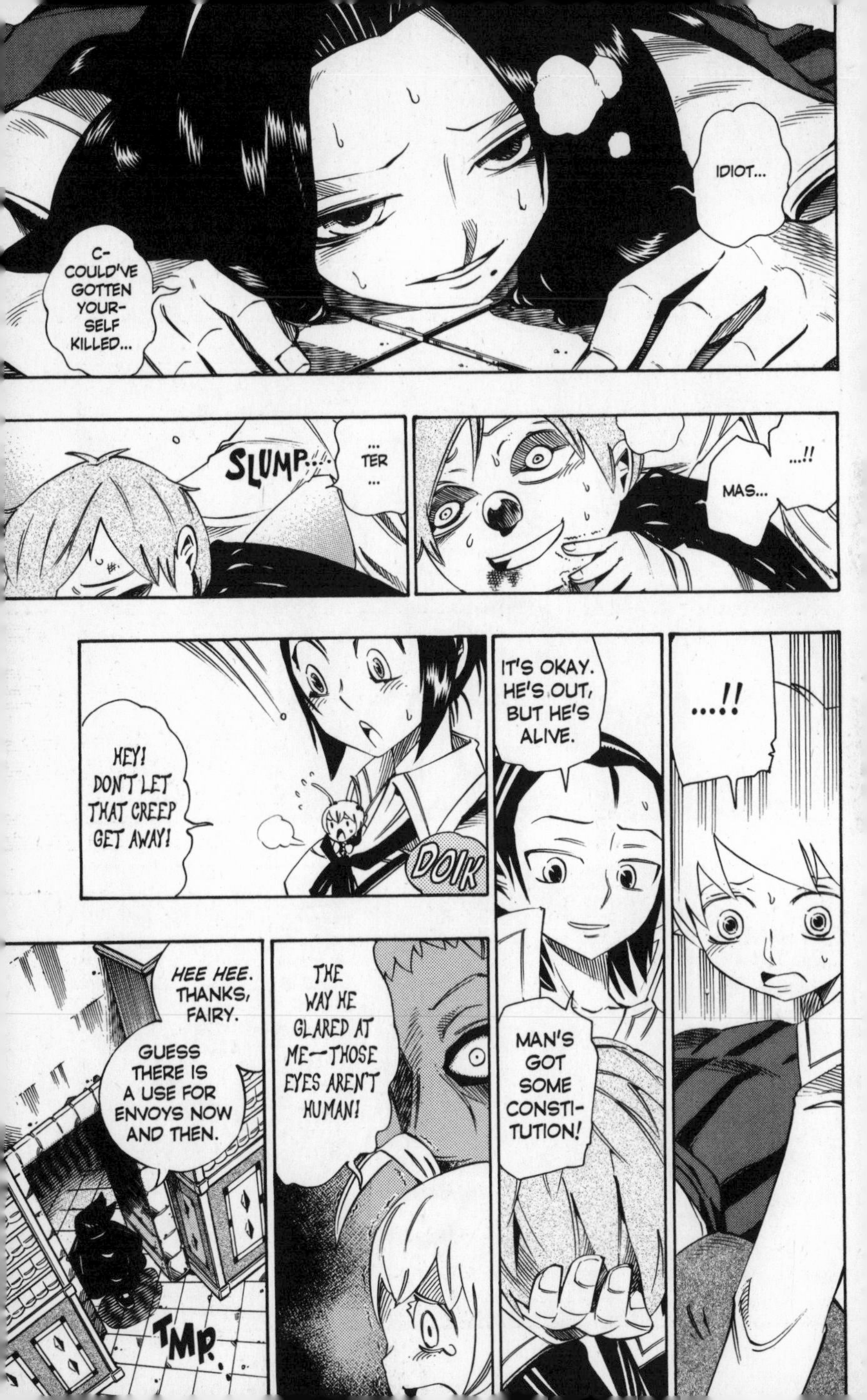
IDIOT...
C-COULD'VE GOTTEN YOURSELF KILLED...
...!!
MAS...
...TER...
SLUMP...
...!!
IT'S OKAY. HE'S OUT, BUT HE'S ALIVE.
MAN'S GOT SOME CONSTITUTION!
HEY! DON'T LET THAT CREEP GET AWAY!
DOIK
THE WAY HE GLARED AT ME—THOSE EYES AREN'T HUMAN!
HEE HEE. THANKS, FAIRY.
GUESS THERE IS A USE FOR ENVOYS NOW AND THEN.
TMP.

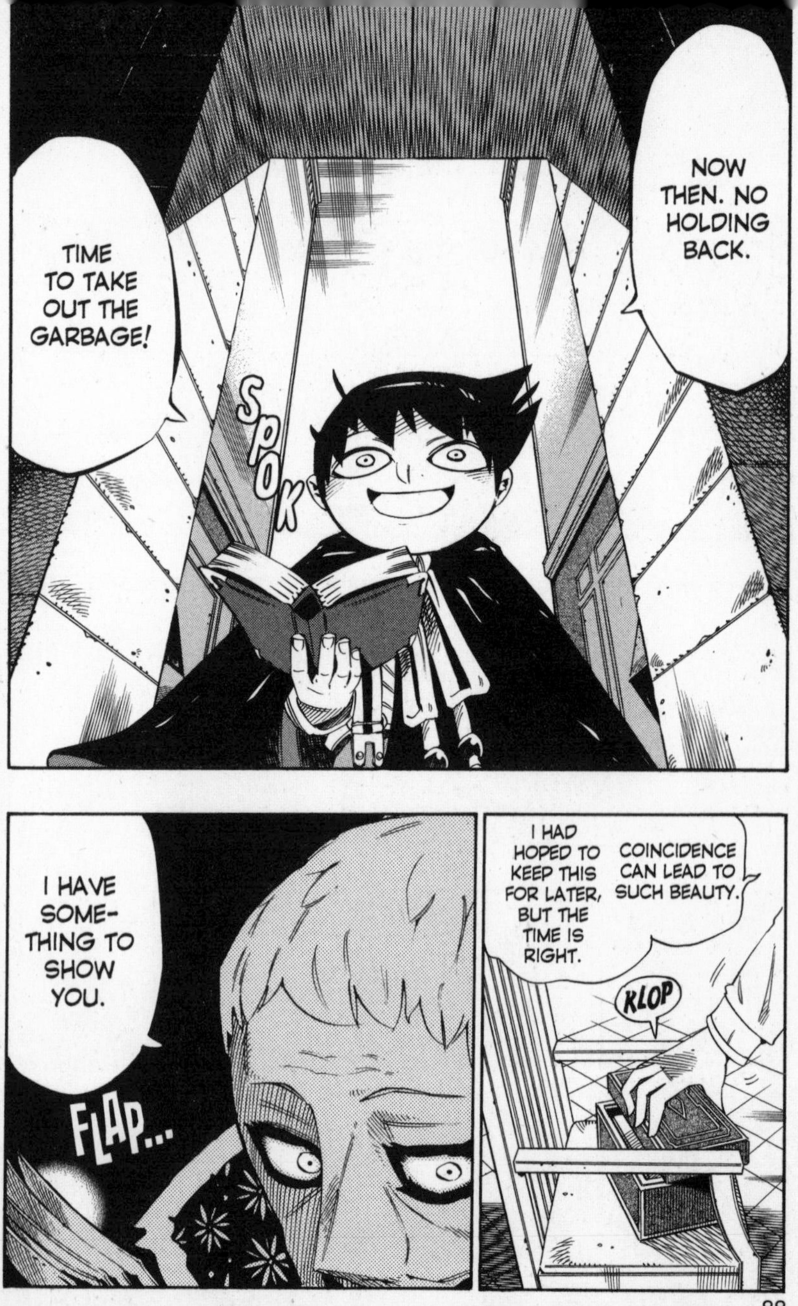
NOW THEN. NO HOLDING BACK.
TIME TO TAKE OUT THE GARBAGE!
SPOK
COINCIDENCE CAN LEAD TO SUCH BEAUTY.
I HAD HOPED TO KEEP THIS FOR LATER, BUT THE TIME IS RIGHT.
KLOP
I HAVE SOME-THING TO SHOW YOU.
FLAP...

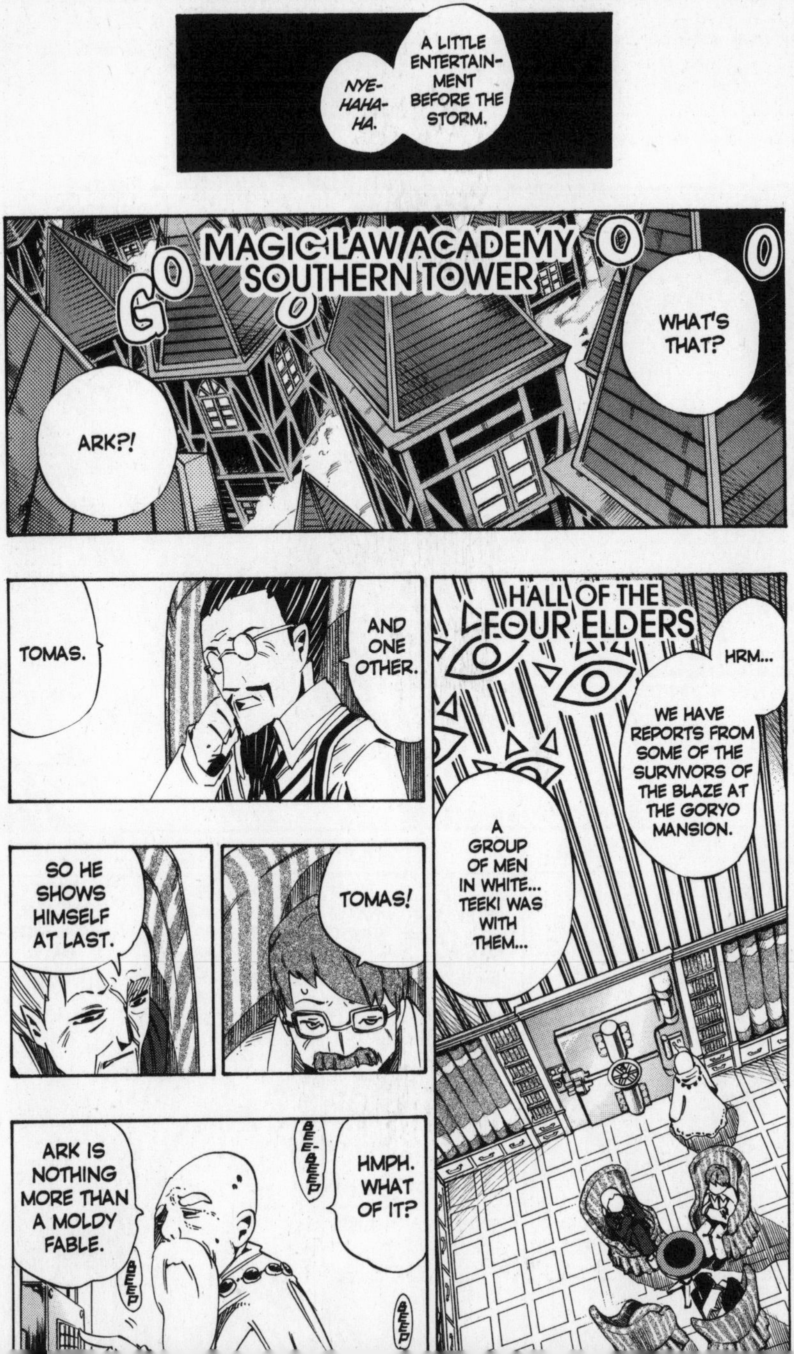
A LITTLE ENTERTAIN-MENT BEFORE THE STORM.
NYE-HAHA-HA.
MAGIC LAW ACADEMY SOUTHERN TOWER
GOOOO
WHAT'S THAT?
ARK?!
HALL OF THE FOUR ELDERS
HRM...
WE HAVE REPORTS FROM SOME OF THE SURVIVORS OF THE BLAZE AT THE GORYO MANSION.
A GROUP OF MEN IN WHITE... TEEKI WAS WITH THEM...
AND ONE OTHER.
TOMAS.
TOMAS!
SO HE SHOWS HIMSELF AT LAST.
HMPH. WHAT OF IT?
BEE-BEEP
ARK IS NOTHING MORE THAN A MOLDY FABLE.
BEEP
BEEP

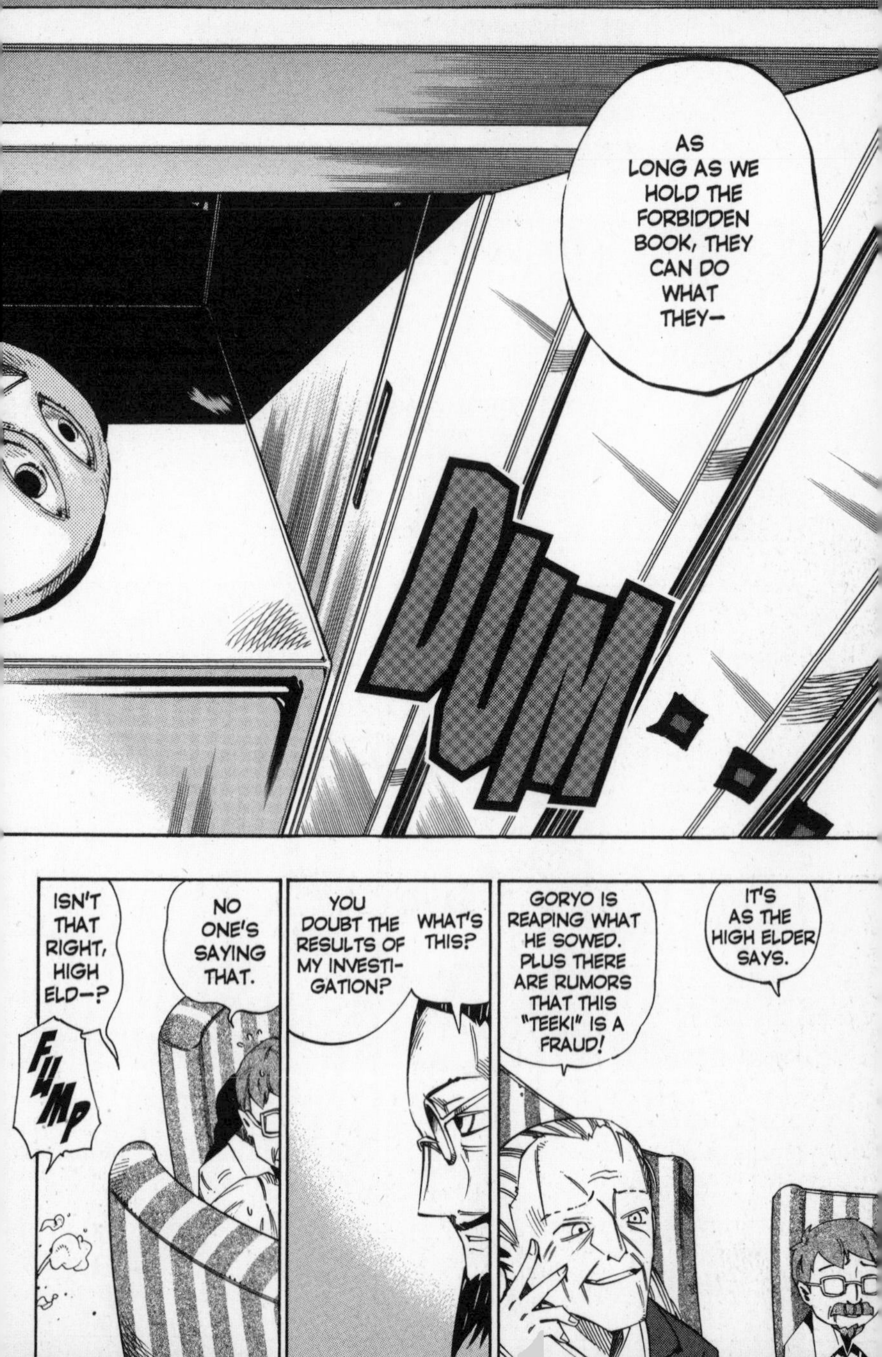
AS LONG AS WE HOLD THE FORBIDDEN BOOK, THEY CAN DO WHAT THEY—
DUM...
IT'S AS THE HIGH ELDER SAYS.
GORYO IS REAPING WHAT HE SOWED. PLUS THERE ARE RUMORS THAT THIS "TEEKI" IS A FRAUD!
WHAT'S THIS?
YOU DOUBT THE RESULTS OF MY INVESTI-GATION?
NO ONE'S SAYING THAT.
ISN'T THAT RIGHT, HIGH ELD—?
FUMP

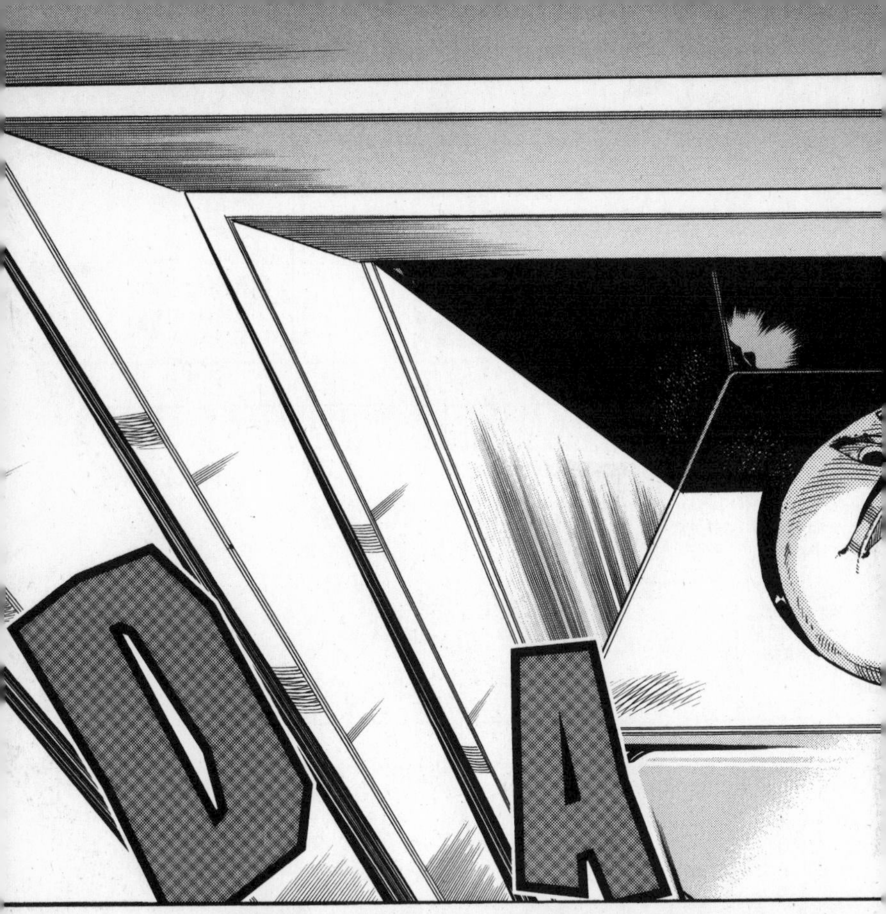
DA
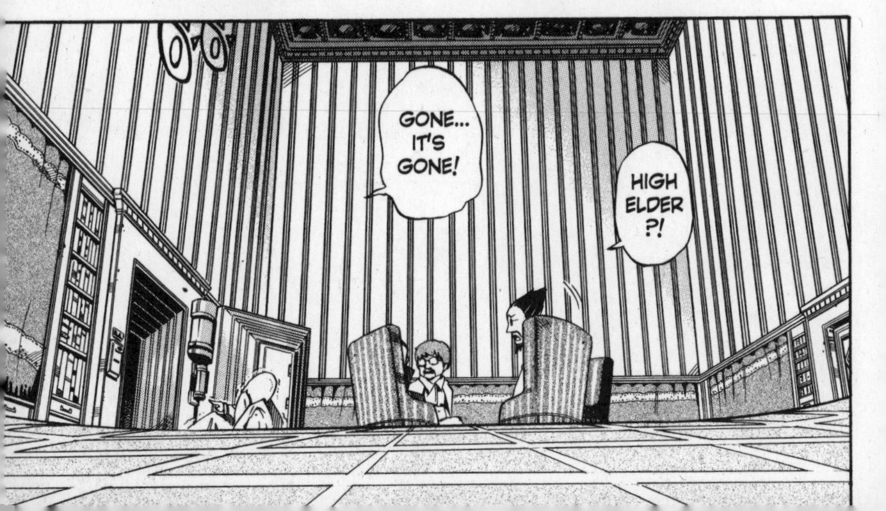
GONE... IT'S GONE!
HIGH ELDER ?!

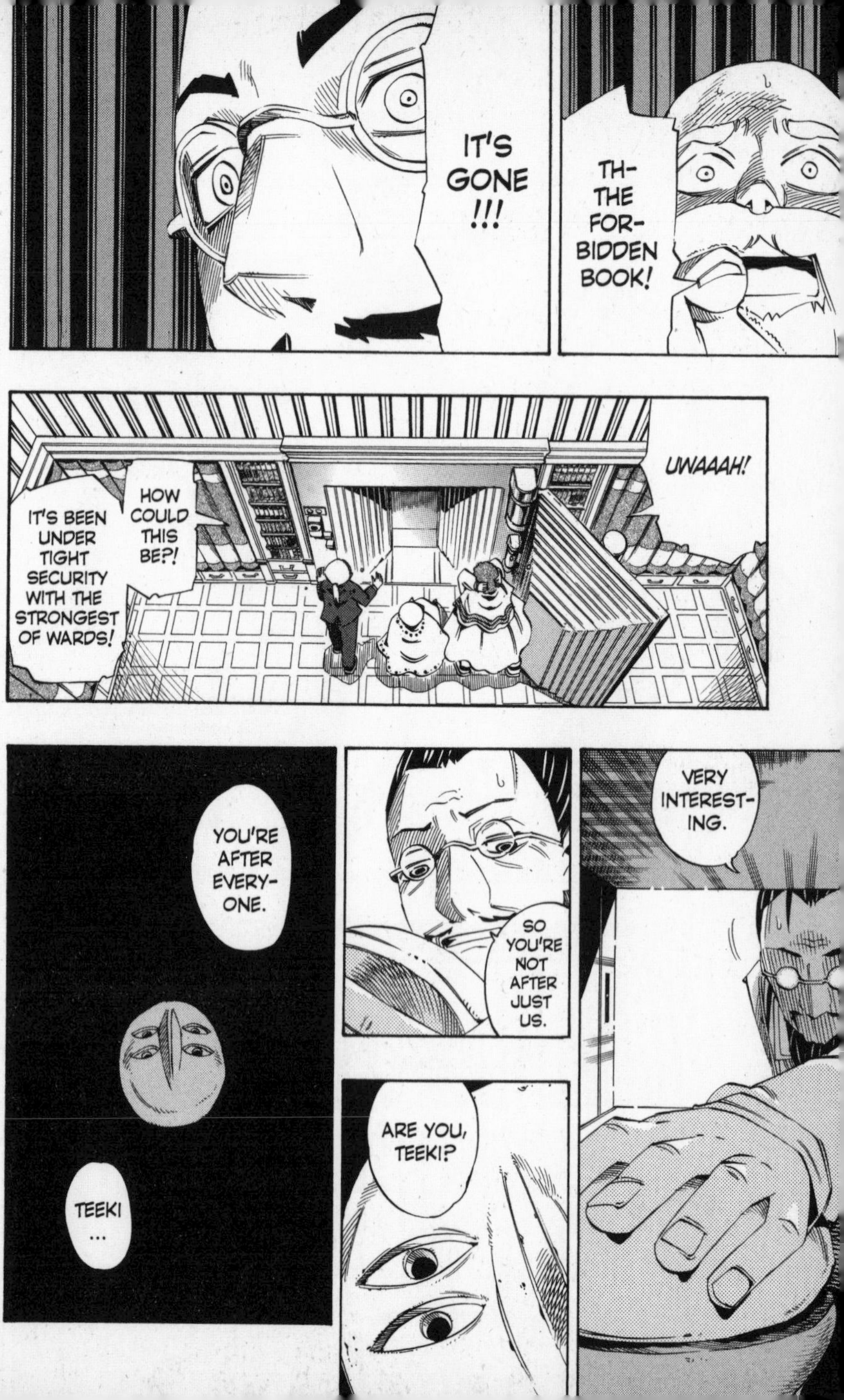
TH- THE FOR- BIDDEN BOOK!
IT'S GONE !!!
UWAAAH!
HOW COULD THIS BE?!
IT'S BEEN UNDER TIGHT SECURITY WITH THE STRONGEST OF WARDS!
VERY INTEREST- ING.
SO YOU'RE NOT AFTER JUST US.
ARE YOU, TEEKI?
YOU'RE AFTER EVERY- ONE.
TEEKI ...

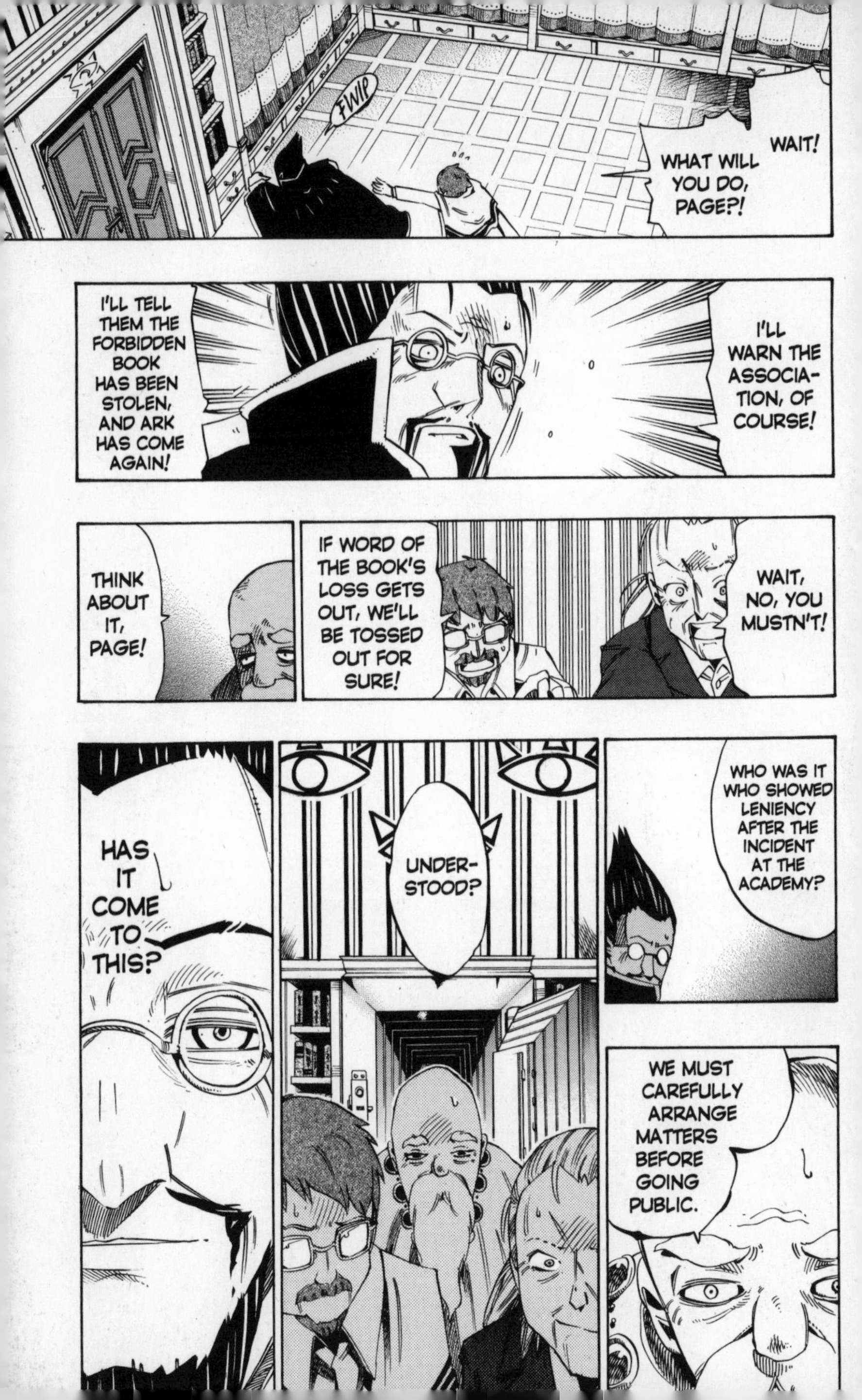
WAIT!
WHAT WILL YOU DO, PAGE?!
FWIP
I'LL WARN THE ASSOCIATION, OF COURSE!
I'LL TELL THEM THE FORBIDDEN BOOK HAS BEEN STOLEN, AND ARK HAS COME AGAIN!
WAIT, NO, YOU MUSTN'T!
IF WORD OF THE BOOK'S LOSS GETS OUT, WE'LL BE TOSSED OUT FOR SURE!
THINK ABOUT IT, PAGE!
WHO WAS IT WHO SHOWED LENIENCY AFTER THE INCIDENT AT THE ACADEMY?
WE MUST CAREFULLY ARRANGE MATTERS BEFORE GOING PUBLIC.
UNDER-STOOD?
HAS IT COME TO THIS?

Q: I KNOW MUHYO, BIKO, YOICHI, AND ENCHU ALL WENT TO MAGIC LAW SCHOOL, BUT WHAT ABOUT ELEMENTARY AND JUNIOR HIGH?
—N.S., MIYAGI PREFECTURE

A: THE M.L.S. TEACHES REGULAR SUBJECTS ALONGSIDE MAGIC LAW, LIKE MATH AND SCIENCE, SO IT COUNTS AS REGULAR SCHOOL, TOO.

AT LEAST, THAT'S WHAT I THINK. BUT LET'S ASK, JUST TO BE SURE.

(ME)   WELL?
(BIKO) YUP. WE HAD GYM AND ENGLISH CLASS TOO.
(ME)   HUH. WHICH CLASS DID YOU LIKE THE MOST?
(BIKO) SCIENCE AND HOME ECONOMICS.
(ME)   RIGHT, THAT MAKES SENSE. HOW LONG WERE SCHOOL HOURS?
(BIKO) OH, WE WENT TO FIVE O'CLOCK, EVEN ON SATURDAYS.
(ME)   YIKES! COUNT ME OUT!

THERE YOU HAVE IT. M.L.S. IS NO PICNIC APPARENTLY.

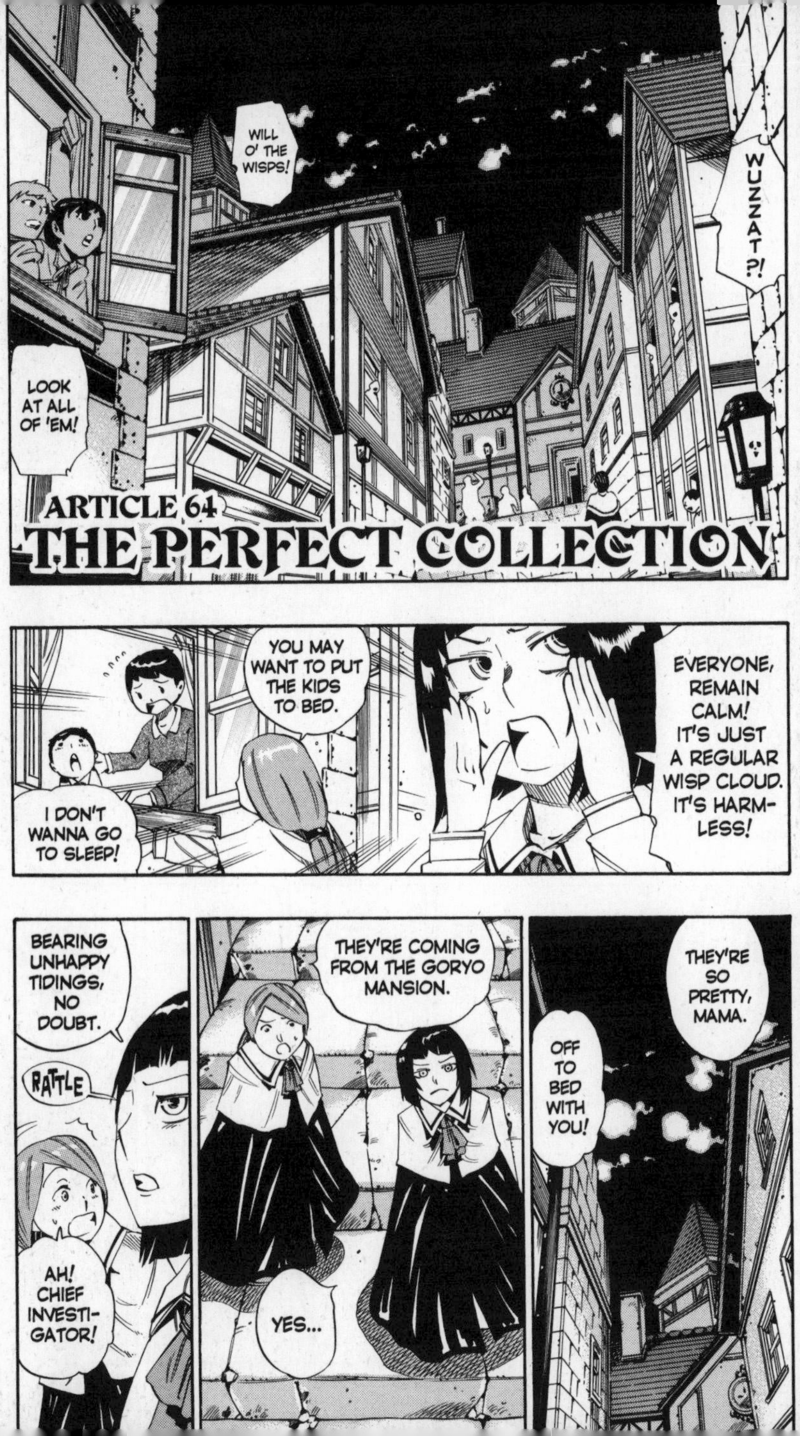
WUZZAT?!
WILL O' THE WISPS!
LOOK AT ALL OF 'EM!
ARTICLE 64
THE PERFECT COLLECTION
EVERYONE, REMAIN CALM! IT'S JUST A REGULAR WISP CLOUD. IT'S HARMLESS!
YOU MAY WANT TO PUT THE KIDS TO BED.
I DON'T WANNA GO TO SLEEP!
THEY'RE SO PRETTY, MAMA.
OFF TO BED WITH YOU!
THEY'RE COMING FROM THE GORYO MANSION.
YES...
BEARING UNHAPPY TIDINGS, NO DOUBT.
RATTLE
AH! CHIEF INVESTIGATOR!

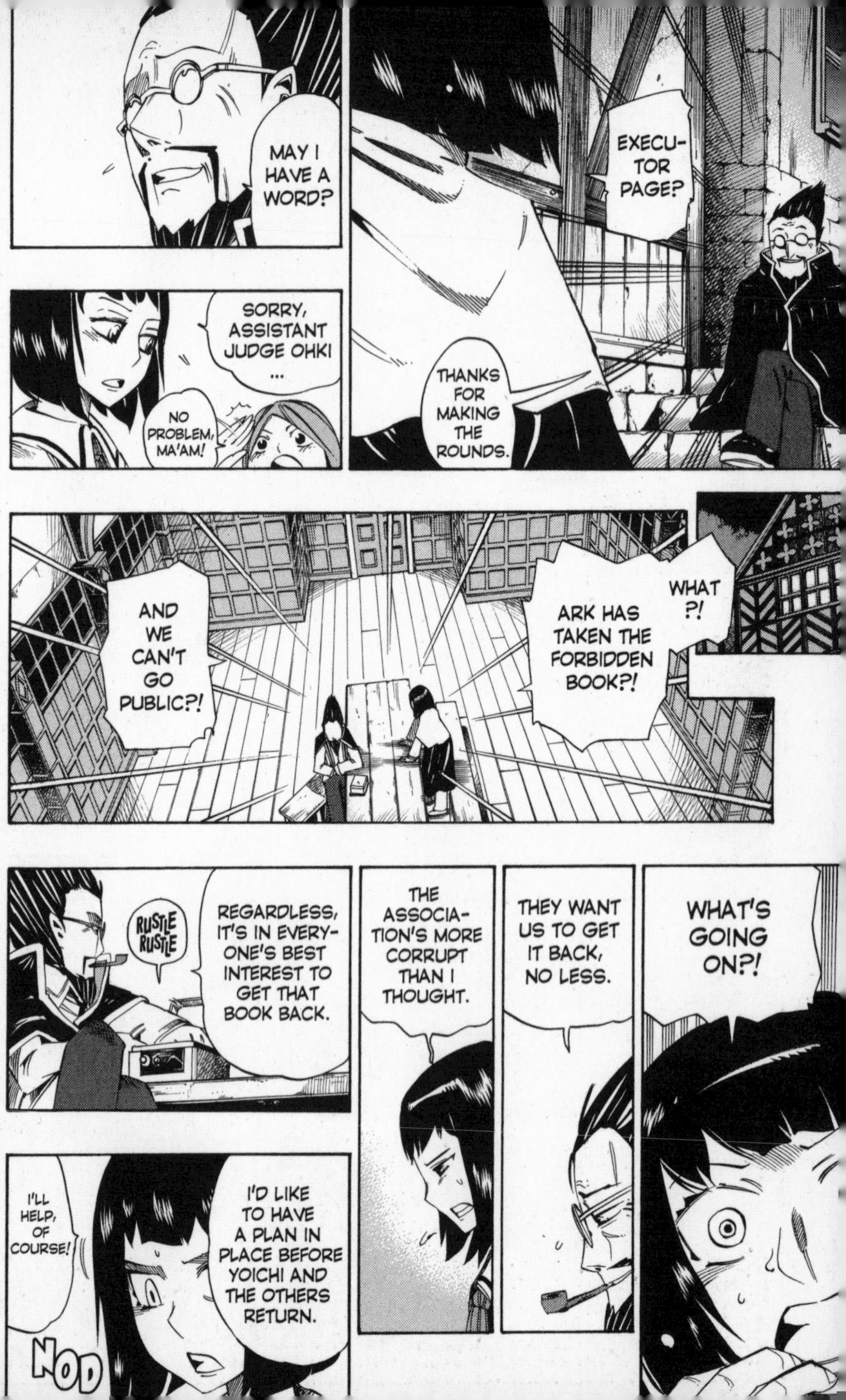
EXECU-TOR PAGE?
THANKS FOR MAKING THE ROUNDS.
MAY I HAVE A WORD?
SORRY, ASSISTANT JUDGE OHKI ...
NO PROBLEM, MA'AM!
WHAT ?!
ARK HAS TAKEN THE FORBIDDEN BOOK?!
AND WE CAN'T GO PUBLIC?!
WHAT'S GOING ON?!
THEY WANT US TO GET IT BACK, NO LESS.
THE ASSOCIA-TION'S MORE CORRUPT THAN I THOUGHT.
REGARDLESS, IT'S IN EVERY-ONE'S BEST INTEREST TO GET THAT BOOK BACK.
RUSTLE RUSTLE
I'D LIKE TO HAVE A PLAN IN PLACE BEFORE YOICHI AND THE OTHERS RETURN.
I'LL HELP, OF COURSE!
NOD

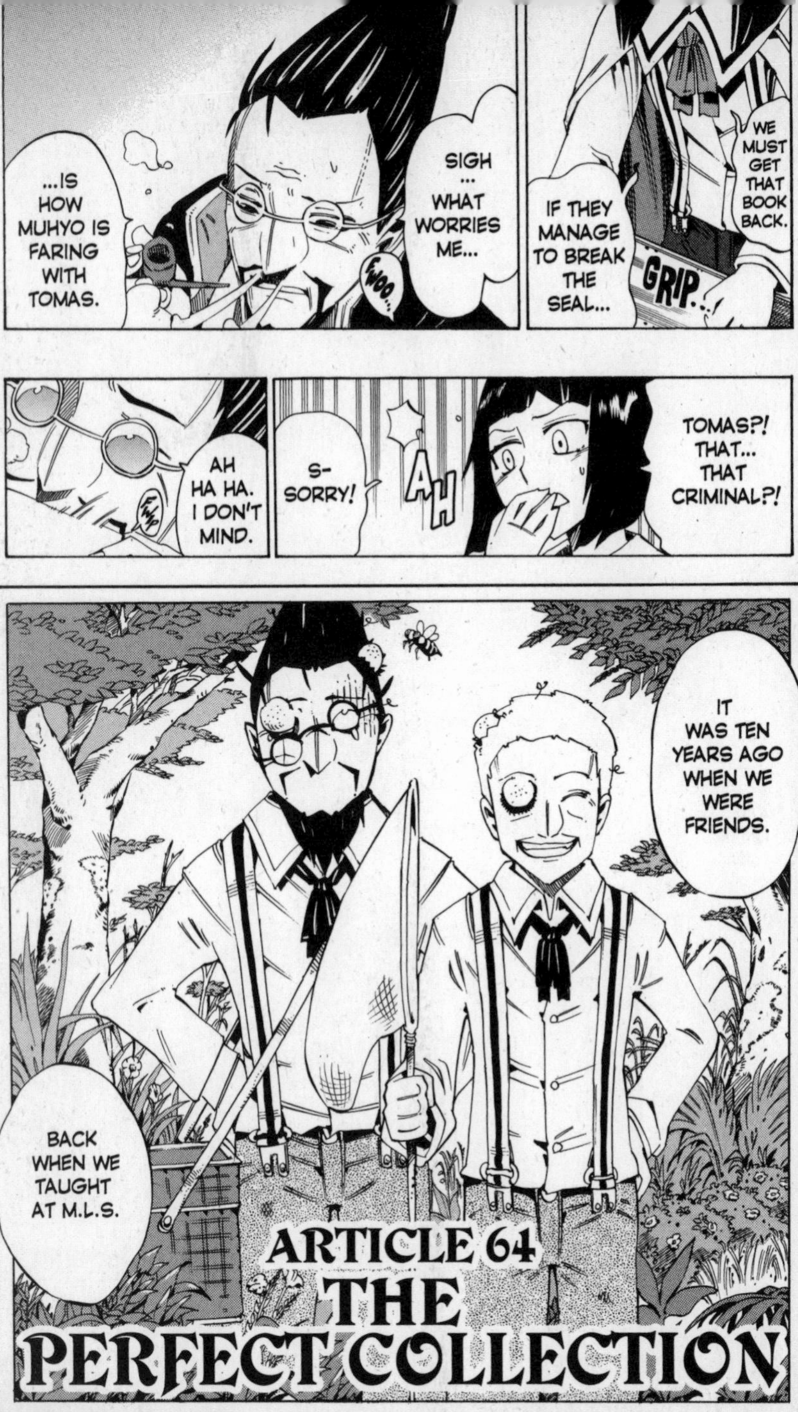
WE MUST GET THAT BOOK BACK.
GRIP...
IF THEY MANAGE TO BREAK THE SEAL...
SIGH ... WHAT WORRIES ME...
FWOO...
...IS HOW MUHYO IS FARING WITH TOMAS.
TOMAS?! THAT... THAT CRIMINAL?!
AH
S-SORRY!
AH HA HA. I DON'T MIND.
IT WAS TEN YEARS AGO WHEN WE WERE FRIENDS.
BACK WHEN WE TAUGHT AT M.L.S.
ARTICLE 64
THE PERFECT COLLECTION

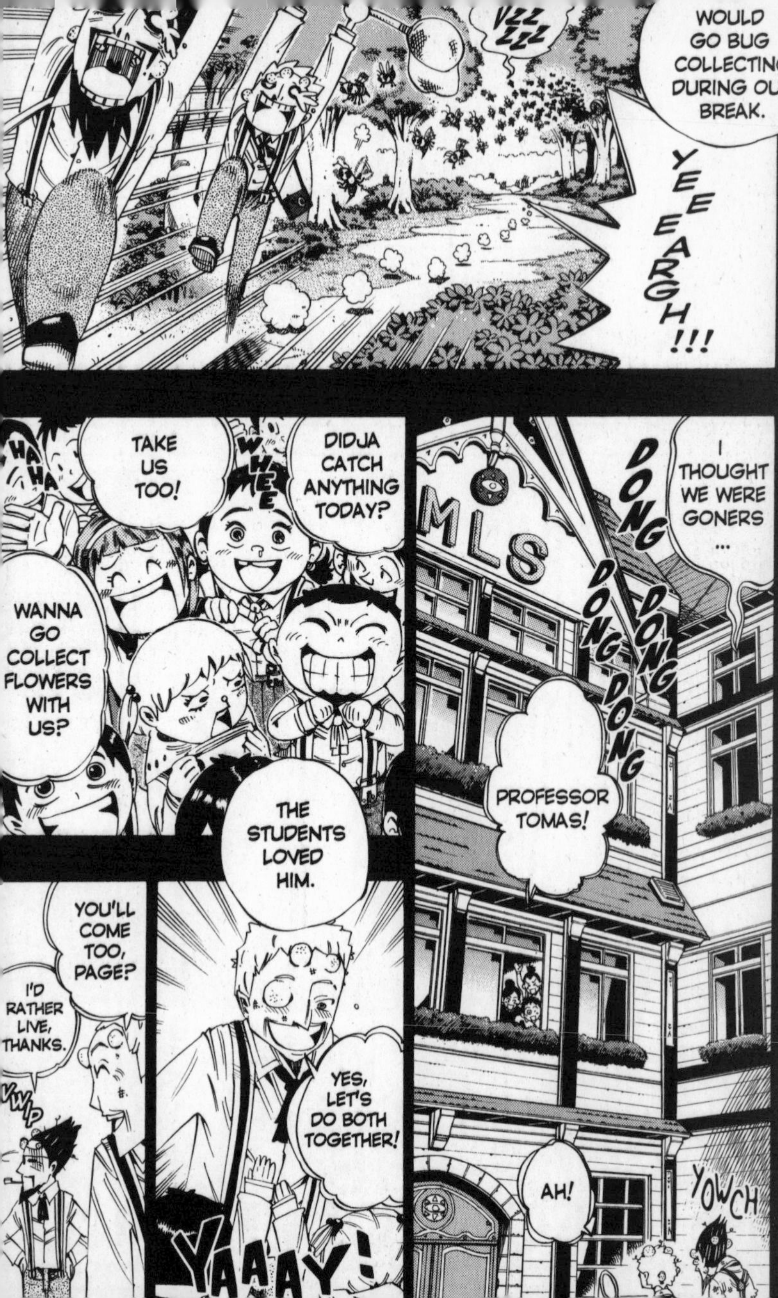
WOULD GO BUG COLLECTING DURING OUR BREAK.
VZZ ZZZ
YEEEARGH!!!
I THOUGHT WE WERE GONERS ...
DONG DONG DONG DONG DONG
PROFESSOR TOMAS!
AH!
YOWCH
DIDJA CATCH ANYTHING TODAY?
WHEEE
TAKE US TOO!
HAHA
WANNA GO COLLECT FLOWERS WITH US?
THE STUDENTS LOVED HIM.
YES, LET'S DO BOTH TOGETHER!
YAAAY!
YOU'LL COME TOO, PAGE?
I'D RATHER LIVE, THANKS.
VWIP

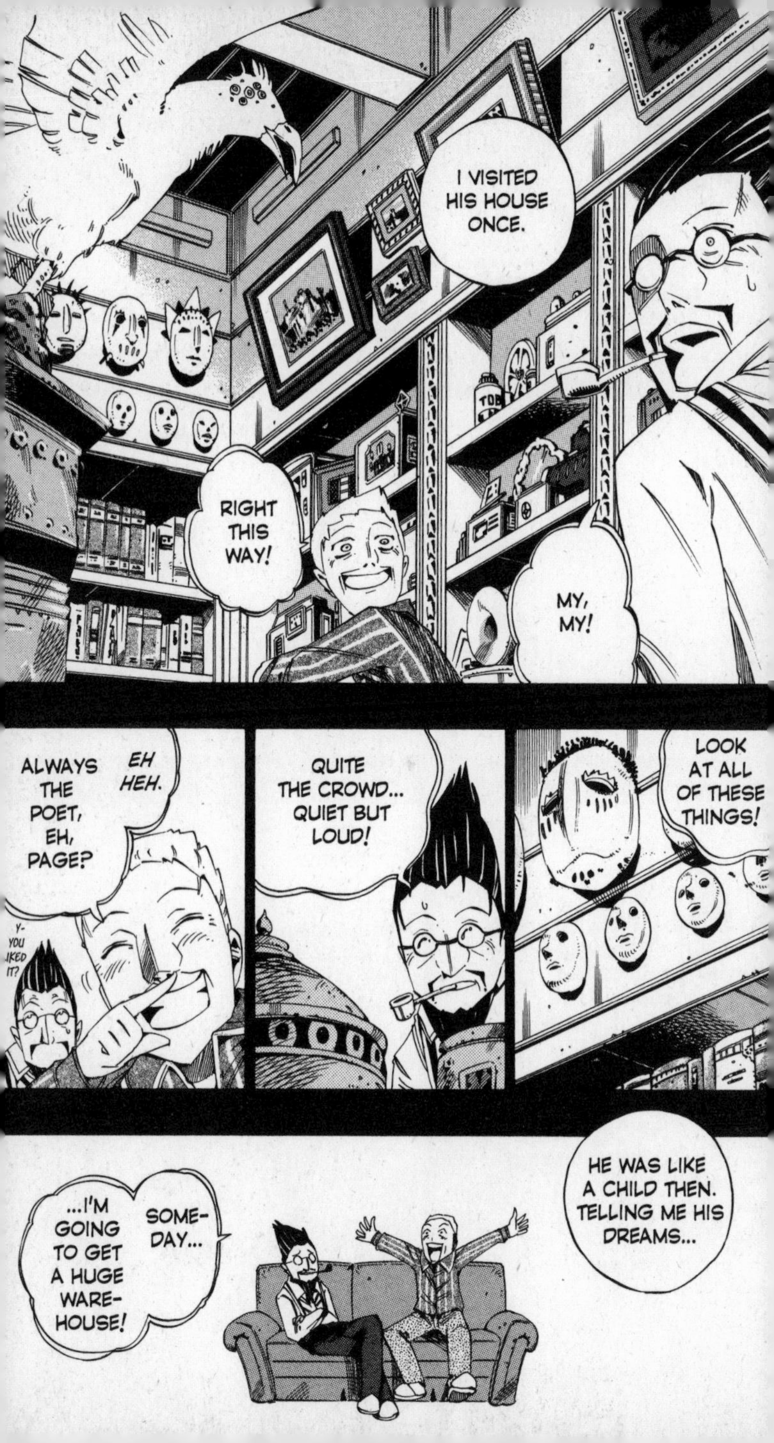
I VISITED HIS HOUSE ONCE.
RIGHT THIS WAY!
MY, MY!
LOOK AT ALL OF THESE THINGS!
QUITE THE CROWD... QUIET BUT LOUD!
ALWAYS THE POET, EH, PAGE?
EH HEH.
Y- YOU LIKED IT?
HE WAS LIKE A CHILD THEN. TELLING ME HIS DREAMS...
SOME-DAY...
...I'M GOING TO GET A HUGE WARE-HOUSE!

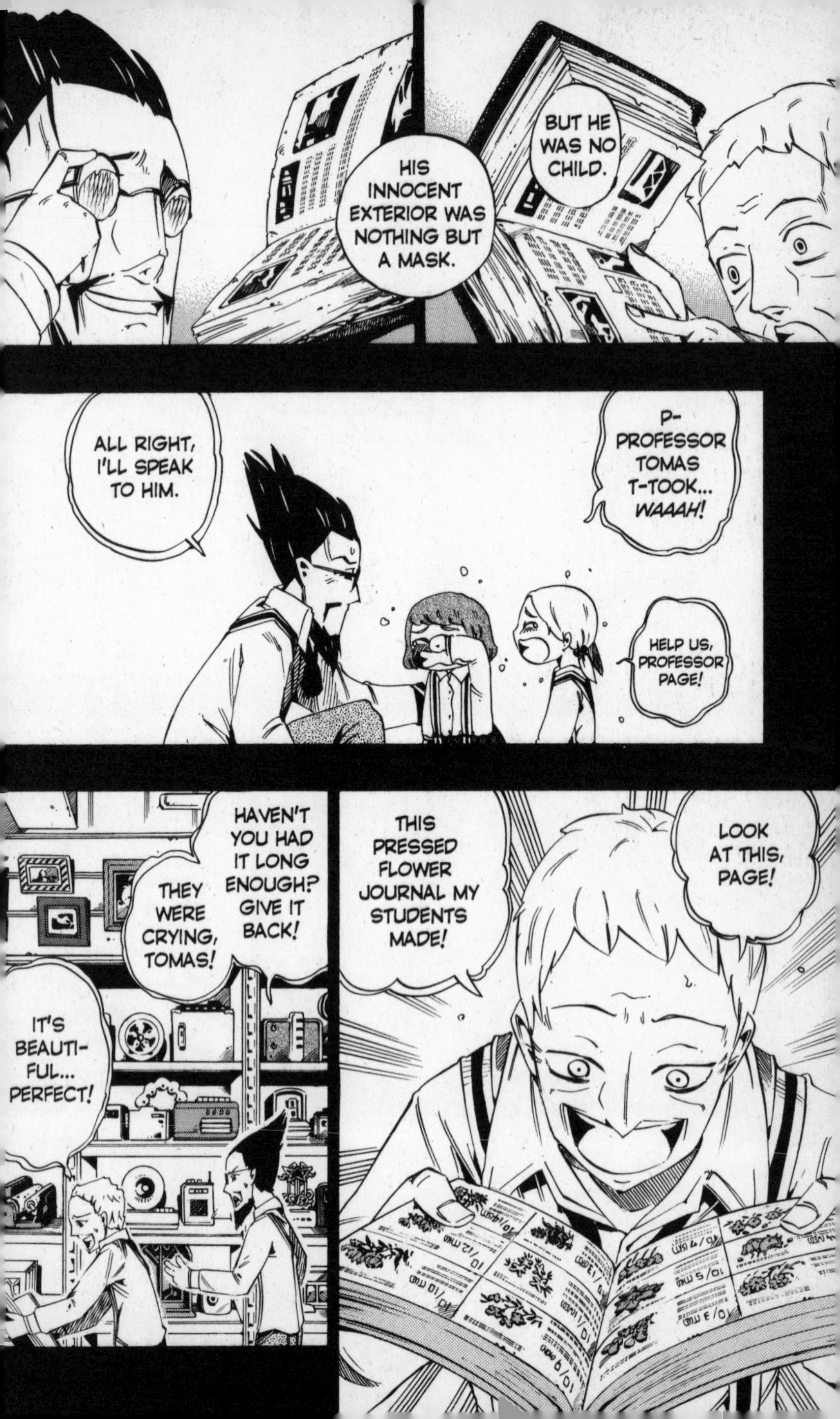
BUT HE WAS NO CHILD.
HIS INNOCENT EXTERIOR WAS NOTHING BUT A MASK.
P-PROFESSOR TOMAS T-TOOK... *WAAAH!*
HELP US, PROFESSOR PAGE!
ALL RIGHT, I'LL SPEAK TO HIM.
LOOK AT THIS, PAGE!
THIS PRESSED FLOWER JOURNAL MY STUDENTS MADE!
HAVEN'T YOU HAD IT LONG ENOUGH? GIVE IT BACK!
THEY WERE CRYING, TOMAS!
IT'S BEAUTIFUL... PERFECT!

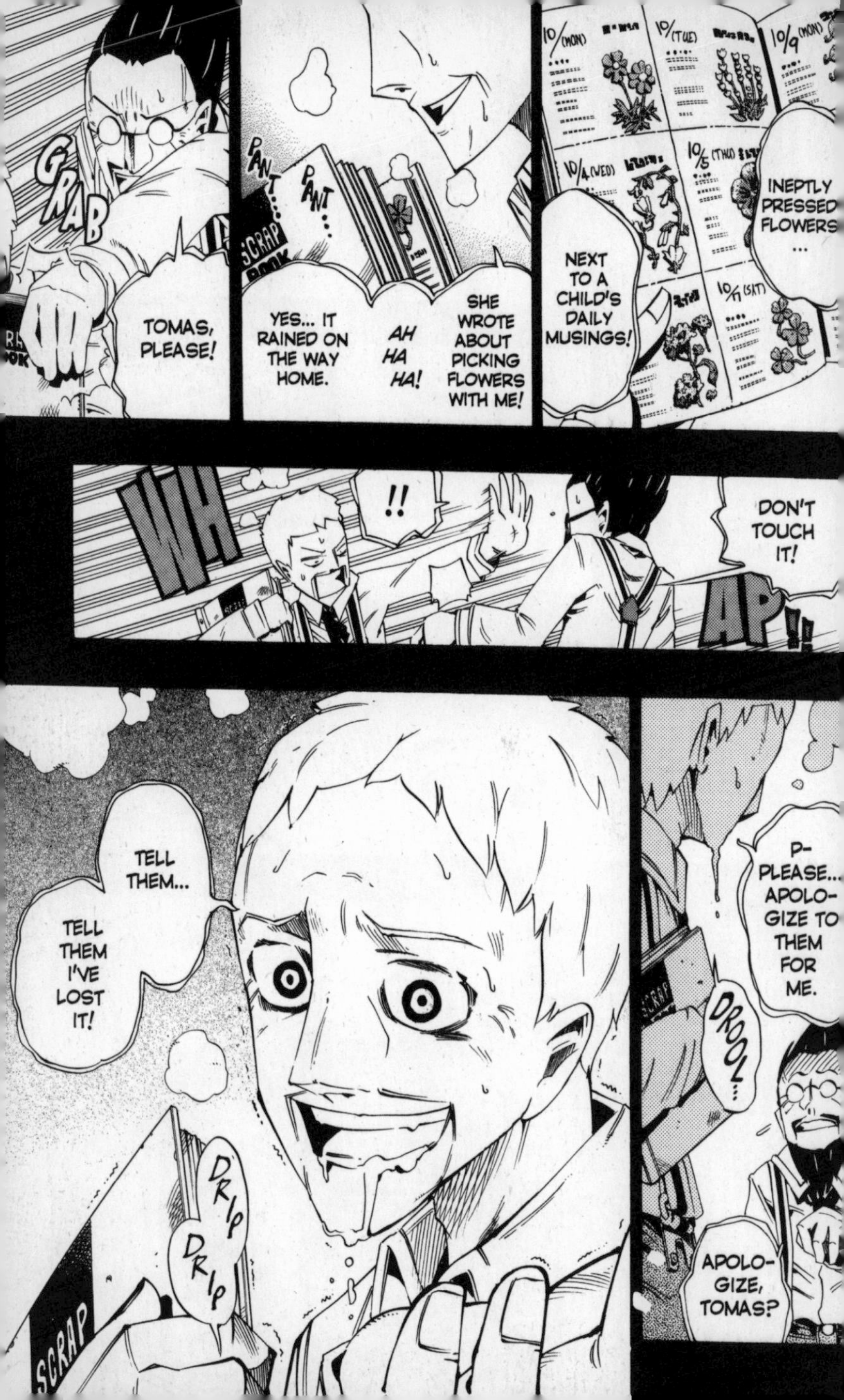
INEPTLY PRESSED FLOWERS...
NEXT TO A CHILD'S DAILY MUSINGS!
SHE WROTE ABOUT PICKING FLOWERS WITH ME!
AH HA HA!
YES... IT RAINED ON THE WAY HOME.
PANT...
PANT...
SCRAP BOOK
TOMAS, PLEASE!
GRAB
DON'T TOUCH IT!
!!
WHAP!!
P-PLEASE... APOLOGIZE TO THEM FOR ME.
DROOL...
APOLOGIZE, TOMAS?
TELL THEM...
TELL THEM I'VE LOST IT!
DRIP
DRIP
DRIP
SCRAP

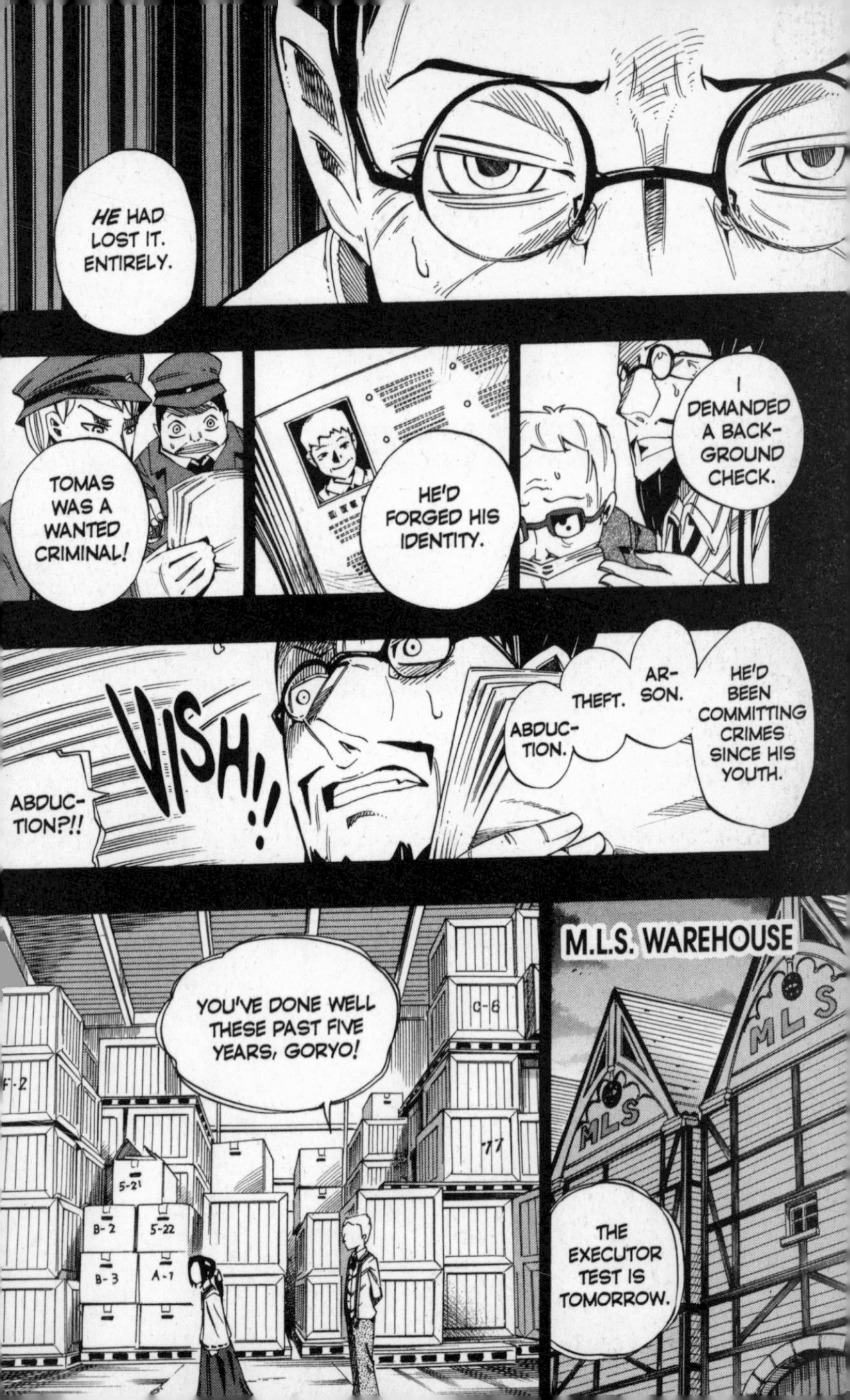
HE HAD LOST IT. ENTIRELY.
I DEMANDED A BACK-GROUND CHECK.
HE'D FORGED HIS IDENTITY.
TOMAS WAS A WANTED CRIMINAL!
HE'D BEEN COMMITTING CRIMES SINCE HIS YOUTH.
AR-SON.
THEFT.
ABDUC-TION.
VISH!!
ABDUC-TION?!!
M.L.S. WAREHOUSE
THE EXECUTOR TEST IS TOMORROW.
YOU'VE DONE WELL THESE PAST FIVE YEARS, GORYO!

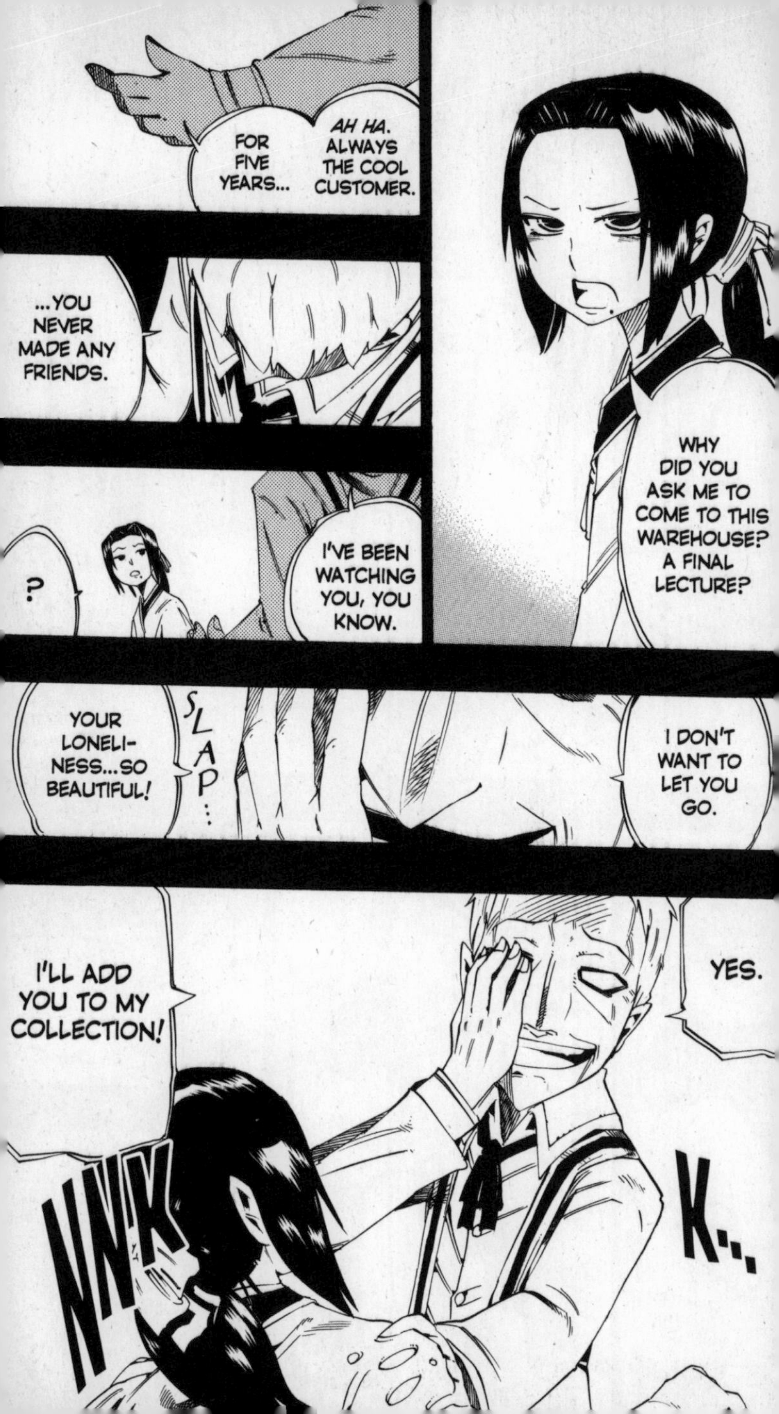
WHY DID YOU ASK ME TO COME TO THIS WAREHOUSE? A FINAL LECTURE?
AH HA. ALWAYS THE COOL CUSTOMER.
FOR FIVE YEARS...
...YOU NEVER MADE ANY FRIENDS.
I'VE BEEN WATCHING YOU, YOU KNOW.
?
I DON'T WANT TO LET YOU GO.
SLAP...
YOUR LONELI-NESS...SO BEAUTIFUL!
YES.
I'LL ADD YOU TO MY COLLECTION!
NNK
K...

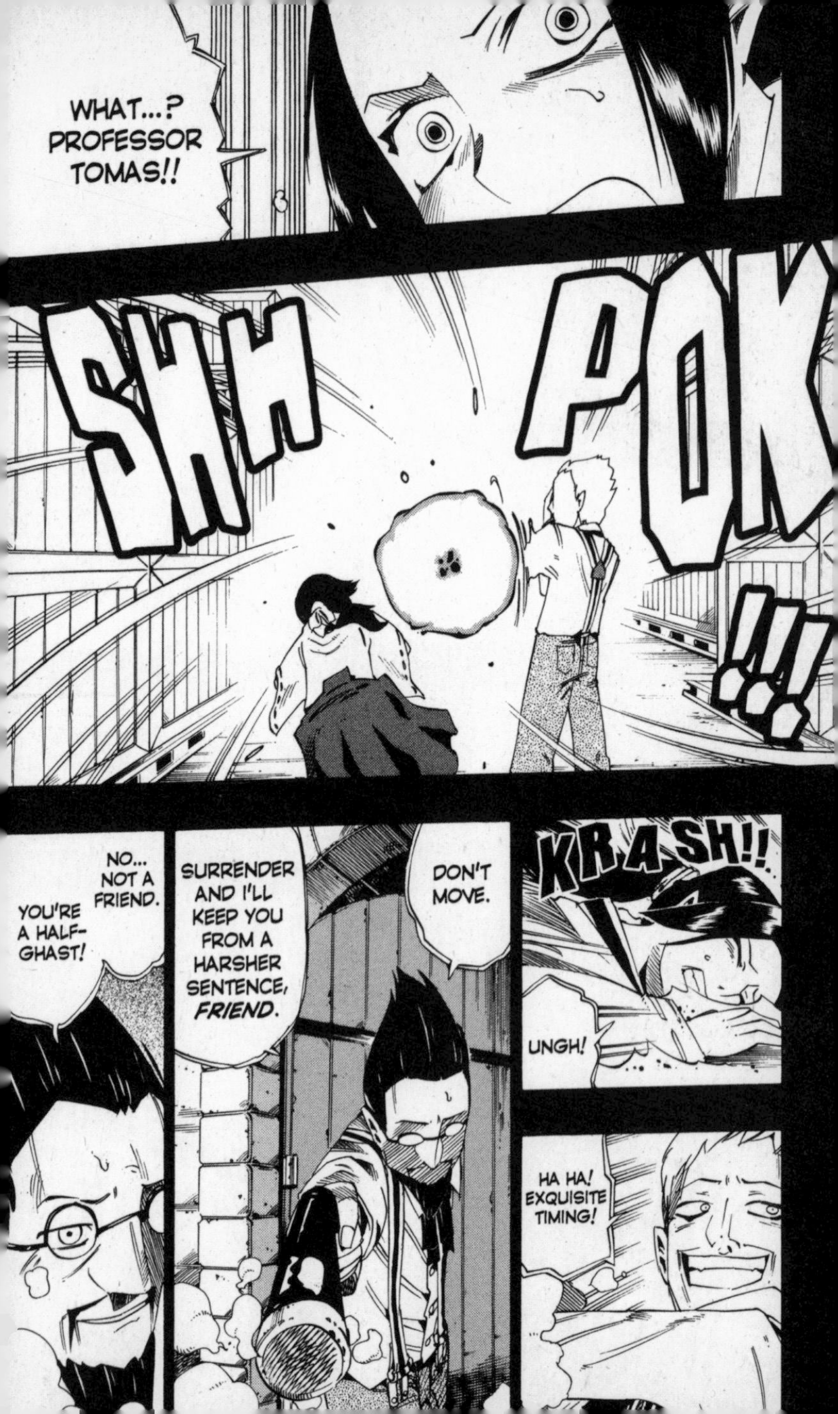
WHAT...? PROFESSOR TOMAS!!
SHH POK!!!
KRASH!!
UNGH!
HA HA! EXQUISITE TIMING!
DON'T MOVE.
SURRENDER AND I'LL KEEP YOU FROM A HARSHER SENTENCE, *FRIEND*.
NO... NOT A FRIEND.
YOU'RE A HALF-GHAST!

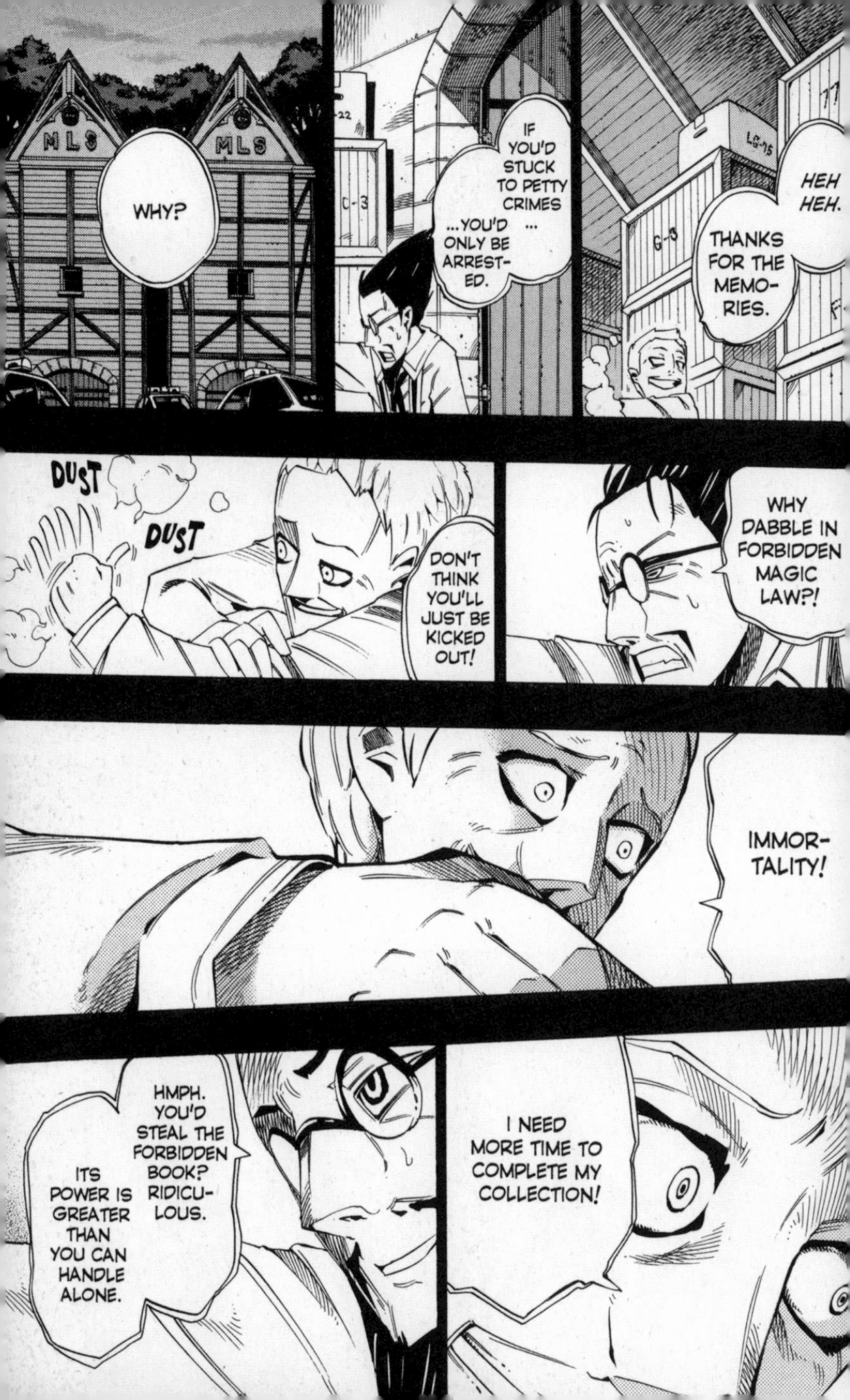
HEH HEH.
THANKS FOR THE MEMORIES.
IF YOU'D STUCK TO PETTY CRIMES ...
...YOU'D ONLY BE ARRESTED.
MLS
MLS
WHY?
WHY DABBLE IN FORBIDDEN MAGIC LAW?!
DUST
DUST
DON'T THINK YOU'LL JUST BE KICKED OUT!
IMMORTALITY!
I NEED MORE TIME TO COMPLETE MY COLLECTION!
HMPH. YOU'D STEAL THE FORBIDDEN BOOK? RIDICULOUS.
ITS POWER IS GREATER THAN YOU CAN HANDLE ALONE.

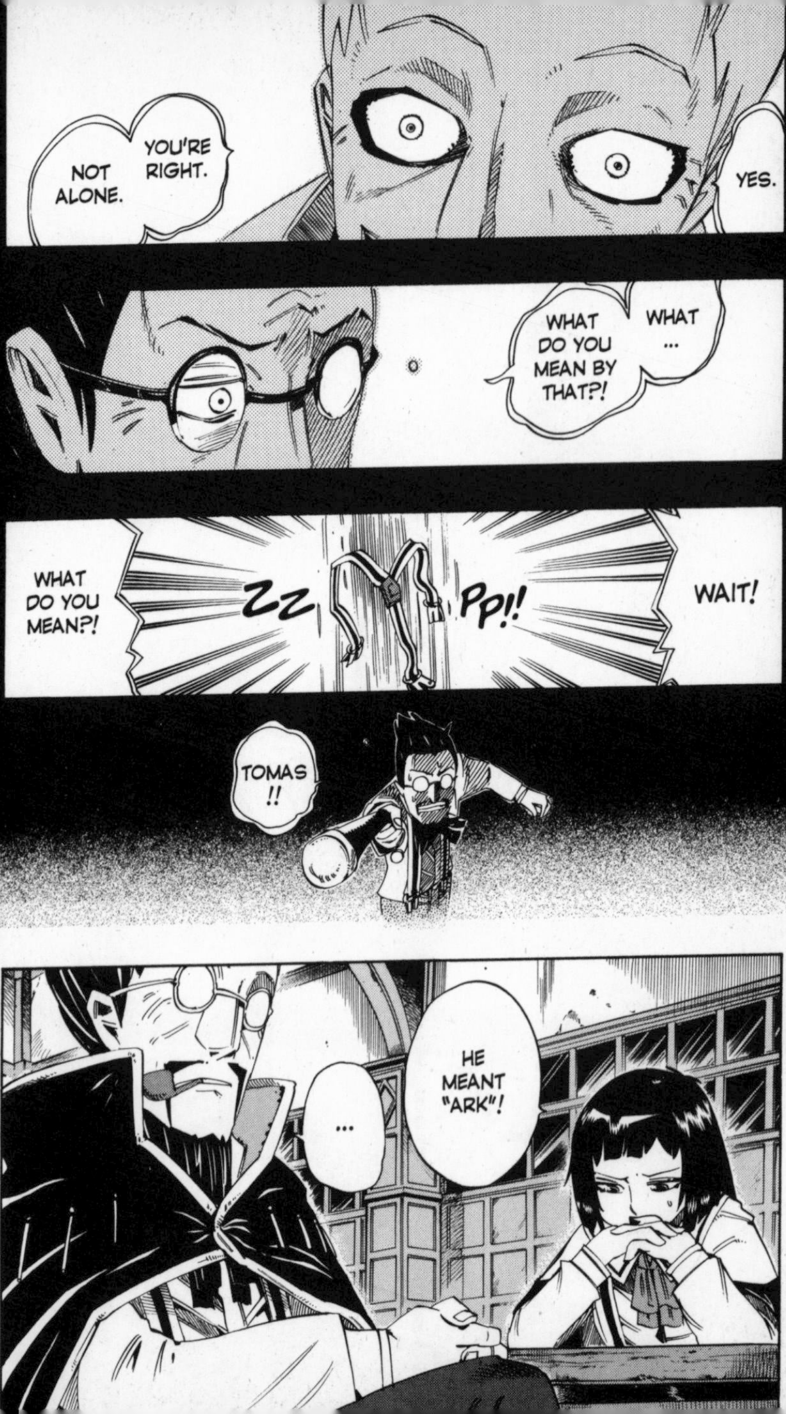
YES.
YOU'RE RIGHT. NOT ALONE.
WHAT ...
WHAT DO YOU MEAN BY THAT?!
WAIT!
ZZPP!!
WHAT DO YOU MEAN?!
TOMAS !!
HE MEANT "ARK"!
...

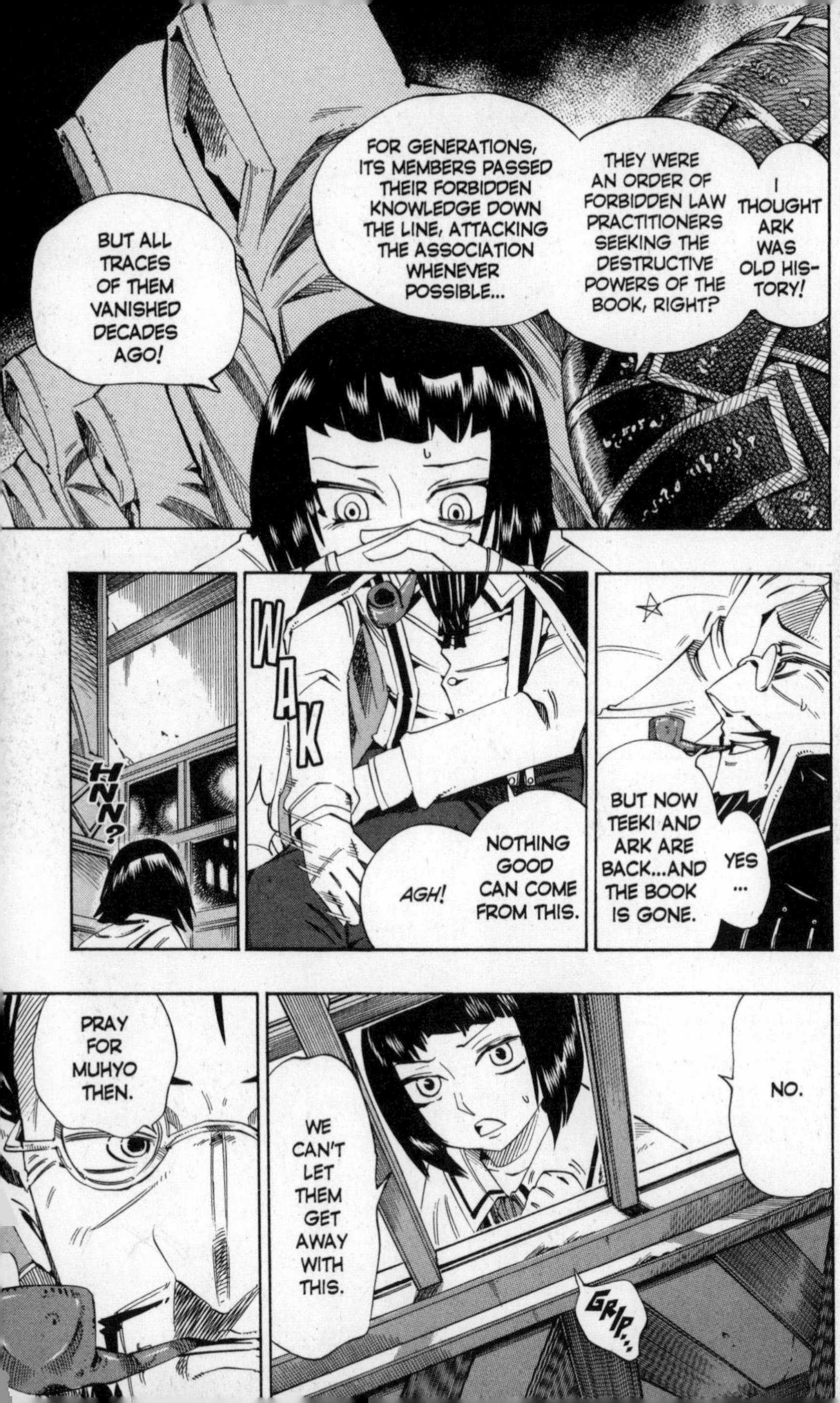
I THOUGHT ARK WAS OLD HISTORY!
THEY WERE AN ORDER OF FORBIDDEN LAW PRACTITIONERS SEEKING THE DESTRUCTIVE POWERS OF THE BOOK, RIGHT?
FOR GENERATIONS, ITS MEMBERS PASSED THEIR FORBIDDEN KNOWLEDGE DOWN THE LINE, ATTACKING THE ASSOCIATION WHENEVER POSSIBLE...
BUT ALL TRACES OF THEM VANISHED DECADES AGO!
YES ...
BUT NOW TEEKI AND ARK ARE BACK...AND THE BOOK IS GONE.
WAK
NOTHING GOOD CAN COME FROM THIS.
AGH!
HNN?
NO.
WE CAN'T LET THEM GET AWAY WITH THIS.
GRIP...
PRAY FOR MUHYO THEN.

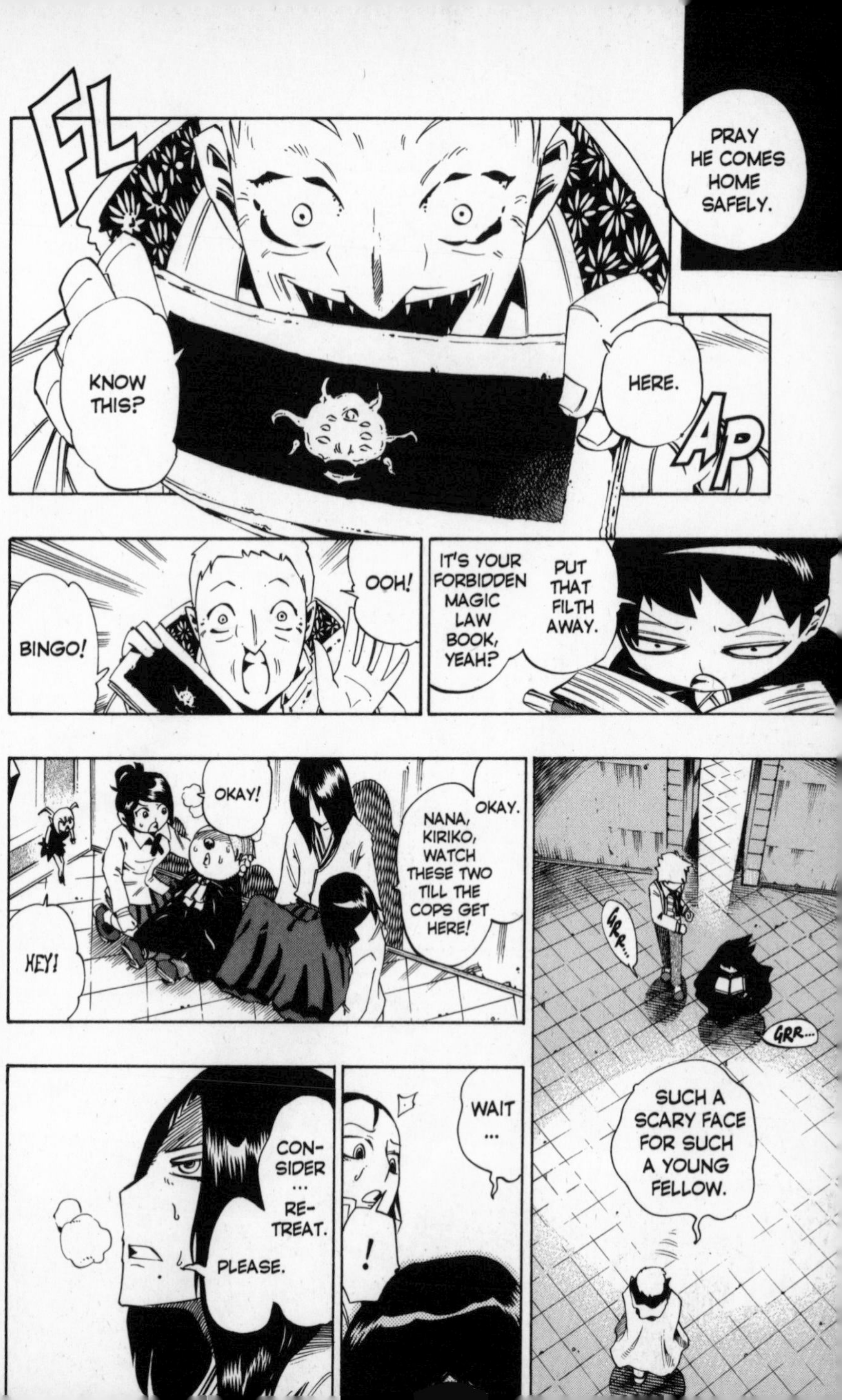
PRAY HE COMES HOME SAFELY.
HERE.
FL
AP
KNOW THIS?
PUT THAT FILTH AWAY.
IT'S YOUR FORBIDDEN MAGIC LAW BOOK, YEAH?
OOH!
BINGO!
GRR...
GRR...
SUCH A SCARY FACE FOR SUCH A YOUNG FELLOW.
OKAY.
NANA, KIRIKO, WATCH THESE TWO TILL THE COPS GET HERE!
OKAY!
HEY!
WAIT ...
!
CON-SIDER ...
RE-TREAT.
PLEASE.

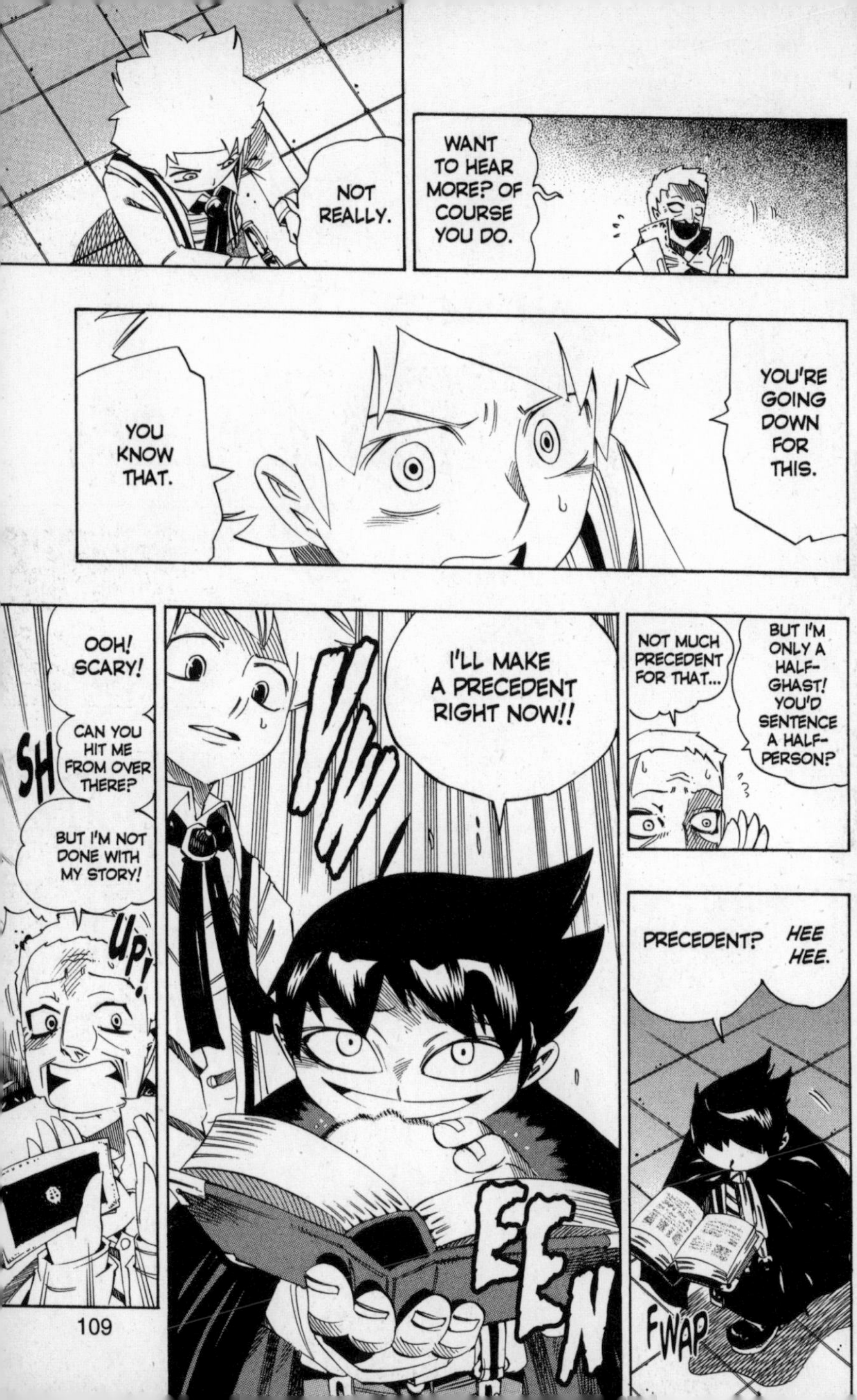
WANT TO HEAR MORE? OF COURSE YOU DO.
NOT REALLY.
YOU'RE GOING DOWN FOR THIS.
YOU KNOW THAT.
BUT I'M ONLY A HALF-GHAST! YOU'D SENTENCE A HALF-PERSON?
NOT MUCH PRECEDENT FOR THAT...
PRECEDENT?
HEE HEE.
FWAP
I'LL MAKE A PRECEDENT RIGHT NOW!!
EEN
OOH! SCARY!
SH
CAN YOU HIT ME FROM OVER THERE?
BUT I'M NOT DONE WITH MY STORY!
UP!

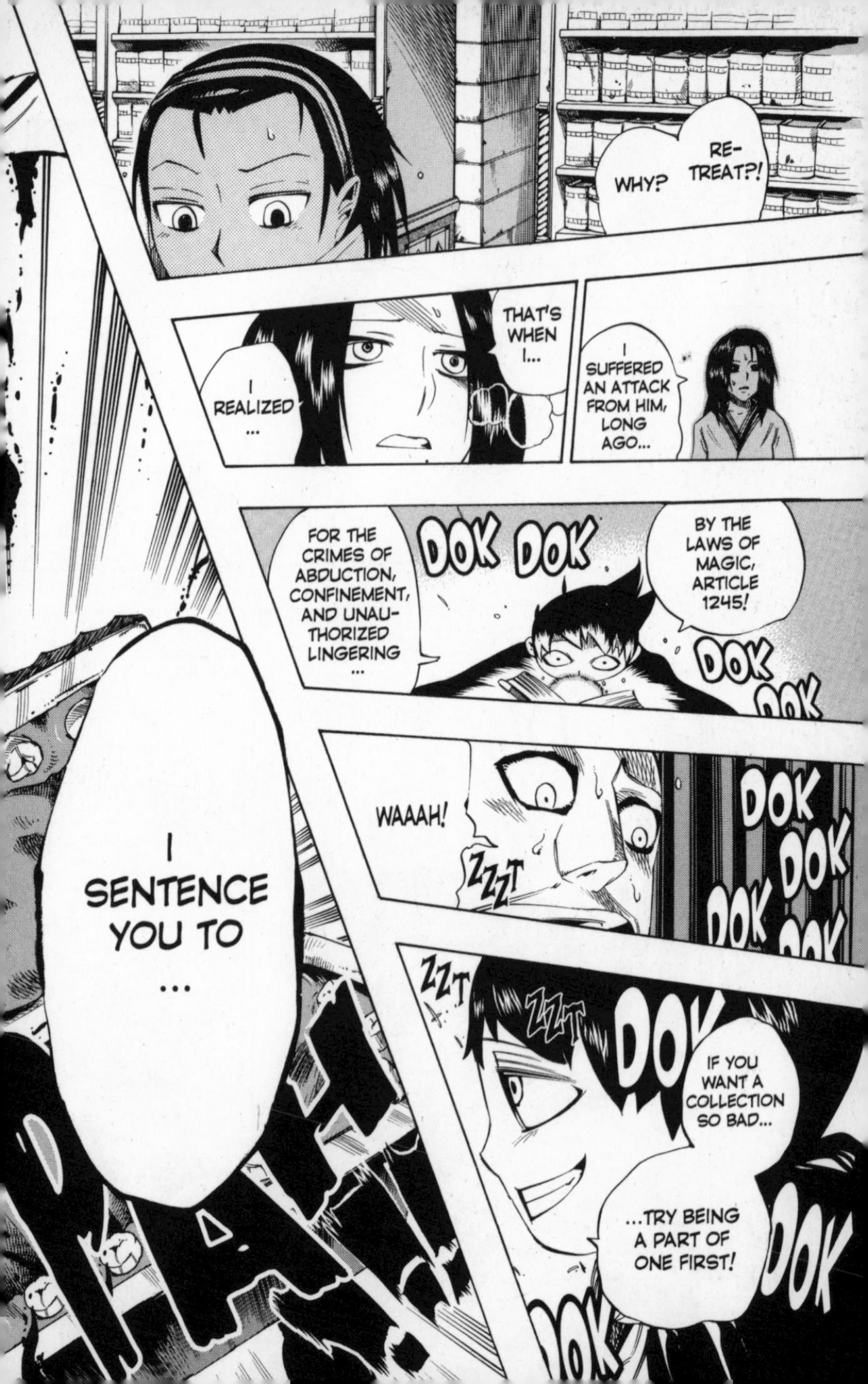
RE-TREAT?!
WHY?
I SUFFERED AN ATTACK FROM HIM, LONG AGO...
THAT'S WHEN I...
I REALIZED ...
BY THE LAWS OF MAGIC, ARTICLE 1245!
DOK DOK
DOK DOK
FOR THE CRIMES OF ABDUCTION, CONFINEMENT, AND UNAUTHORIZED LINGERING ...
DOK DOK DOK
WAAAH!
ZZZT
DOK
ZZZT
ZZZT
IF YOU WANT A COLLECTION SO BAD...
...TRY BEING A PART OF ONE FIRST!
DOK
I SENTENCE YOU TO ...

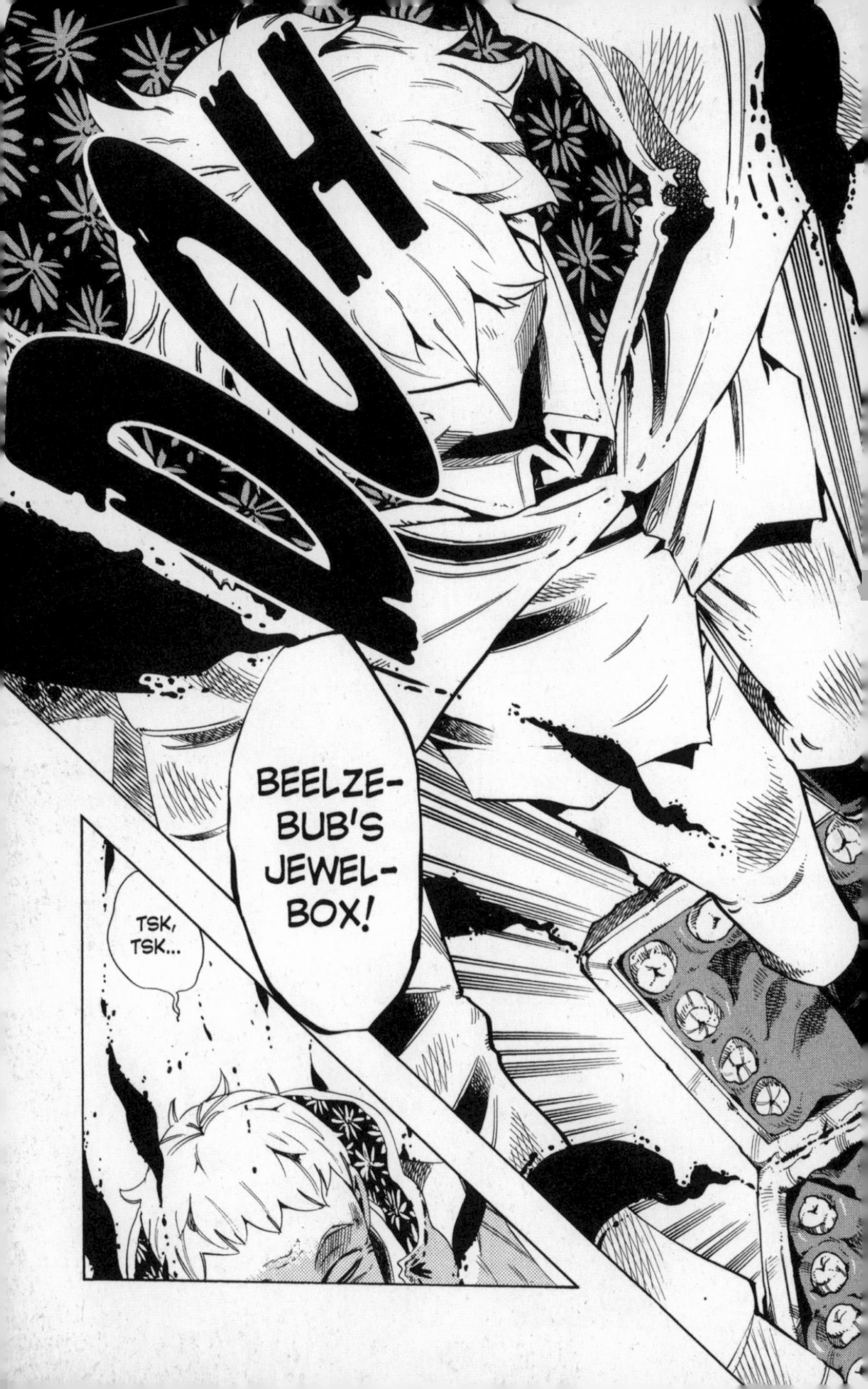
BEELZE-BUB'S JEWEL-BOX!
TSK, TSK...

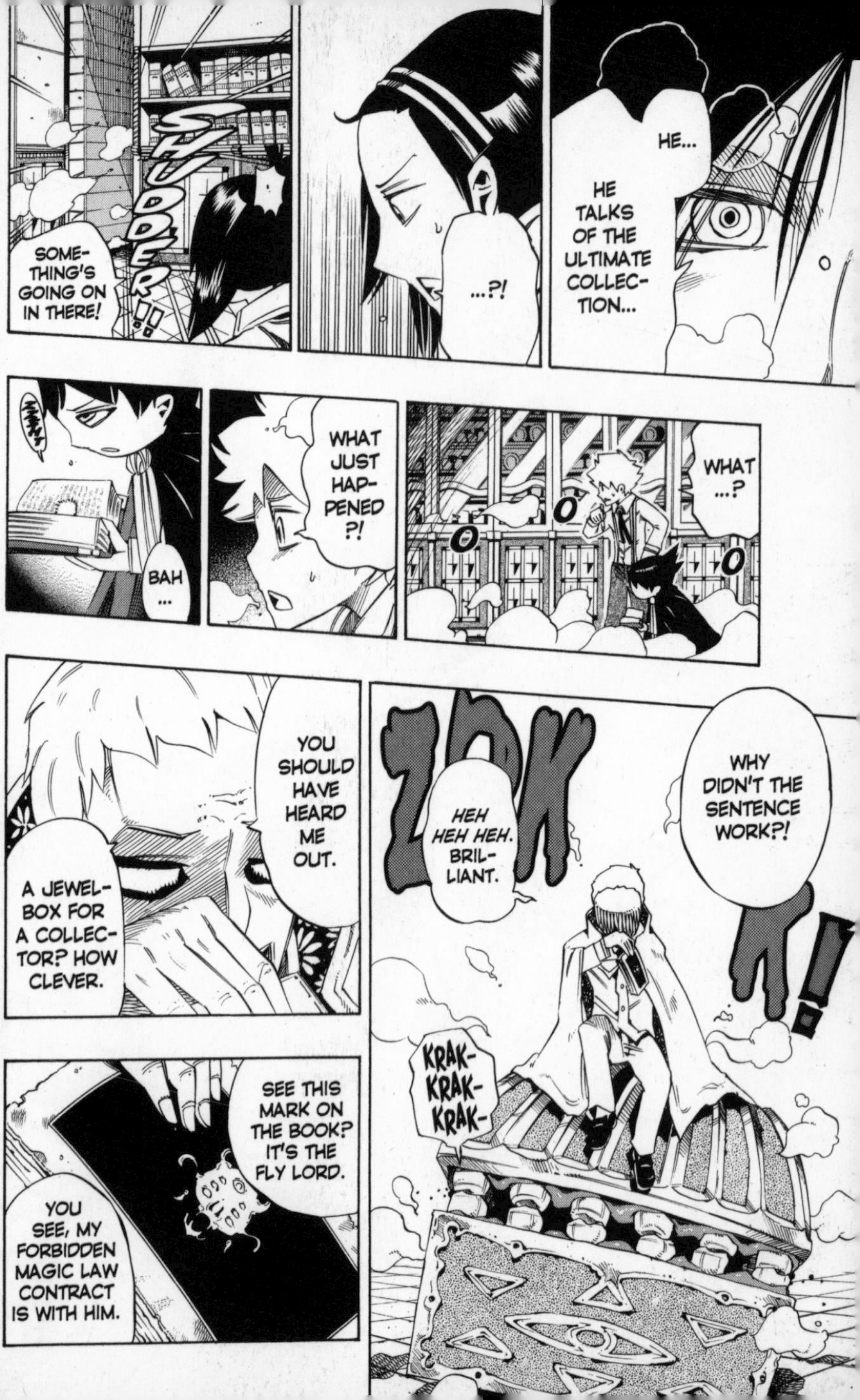

HE...
HE TALKS OF THE ULTIMATE COLLECTION...
...?!
SHUDDER!!
SOMETHING'S GOING ON IN THERE!
WHAT ...?
WHAT JUST HAPPENED?!
BAH ...
WHY DIDN'T THE SENTENCE WORK?!
ZOKK!
HEH HEH HEH. BRILLIANT.
KRAK-KRAK-KRAK-
YOU SHOULD HAVE HEARD ME OUT.
A JEWELBOX FOR A COLLECTOR? HOW CLEVER.
SEE THIS MARK ON THE BOOK? IT'S THE FLY LORD.
YOU SEE, MY FORBIDDEN MAGIC LAW CONTRACT IS WITH HIM.

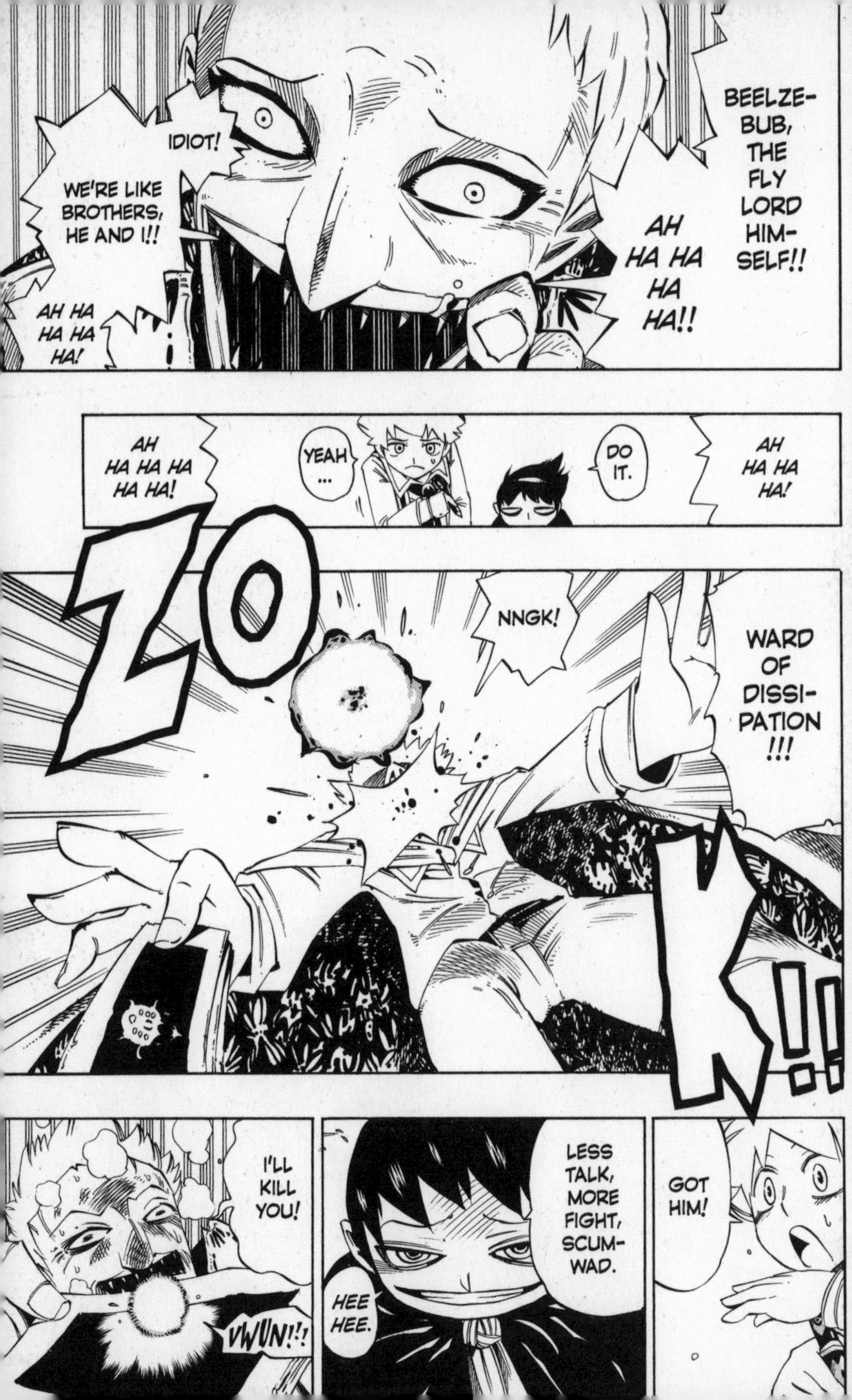
BEELZE-BUB, THE FLY LORD HIM-SELF!!
AH HA HA HA HA!!
IDIOT!
WE'RE LIKE BROTHERS, HE AND I!!
AH HA HA HA HA!
AH HA HA HA!
DO IT.
YEAH ...
AH HA HA HA HA HA!
WARD OF DISSI-PATION!!!
NNGK!
ZOK!!
GOT HIM!
LESS TALK, MORE FIGHT, SCUM-WAD.
HEE HEE.
I'LL KILL YOU!
VWUN!!!

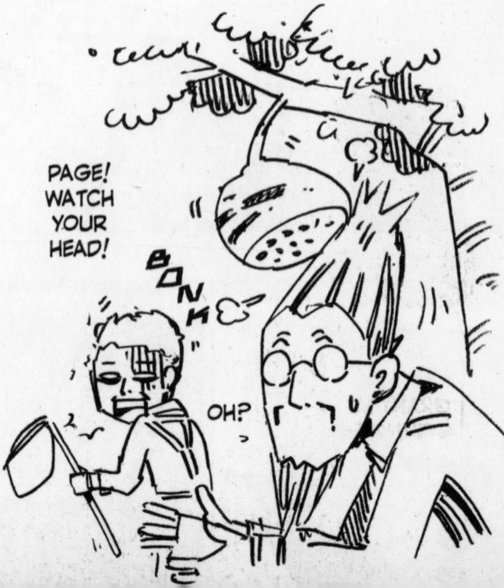
PAGE! WATCH YOUR HEAD!
BONK
OH?

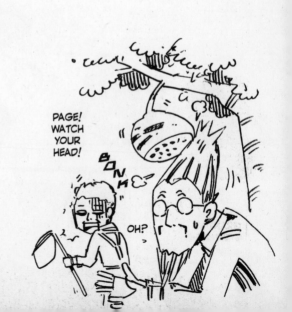

ARTICLE 65
ARMOR OF FLIES

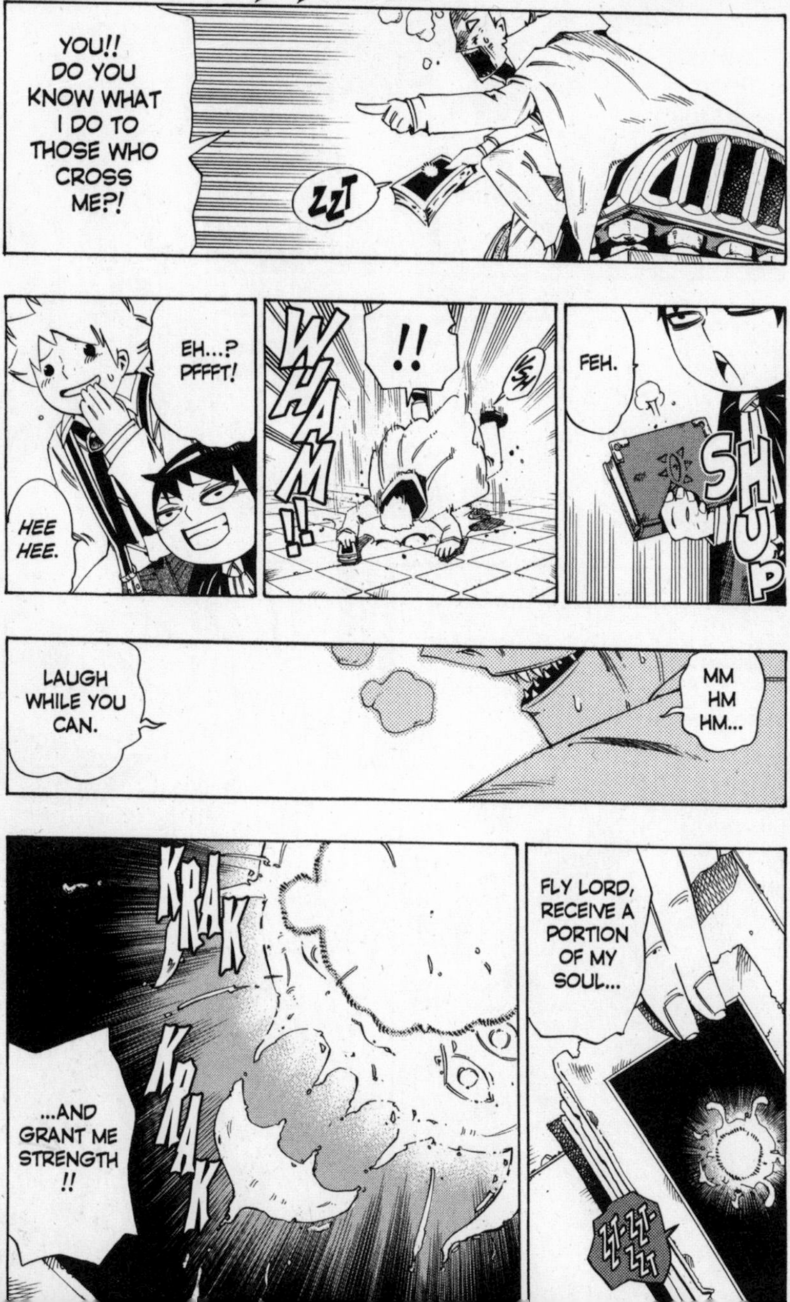
YOU!! DO YOU KNOW WHAT I DO TO THOSE WHO CROSS ME?!
ZZT
FEH.
SHUP
!!
WHAM!!
EH...? PFFFT!
HEE HEE.
MM HM HM...
LAUGH WHILE YOU CAN.
FLY LORD, RECEIVE A PORTION OF MY SOUL...
KRAK
KRAK
...AND GRANT ME STRENGTH!!

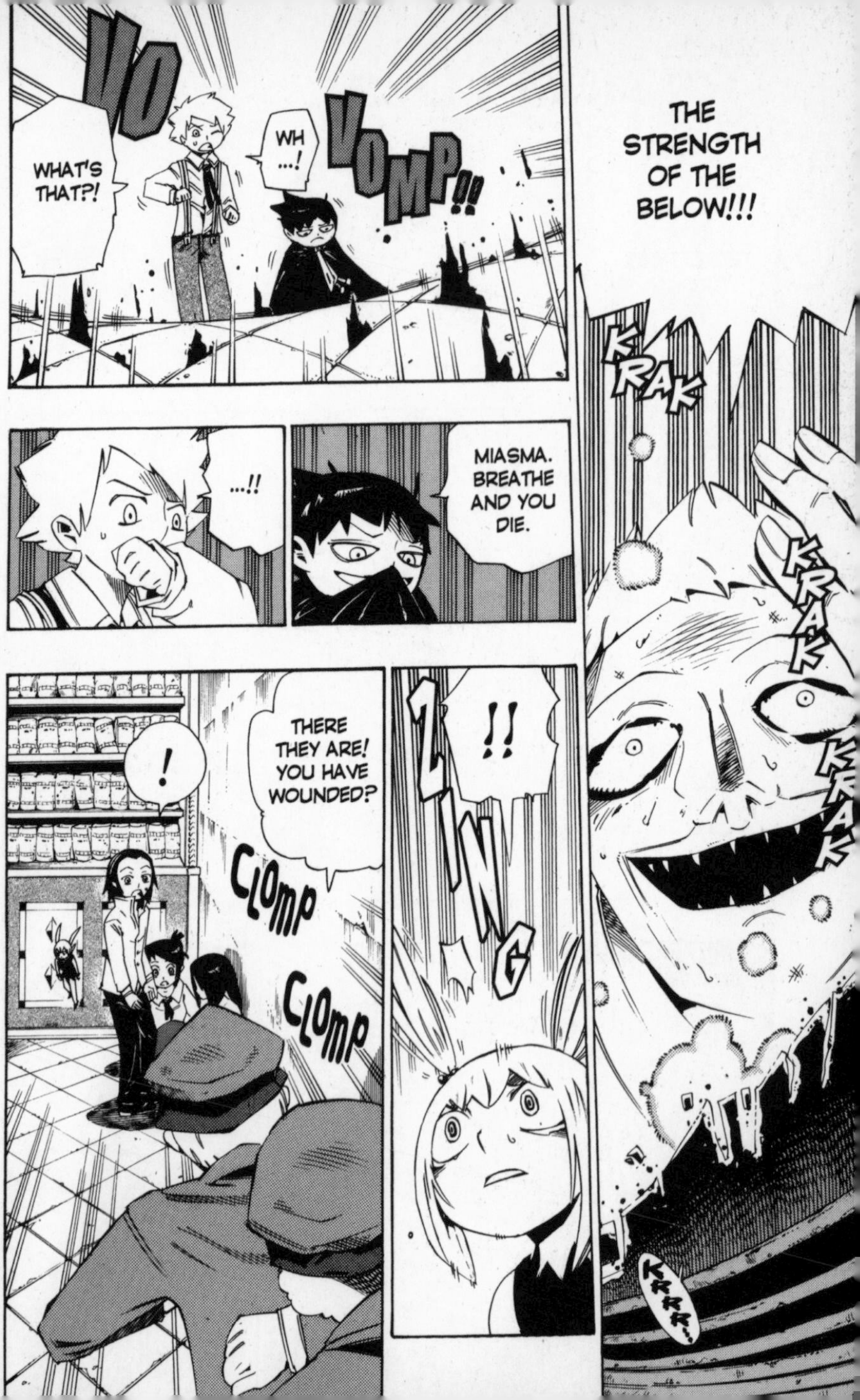
THE STRENGTH OF THE BELOW!!!
KRAK
KRAK
KRAK
KRRR!
VOMP!!
WH ...!
VO
WHAT'S THAT?!
MIASMA. BREATHE AND YOU DIE.
...!!
!!
ZING
THERE THEY ARE! YOU HAVE WOUNDED?
!
CLOMP
CLOMP

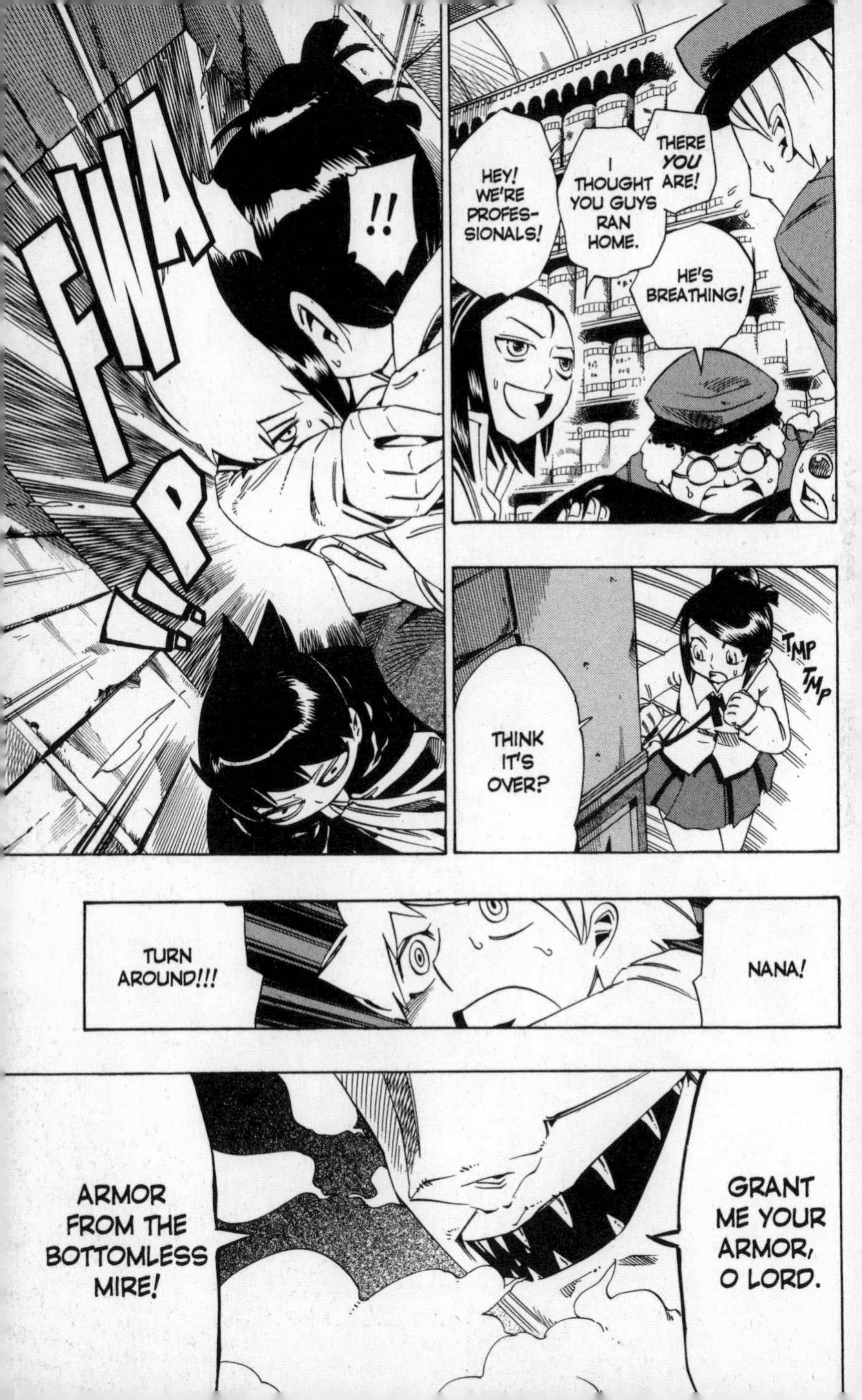
THERE YOU ARE!
I THOUGHT YOU GUYS RAN HOME.
HEY! WE'RE PROFES-SIONALS!
HE'S BREATHING!
TMP TMP
THINK IT'S OVER?
FWAP
!!
NANA!
TURN AROUND!!!
GRANT ME YOUR ARMOR, O LORD.
ARMOR FROM THE BOTTOMLESS MIRE!

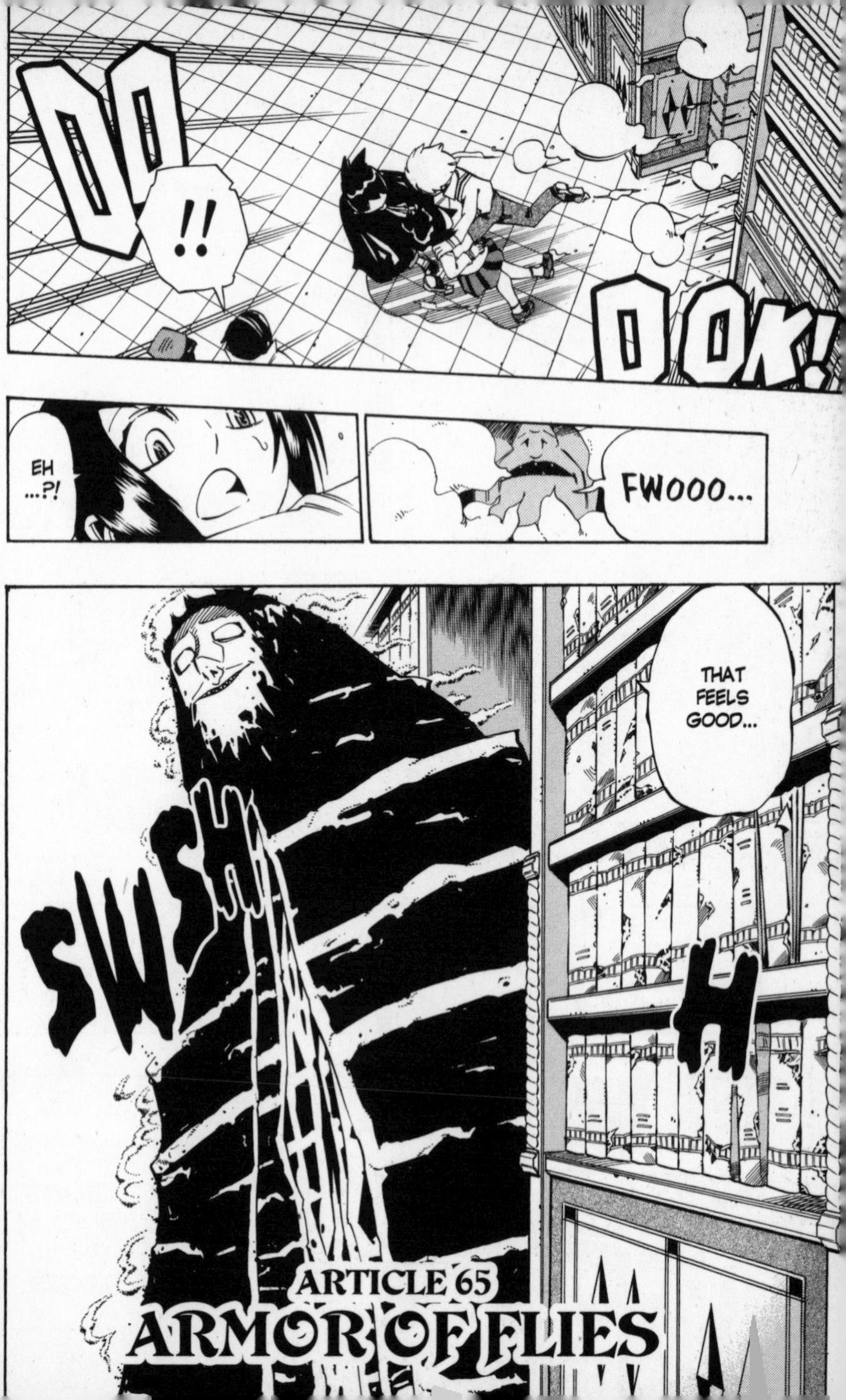
DO
!!
DOK!
FWOOO...
EH ...?!
THAT FEELS GOOD...
SWSHH
ARTICLE 65
ARMOR OF FLIES

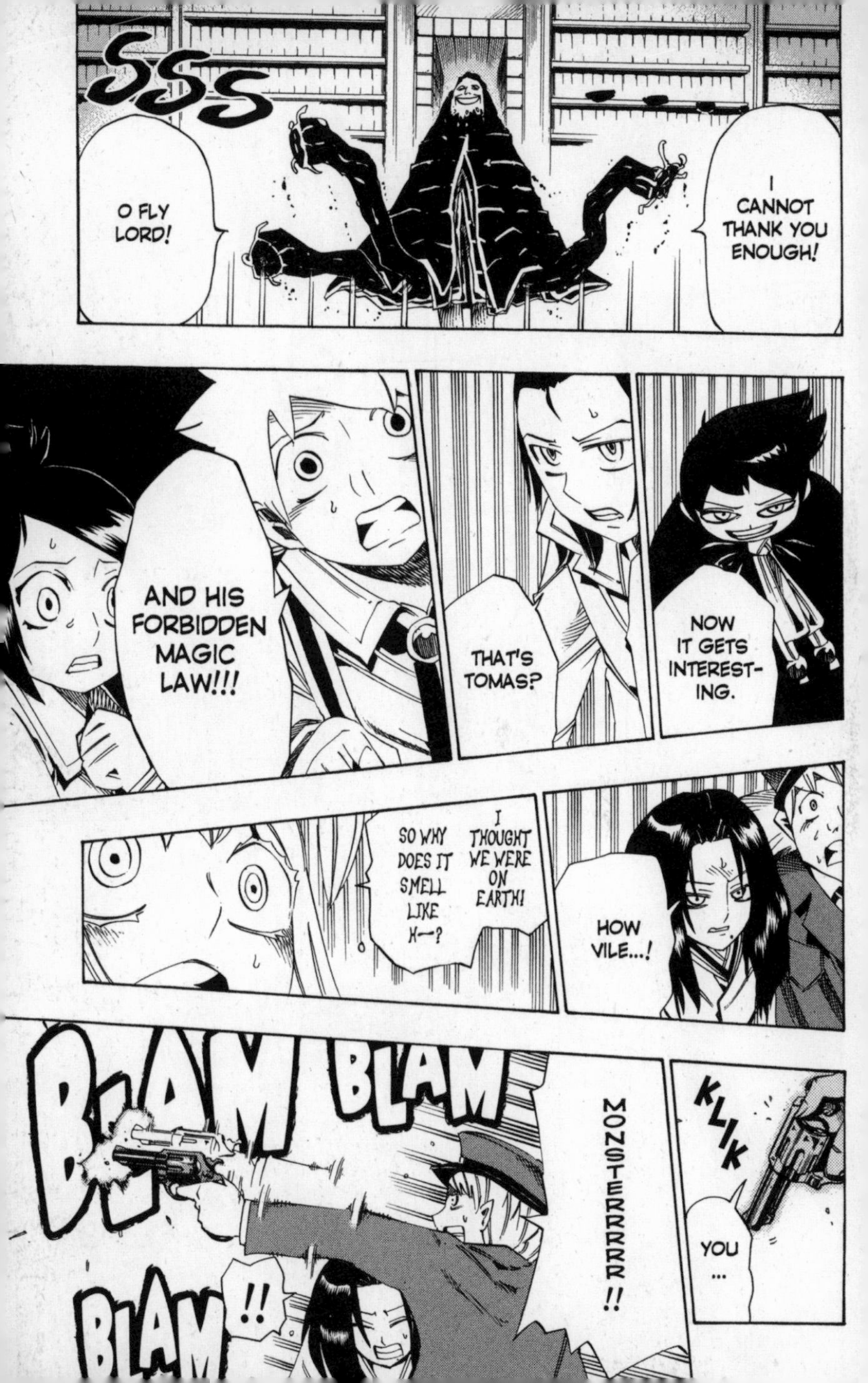
SSS
O FLY LORD!
I CANNOT THANK YOU ENOUGH!
NOW IT GETS INTEREST-ING.
THAT'S TOMAS?
AND HIS FORBIDDEN MAGIC LAW!!!
HOW VILE...!
I THOUGHT WE WERE ON EARTH!
SO WHY DOES IT SMELL LIKE H—?
KLIK
YOU ...
MONSTERRRRR!!
BLAM
BLAM
BLAM!!

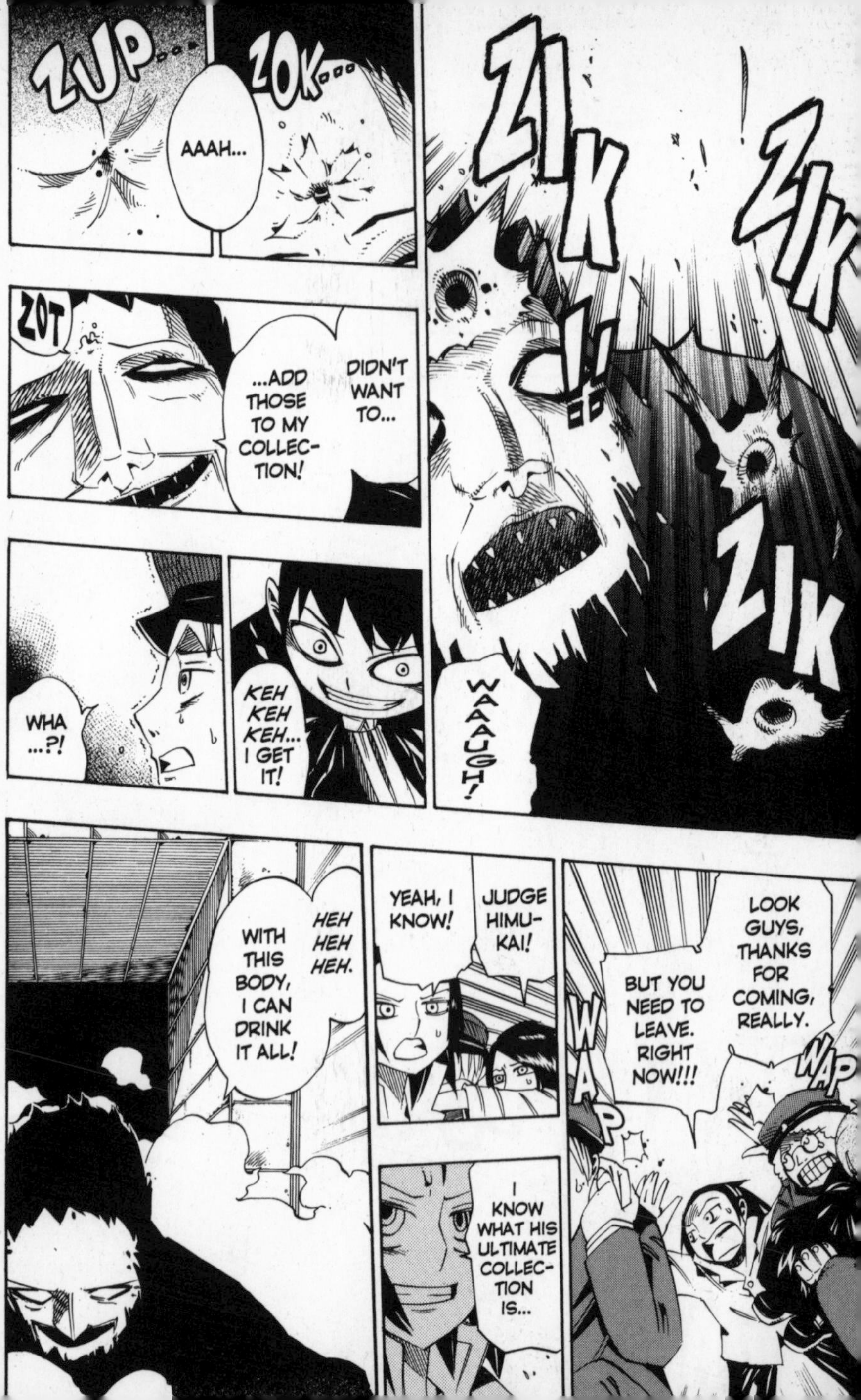
ZIK
ZIK
!!
ZIK
WAAAUGH!
ZOK...
AAAH...
ZUP...
DIDN'T WANT TO...
...ADD THOSE TO MY COLLECTION!
ZOT
KEH KEH KEH... I GET IT!
WHA ...?!
LOOK GUYS, THANKS FOR COMING, REALLY.
BUT YOU NEED TO LEAVE. RIGHT NOW!!!
WAP
WAP
JUDGE HIMUKAI!
YEAH, I KNOW!
I KNOW WHAT HIS ULTIMATE COLLECTION IS...
HEH HEH HEH.
WITH THIS BODY, I CAN DRINK IT ALL!

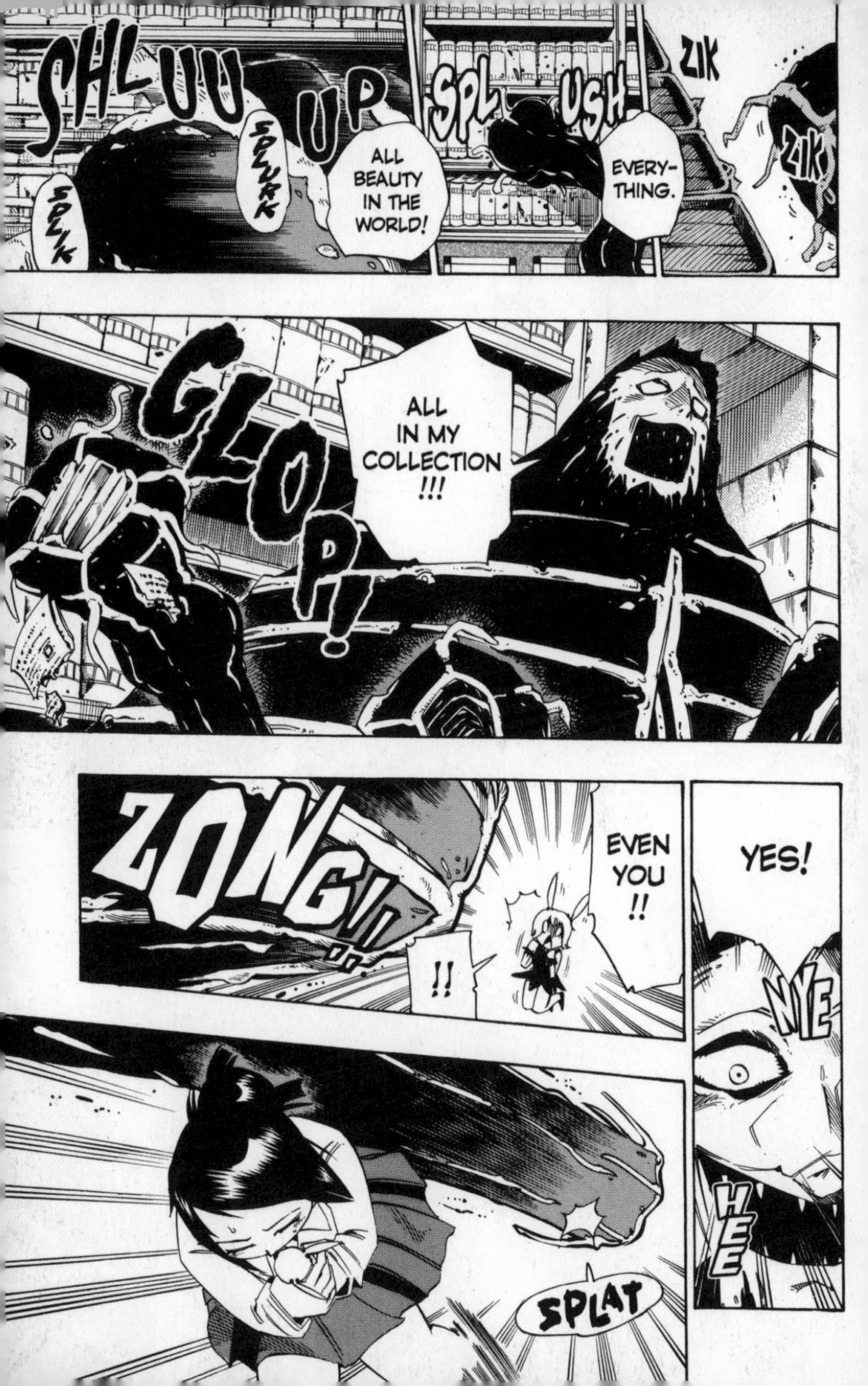
ZIK
ZIK
EVERY-THING.
SPLUSH
ALL BEAUTY IN THE WORLD!
SHLUUUP
SPLURK
SPLIK
ALL IN MY COLLECTION!!!
GLOP!
YES!
NYE
HEE
EVEN YOU!!
!!
ZONG!!
SPLAT

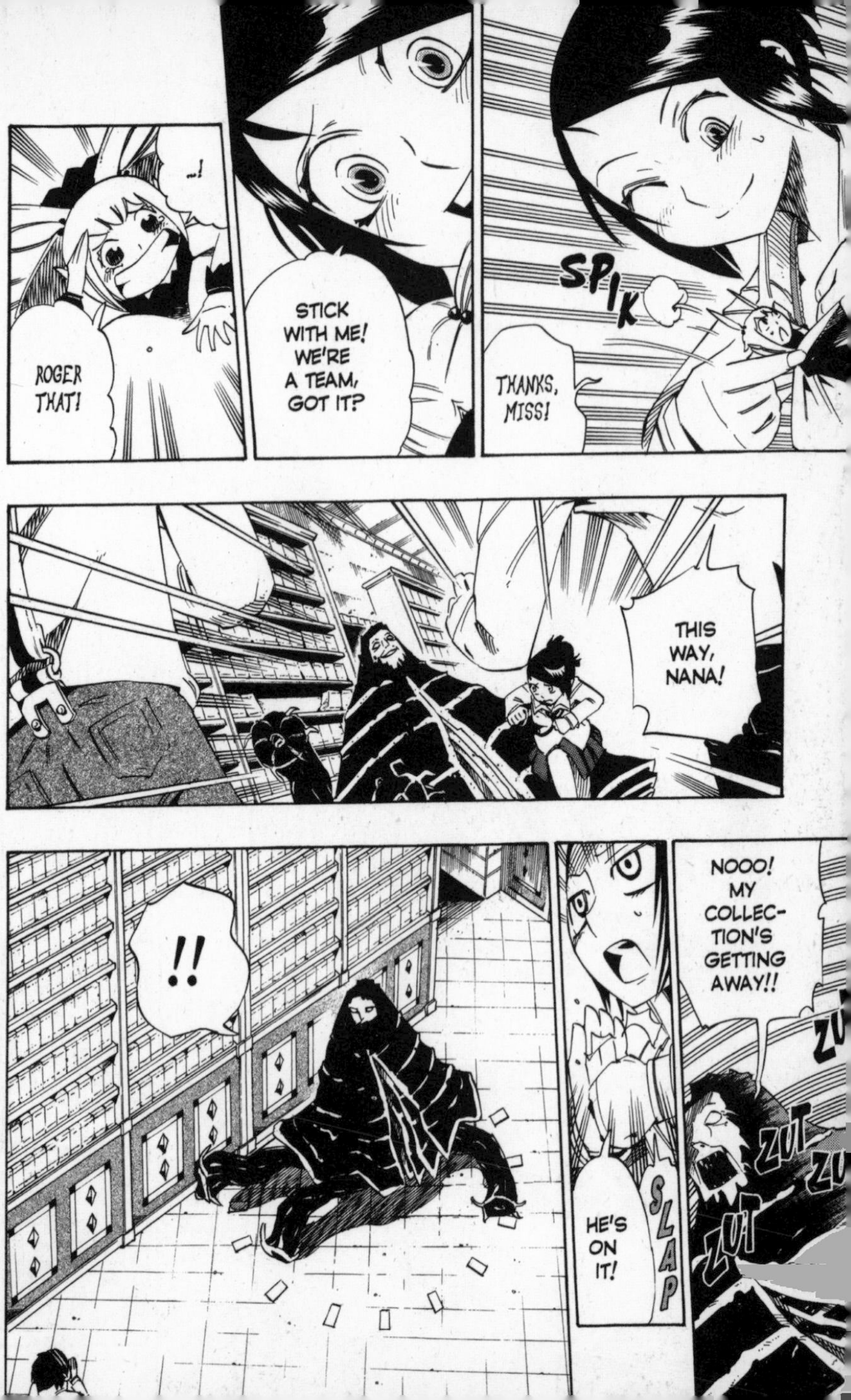
SPIK
THANKS, MISS!
STICK WITH ME! WE'RE A TEAM, GOT IT?
...!
ROGER THAT!
THIS WAY, NANA!
NOOO! MY COLLEC-TION'S GETTING AWAY!!
ZU
ZUT
ZU
ZUT
HE'S ON IT!
SLAP
!!

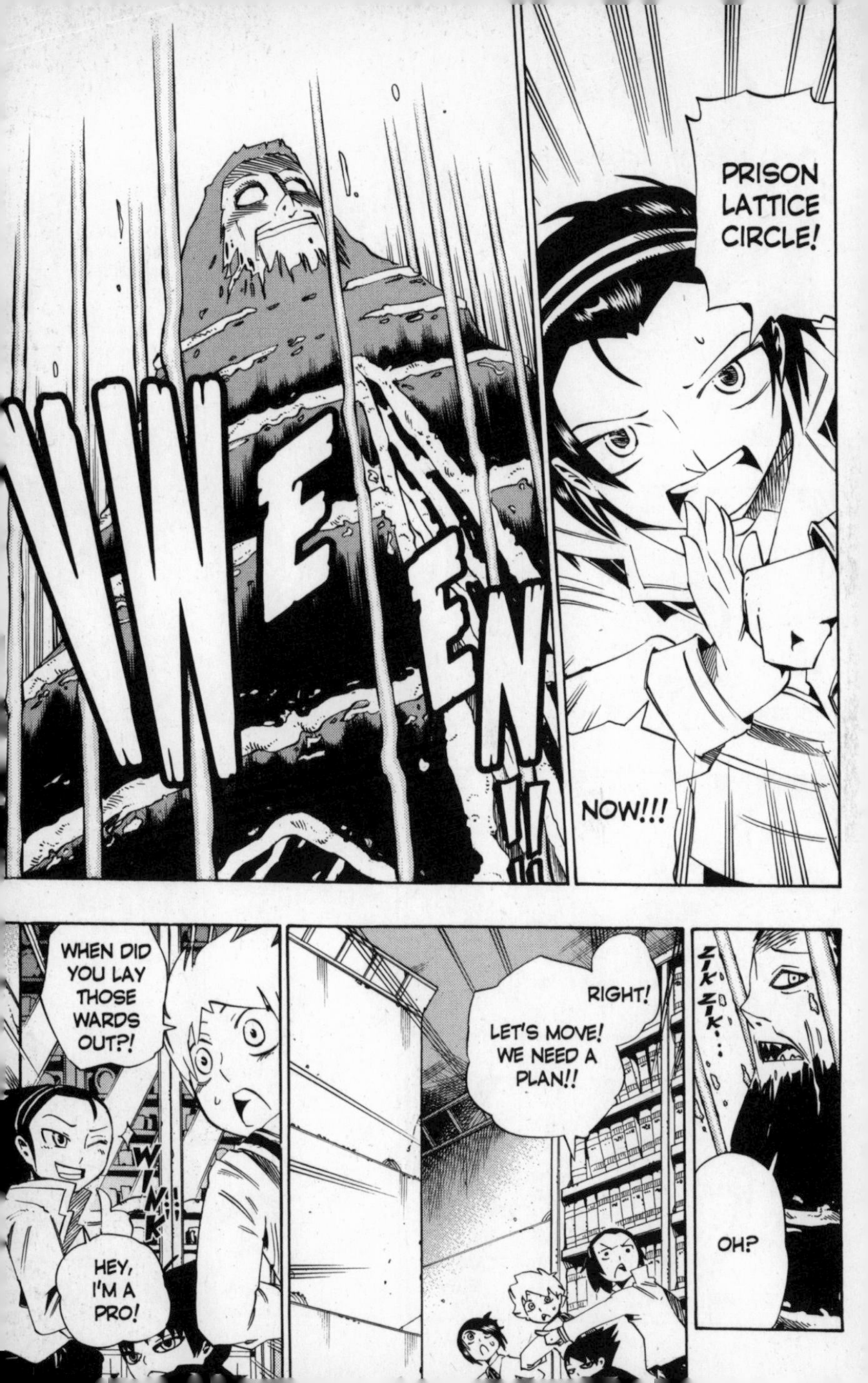
PRISON LATTICE CIRCLE!
NOW!!!
WEEN!!
ZIK ZIK...
OH?
RIGHT!
LET'S MOVE! WE NEED A PLAN!!
WHEN DID YOU LAY THOSE WARDS OUT?!
WINK
HEY, I'M A PRO!

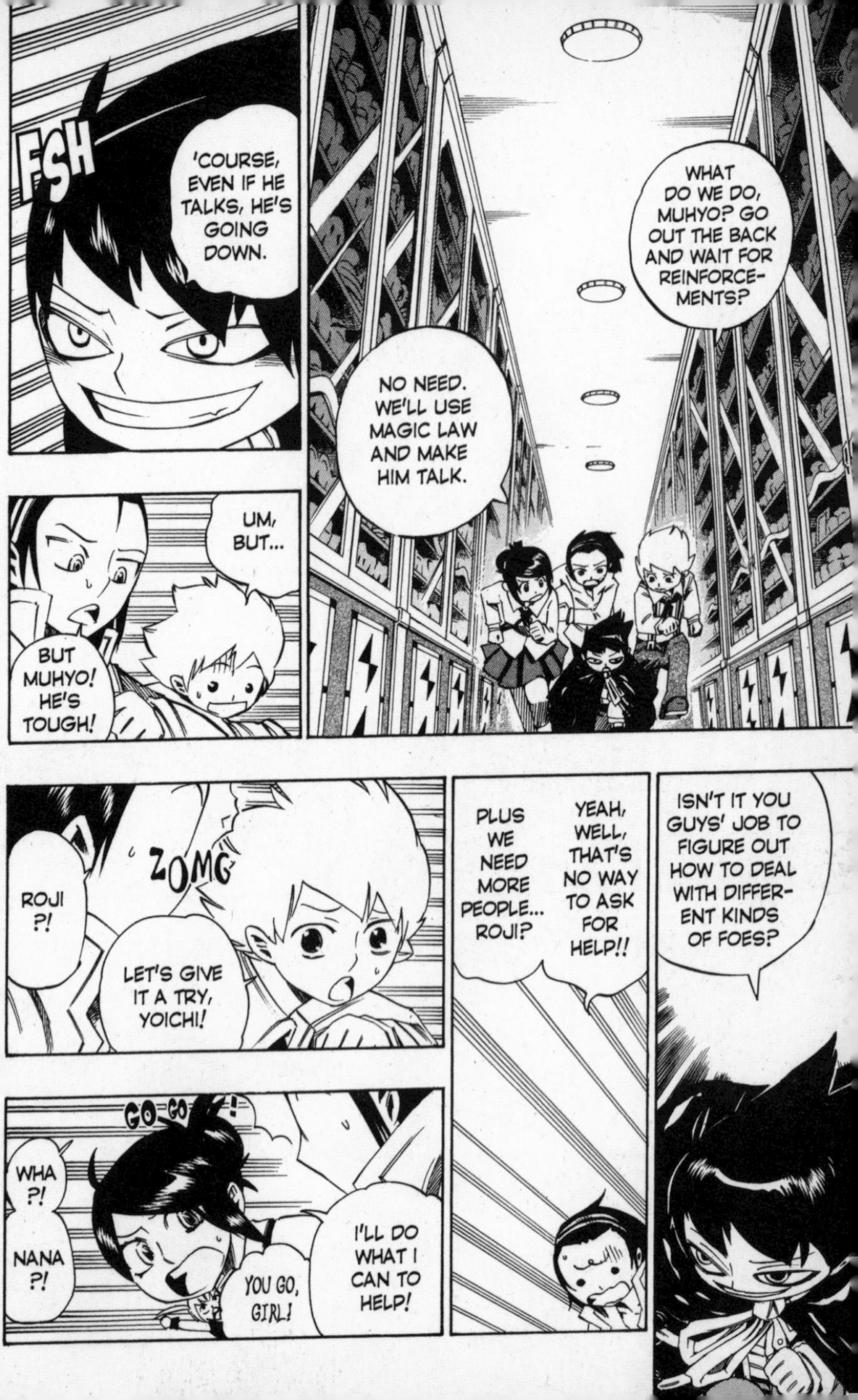
WHAT DO WE DO, MUHYO? GO OUT THE BACK AND WAIT FOR REINFORCE-MENTS?
NO NEED. WE'LL USE MAGIC LAW AND MAKE HIM TALK.
FSH
'COURSE, EVEN IF HE TALKS, HE'S GOING DOWN.
UM, BUT...
BUT MUHYO! HE'S TOUGH!
ISN'T IT YOU GUYS' JOB TO FIGURE OUT HOW TO DEAL WITH DIFFER-ENT KINDS OF FOES?
YEAH, WELL, THAT'S NO WAY TO ASK FOR HELP!!
PLUS WE NEED MORE PEOPLE... ROJI?
ZOMG
ROJI ?!
LET'S GIVE IT A TRY, YOICHI!
GO-GO
I'LL DO WHAT I CAN TO HELP!
YOU GO, GIRL!
WHA ?!
NANA ?!

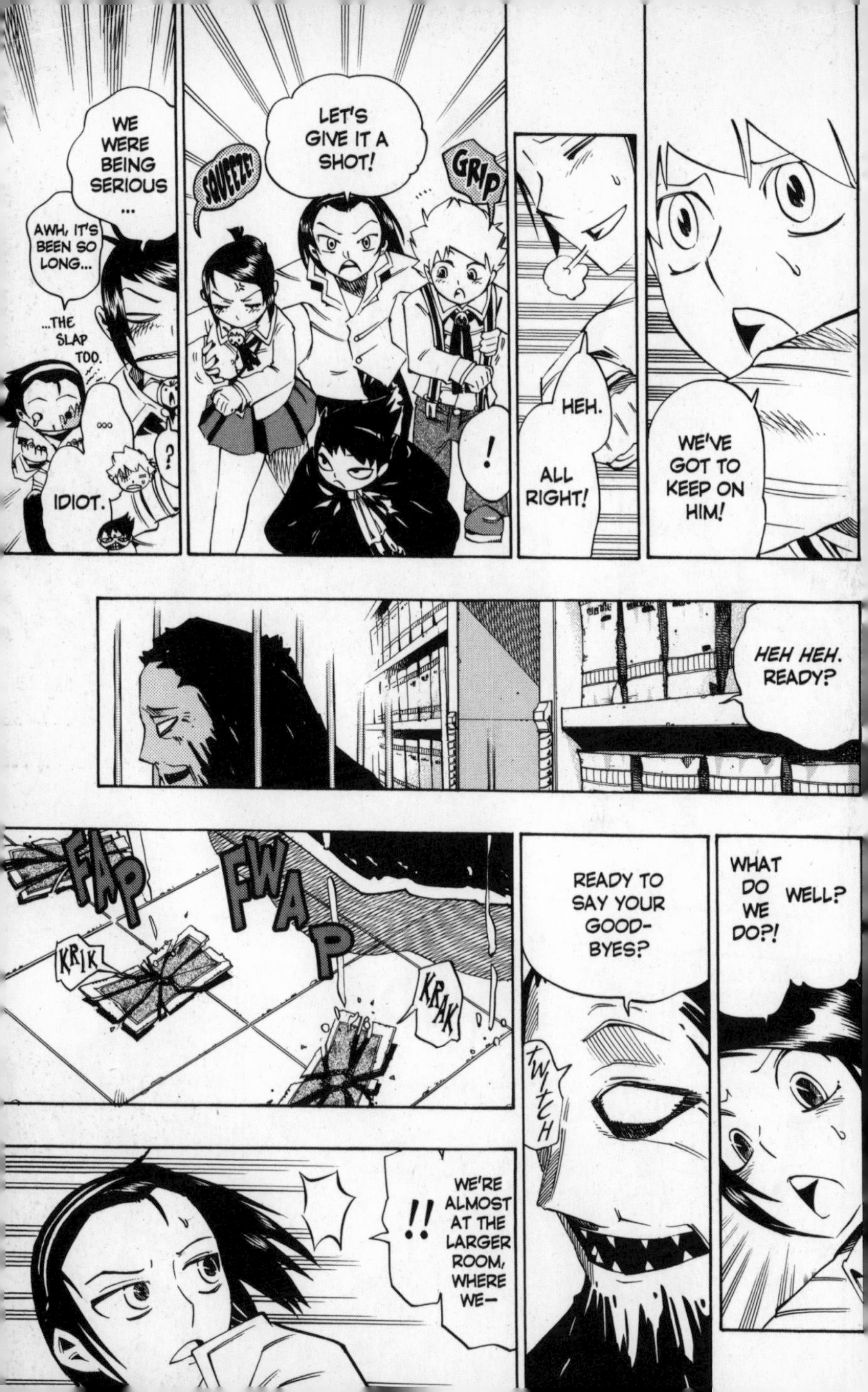
WE'VE GOT TO KEEP ON HIM!
HEH.
ALL RIGHT!
LET'S GIVE IT A SHOT!
GRIP
...
SQUEEZE!
!
WE WERE BEING SERIOUS ...
AWH, IT'S BEEN SO LONG...
...THE SLAP TOO.
...
?
IDIOT.
HEH HEH. READY?
WELL?
WHAT DO WE DO?!
READY TO SAY YOUR GOOD-BYES?
TWITCH
FWAP
FAP
KRIK
KRAK
WE'RE ALMOST AT THE LARGER ROOM, WHERE WE—
!!

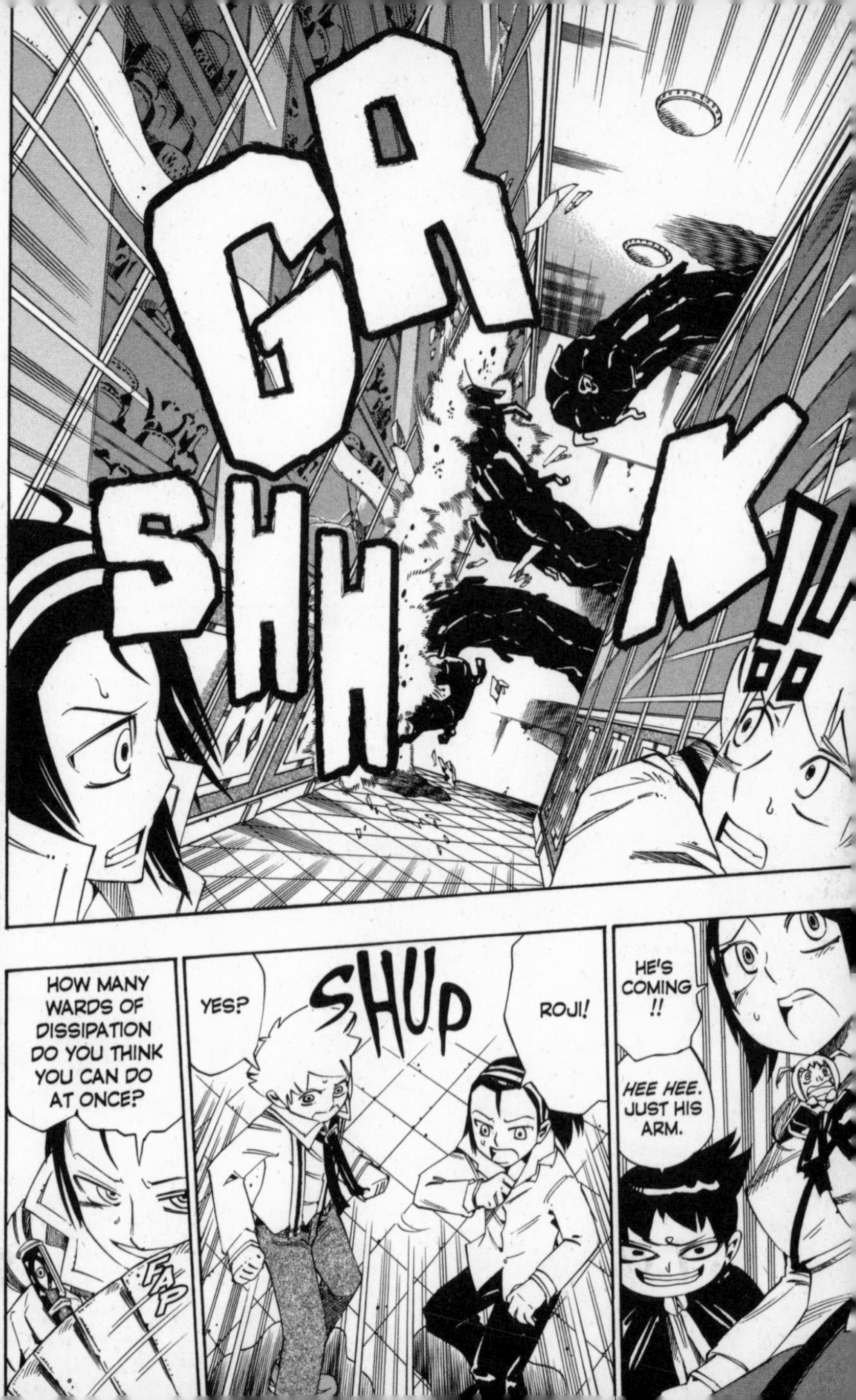
CRSHHK!!
HE'S COMING!!
HEE HEE. JUST HIS ARM.
ROJI!
SHUP
YES?
HOW MANY WARDS OF DISSIPATION DO YOU THINK YOU CAN DO AT ONCE?
FAP

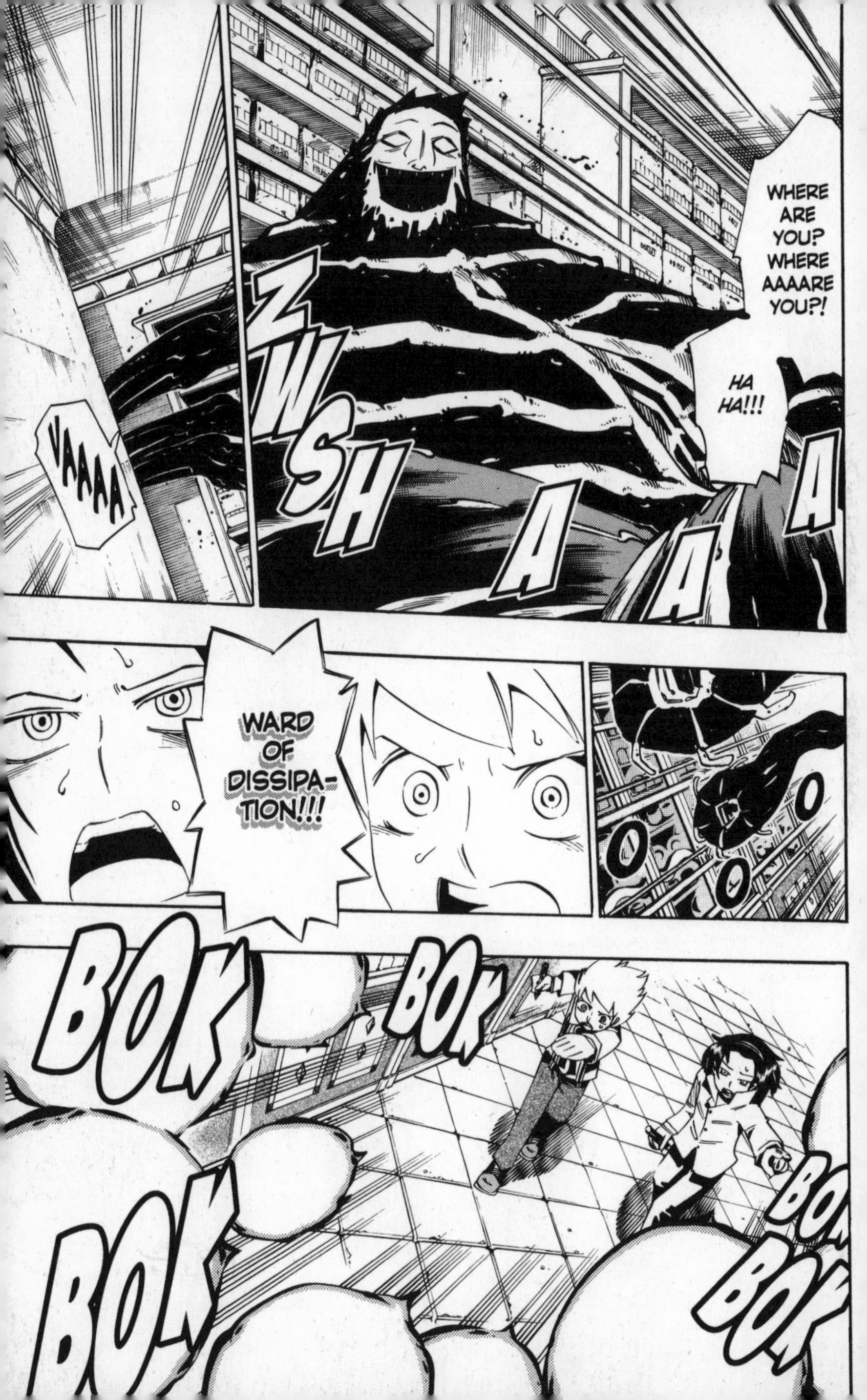
WHERE ARE YOU? WHERE AAAARE YOU?!
HA HA!!!
A A A A
ZWSH
VAAAA
WARD OF DISSIPA-TION!!!
BOK
BOK
BOK
BOK
BOK
BOK

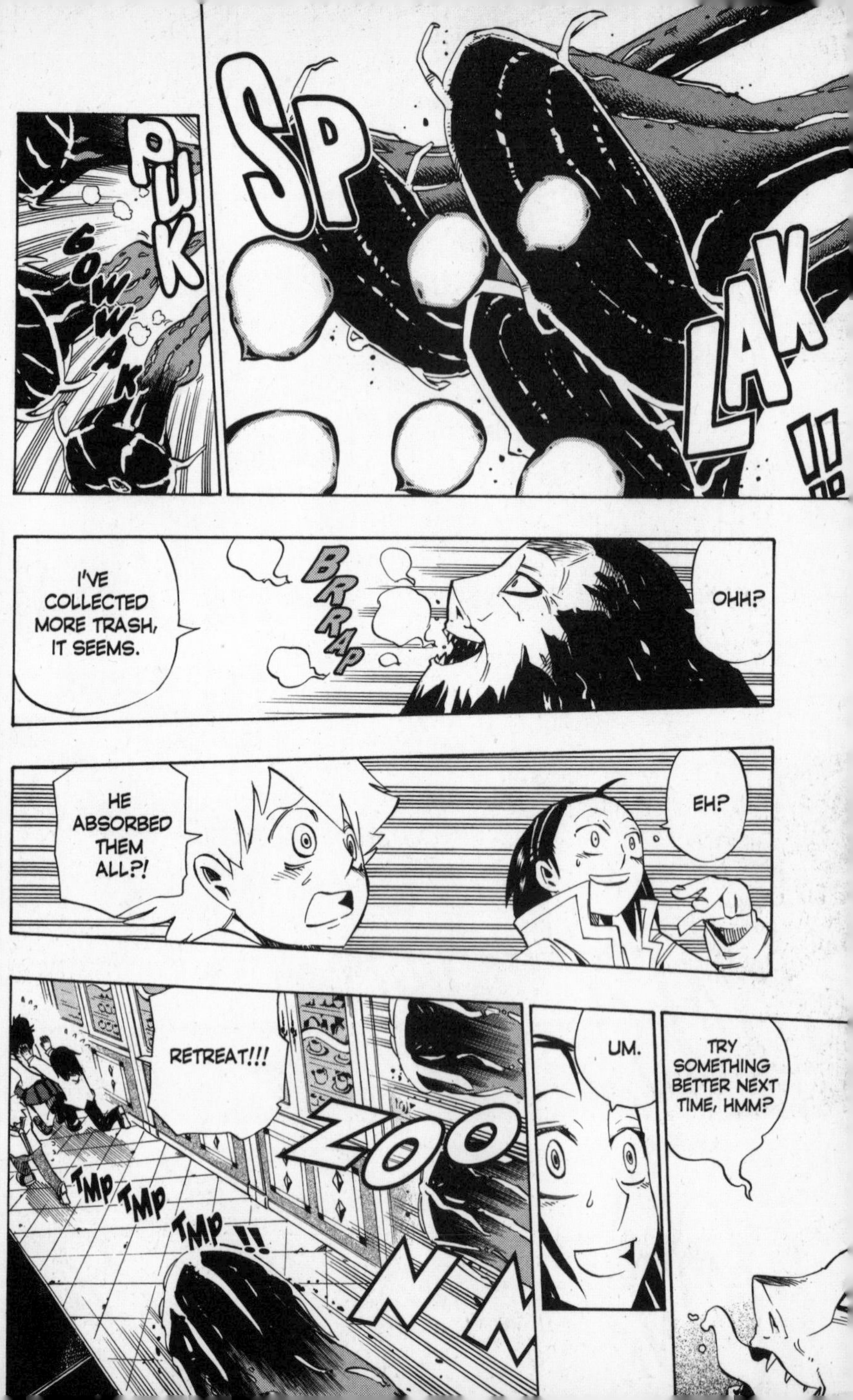
SPLAK!!
PUK
GOWWAK
OHH?
BRRAP
I'VE COLLECTED MORE TRASH, IT SEEMS.
EH?
HE ABSORBED THEM ALL?!
TRY SOMETHING BETTER NEXT TIME, HMM?
UM.
ZOO
NM
RETREAT!!!
TMP TMP TMP!!

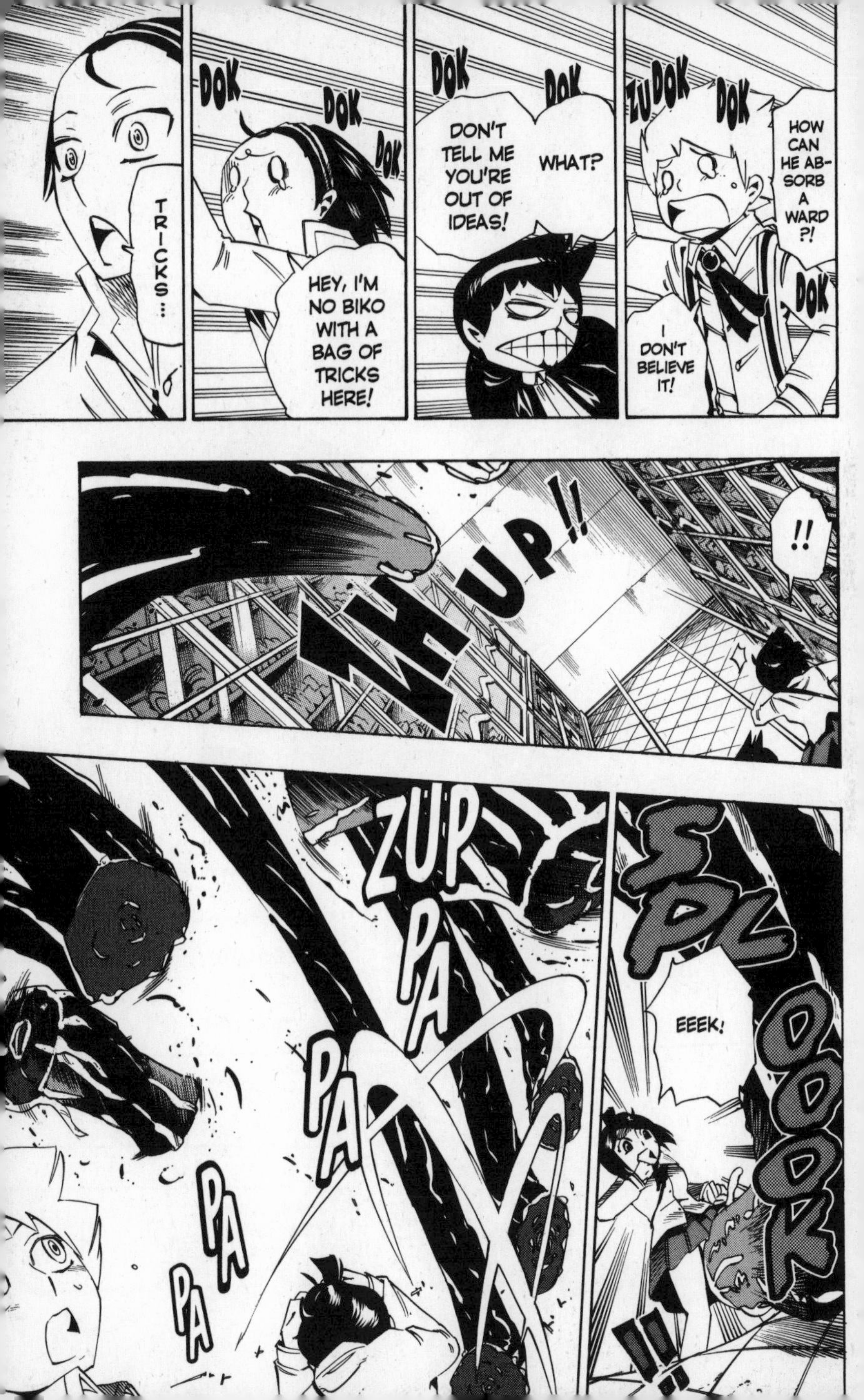
ZU
DOK
DOK
HOW CAN HE AB-SORB A WARD?!
DOK
I DON'T BELIEVE IT!
DOK
DOK
WHAT?
DON'T TELL ME YOU'RE OUT OF IDEAS!
DOK
DOK
DOK
HEY, I'M NO BIKO WITH A BAG OF TRICKS HERE!
TRICKS...
!!
THUP!!
SPLOOOOK
EEEK!
!!
ZUP
PA
PA
PA
PA

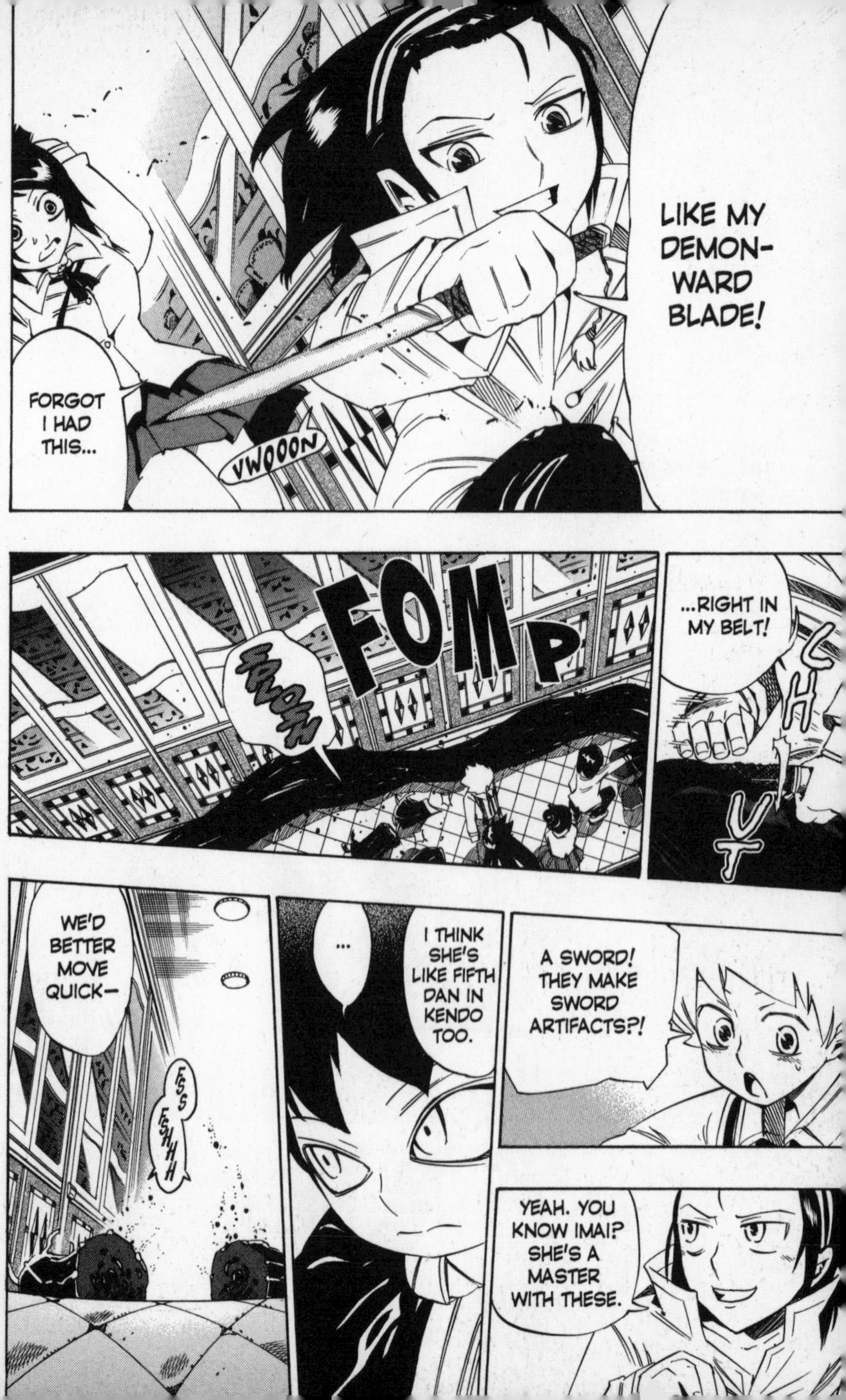
LIKE MY DEMON-WARD BLADE!
FORGOT I HAD THIS...
VWOOON
...RIGHT IN MY BELT!
CHYT
FOMP
VWOOM
A SWORD! THEY MAKE SWORD ARTIFACTS?!
YEAH. YOU KNOW IMAI? SHE'S A MASTER WITH THESE.
I THINK SHE'S LIKE FIFTH DAN IN KENDO TOO.
...
WE'D BETTER MOVE QUICK—
FSS FSHHH

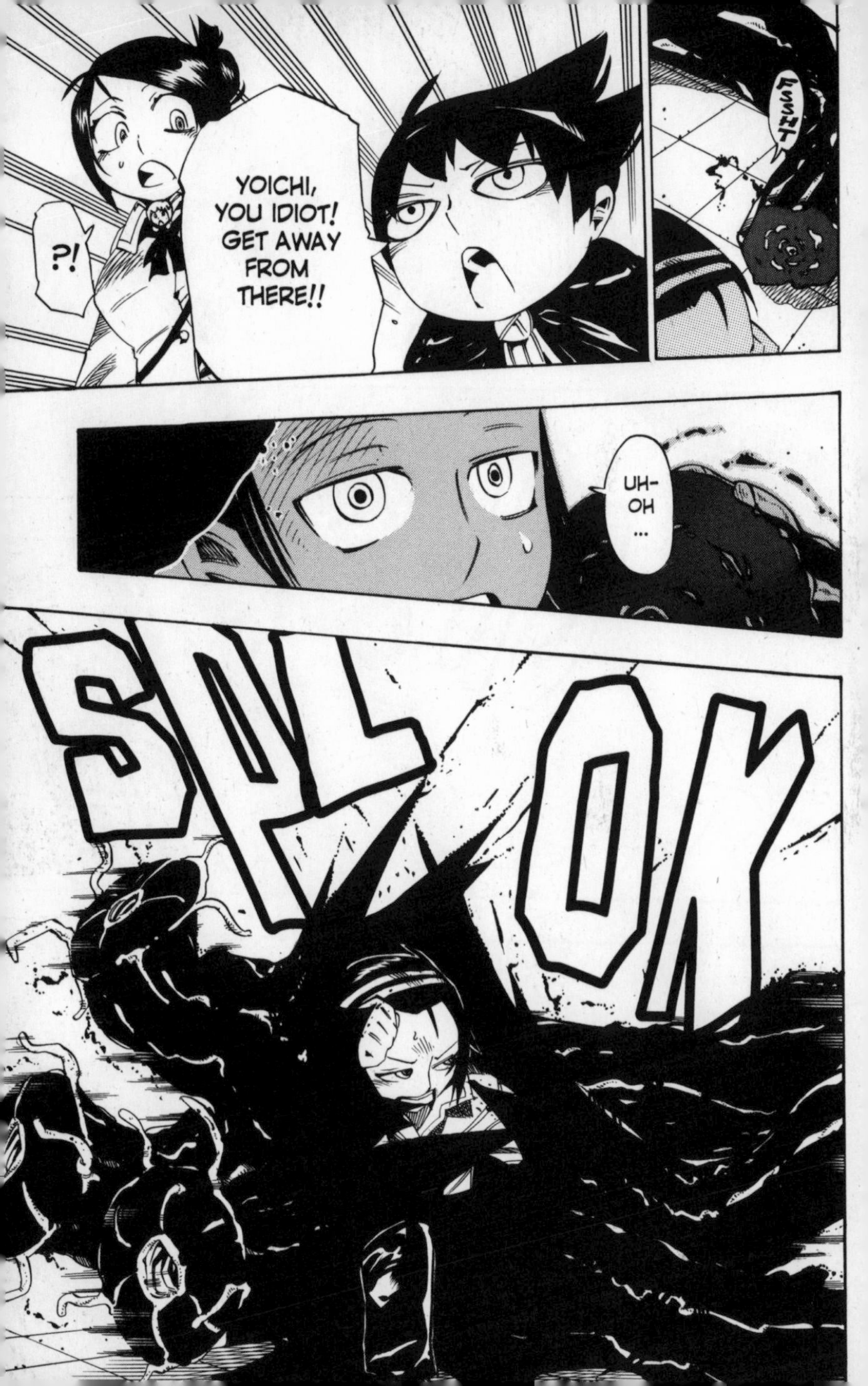
FSSHT
YOICHI, YOU IDIOT! GET AWAY FROM THERE!!
?!
UH-OH ...
SPL
OK

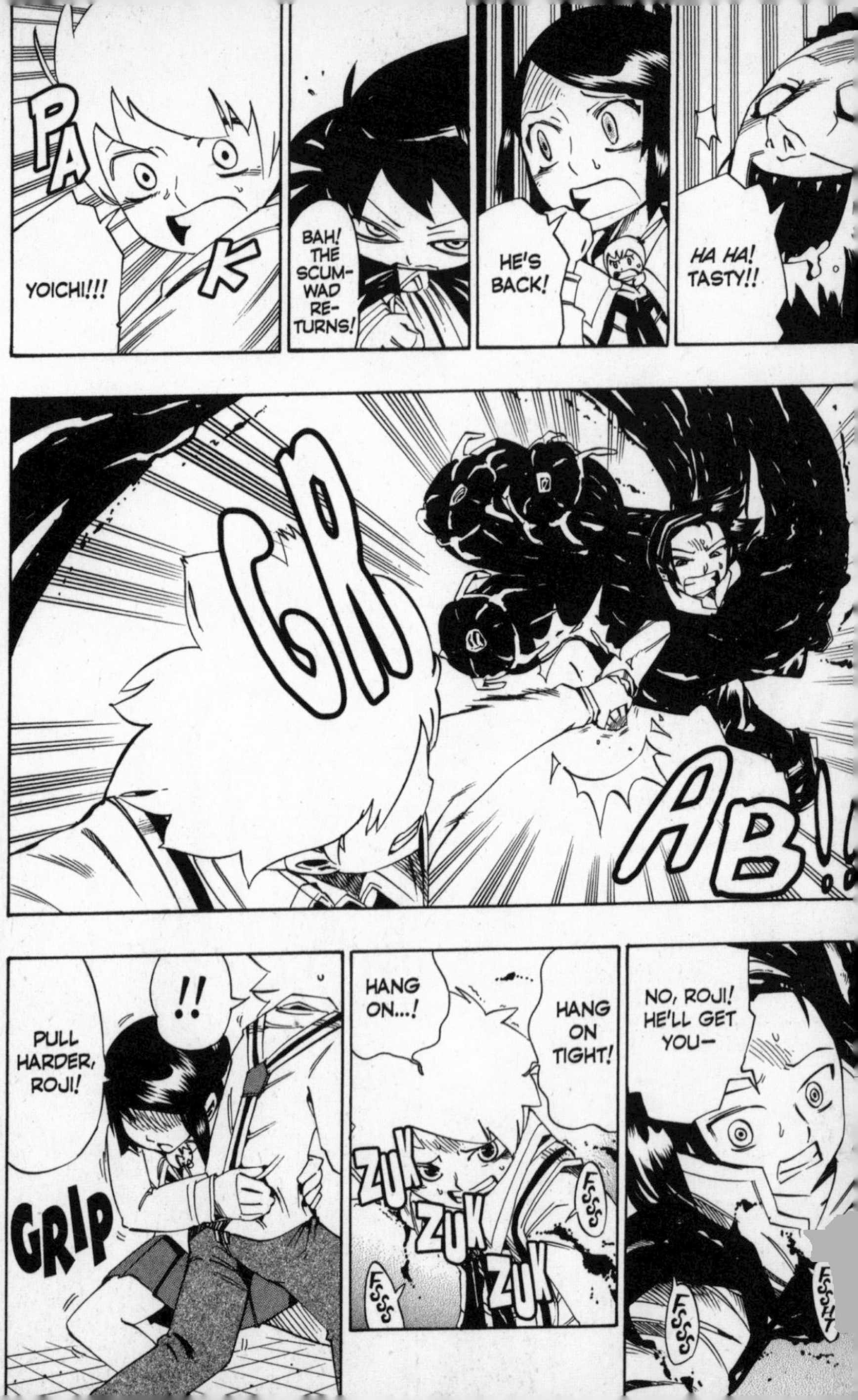
HA HA! TASTY!!
HE'S BACK!
BAH! THE SCUMWAD RETURNS!
YOICHI!!!
PAK
GRAB!!
NO, ROJI! HE'LL GET YOU—
FSSHT
FSSS
HANG ON TIGHT!
HANG ON...!
FSSS
ZUK ZUK ZUK
FSSS
!!
PULL HARDER, ROJI!
GRIP

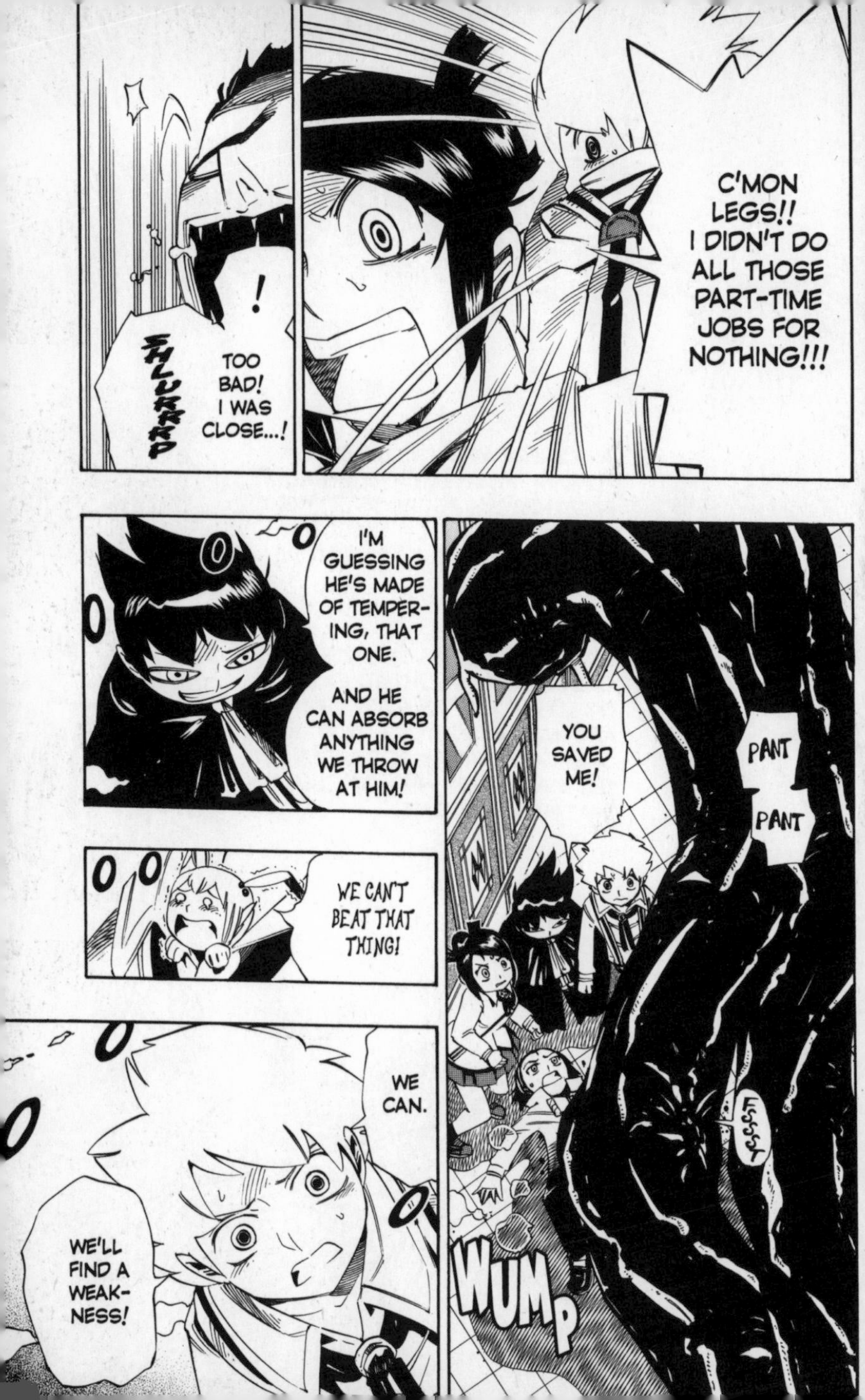
C'MON LEGS!! I DIDN'T DO ALL THOSE PART-TIME JOBS FOR NOTHING!!!
!
SHLURRRP
TOO BAD! I WAS CLOSE...!
YOU SAVED ME!
PANT
PANT
FSSSH
WUMP
I'M GUESSING HE'S MADE OF TEMPER-ING, THAT ONE.
AND HE CAN ABSORB ANYTHING WE THROW AT HIM!
WE CAN'T BEAT THAT THING!
WE CAN.
WE'LL FIND A WEAK-NESS!

Q: ARE THERE A FEW KINDS OF "UNDERSPEAK" (MUHYO'S "ARO..." AND GORYO'S "SORIADE...")? IS IT DIFFERENT FOR EACH EXECUTOR?
—T., YAMANASHI PREFECTURE

A: SEVERAL DIALECTS OF UNDERSPEAK ARE THOUGHT TO EXIST, OR MAYBE THEY'RE MORE LIKE ACCENTS. EXECUTORS PROBABLY CHANGE THEIR DIALECT BASED ON THE ENVOY THEY WISH TO SUMMON. THAT'S WHAT I HEAR.

ARTICLE 66
ABSORPTION

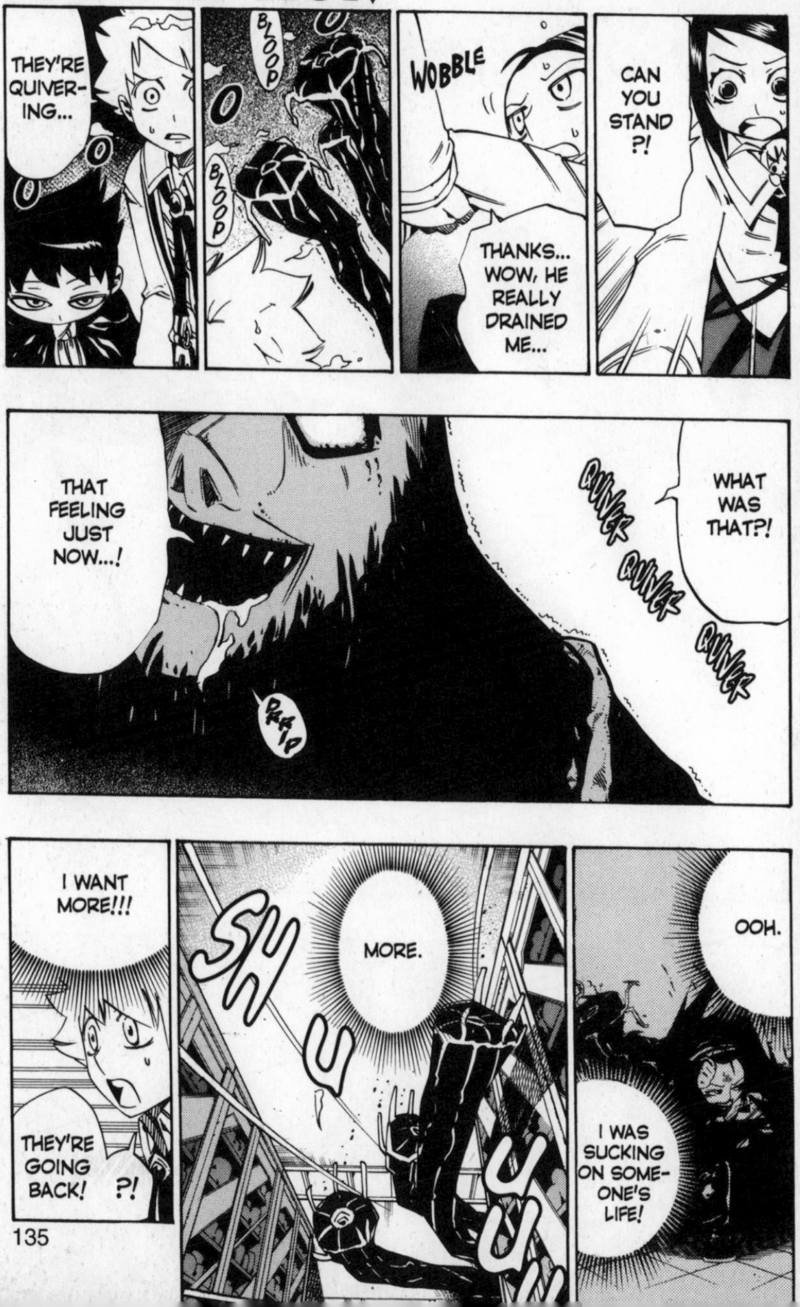
CAN YOU STAND?!
WOBBLE
THANKS... WOW, HE REALLY DRAINED ME...
BLOOP
BLOOP
THEY'RE QUIVERING...
WHAT WAS THAT?!
QUIVER
QUIVER
QUIVER
THAT FEELING JUST NOW...!
DRIP
OOH.
I WAS SUCKING ON SOME-ONE'S LIFE!
MORE.
SHUUU
I WANT MORE!!!
THEY'RE GOING BACK!
?!

ARTICLE 66
ABSORPTION

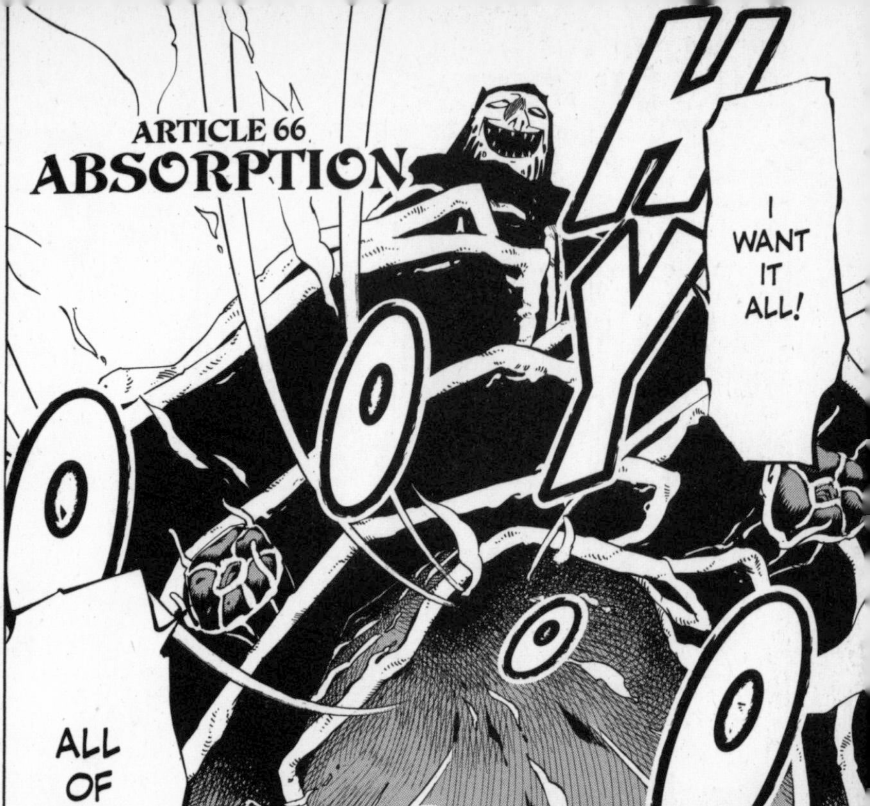

I WANT IT ALL!
ALL OF IT!!!

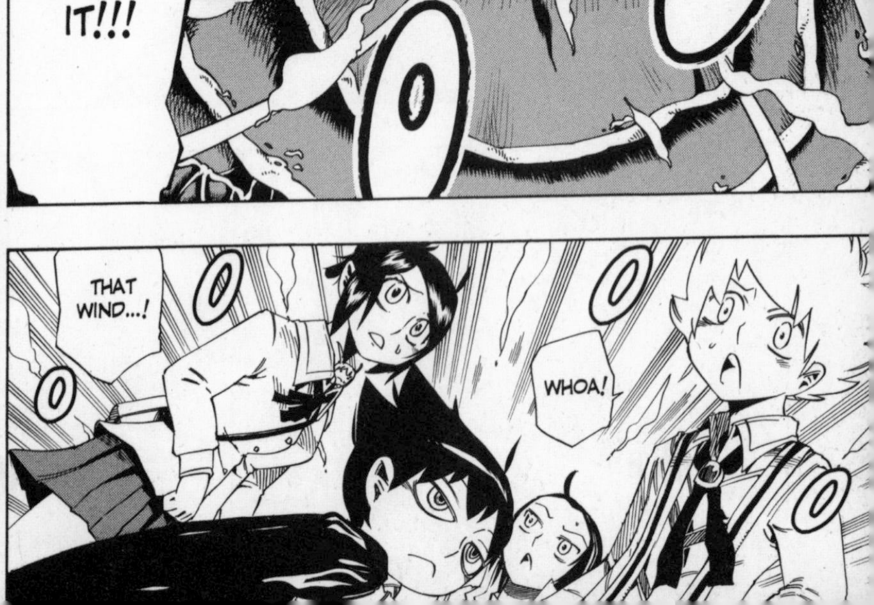

WHOA!
THAT WIND...!

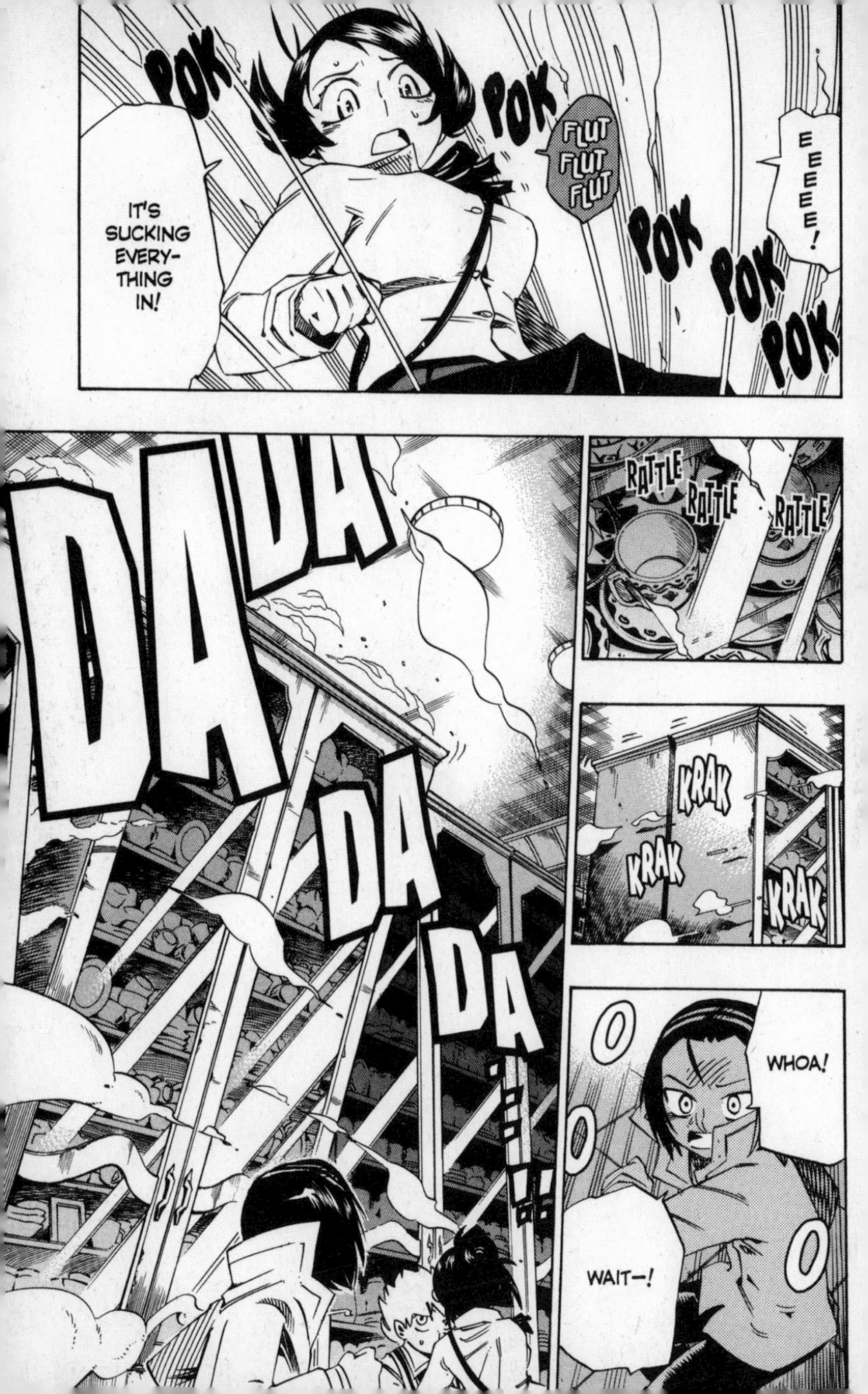
EEEEE!
POK POK POK
FLUT FLUT FLUT
POK POK
IT'S SUCKING EVERY-THING IN!
RATTLE RATTLE RATTLE
KRAK KRAK KRAK
WHOA!
WAIT—!
DA DA DA DA DA DA...!!

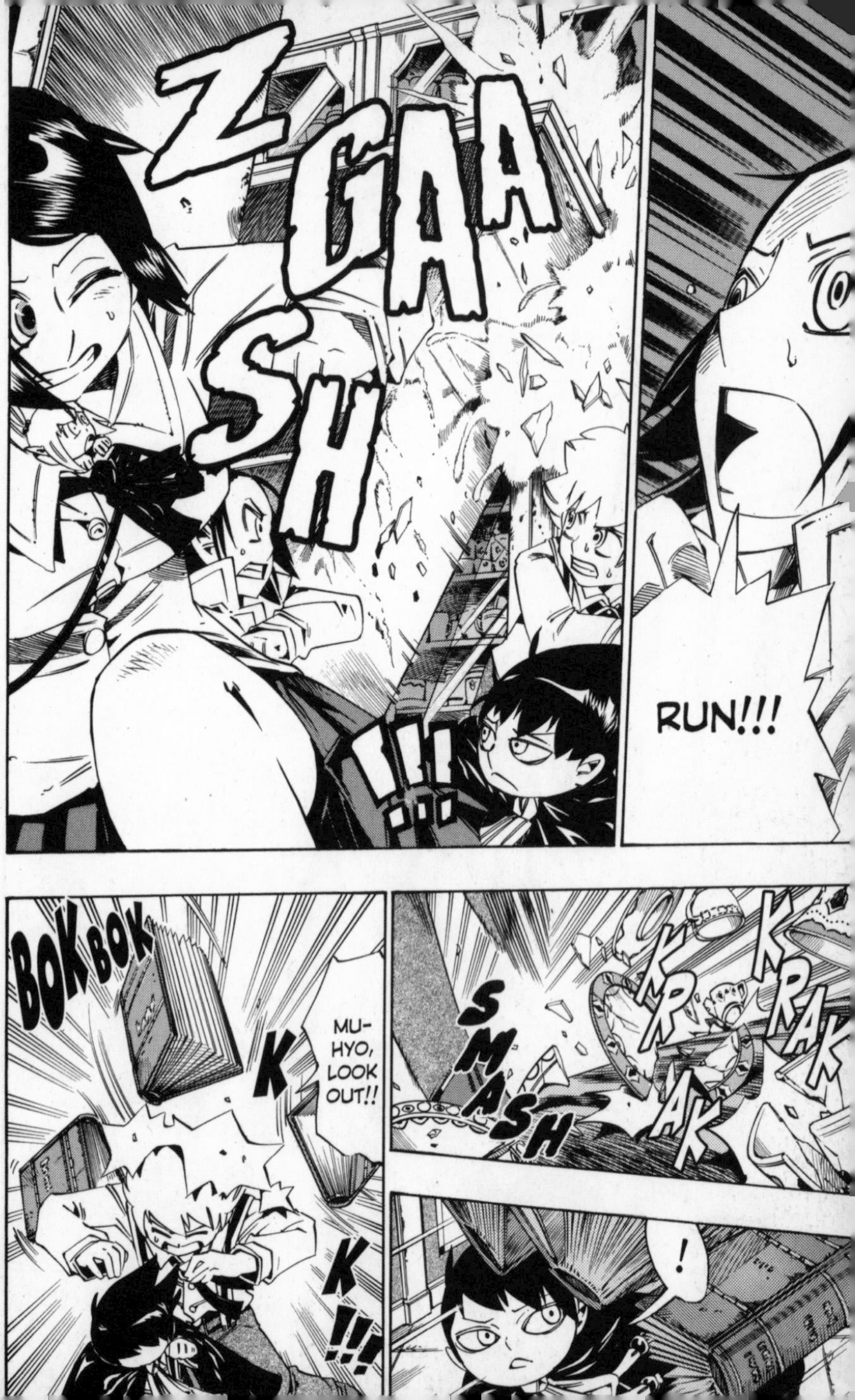
RUN!!!
ZGAASH
!!!
KRAK KRAK
SMASH
!
BOK BOK
MU-HYO, LOOK OUT!!
KK!!!

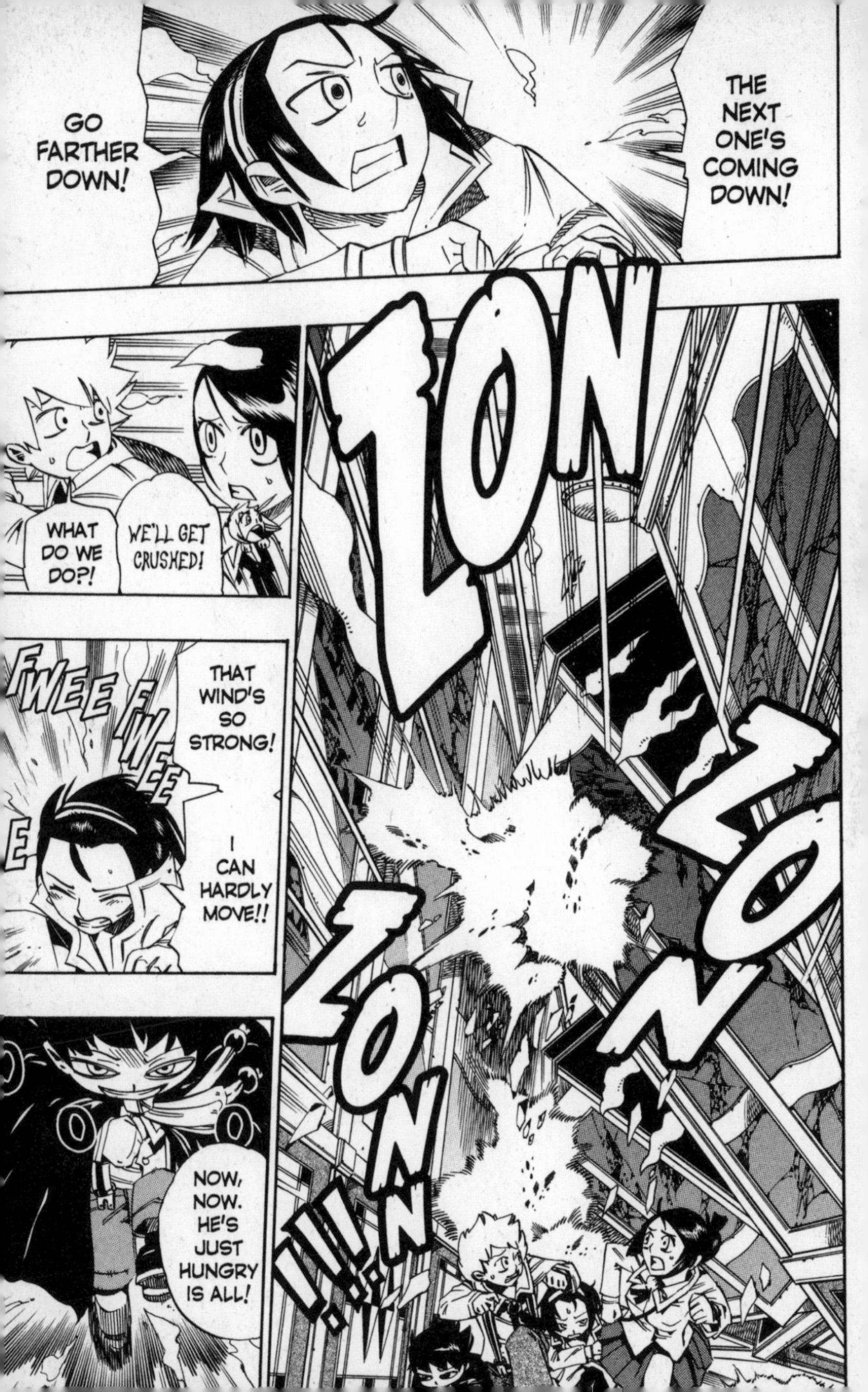
THE NEXT ONE'S COMING DOWN!
GO FARTHER DOWN!
ZON
ZON
ZONNN...!!!
WE'LL GET CRUSHED!
WHAT DO WE DO?!
FWEE
FWEEE
E
THAT WIND'S SO STRONG!
I CAN HARDLY MOVE!!
NOW, NOW. HE'S JUST HUNGRY IS ALL!

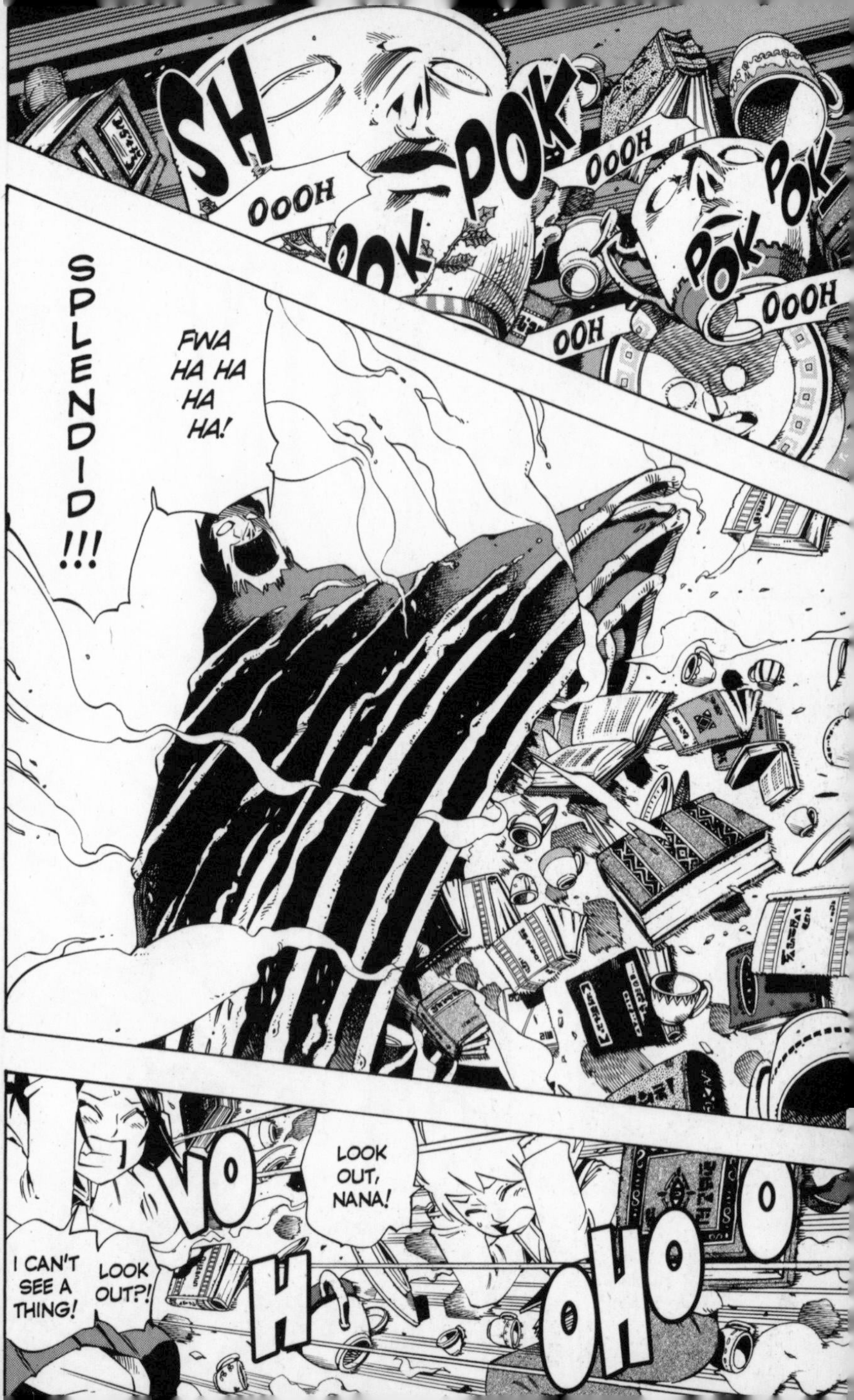

POK POK
OOOH
OOOH
POK
POK
OOOH
SH
OOOH
OOH
FWA HA HA HA HA!
SPLENDID!!!
VO
O
OHO
H
LOOK OUT, NANA!
LOOK OUT?!
I CAN'T SEE A THING!

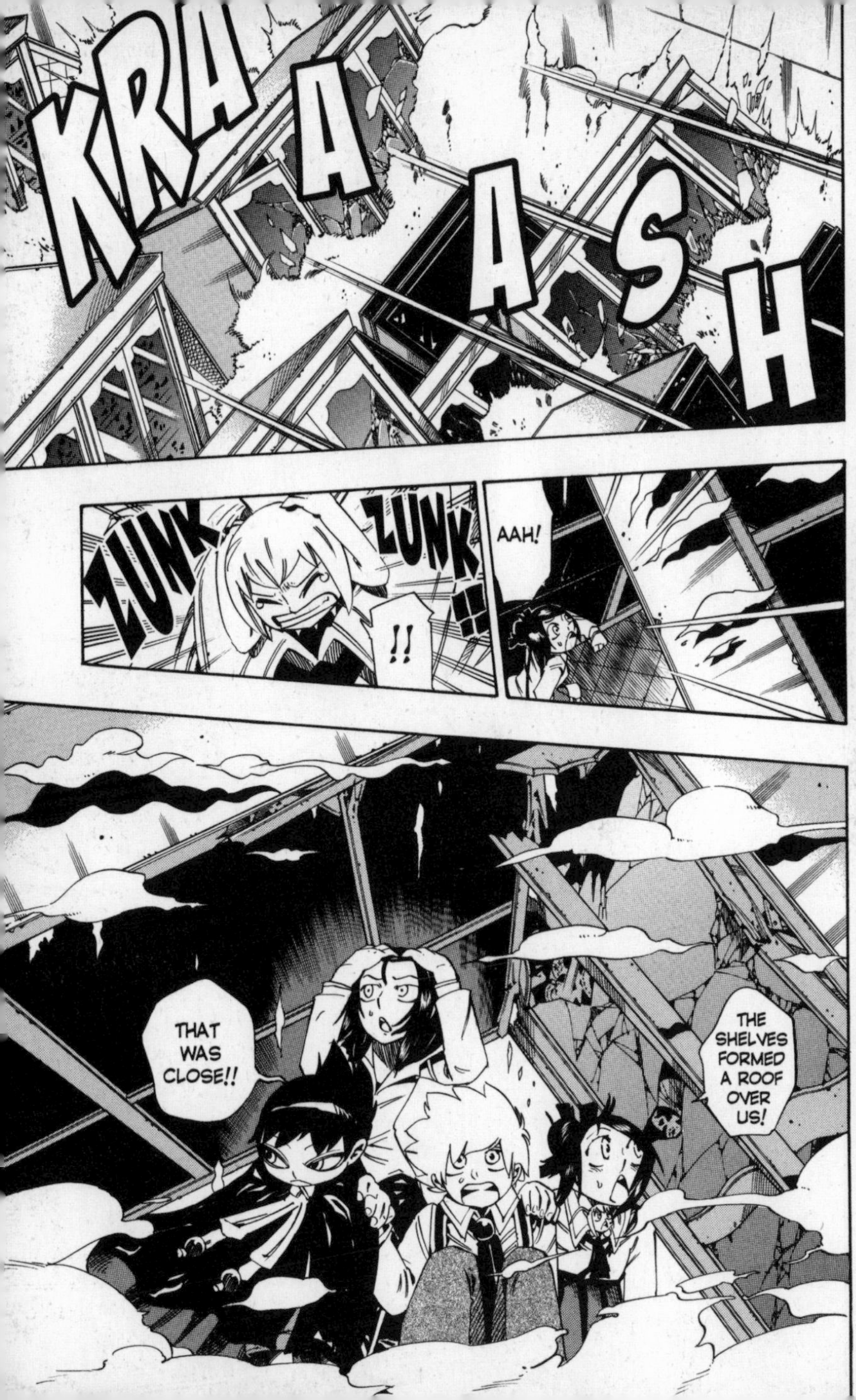
KRAAASH
AAH!
ZUNK
ZUNK
!!
THE SHELVES FORMED A ROOF OVER US!
THAT WAS CLOSE!!

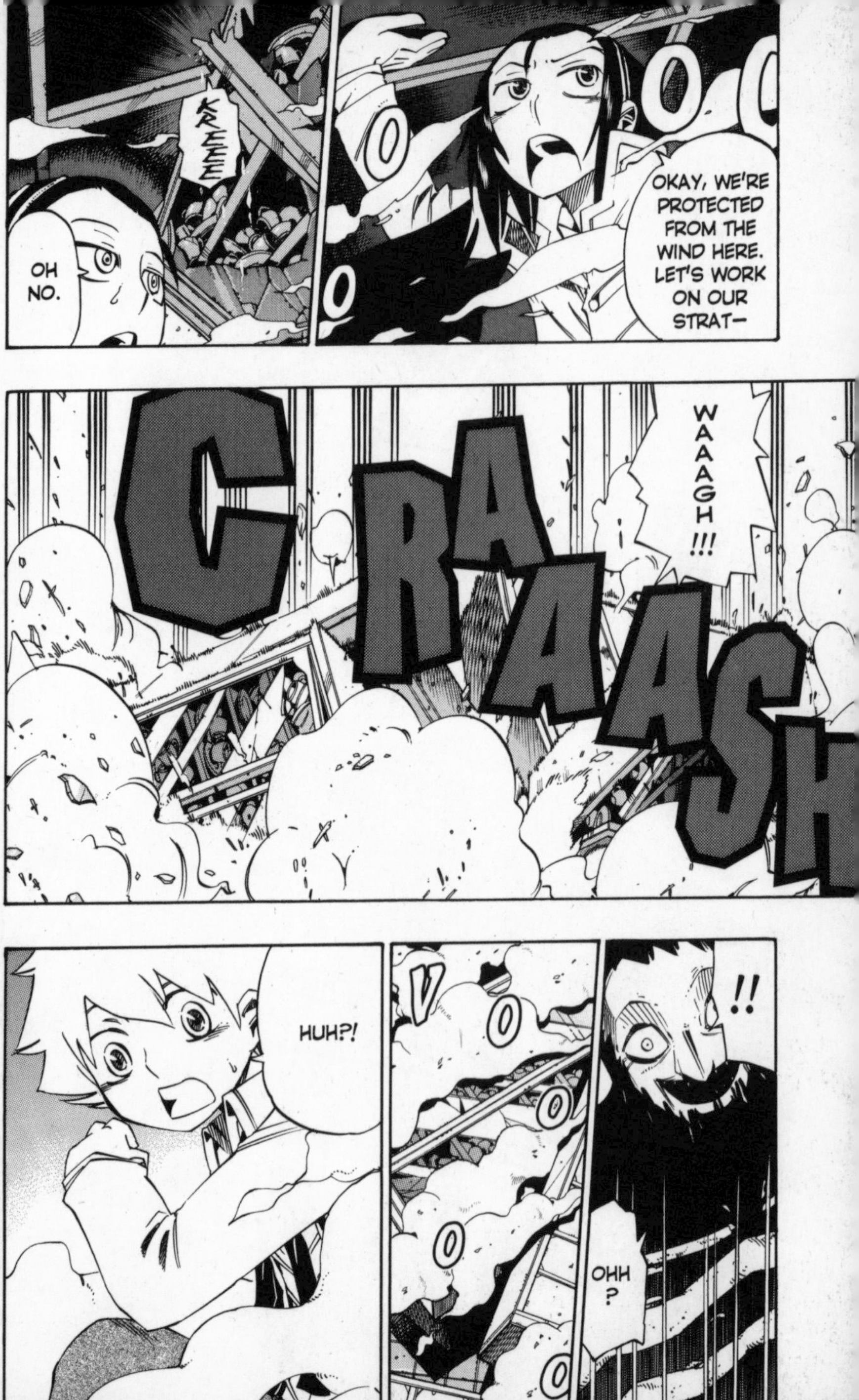
OKAY, WE'RE PROTECTED FROM THE WIND HERE. LET'S WORK ON OUR STRAT—
KREEEE
OH NO.
WAAAGH!!!
CRAAASH
!!
OHH ?
HUH?!

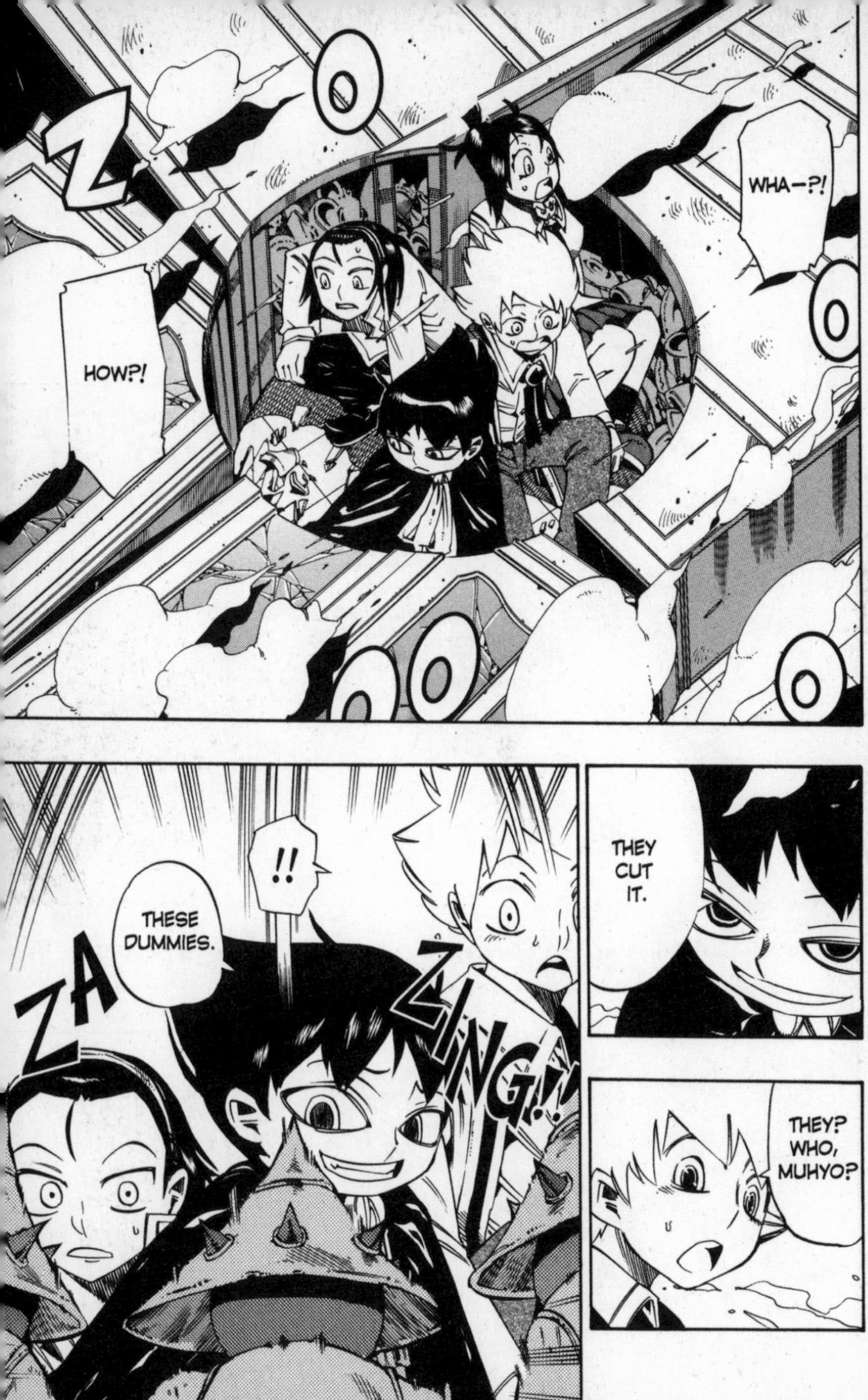
WHA—?!
HOW?!
THEY CUT IT.
THEY? WHO, MUHYO?
!!
THESE DUMMIES.
ZA
ZING!!

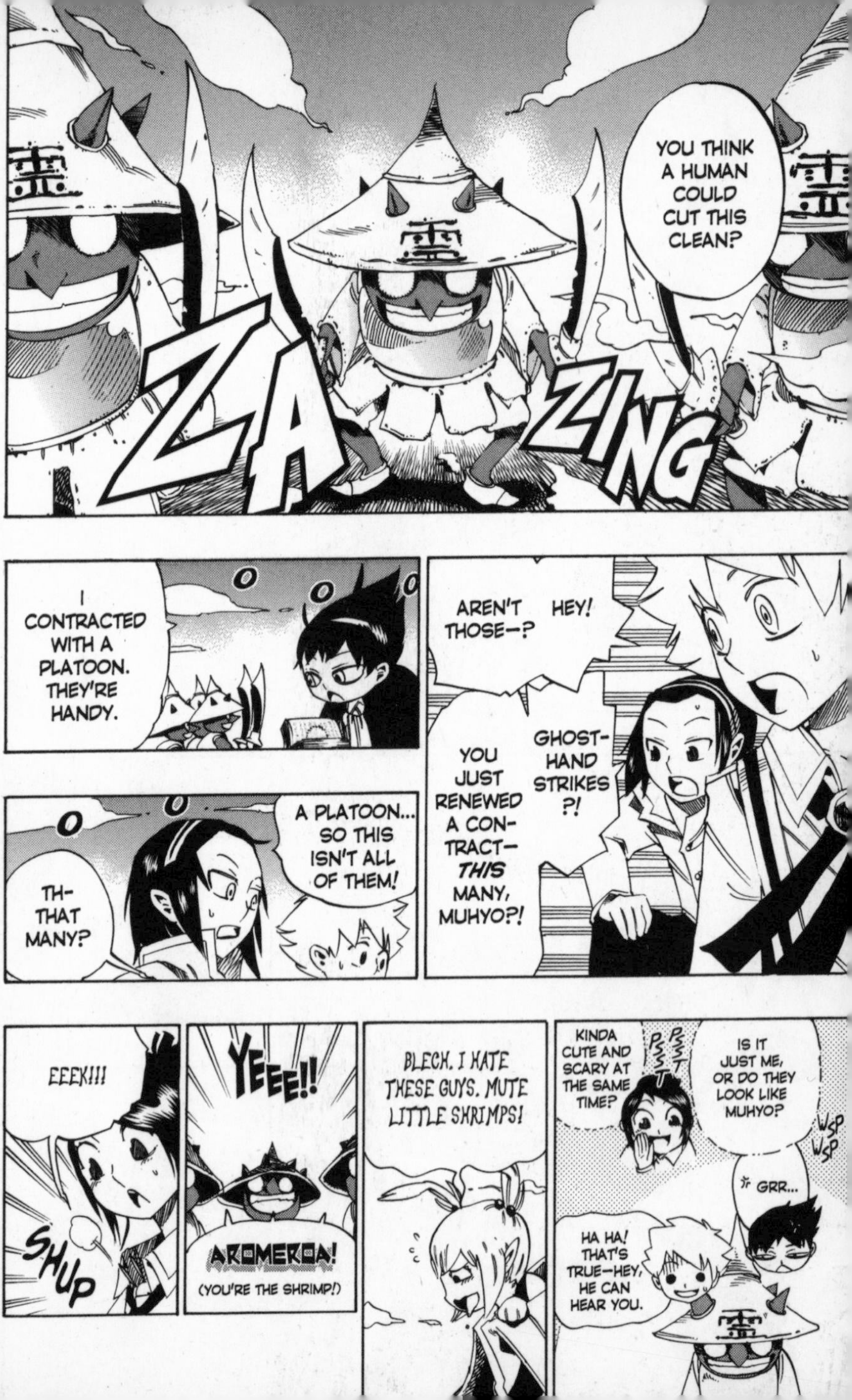
YOU THINK A HUMAN COULD CUT THIS CLEAN?
ZA
ZING
HEY!
AREN'T THOSE—?
GHOST-HAND STRIKES?!
YOU JUST RENEWED A CONTRACT—*THIS* MANY, MUHYO?!
I CONTRACTED WITH A PLATOON. THEY'RE HANDY.
A PLATOON... SO THIS ISN'T ALL OF THEM!
TH-THAT MANY?
IS IT JUST ME, OR DO THEY LOOK LIKE MUHYO?
WSP WSP
PSST
KINDA CUTE AND SCARY AT THE SAME TIME?
GRR...
HA HA! THAT'S TRUE—HEY, HE CAN HEAR YOU.
BLECH. I HATE THESE GUYS. MUTE LITTLE SHRIMPS!
YEEE!!
AROMEROA!
(YOU'RE THE SHRIMP!)
EEEK!!!
SHUP

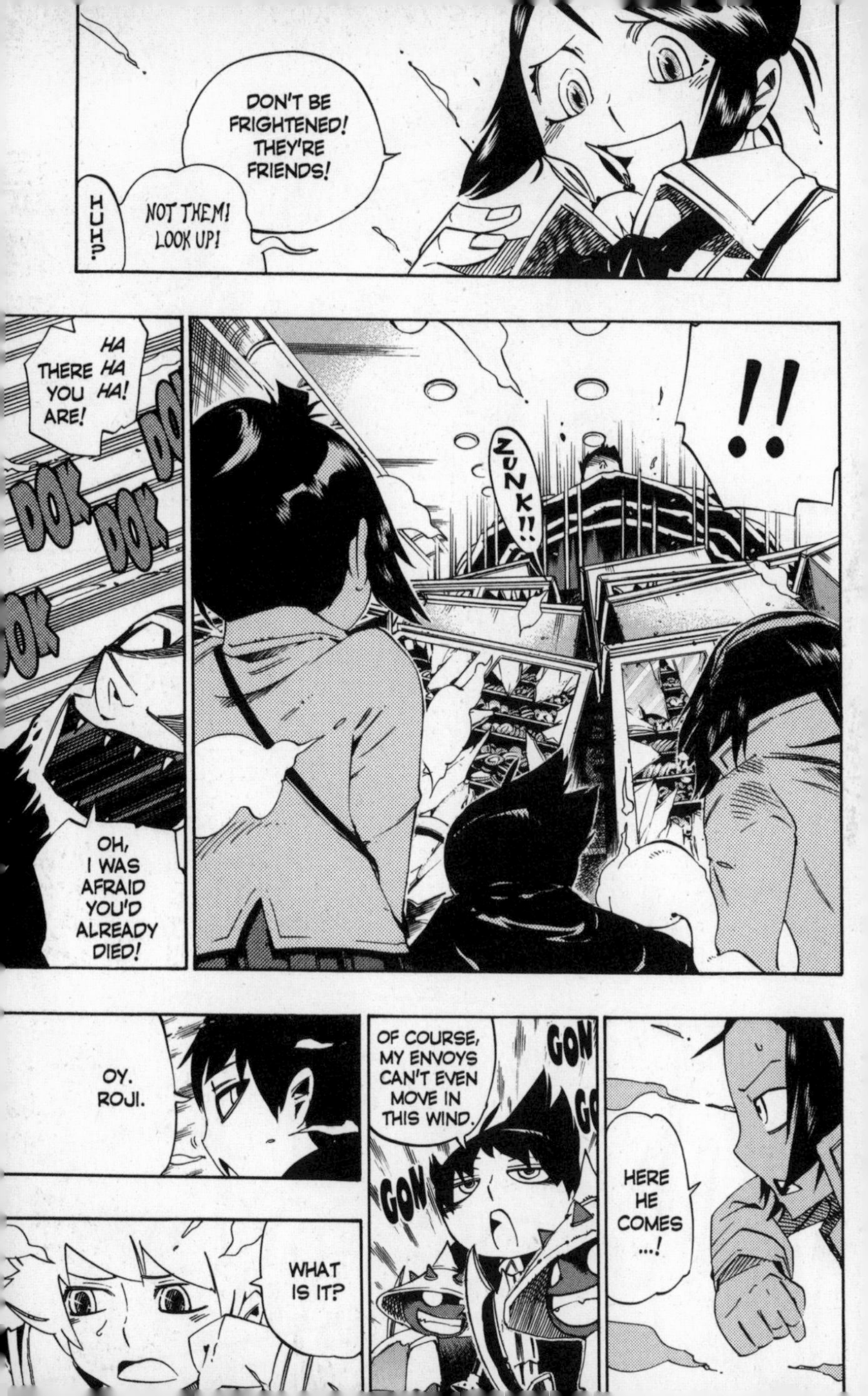
DON'T BE FRIGHTENED! THEY'RE FRIENDS!
HUH?
NOT THEM! LOOK UP!
!!
ZUNK!!
HA HA HA! THERE YOU ARE!
DOK DOK DOK DOK
OH, I WAS AFRAID YOU'D ALREADY DIED!
HERE HE COMES...!
GON GO
OF COURSE, MY ENVOYS CAN'T EVEN MOVE IN THIS WIND.
GON
OY. ROJI.
WHAT IS IT?

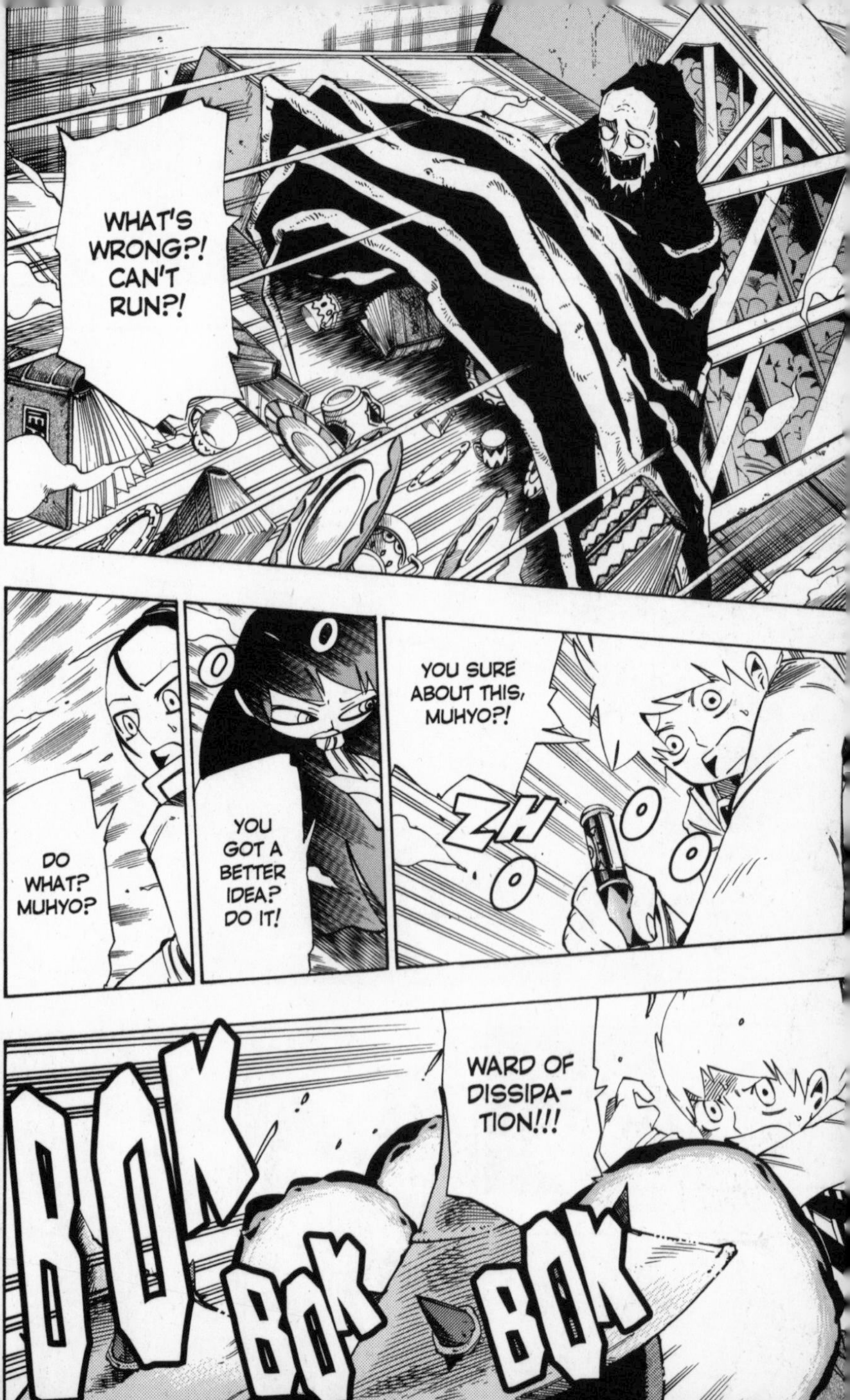
WHAT'S WRONG?! CAN'T RUN?!
YOU SURE ABOUT THIS, MUHYO?!
ZH
YOU GOT A BETTER IDEA? DO IT!
DO WHAT? MUHYO?
WARD OF DISSIPA-TION!!!
BOK
BOK
BOK

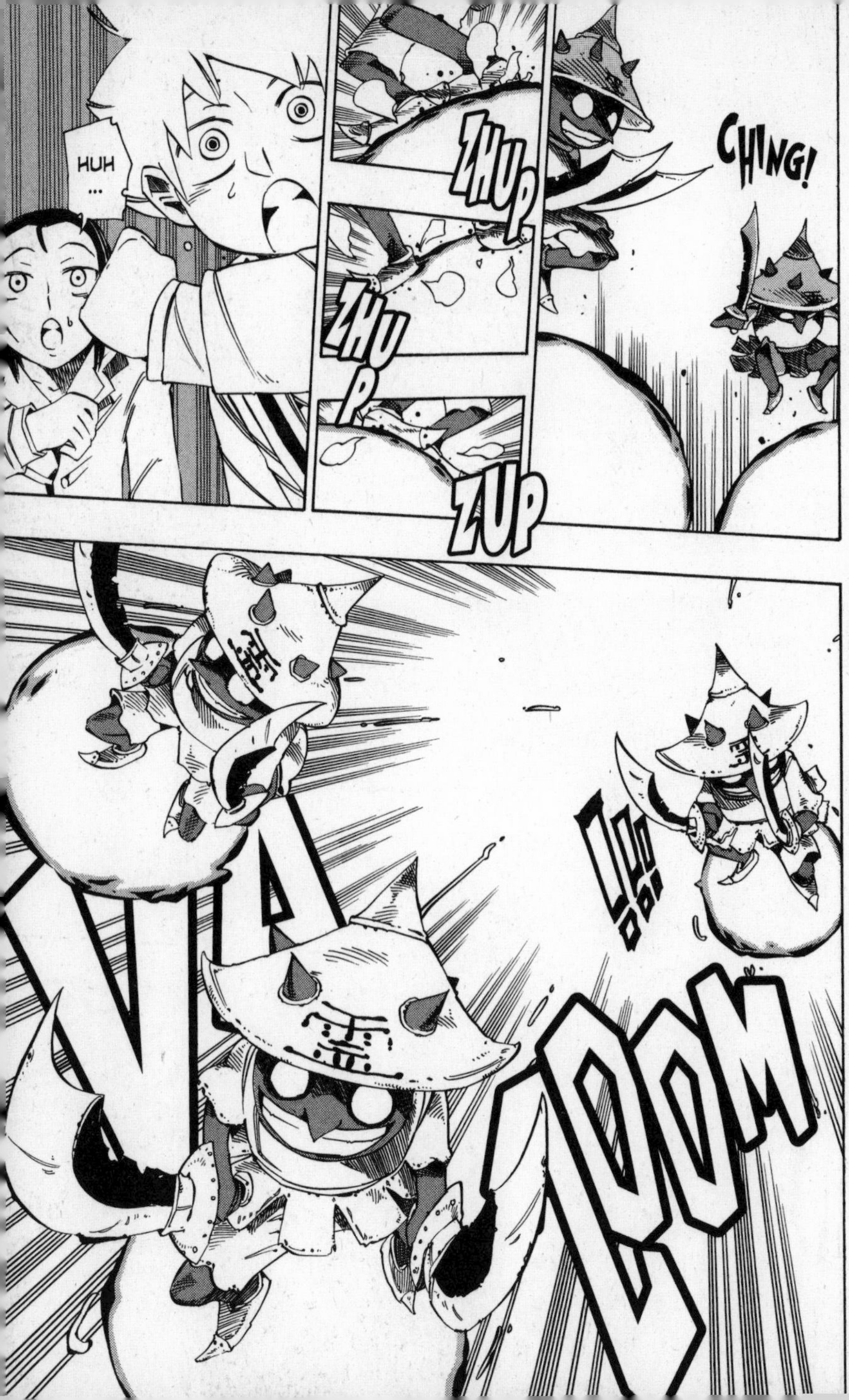

CHING!
ZHUP
ZHUP
ZUP
HUH ...
ZOOM

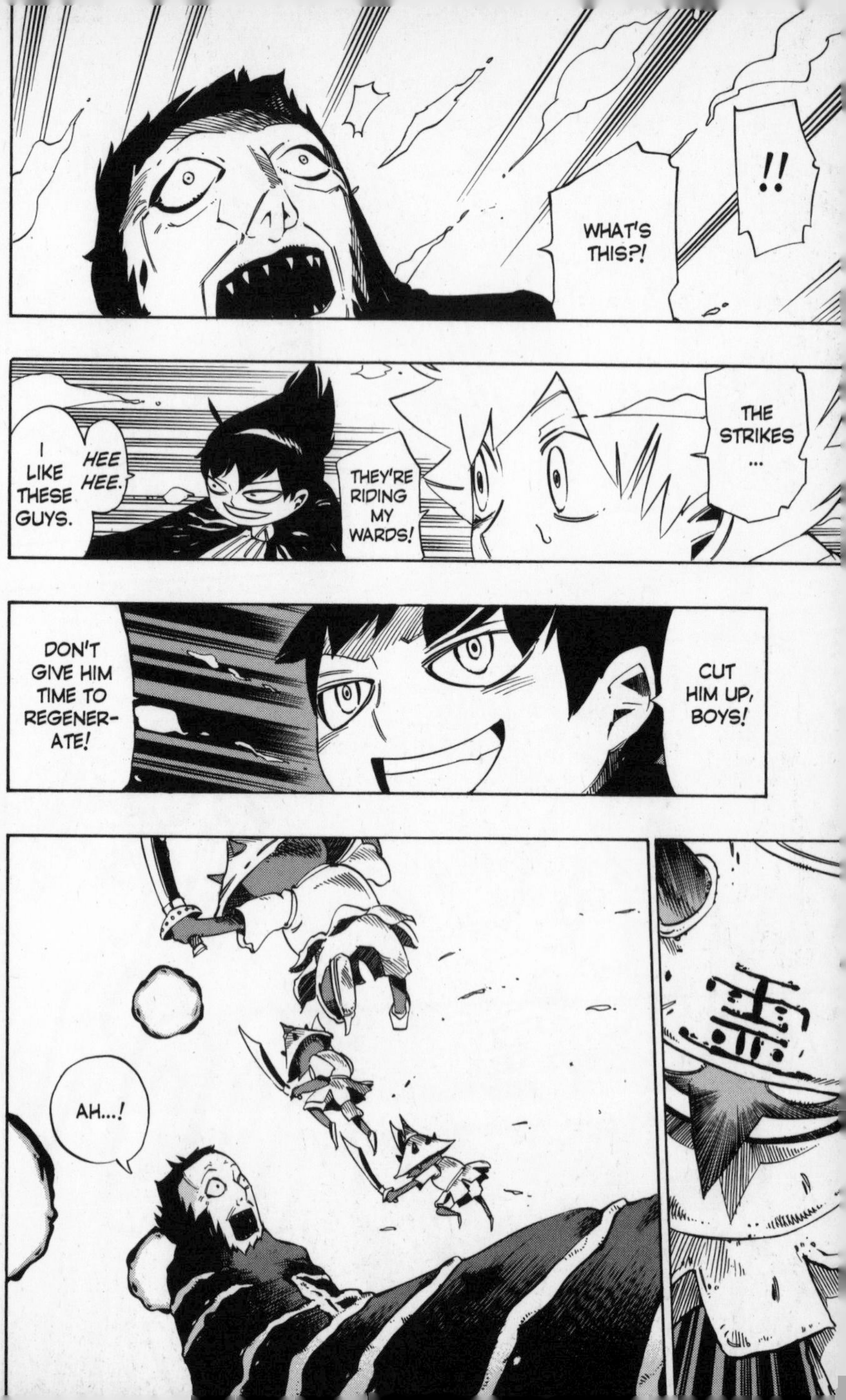
!!
WHAT'S THIS?!
THE STRIKES ...
THEY'RE RIDING MY WARDS!
HEE HEE.
I LIKE THESE GUYS.
CUT HIM UP, BOYS!
DON'T GIVE HIM TIME TO REGENER-ATE!
AH...!

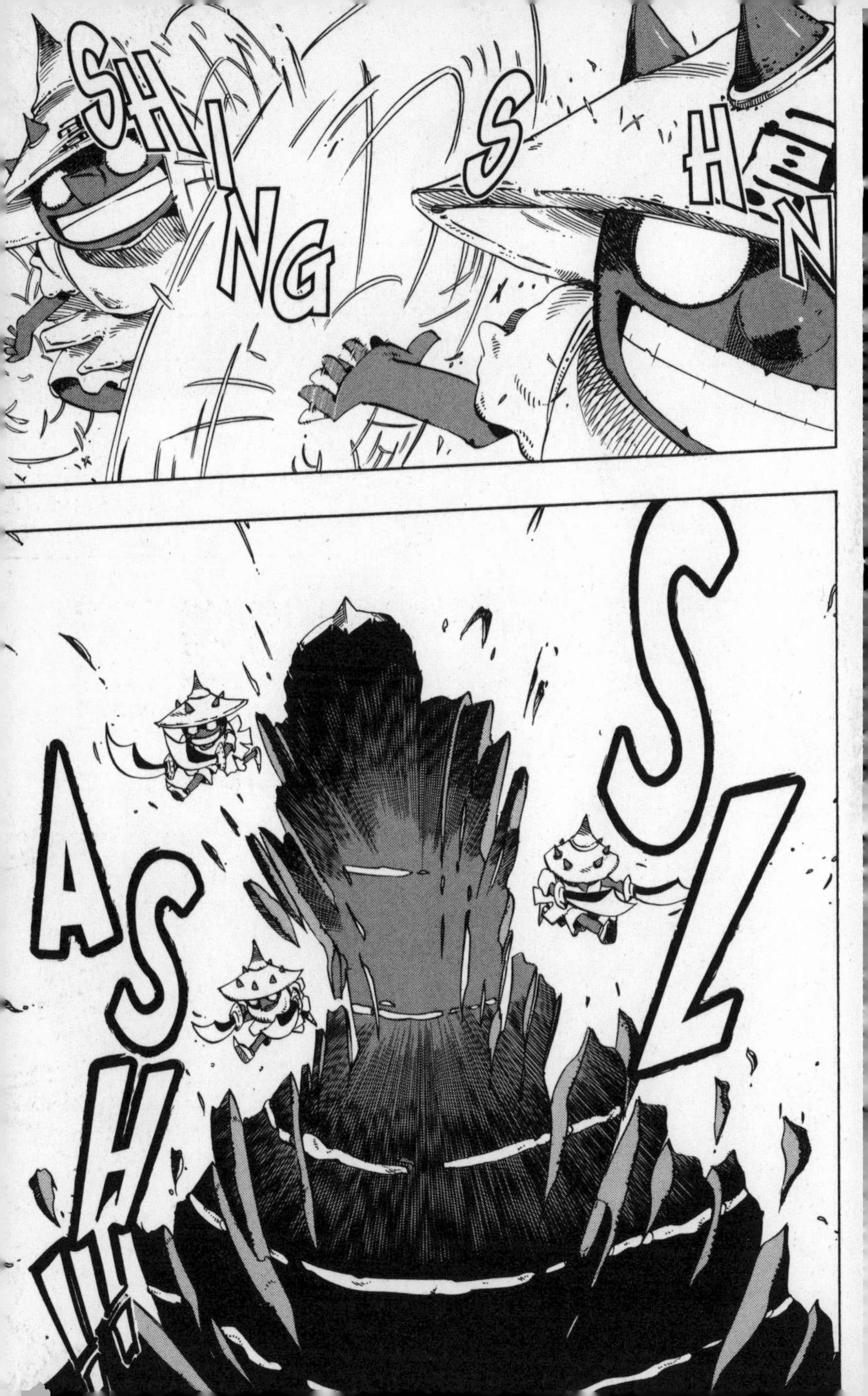
SHEN
SHING
SLASH!!

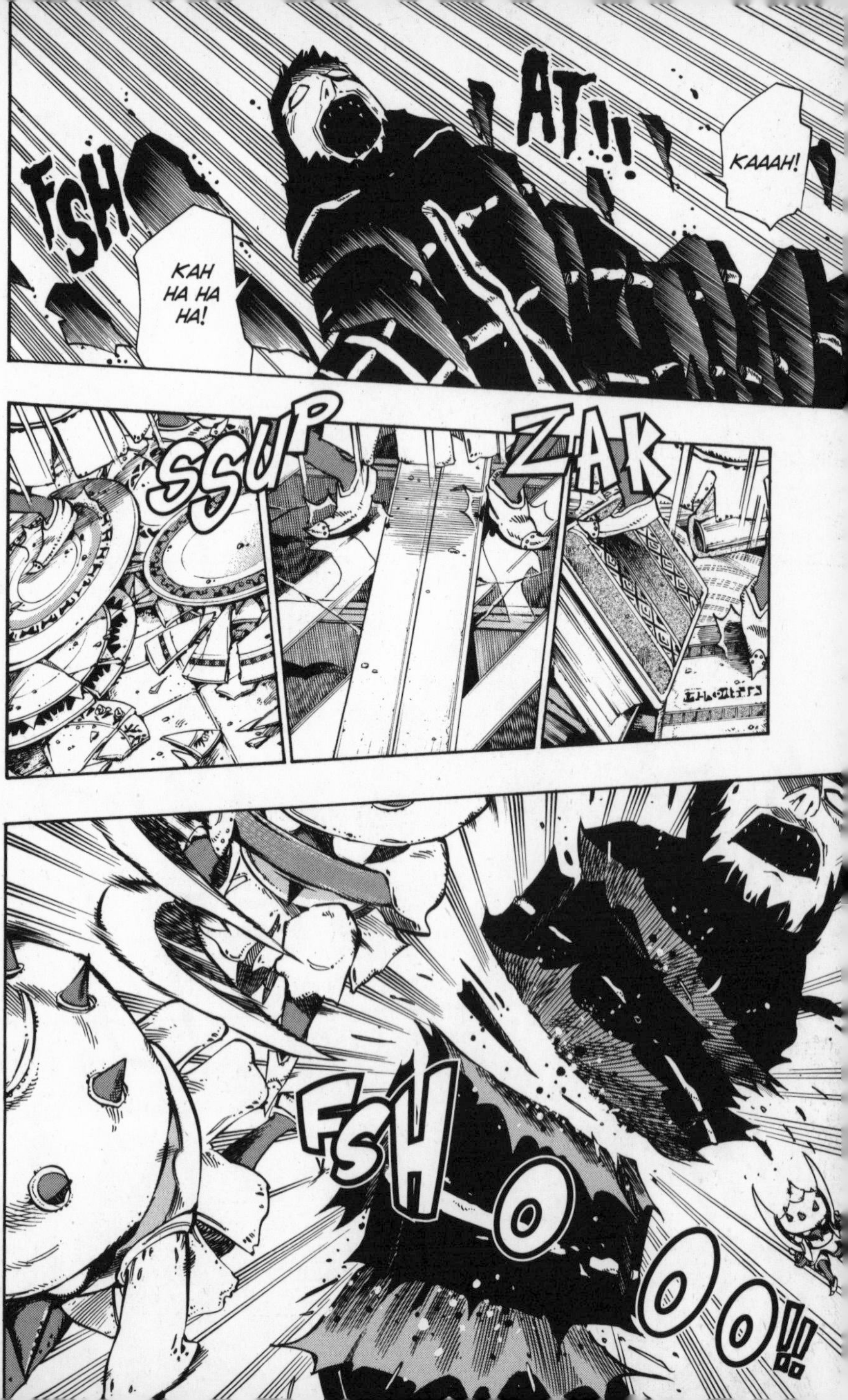
KAAAH!
AT!!
FSH
KAH HA HA HA!
ZAK
SSUP
FSHOOOOO!!!

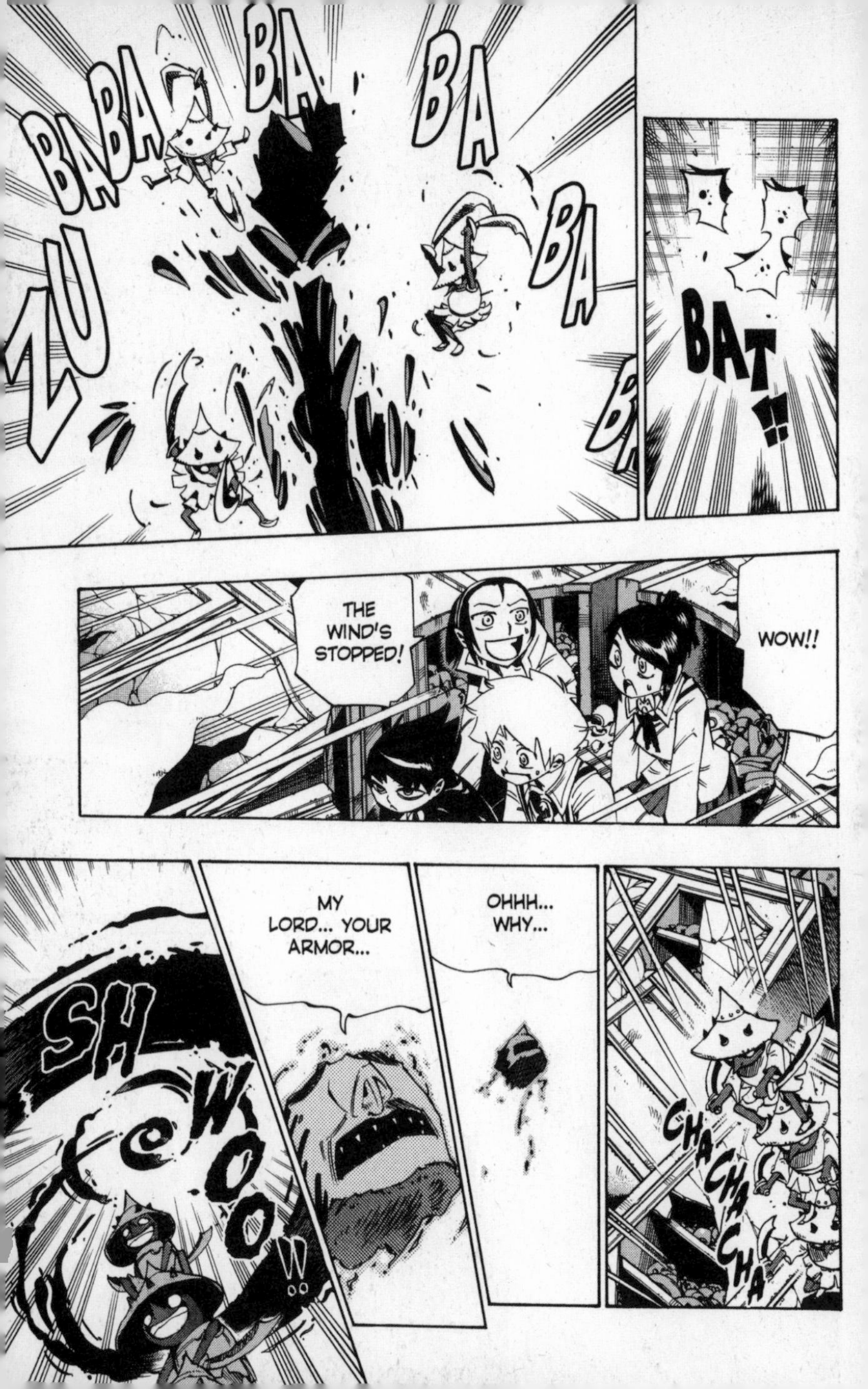
BAT!!
BA BA
BA
BA
ZUBABA
WOW!!
THE WIND'S STOPPED!
CHACHACHACHA
OHHH... WHY...
MY LORD... YOUR ARMOR...
SHWOOO!!

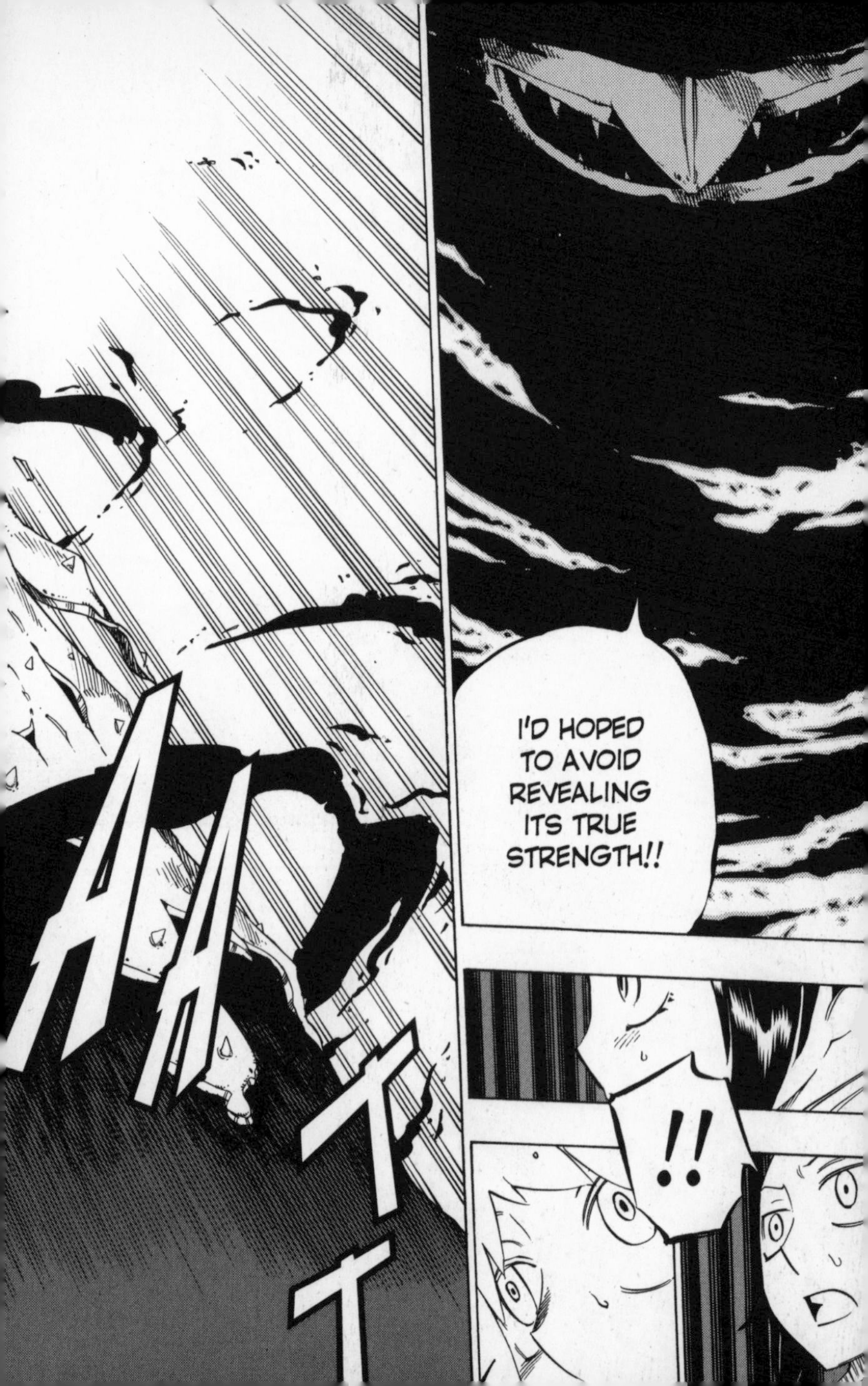
I'D HOPED TO AVOID REVEALING ITS TRUE STRENGTH!!
!!
AA

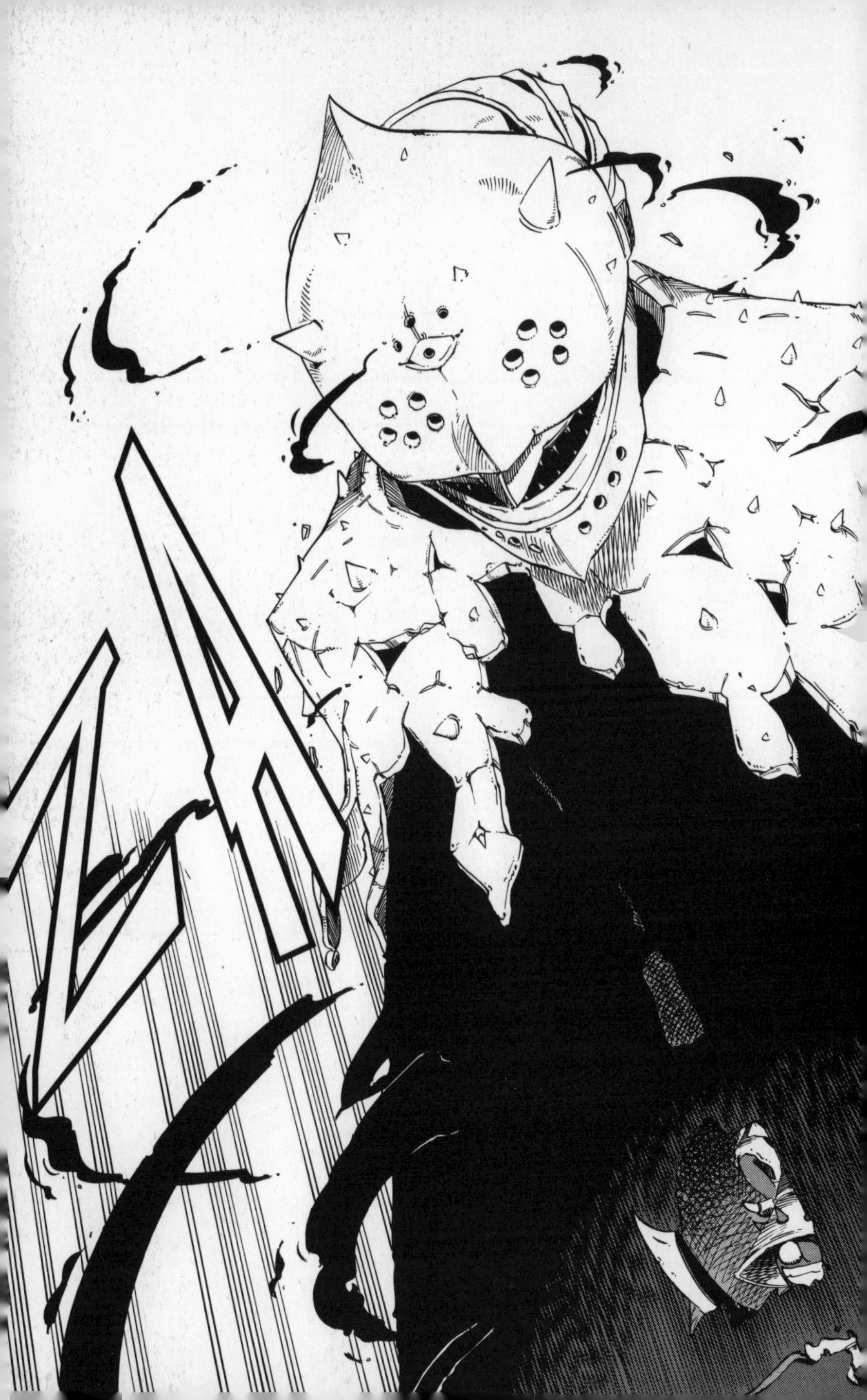
ZA

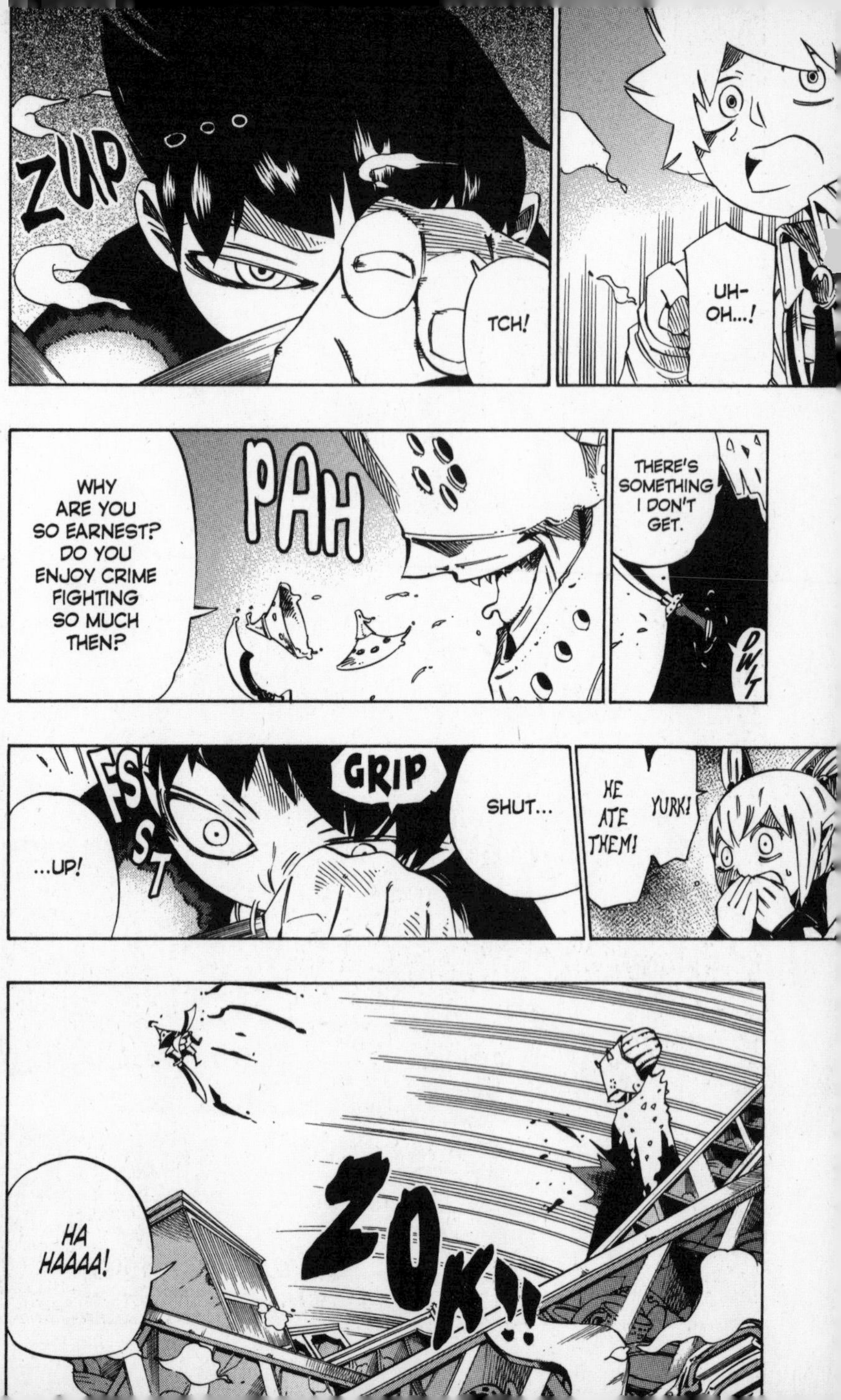
UH-OH...!
TCH!
ZUP
THERE'S SOMETHING I DON'T GET.
DWIT
PAH
WHY ARE YOU SO EARNEST? DO YOU ENJOY CRIME FIGHTING SO MUCH THEN?
YURK!
HE ATE THEM!
SHUT...
GRIP
FSST
...UP!
ZOK!!
HA HAAAA!

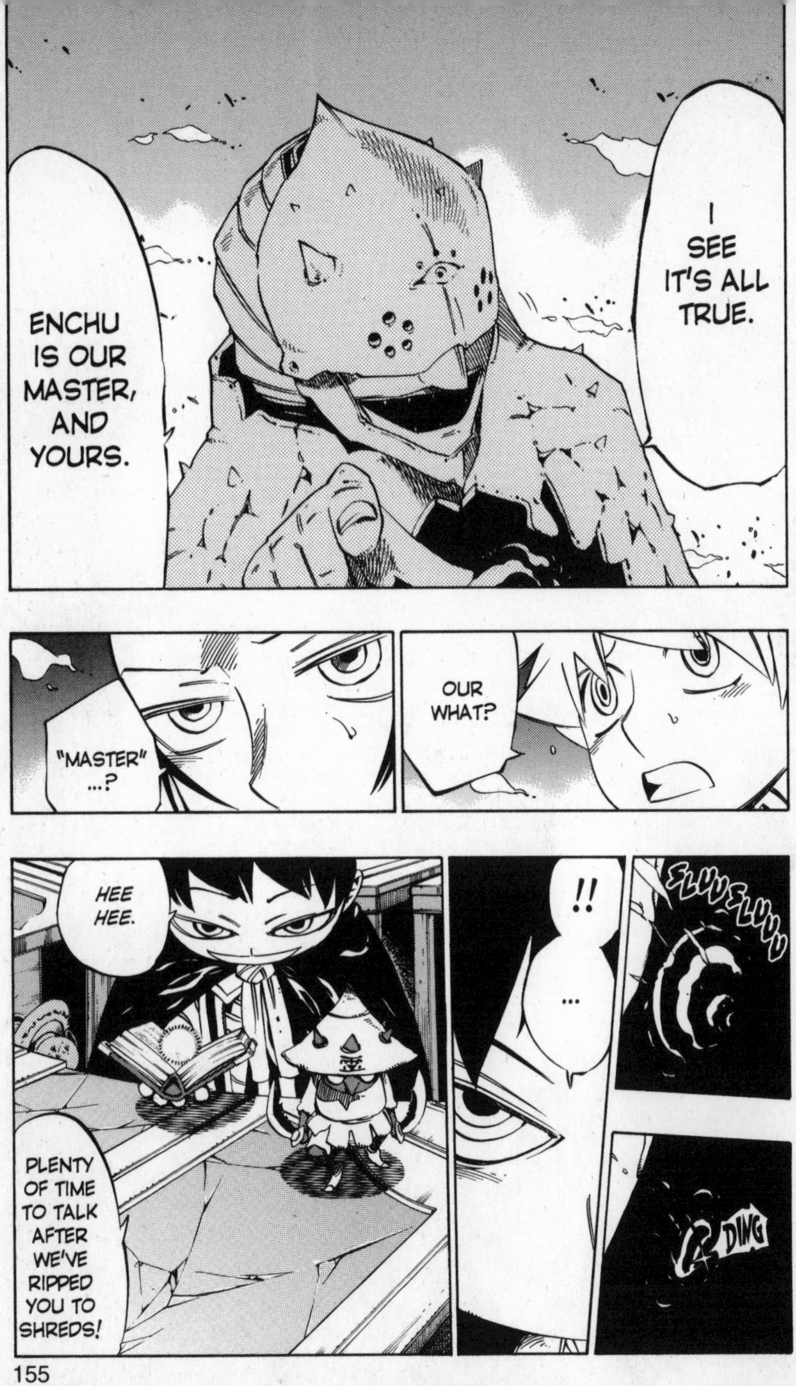
I SEE IT'S ALL TRUE.
ENCHU IS OUR MASTER, AND YOURS.
OUR WHAT?
"MASTER" ...?
ELUU ELUUU
DING
!!
...
HEE HEE.
PLENTY OF TIME TO TALK AFTER WE'VE RIPPED YOU TO SHREDS!

Q: IN VOLUME 7, ARTICLE 55, MUHYO OPENS HIS REGISTRY AND IT'S SOLID BLACK. JUST HOW MANY THINGS HAS HE MADE A CONTRACT WITH?
   -ANONYMOUS,
    KAGOSHIMA PREFECTURE

A: OVER 100, I'D SAY. THERE ARE A VARIETY OF SENTENCES IN MAGIC LAW, AND NOT ALL REQUIRE THEIR OWN UNIQUE ENVOY. SOME ENVOYS ARE RESPONSIBLE FOR CARRYING OUT SEVERAL DIFFERENT SENTENCES. WHILE THERE ARE MANY THOUSANDS OF CRIMES, THERE ARE SEVERAL HUNDRED ENVOYS. EVEN SOMEONE WITH A FULL REGISTRY LIKE MUHYO HASN'T SEEN THEM ALL. THAT SAID, ONLY A FEW EXECTUORS HAVE A REGISTRY AS FULL AS HIS.

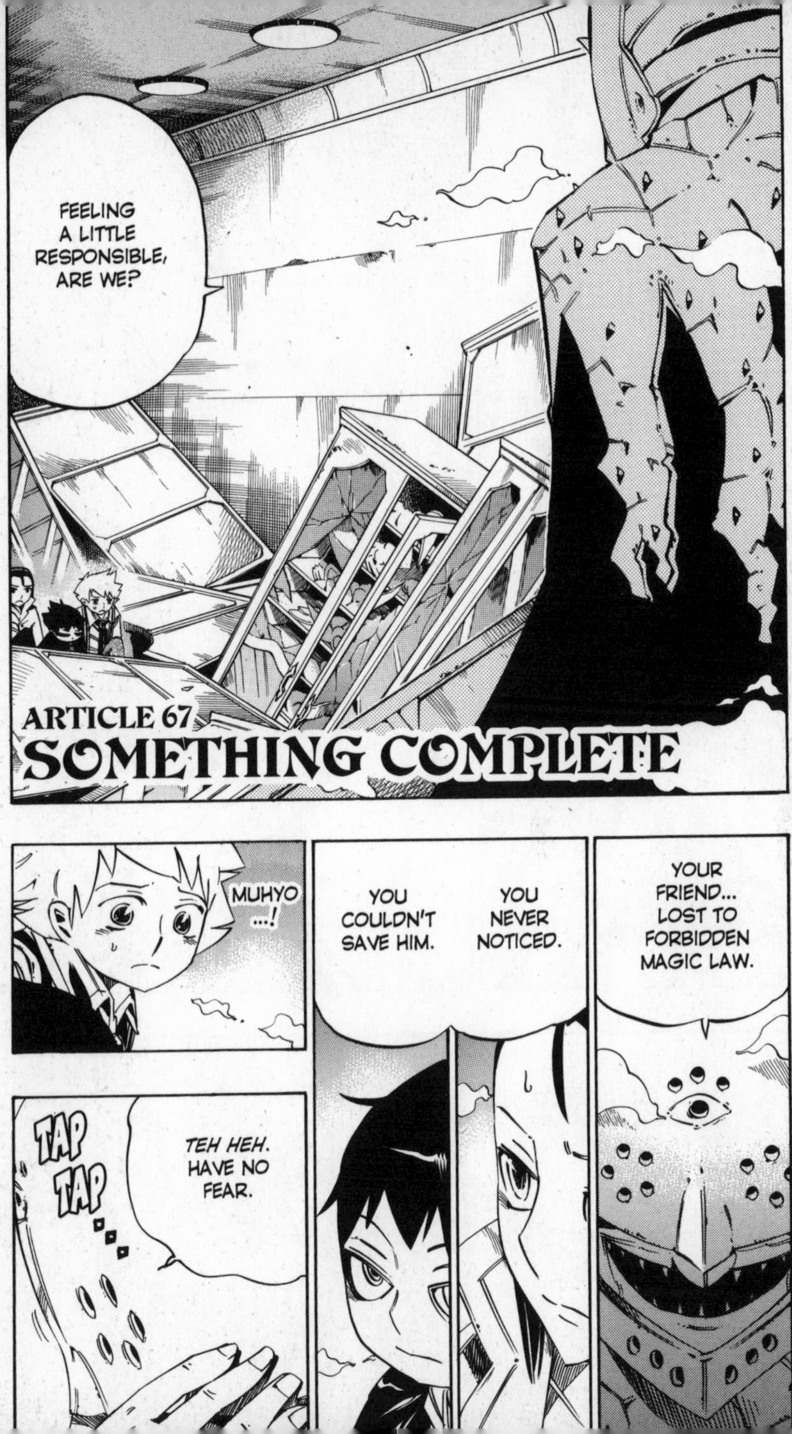
FEELING A LITTLE RESPONSIBLE, ARE WE?
ARTICLE 67
SOMETHING COMPLETE
YOUR FRIEND... LOST TO FORBIDDEN MAGIC LAW.
YOU NEVER NOTICED.
YOU COULDN'T SAVE HIM.
MUHYO ...!
TEH HEH. HAVE NO FEAR.
TAP TAP

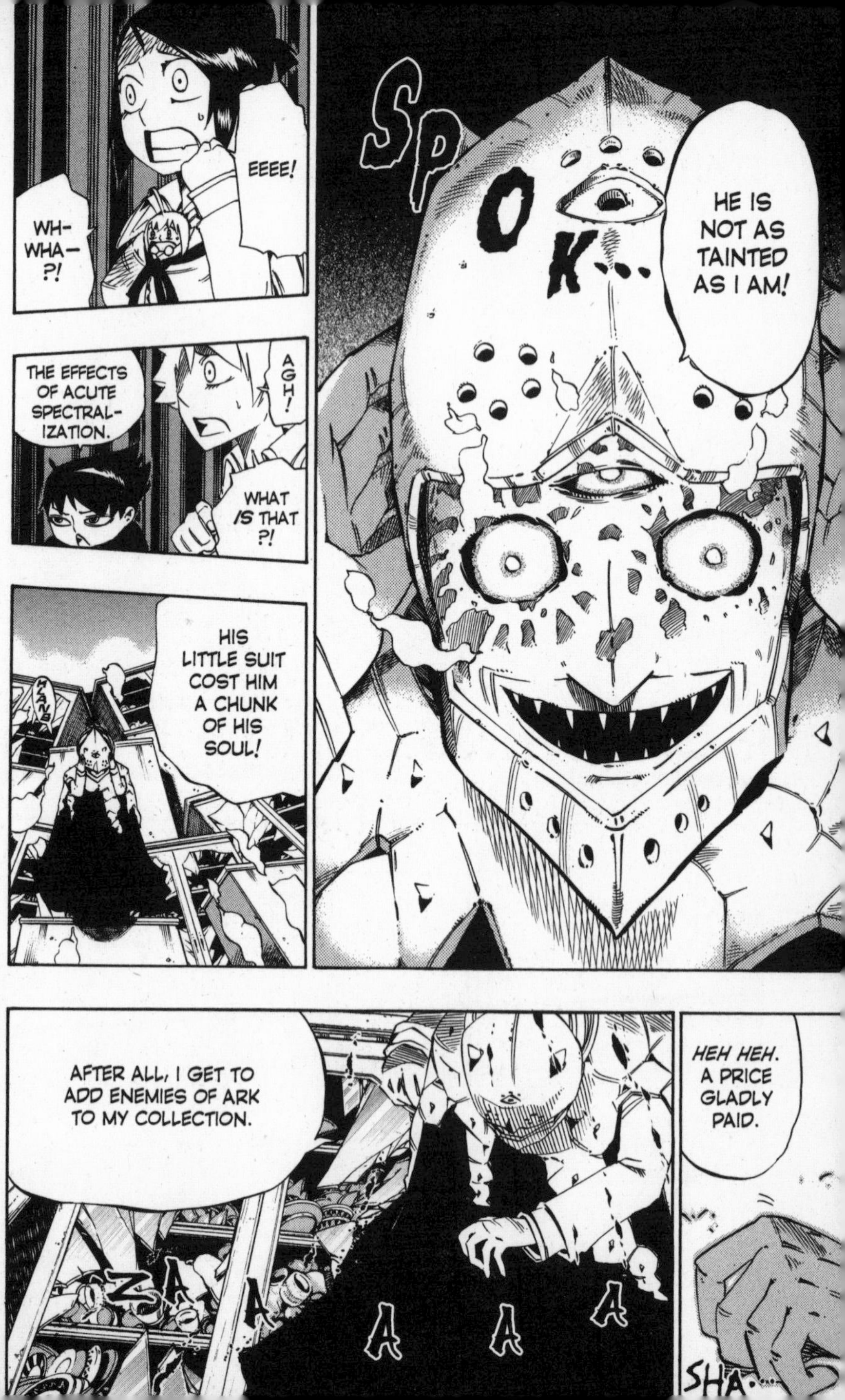
SPOK...
HE IS NOT AS TAINTED AS I AM!
EEEE!
WH-WHA-?!
AGH!
WHAT *IS* THAT?!
THE EFFECTS OF ACUTE SPECTRALIZATION.
HIS LITTLE SUIT COST HIM A CHUNK OF HIS SOUL!
HEH HEH. A PRICE GLADLY PAID.
SHA...
AFTER ALL, I GET TO ADD ENEMIES OF ARK TO MY COLLECTION.
ZAAAA

ARTICLE 67
SOMETHING COMPLETE

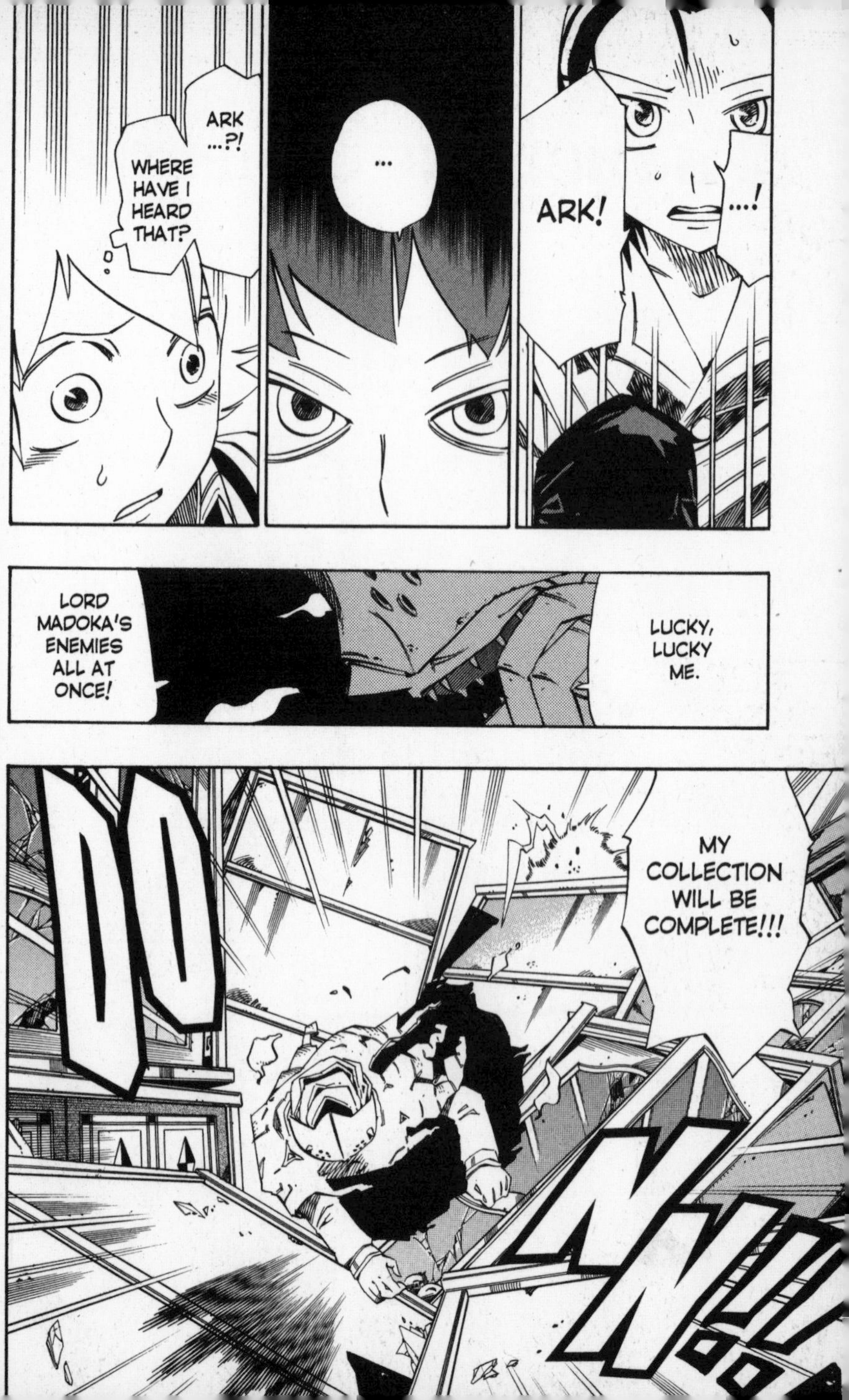
...!
ARK!
...
ARK ...?!
WHERE HAVE I HEARD THAT?
LUCKY, LUCKY ME.
LORD MADOKA'S ENEMIES ALL AT ONCE!
MY COLLECTION WILL BE COMPLETE!!!
DO
N!!

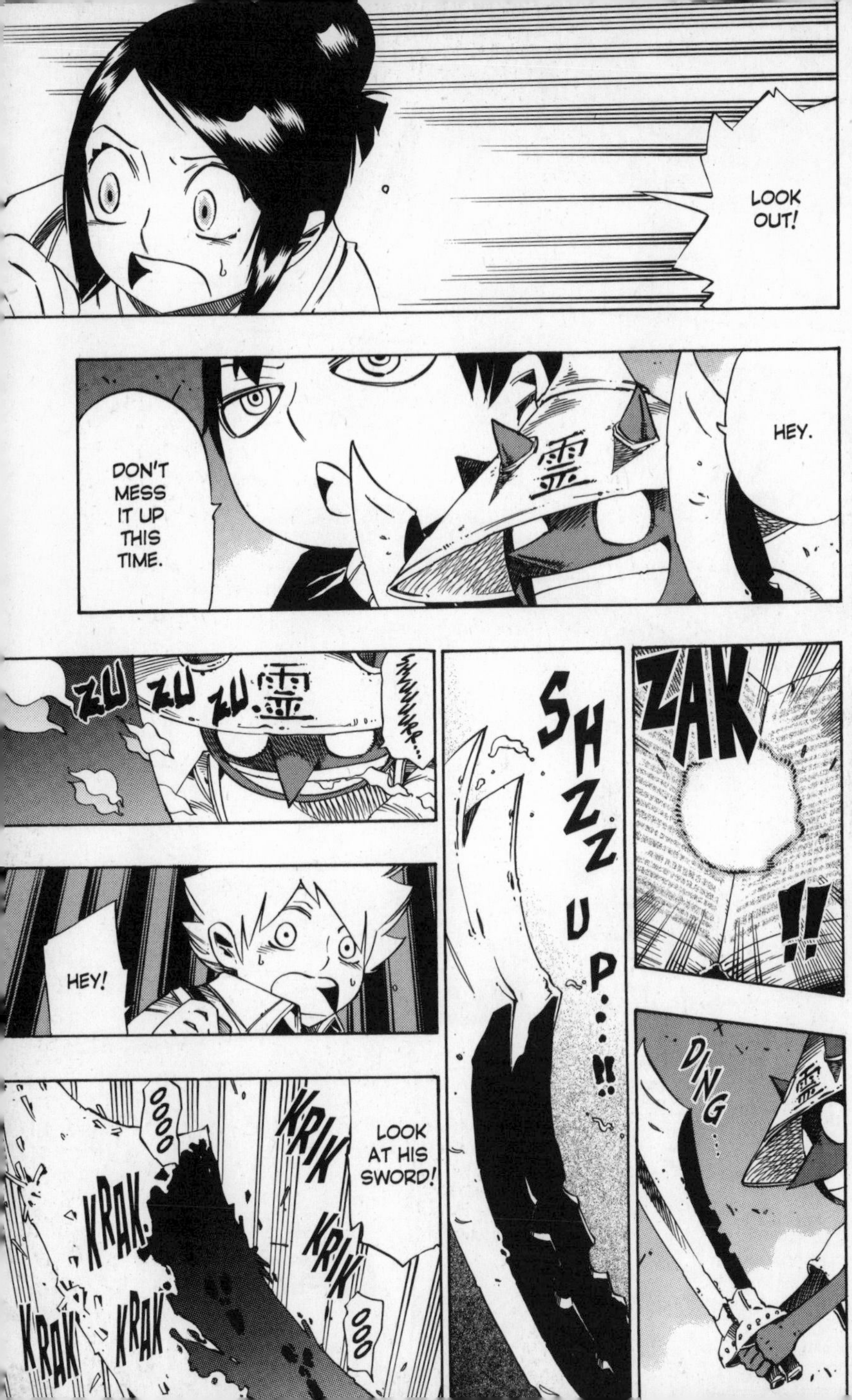
LOOK OUT!
HEY.
DON'T MESS IT UP THIS TIME.
ZAK!!
DING...
SHZZUP...!!
ZU ZU ZU
HEY!
LOOK AT HIS SWORD!
KRIK KRIK
OOOO
KRIK KRIK
OOO
KRAK.
KRAK KRAK

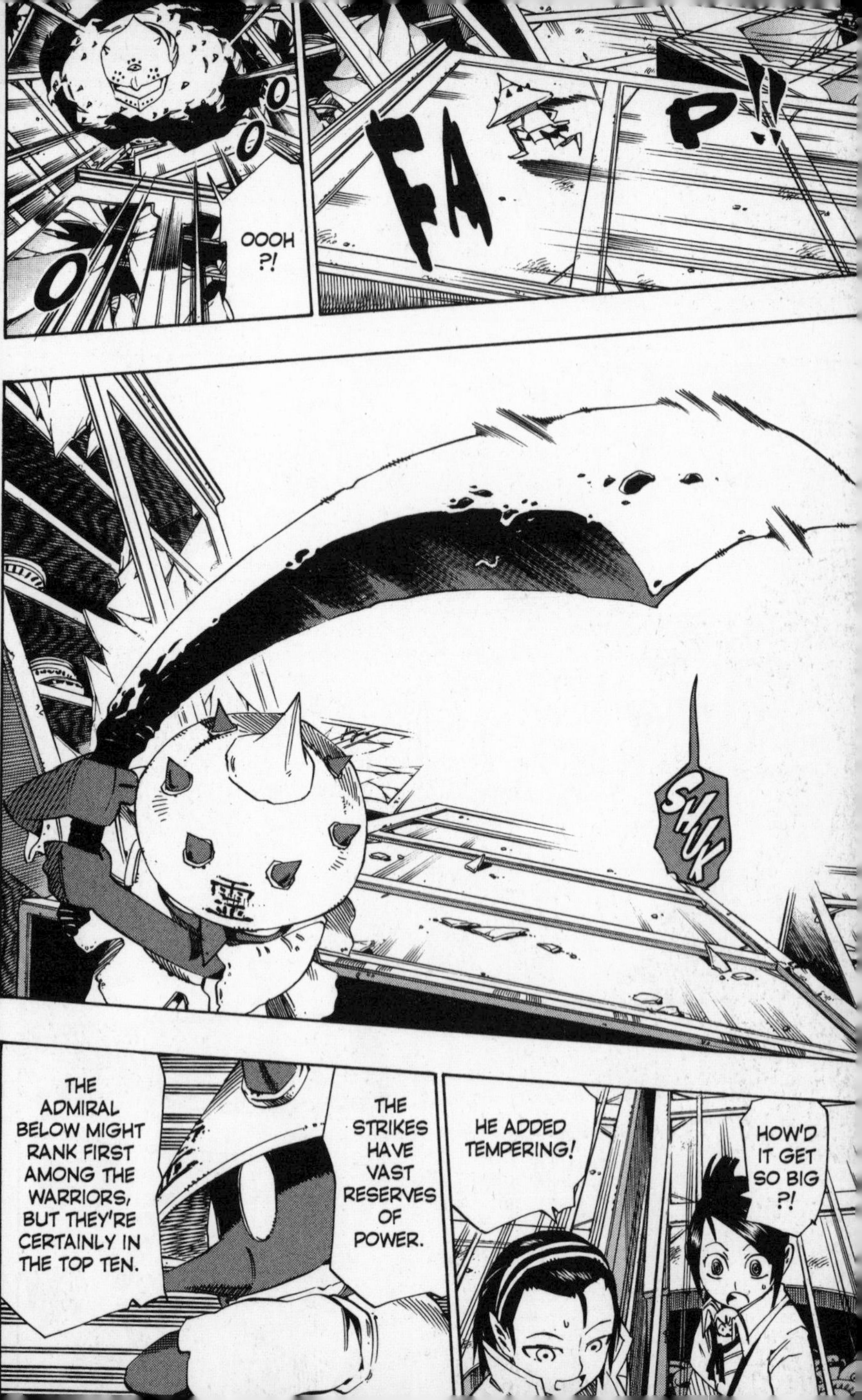
FAP!!
OOOH ?!
SHUK
HOW'D IT GET SO BIG ?!
HE ADDED TEMPERING!
THE STRIKES HAVE VAST RESERVES OF POWER.
THE ADMIRAL BELOW MIGHT RANK FIRST AMONG THE WARRIORS, BUT THEY'RE CERTAINLY IN THE TOP TEN.

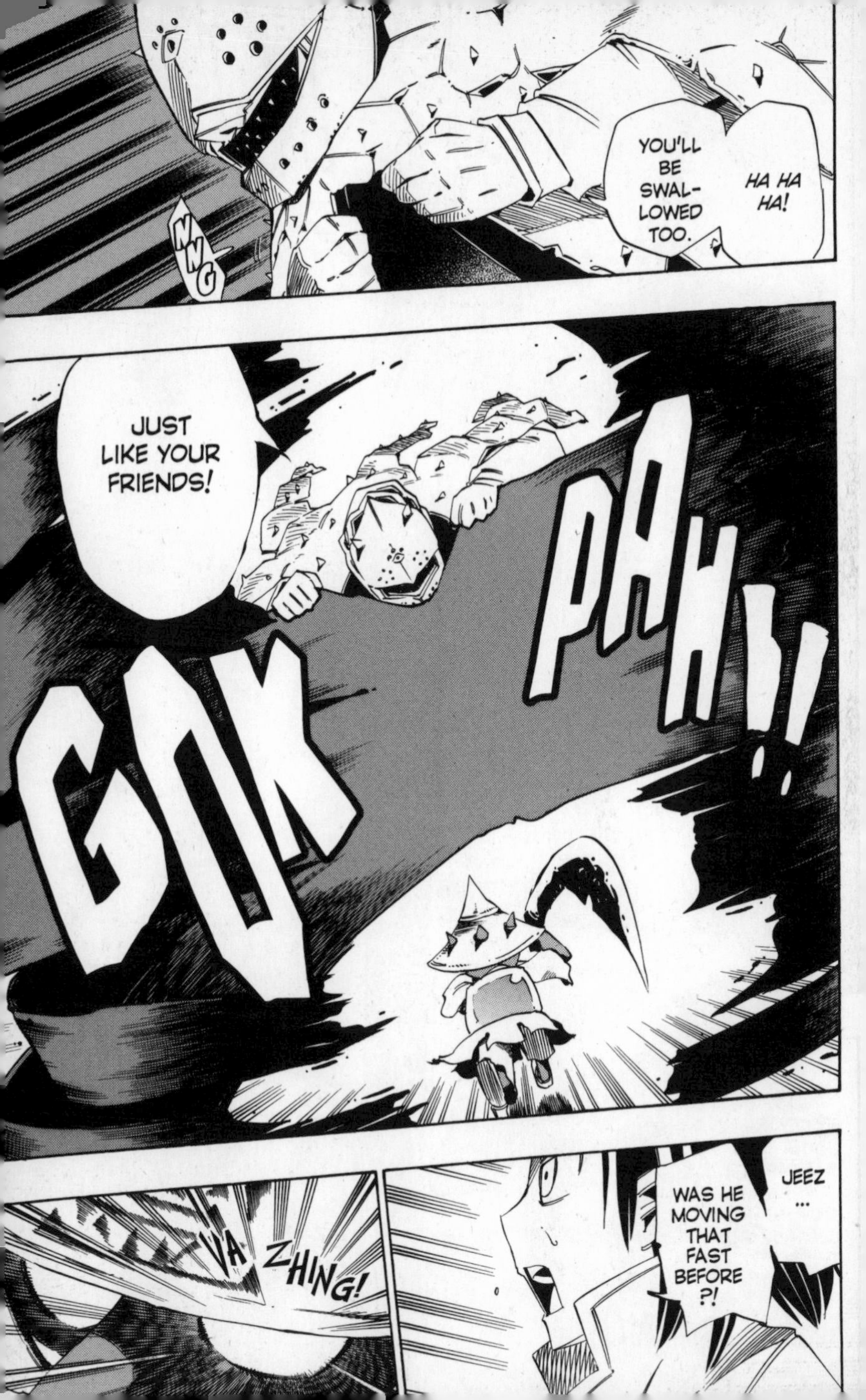
HA HA HA!
YOU'LL BE SWAL-LOWED TOO.
NNG
JUST LIKE YOUR FRIENDS!
PAHH!!
GOK
JEEZ ...
WAS HE MOVING THAT FAST BEFORE ?!
VA ZHING!

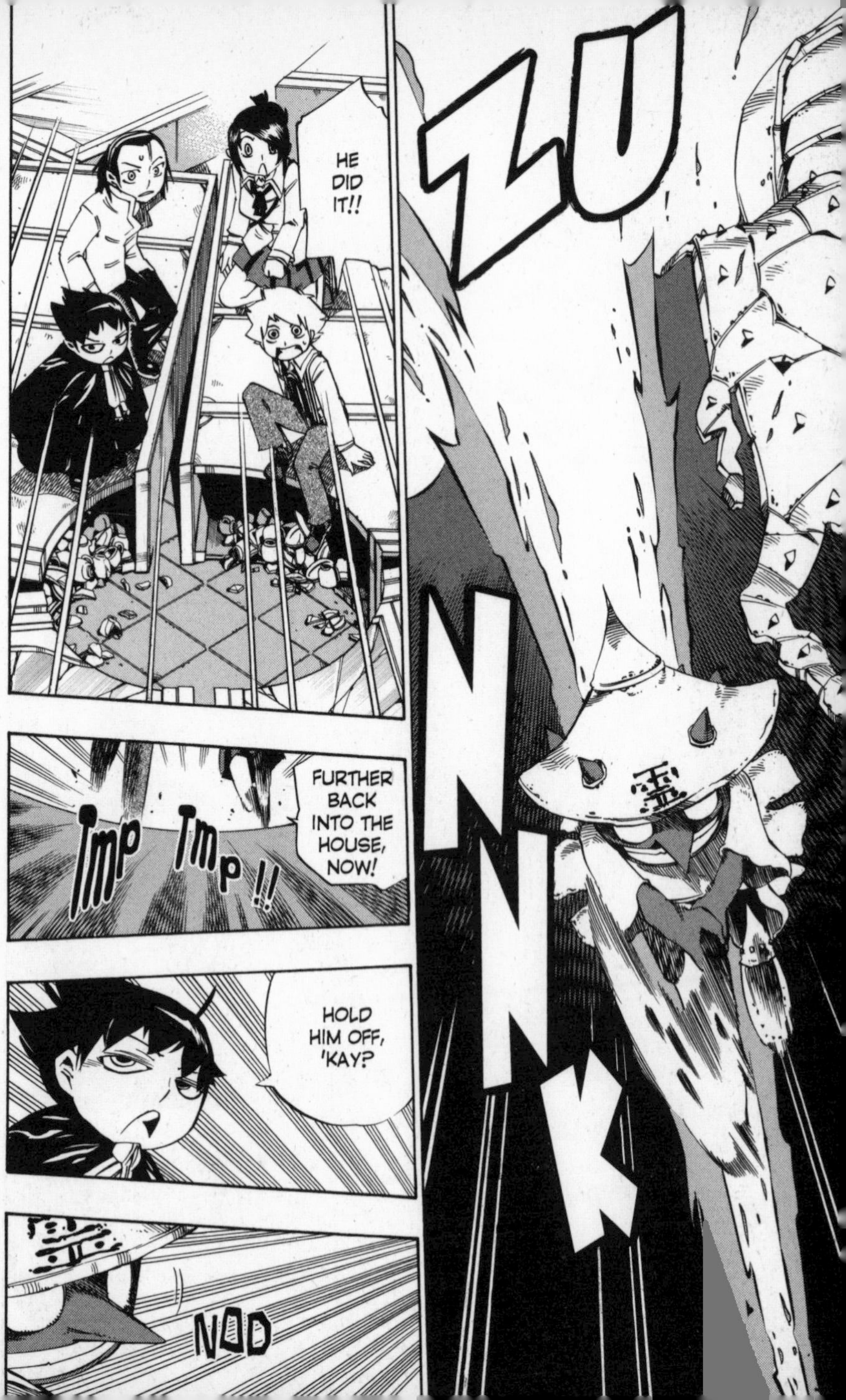
ZU
NNK
HE DID IT!!
FURTHER BACK INTO THE HOUSE, NOW!
Tmp Tmp!!
HOLD HIM OFF, 'KAY?
NOD

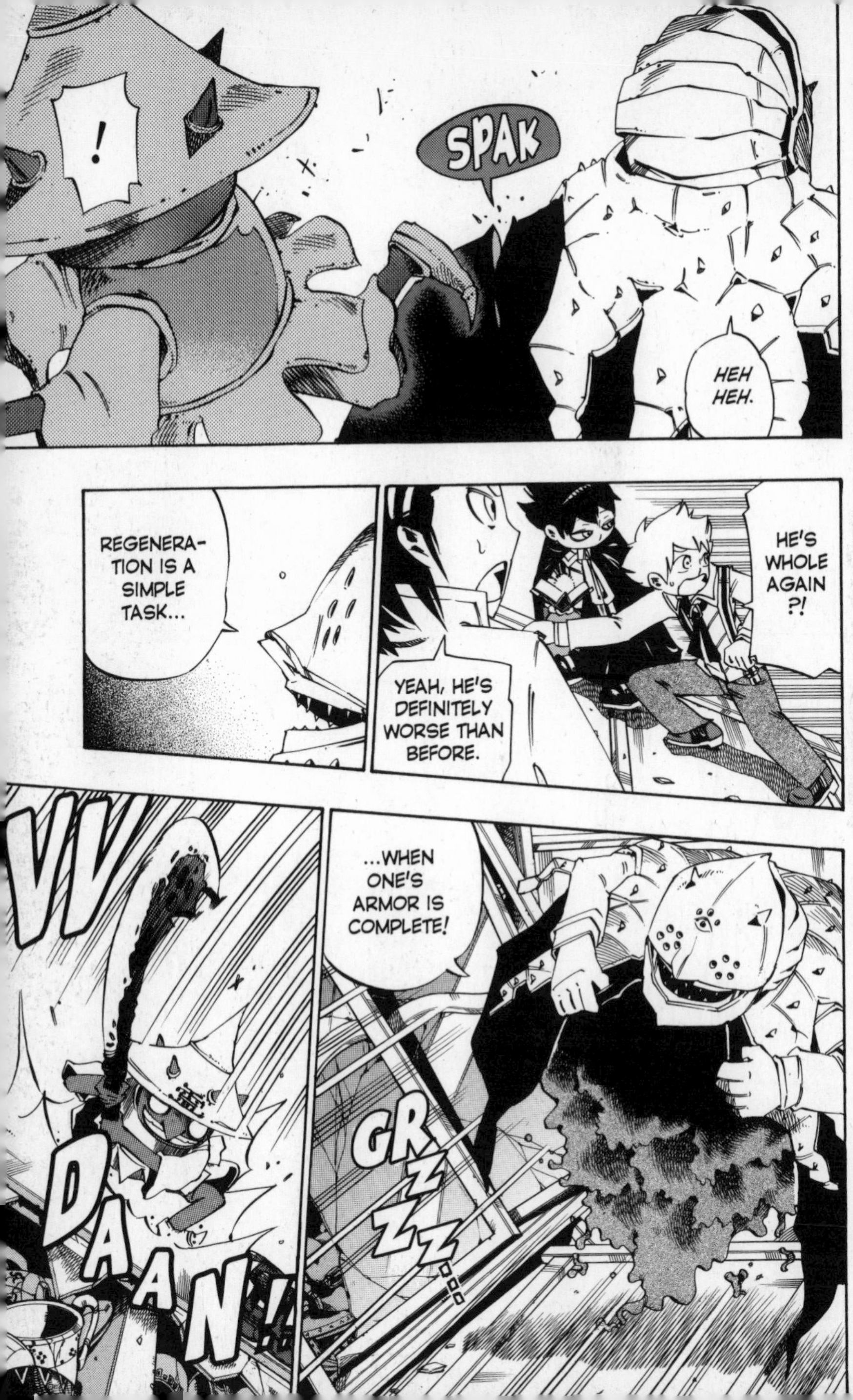
SPAK
HEH HEH.
!
HE'S WHOLE AGAIN ?!
YEAH, HE'S DEFINITELY WORSE THAN BEFORE.
REGENERATION IS A SIMPLE TASK...
...WHEN ONE'S ARMOR IS COMPLETE!
GRZZZ...
DAAN!!

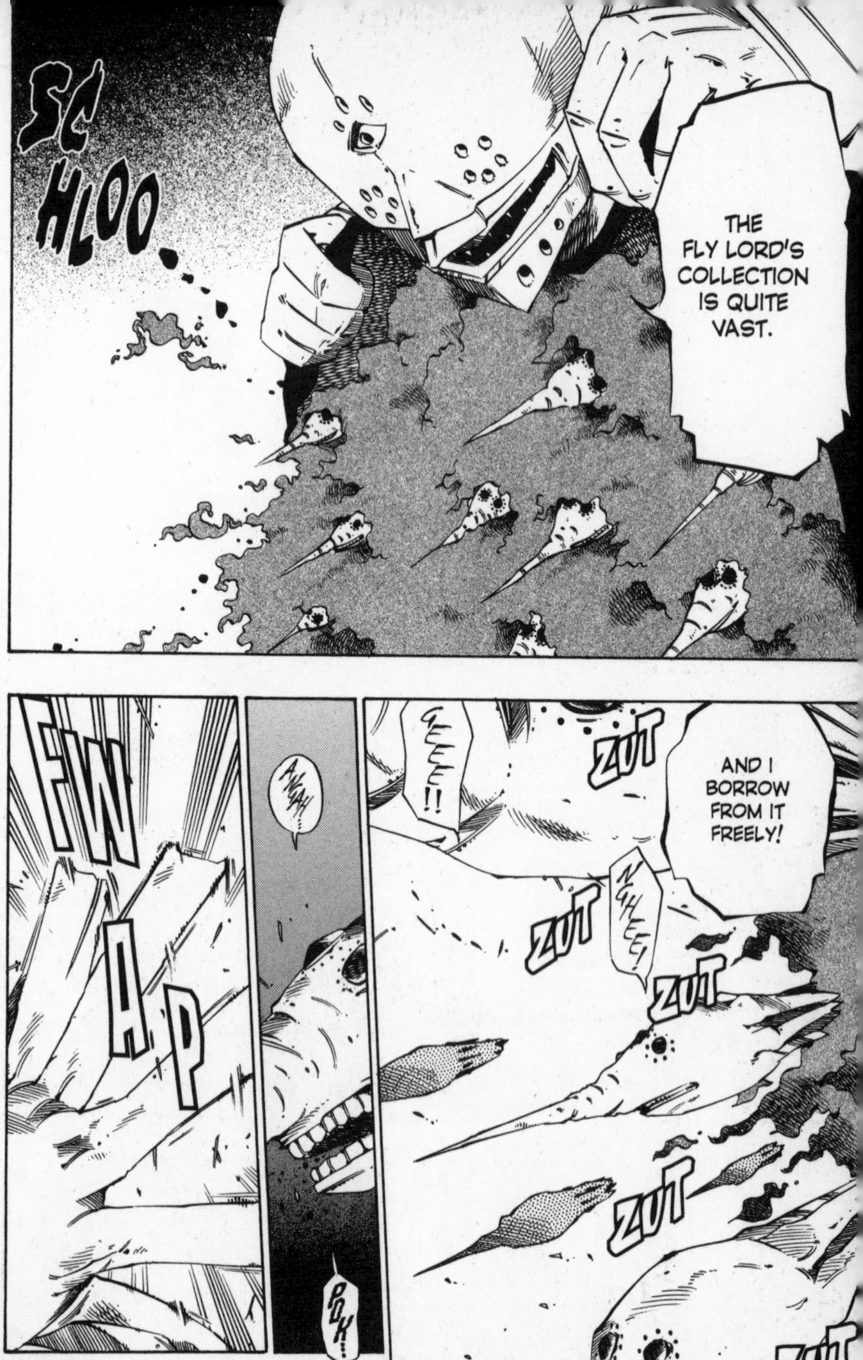
THE FLY LORD'S COLLECTION IS QUITE VAST.
SCHLOO
AND I BORROW FROM IT FREELY!
ZUT
GEEEE!!
NGHEE!
ZUT
ZUT
ZUT
ZUT
AHGAH...
POK...
FWAP

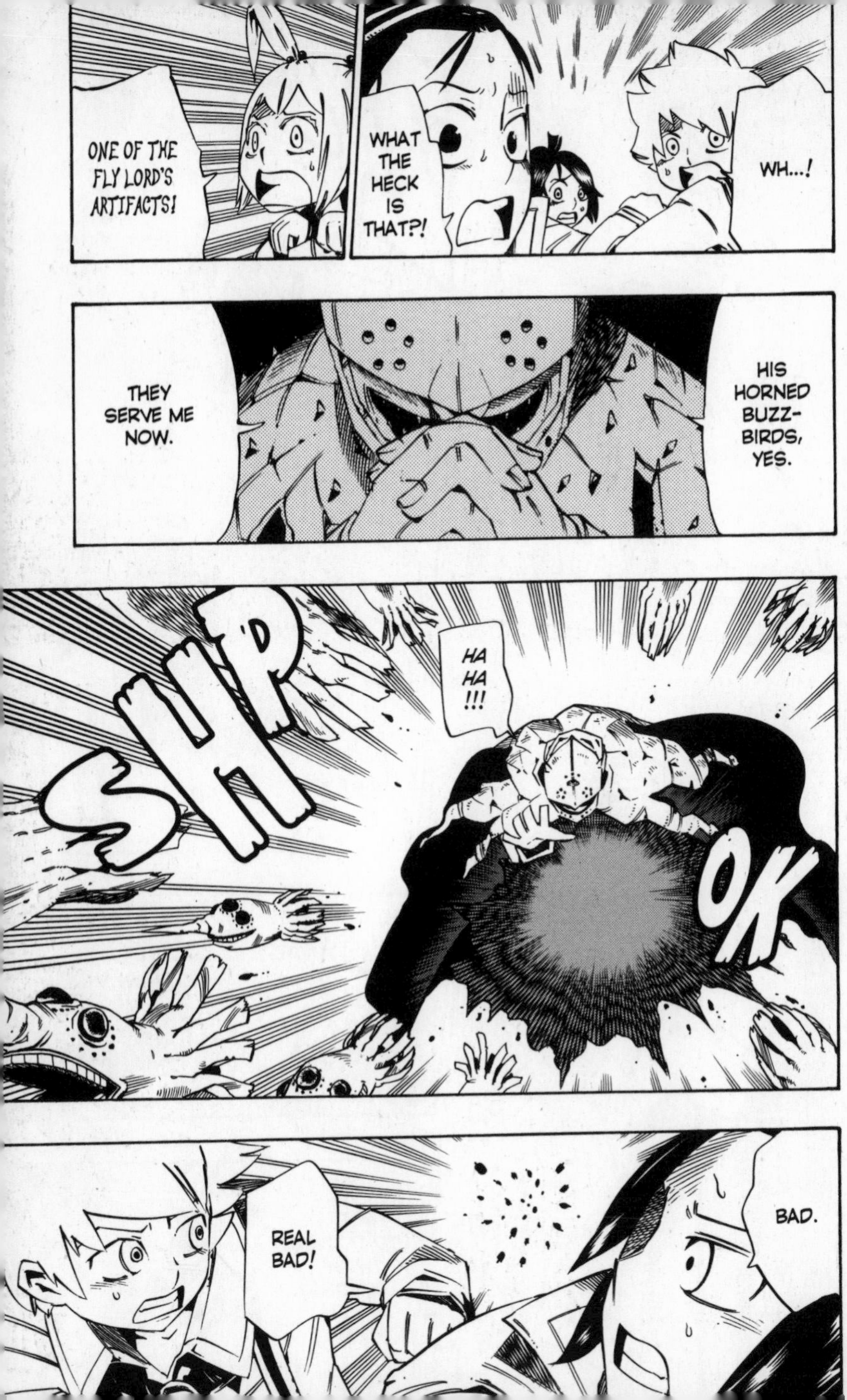
WH...!
WHAT THE HECK IS THAT?!
ONE OF THE FLY LORD'S ARTIFACTS!
HIS HORNED BUZZ-BIRDS, YES.
THEY SERVE ME NOW.
HA HA !!!
SHP'D
OK
BAD.
REAL BAD!

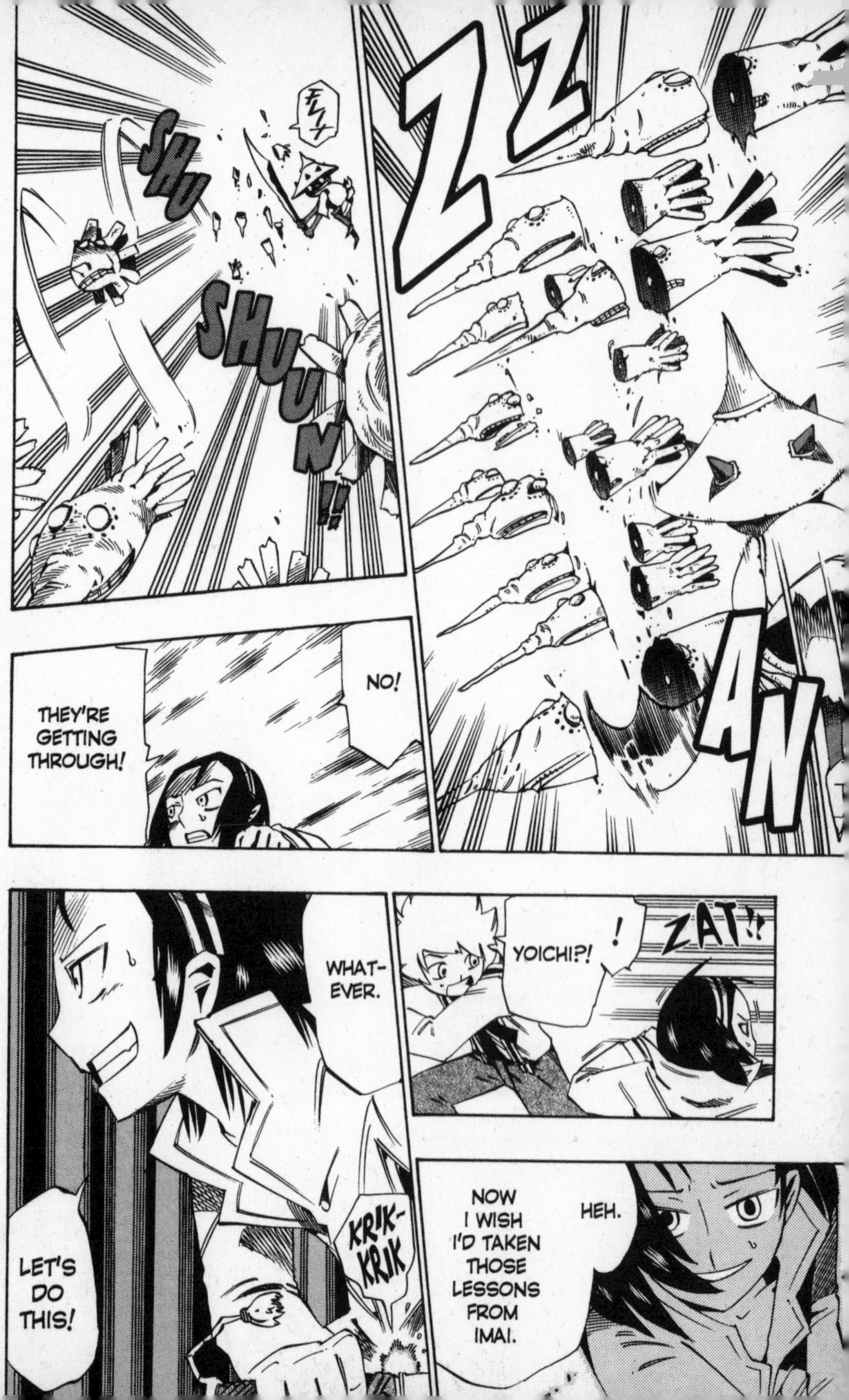
ZZ
AN
SHU
SHUUUN!!
NO!
THEY'RE GETTING THROUGH!
ZAT!!
!
YOICHI?!
HEH.
NOW I WISH I'D TAKEN THOSE LESSONS FROM IMAI.
WHAT-EVER.
KRIK-KRIK
LET'S DO THIS!

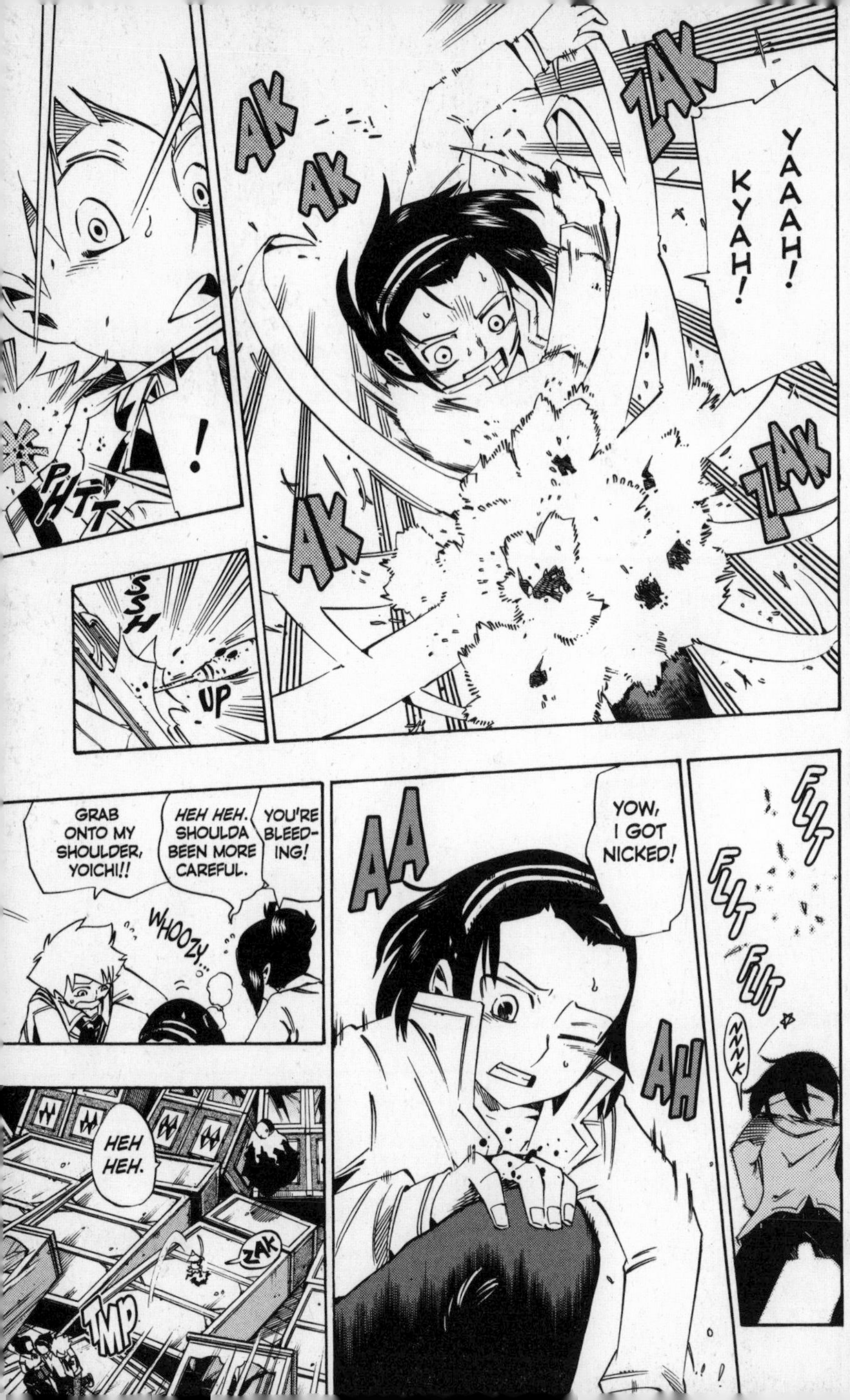
YAAAAH!
KYAAH!
ZAK
ZAK
AK
AK
AK
!
PHTTT
SSH
UP
FLIT
FLIT
FLIT
NNNK
YOW, I GOT NICKED!
AA
AH
YOU'RE BLEEDING!
HEH HEH. SHOULDA BEEN MORE CAREFUL.
GRAB ONTO MY SHOULDER, YOICHI!!
WHOOZY...
HEH HEH.
ZAK
TMP

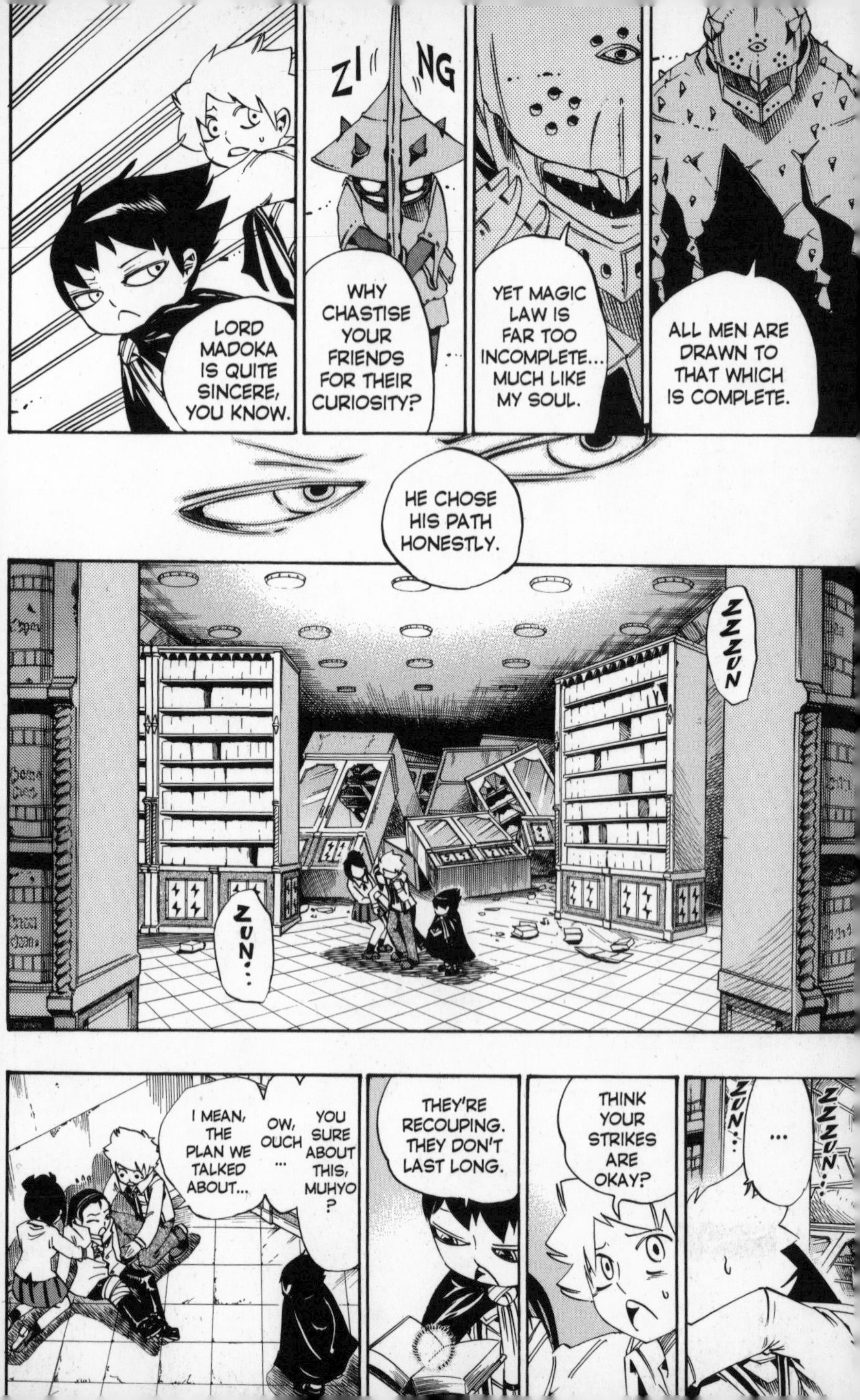
ALL MEN ARE DRAWN TO THAT WHICH IS COMPLETE.
YET MAGIC LAW IS FAR TOO INCOMPLETE... MUCH LIKE MY SOUL.
ZING
WHY CHASTISE YOUR FRIENDS FOR THEIR CURIOSITY?
LORD MADOKA IS QUITE SINCERE, YOU KNOW.
HE CHOSE HIS PATH HONESTLY.
ZZZUN
ZUN...
ZZZUN...
ZUN...
...
THINK YOUR STRIKES ARE OKAY?
THEY'RE RECOUPING. THEY DON'T LAST LONG.
YOU SURE ABOUT THIS, MUHYO?
OW, OUCH ...
I MEAN, THE PLAN WE TALKED ABOUT...

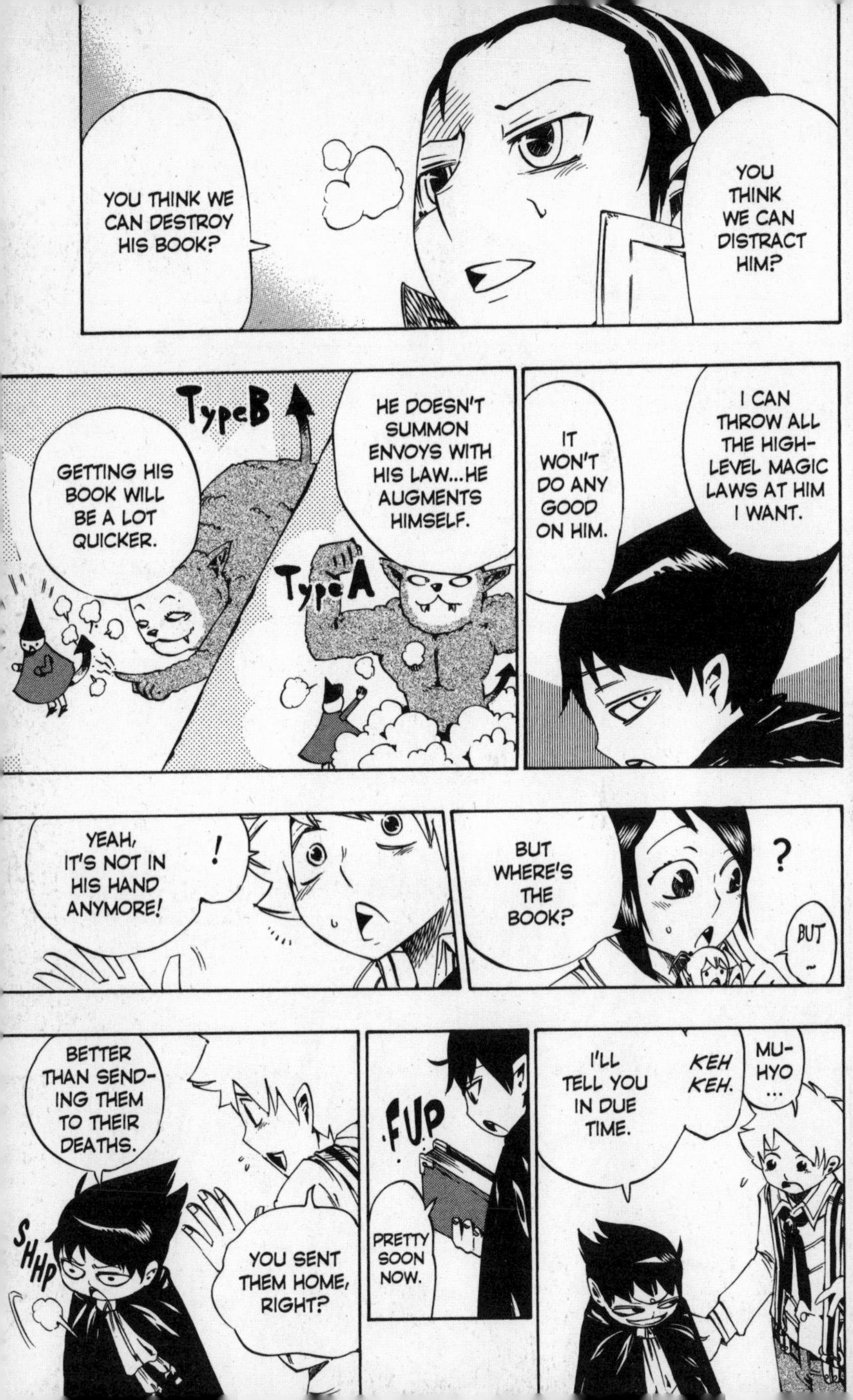
YOU THINK WE CAN DISTRACT HIM?
YOU THINK WE CAN DESTROY HIS BOOK?
I CAN THROW ALL THE HIGH-LEVEL MAGIC LAWS AT HIM I WANT.
IT WON'T DO ANY GOOD ON HIM.
HE DOESN'T SUMMON ENVOYS WITH HIS LAW...HE AUGMENTS HIMSELF.
Type A
Type B
GETTING HIS BOOK WILL BE A LOT QUICKER.
?
BUT ...
BUT WHERE'S THE BOOK?
!
YEAH, IT'S NOT IN HIS HAND ANYMORE!
MU-HYO ...
KEH KEH.
I'LL TELL YOU IN DUE TIME.
FUP
PRETTY SOON NOW.
YOU SENT THEM HOME, RIGHT?
BETTER THAN SENDING THEM TO THEIR DEATHS.
SHHP

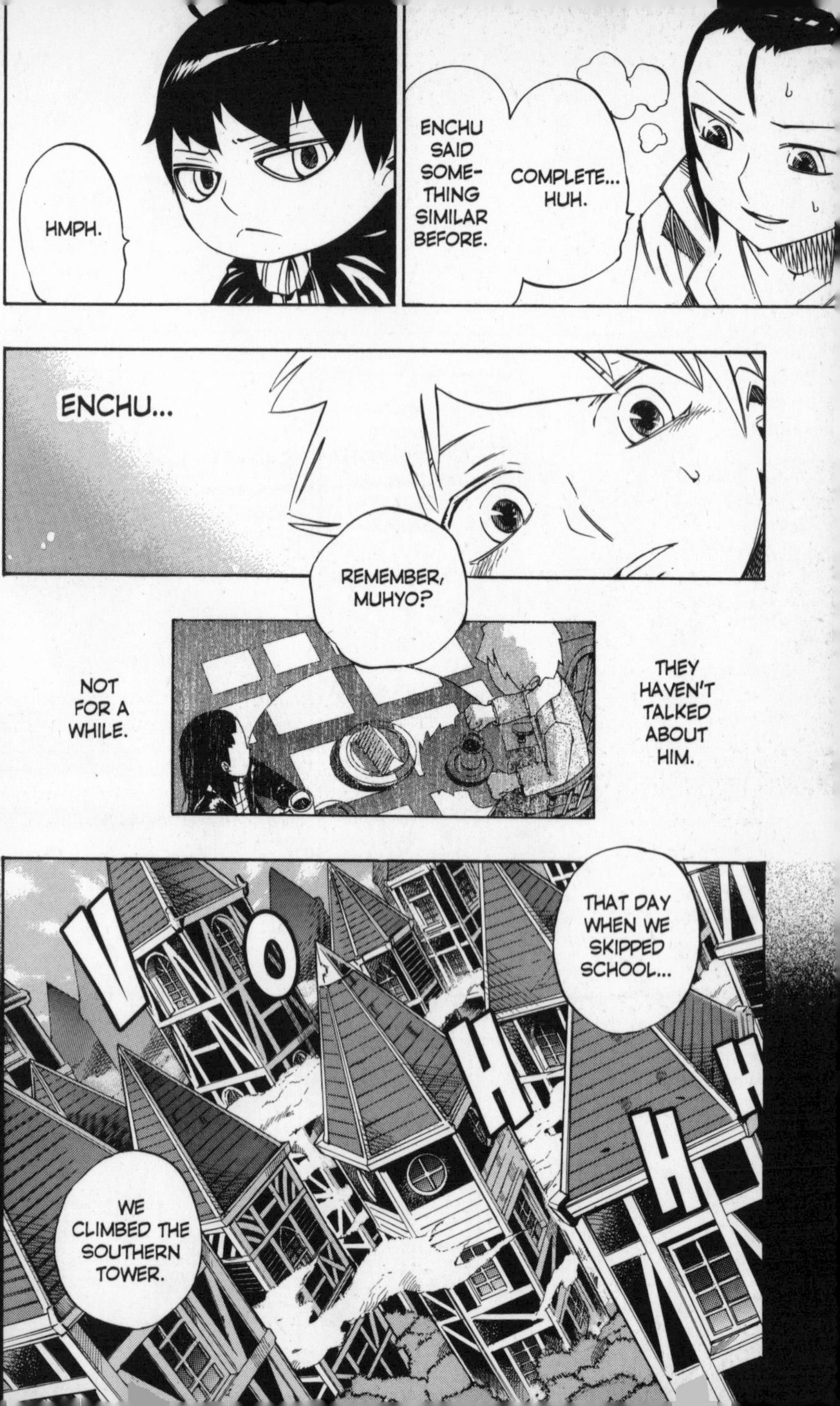
COMPLETE... HUH.
ENCHU SAID SOME-THING SIMILAR BEFORE.
HMPH.
ENCHU...
REMEMBER, MUHYO?
THEY HAVEN'T TALKED ABOUT HIM.
NOT FOR A WHILE.
THAT DAY WHEN WE SKIPPED SCHOOL...
VOHHHH
WE CLIMBED THE SOUTHERN TOWER.

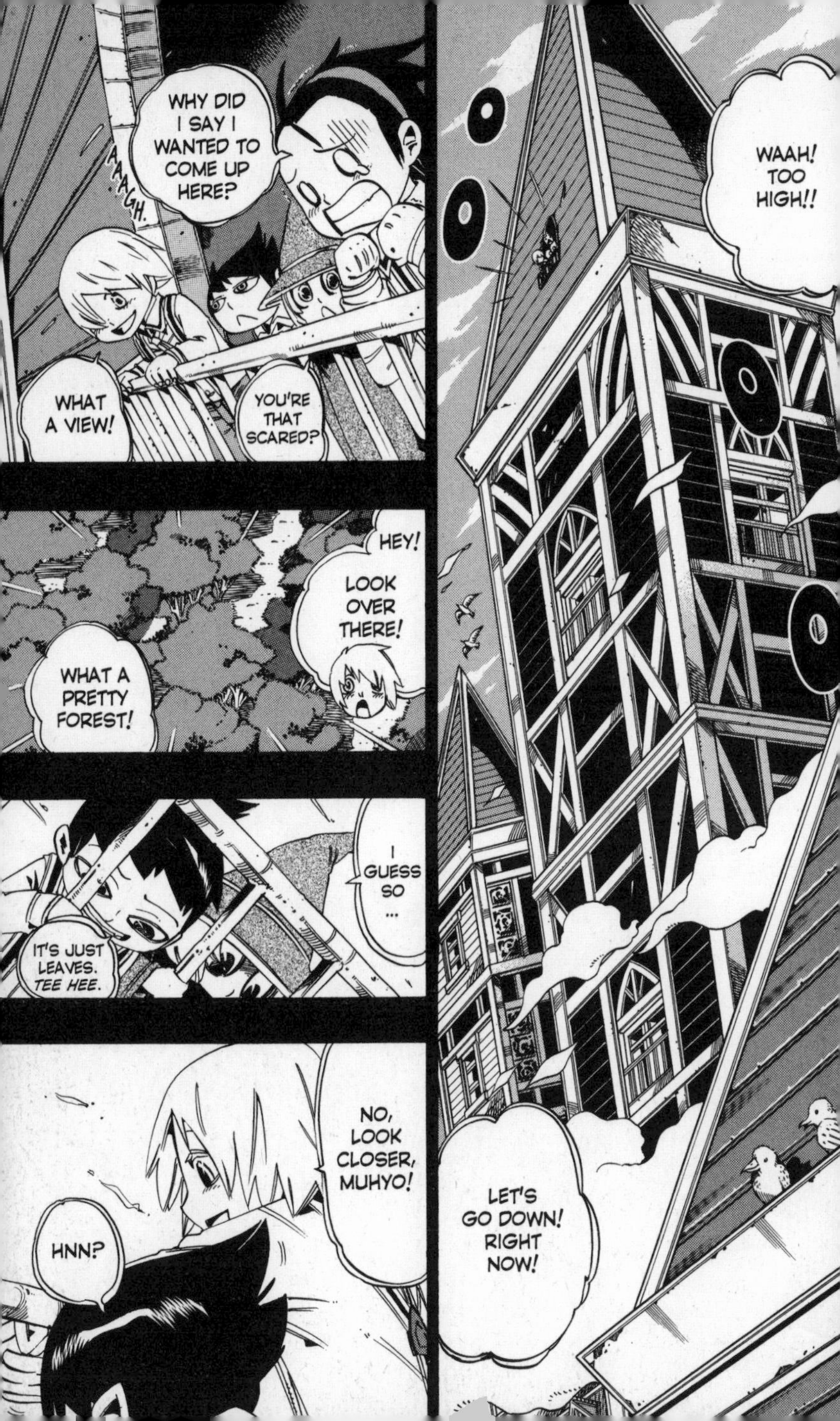
WAAH! TOO HIGH!!
LET'S GO DOWN! RIGHT NOW!
WHY DID I SAY I WANTED TO COME UP HERE?
AAAAGH.
YOU'RE THAT SCARED?
WHAT A VIEW!
HEY! LOOK OVER THERE!
WHAT A PRETTY FOREST!
I GUESS SO ...
IT'S JUST LEAVES. TEE HEE.
NO, LOOK CLOSER, MUHYO!
HNN?

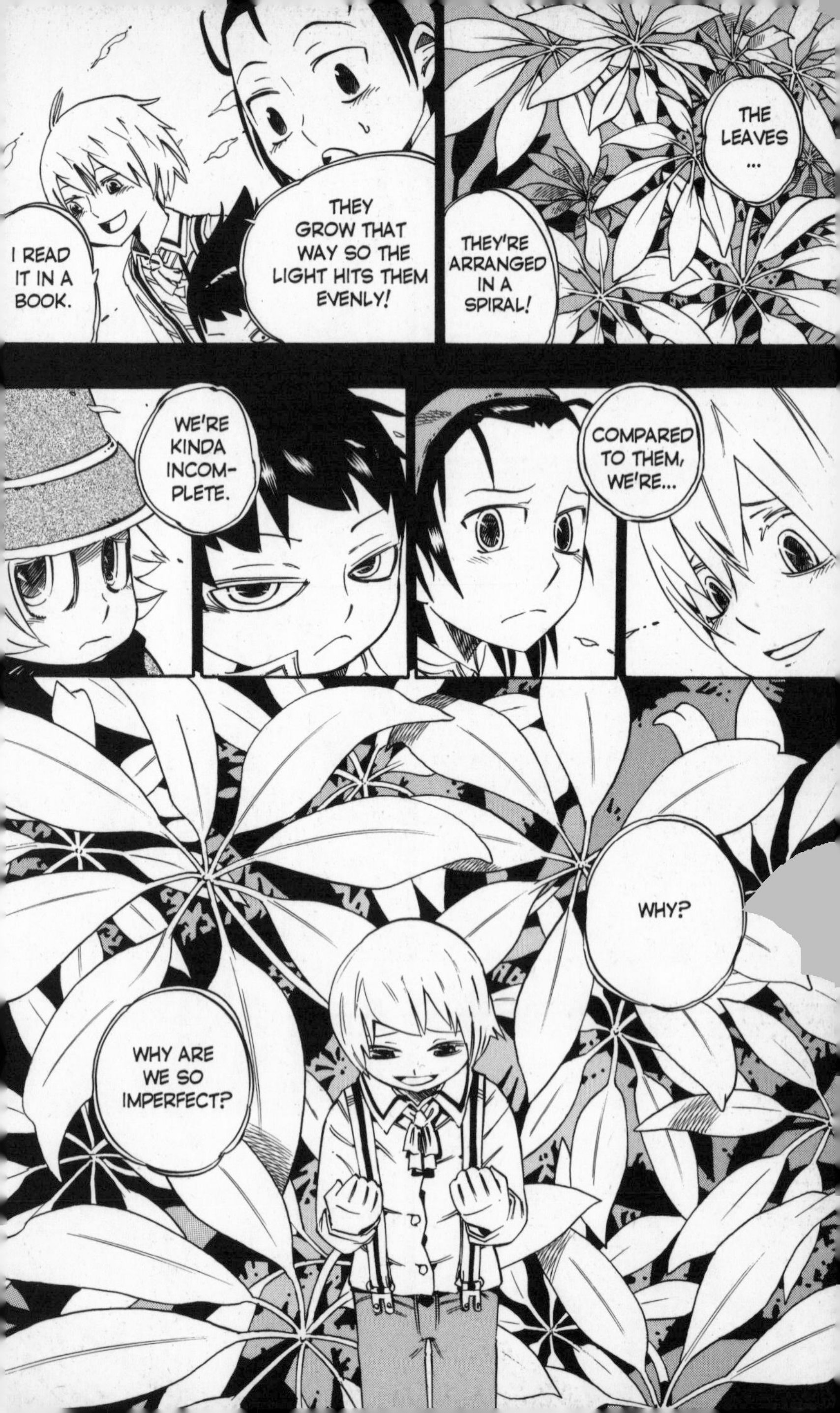
THE LEAVES ...
THEY'RE ARRANGED IN A SPIRAL!
THEY GROW THAT WAY SO THE LIGHT HITS THEM EVENLY!
I READ IT IN A BOOK.
COMPARED TO THEM, WE'RE...
WE'RE KINDA INCOM-PLETE.
WHY?
WHY ARE WE SO IMPERFECT?

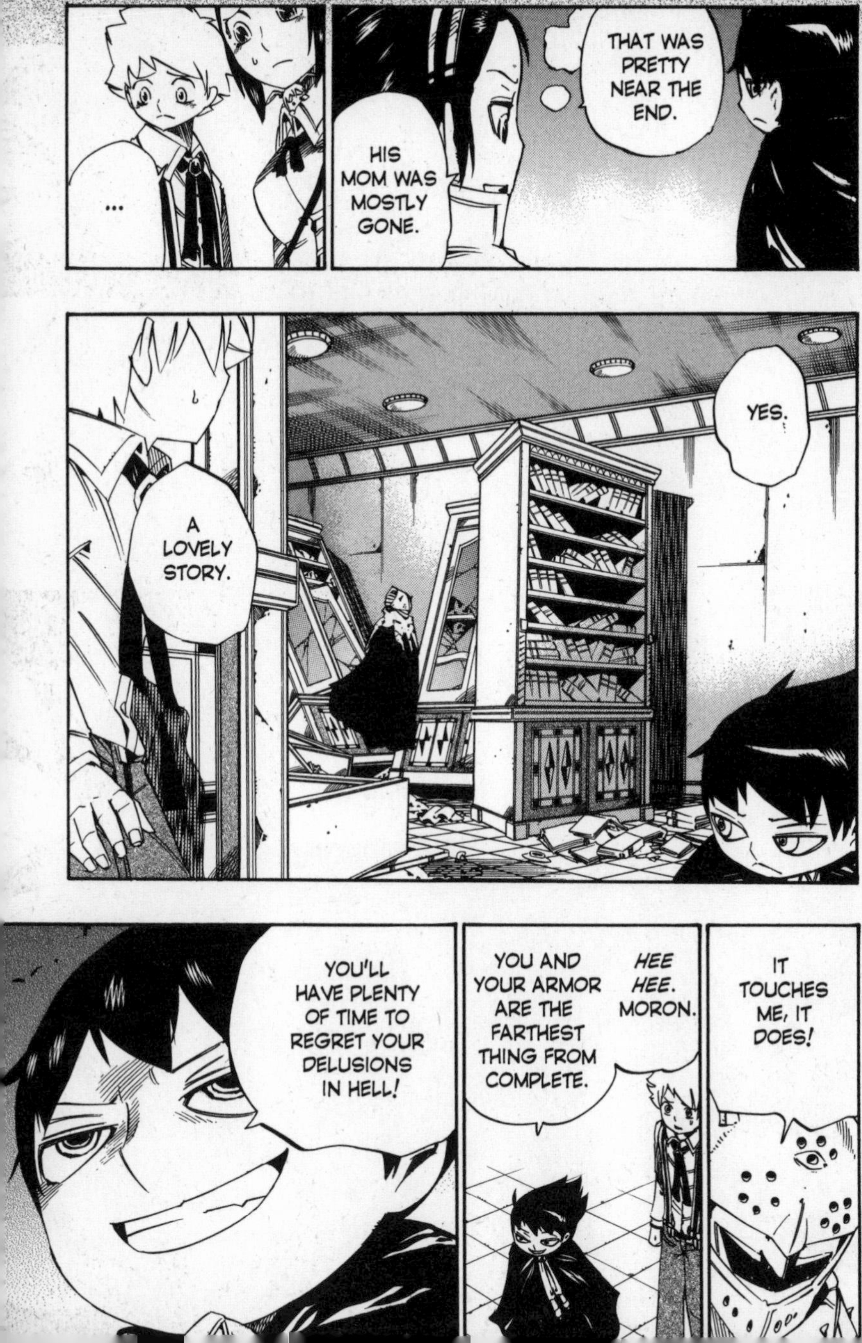

THAT WAS PRETTY NEAR THE END.
HIS MOM WAS MOSTLY GONE.
...
YES.
A LOVELY STORY.
IT TOUCHES ME, IT DOES!
HEE HEE. MORON.
YOU AND YOUR ARMOR ARE THE FARTHEST THING FROM COMPLETE.
YOU'LL HAVE PLENTY OF TIME TO REGRET YOUR DELUSIONS IN HELL!

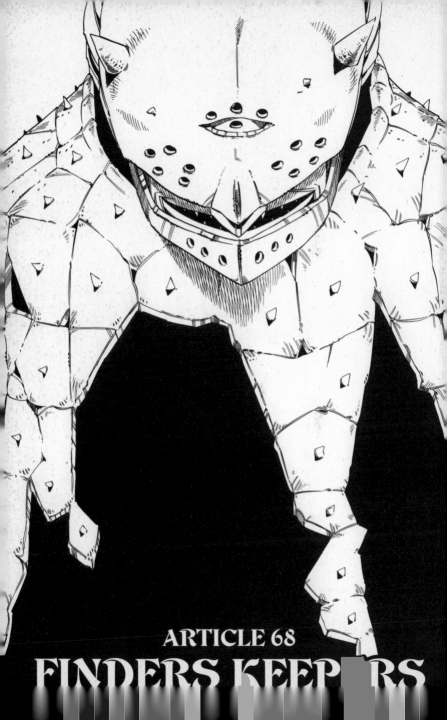

ARTICLE 68
FINDERS KEEPERS

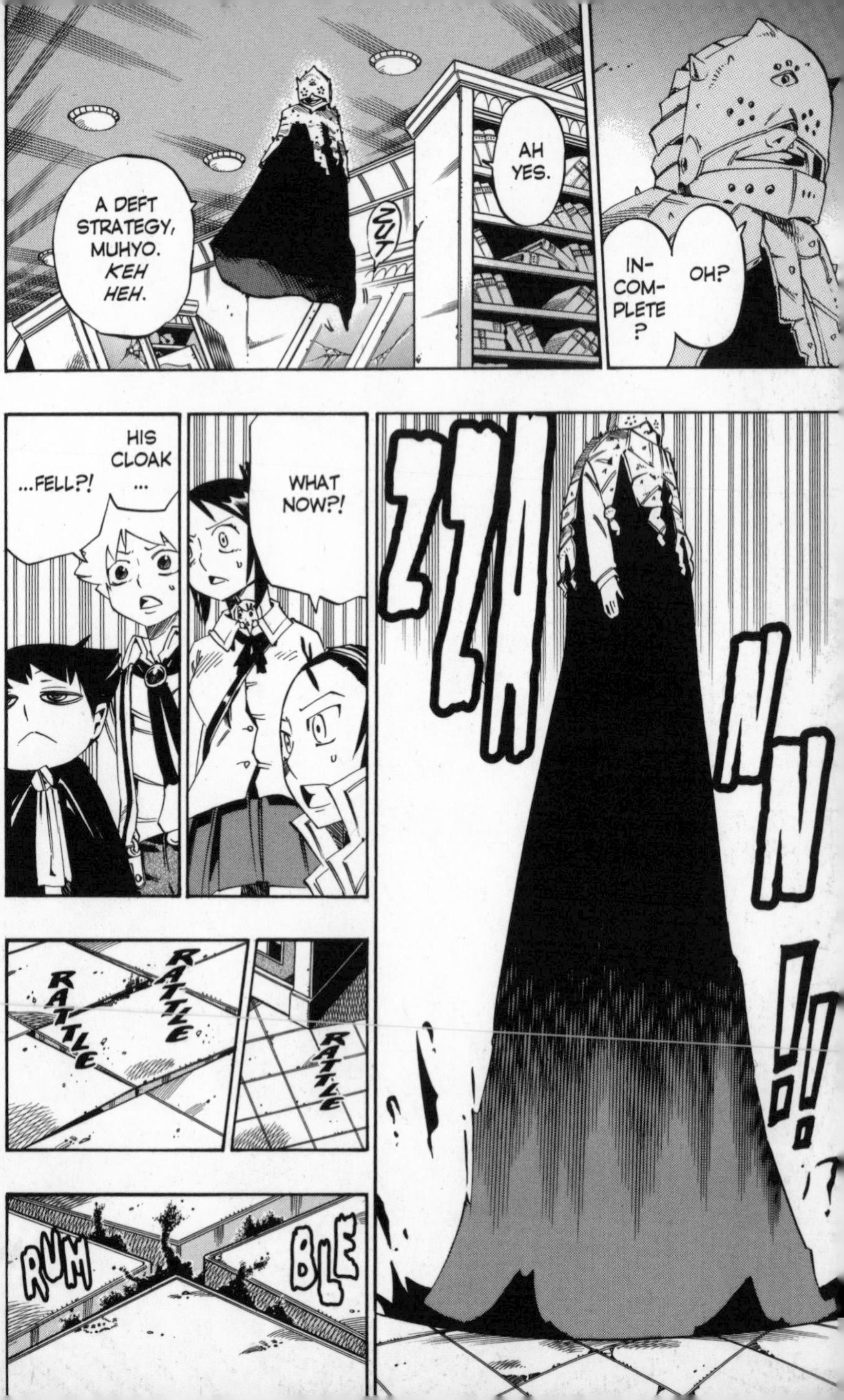
OH?
IN-COMPLETE?
AH YES.
ZUT
A DEFT STRATEGY, MUHYO. *KEH HEH.*
ZZHNN!!
WHAT NOW?!
HIS CLOAK...
...FELL?!
RATTLE
RATTLE
RATTLE
RUMBLE

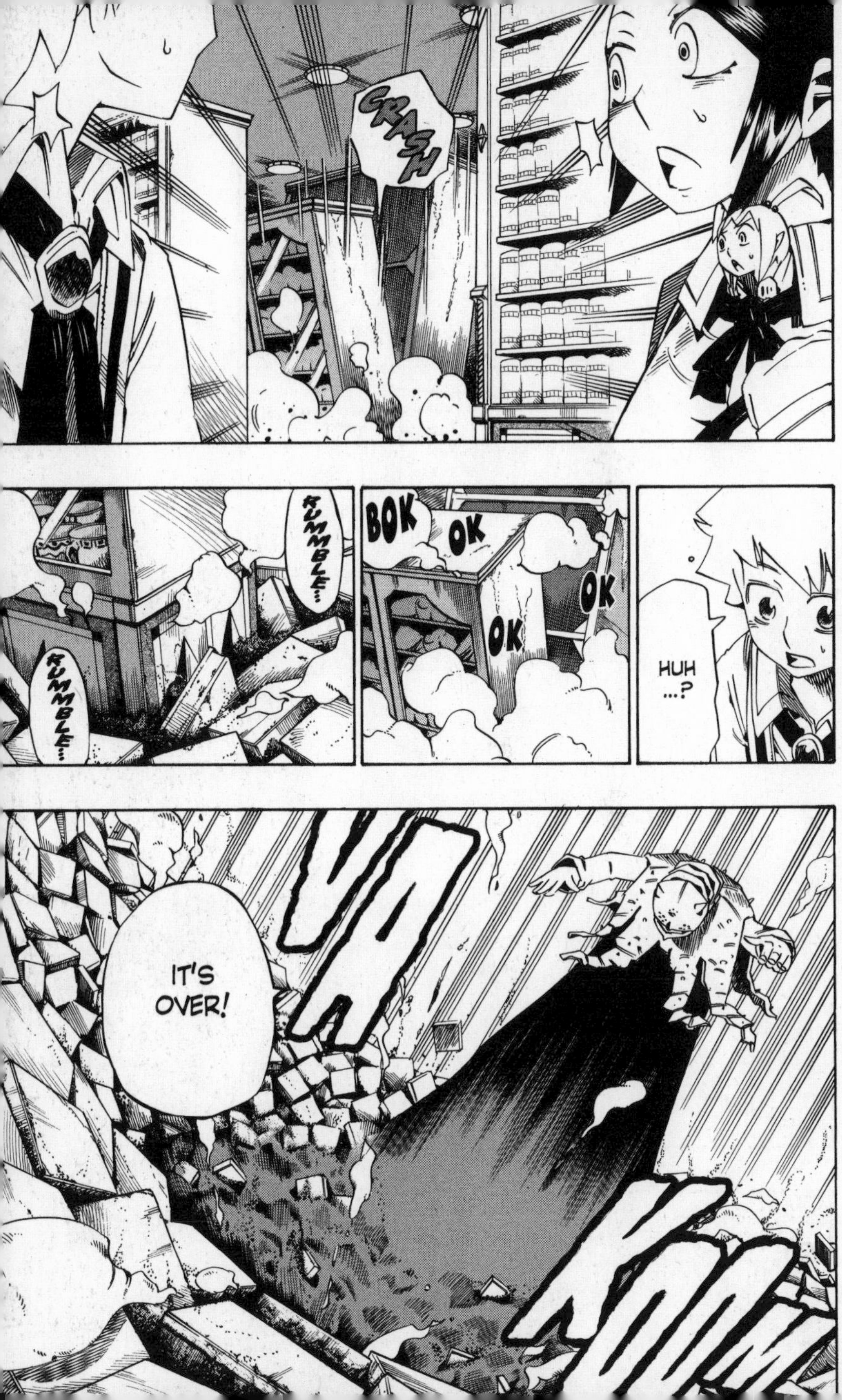
CRASH
HUH ...?
BOK
OK
OK
OK
RUMMBLE...
RUMMBLE...
IT'S OVER!

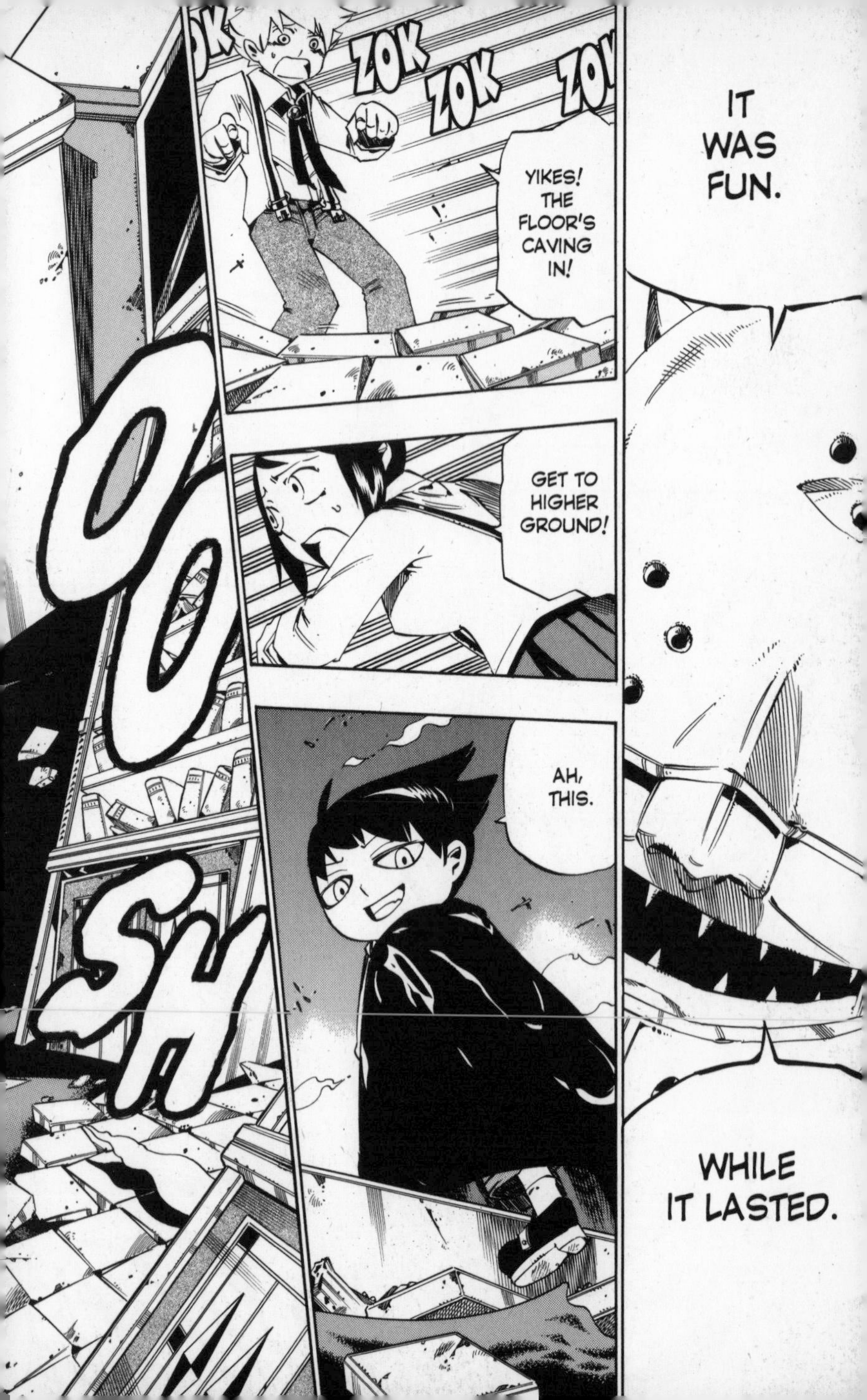
IT WAS FUN.
WHILE IT LASTED.
ZOK
ZOK
ZOK
ZOK
YIKES! THE FLOOR'S CAVING IN!
GET TO HIGHER GROUND!
AH, THIS.
OOSH

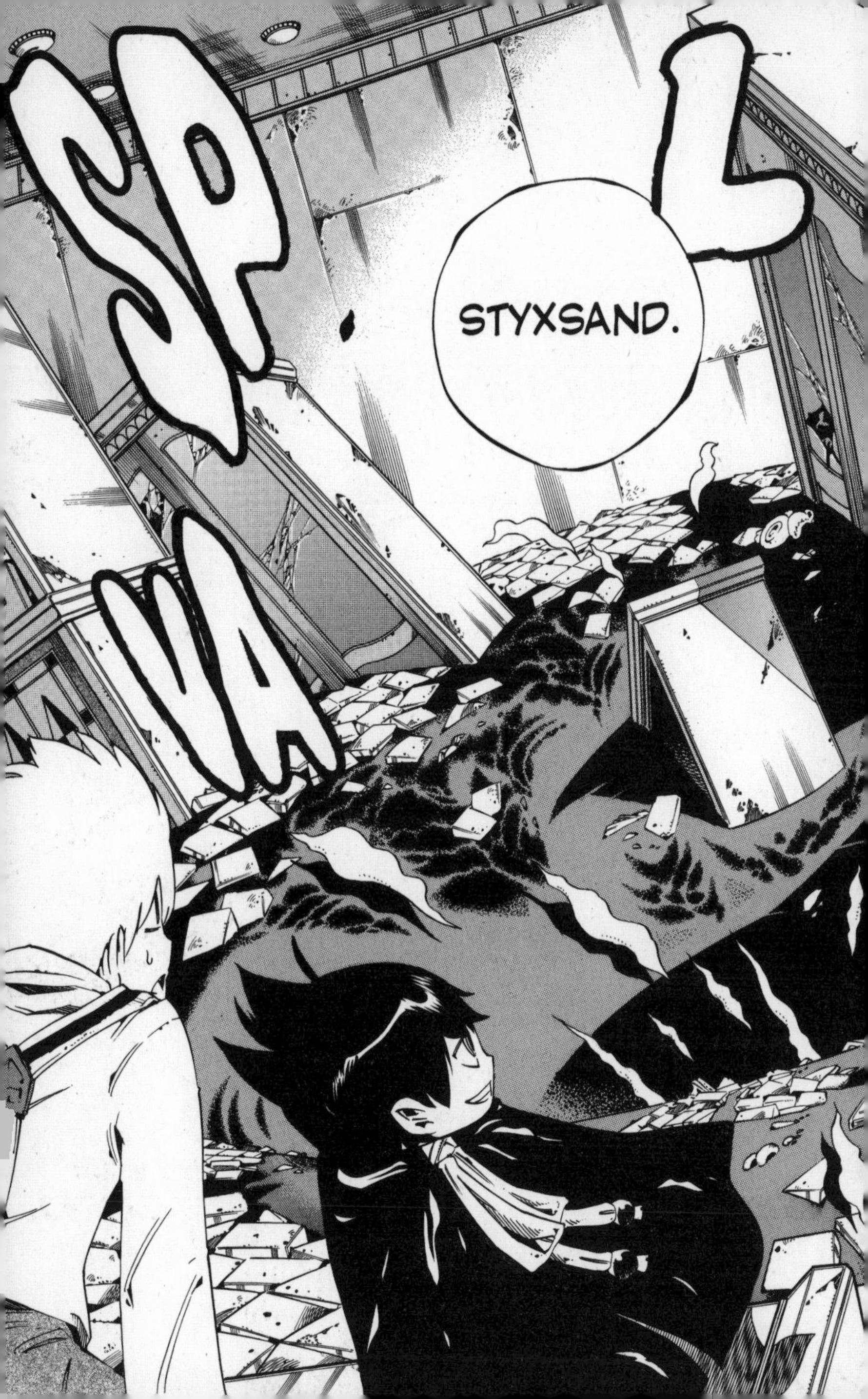
STYXSAND.

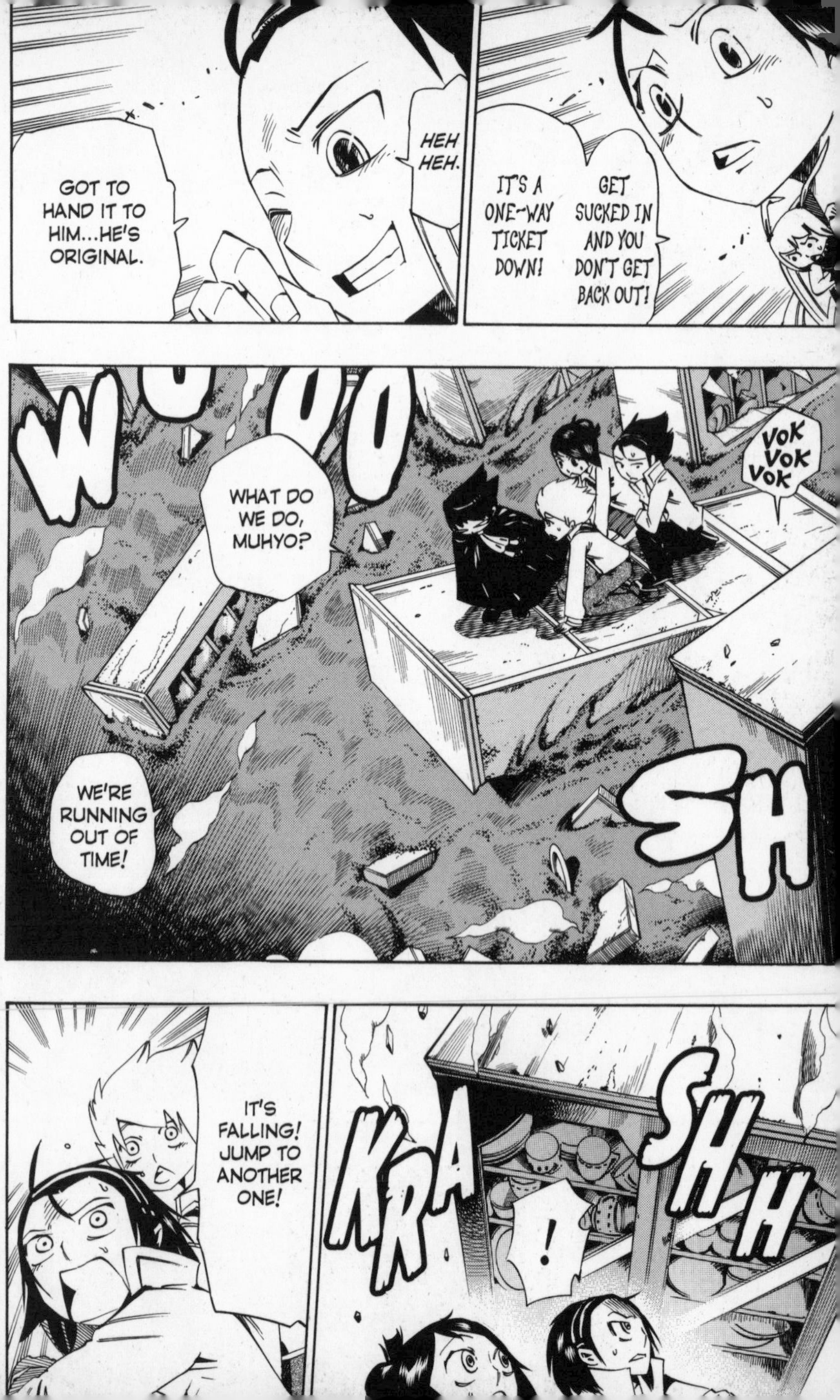
IT'S A ONE-WAY TICKET DOWN! GET SUCKED IN AND YOU DON'T GET BACK OUT!
HEH HEH.
GOT TO HAND IT TO HIM...HE'S ORIGINAL.
VOK VOK VOK
WOOO
WHAT DO WE DO, MUHYO?
SH
WE'RE RUNNING OUT OF TIME!
KRA
SHHH
!
IT'S FALLING! JUMP TO ANOTHER ONE!

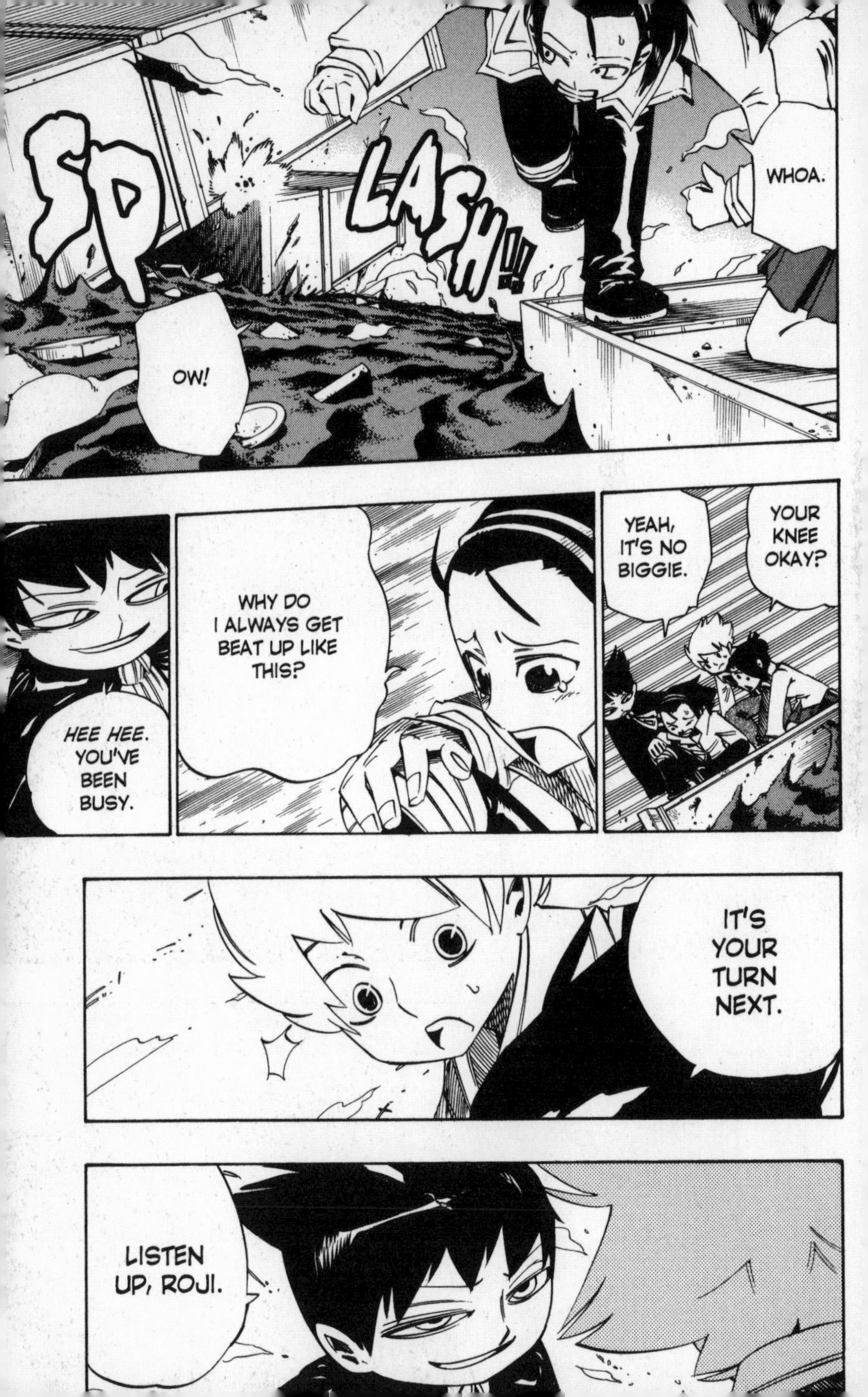
WHOA.
SPLASH!!
OW!
YOUR KNEE OKAY?
YEAH, IT'S NO BIGGIE.
WHY DO I ALWAYS GET BEAT UP LIKE THIS?
HEE HEE. YOU'VE BEEN BUSY.
IT'S YOUR TURN NEXT.
LISTEN UP, ROJI.

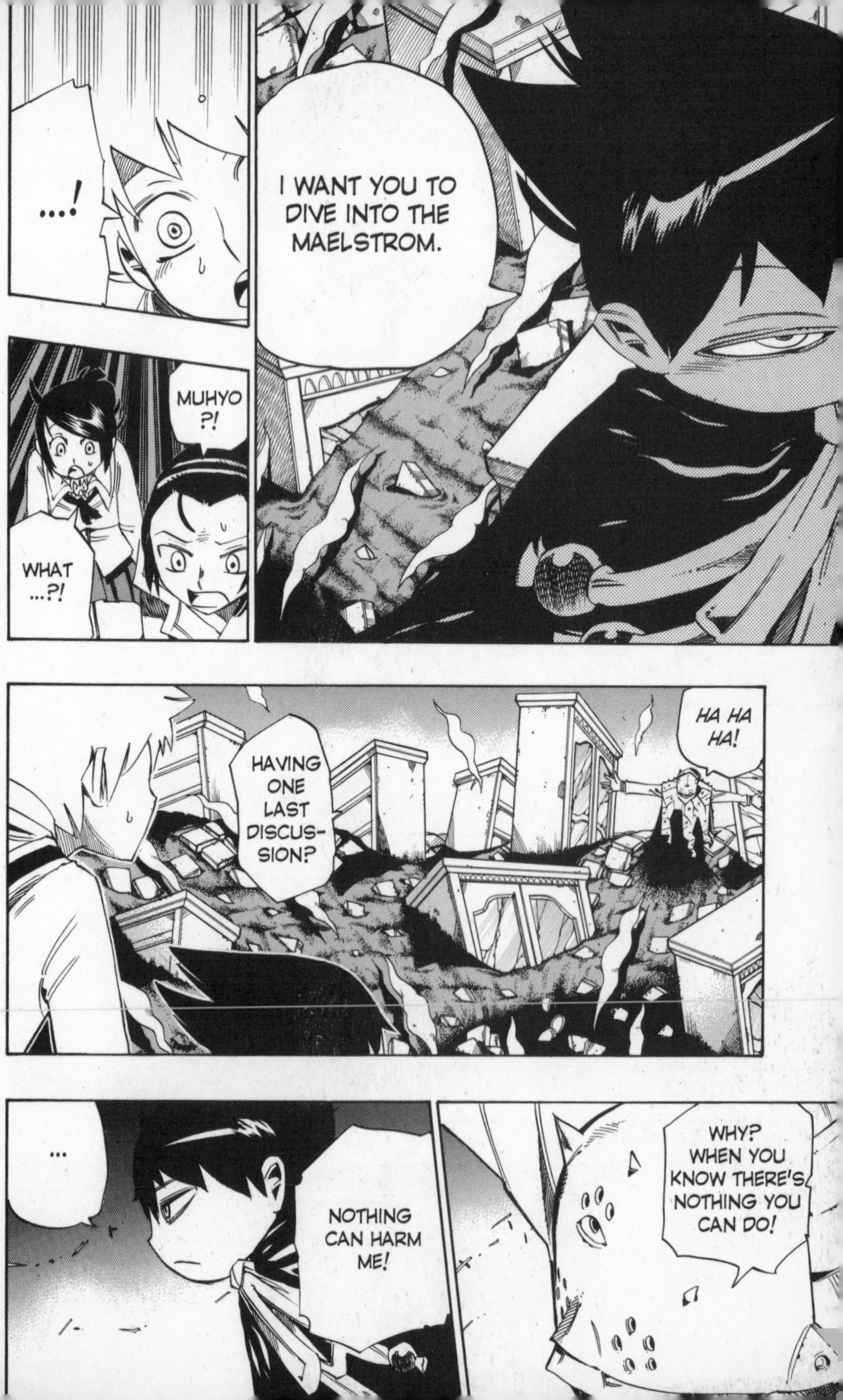
I WANT YOU TO DIVE INTO THE MAELSTROM.
...!
MUHYO ?!
WHAT ...?!
HA HA HA!
HAVING ONE LAST DISCUSSION?
WHY? WHEN YOU KNOW THERE'S NOTHING YOU CAN DO!
NOTHING CAN HARM ME!
...

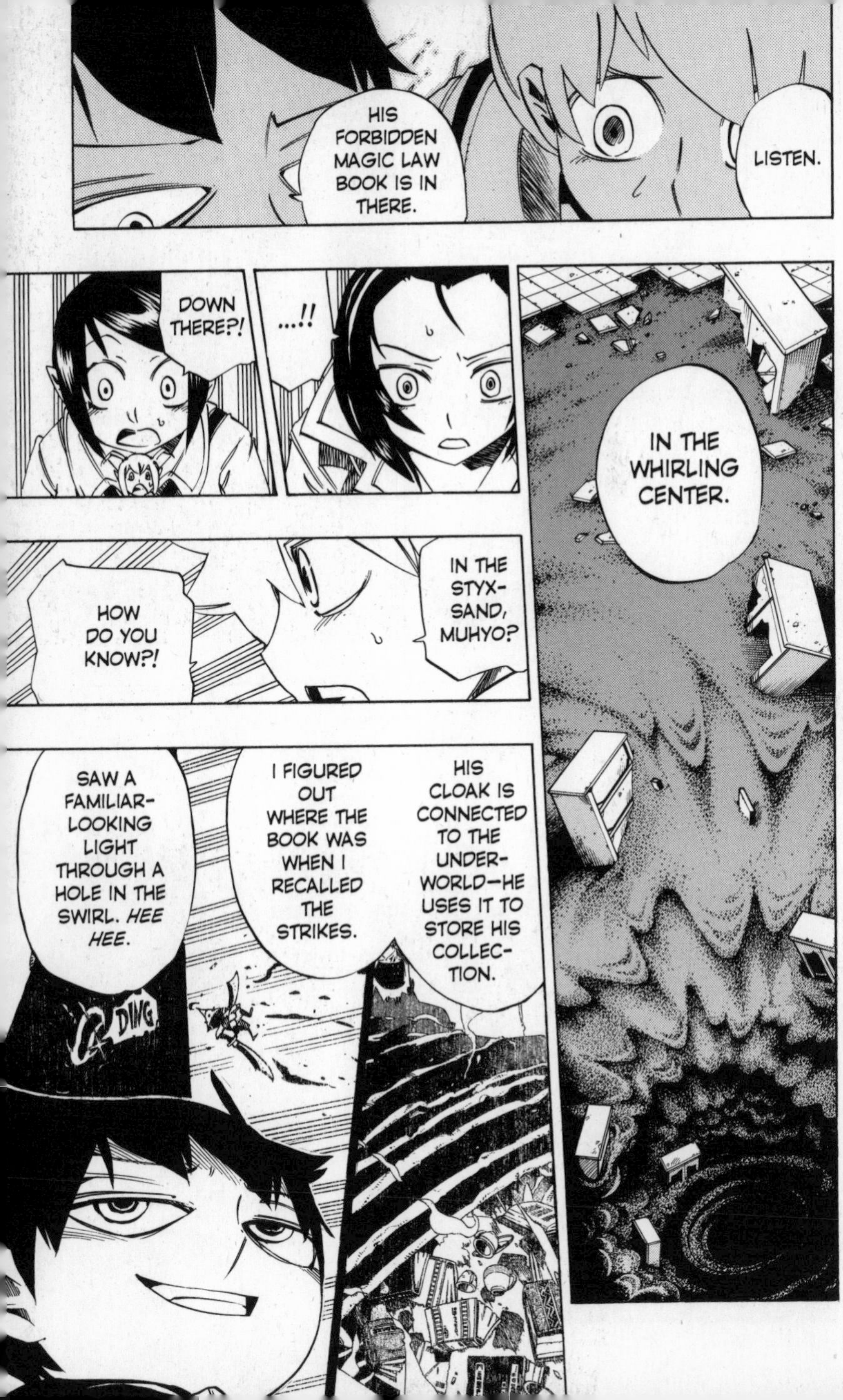
LISTEN.
HIS FORBIDDEN MAGIC LAW BOOK IS IN THERE.
IN THE WHIRLING CENTER.
...!!
DOWN THERE?!
IN THE STYX-SAND, MUHYO?
HOW DO YOU KNOW?!
HIS CLOAK IS CONNECTED TO THE UNDER-WORLD—HE USES IT TO STORE HIS COLLEC-TION.
I FIGURED OUT WHERE THE BOOK WAS WHEN I RECALLED THE STRIKES.
SAW A FAMILIAR-LOOKING LIGHT THROUGH A HOLE IN THE SWIRL. *HEE HEE*.
DING

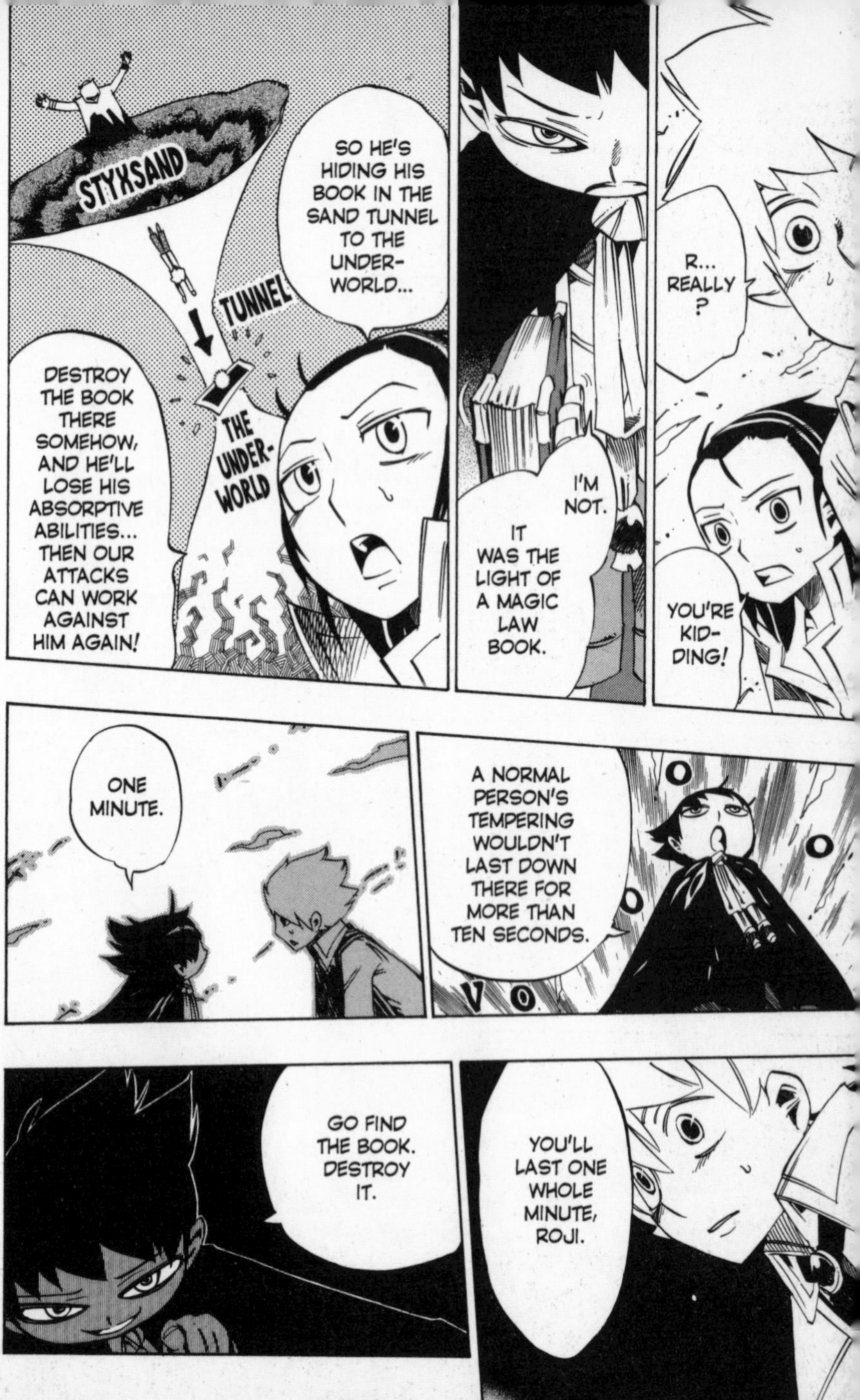
R... REALLY?
YOU'RE KIDDING!
I'M NOT.
IT WAS THE LIGHT OF A MAGIC LAW BOOK.
SO HE'S HIDING HIS BOOK IN THE SAND TUNNEL TO THE UNDERWORLD...
STYXSAND
TUNNEL
THE UNDERWORLD
DESTROY THE BOOK THERE SOMEHOW, AND HE'LL LOSE HIS ABSORPTIVE ABILITIES... THEN OUR ATTACKS CAN WORK AGAINST HIM AGAIN!
A NORMAL PERSON'S TEMPERING WOULDN'T LAST DOWN THERE FOR MORE THAN TEN SECONDS.
VO
ONE MINUTE.
YOU'LL LAST ONE WHOLE MINUTE, ROJI.
GO FIND THE BOOK. DESTROY IT.

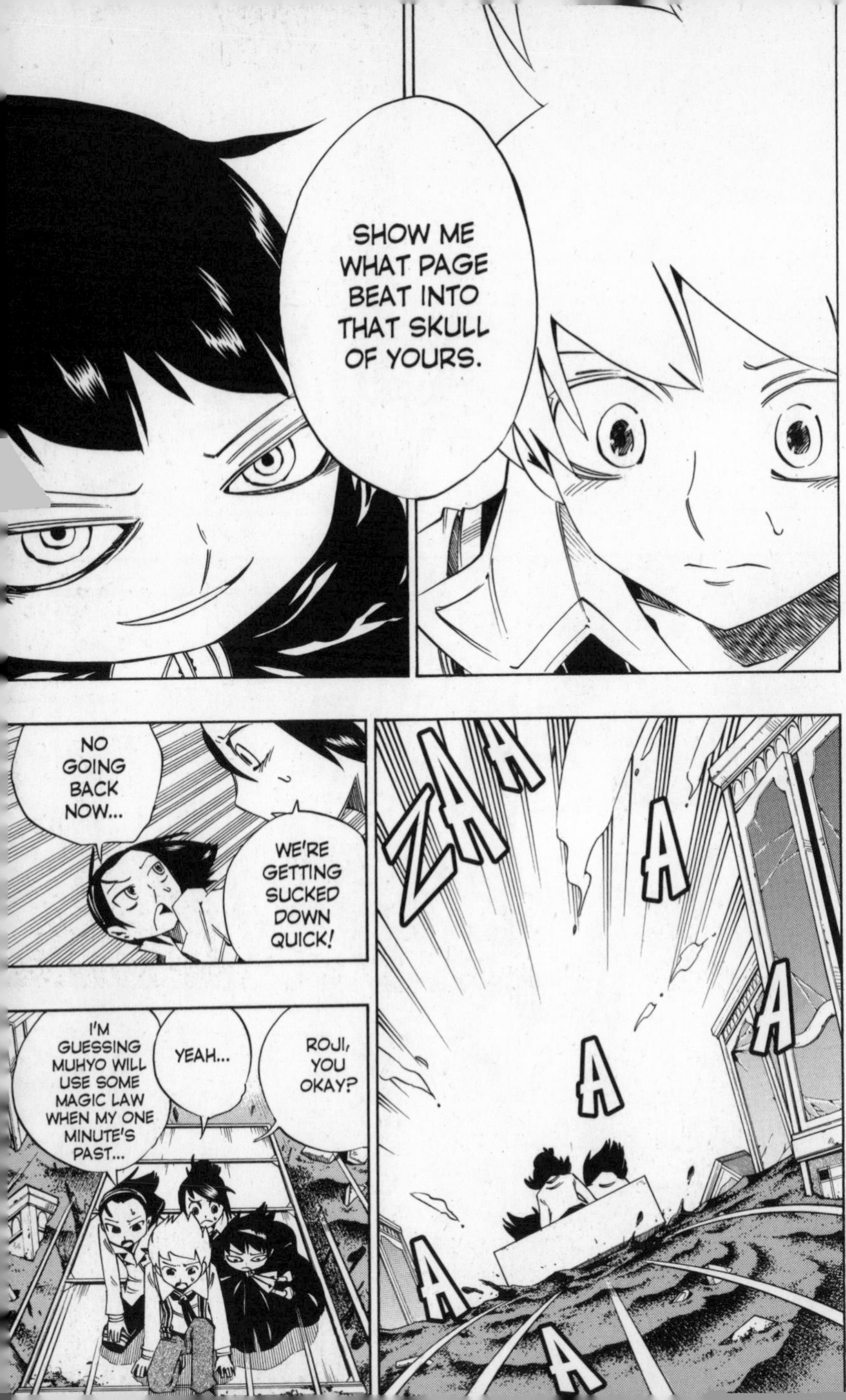
SHOW ME WHAT PAGE BEAT INTO THAT SKULL OF YOURS.
ZAAAAAA
WE'RE GETTING SUCKED DOWN QUICK!
NO GOING BACK NOW...
ROJI, YOU OKAY?
YEAH...
I'M GUESSING MUHYO WILL USE SOME MAGIC LAW WHEN MY ONE MINUTE'S PAST...

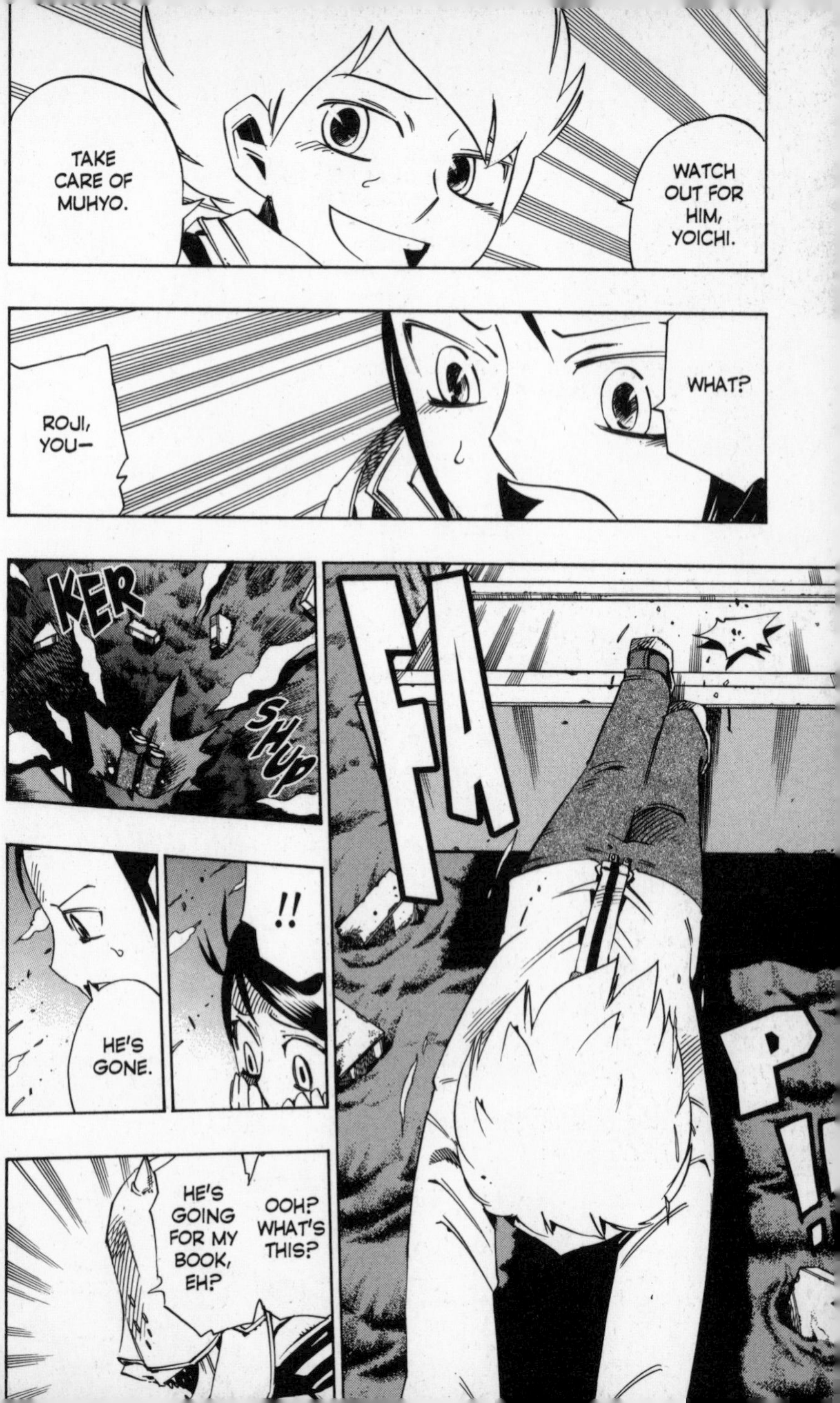
WATCH OUT FOR HIM, YOICHI.
TAKE CARE OF MUHYO.
WHAT?
ROJI, YOU—
FA
P!!
KER
SHUP
!!
HE'S GONE.
OOH? WHAT'S THIS?
HE'S GOING FOR MY BOOK, EH?

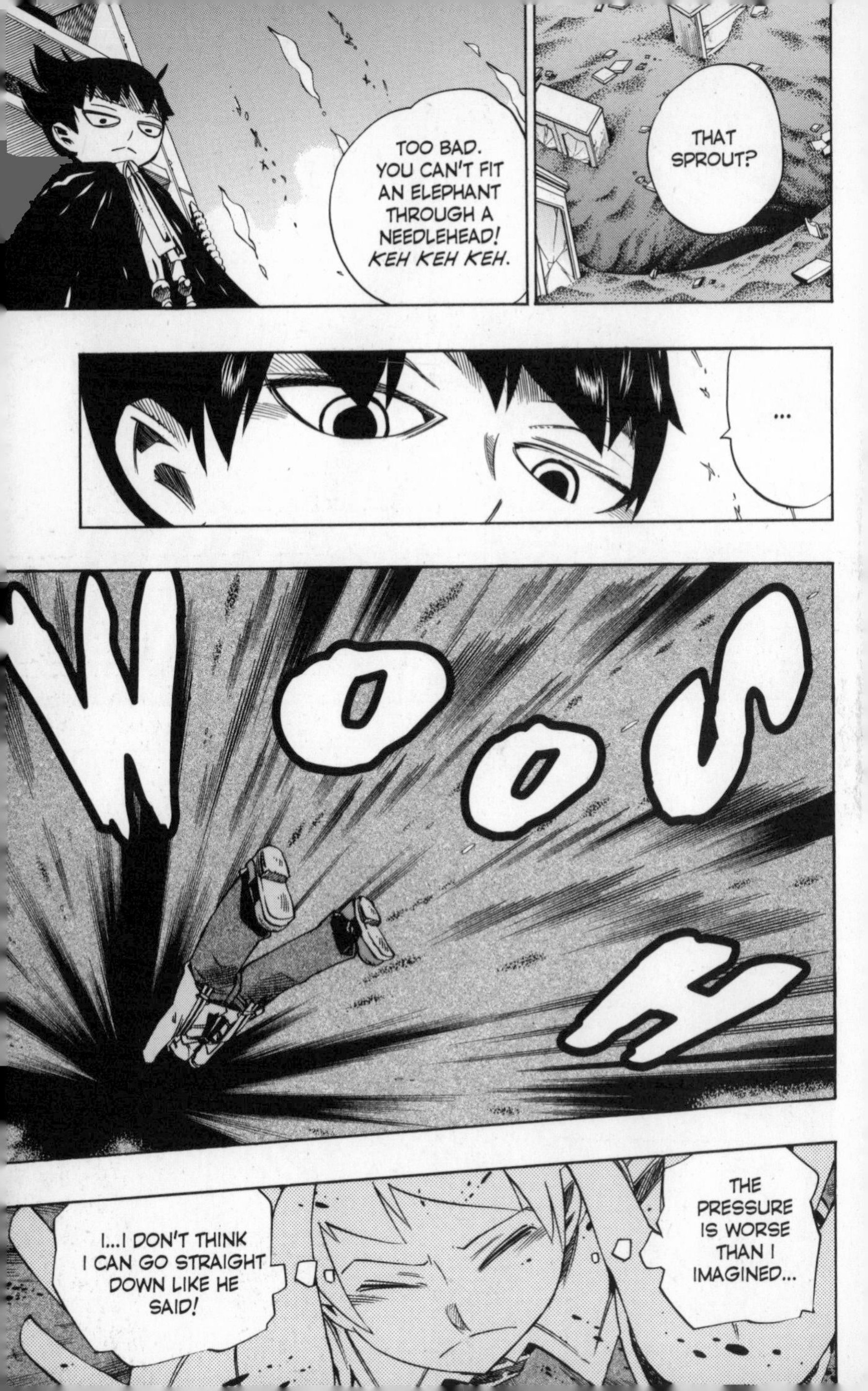
THAT SPROUT?
TOO BAD. YOU CAN'T FIT AN ELEPHANT THROUGH A NEEDLEHEAD! *KEH KEH KEH.*
...
WHOOSH
THE PRESSURE IS WORSE THAN I IMAGINED...
I...I DON'T THINK I CAN GO STRAIGHT DOWN LIKE HE SAID!

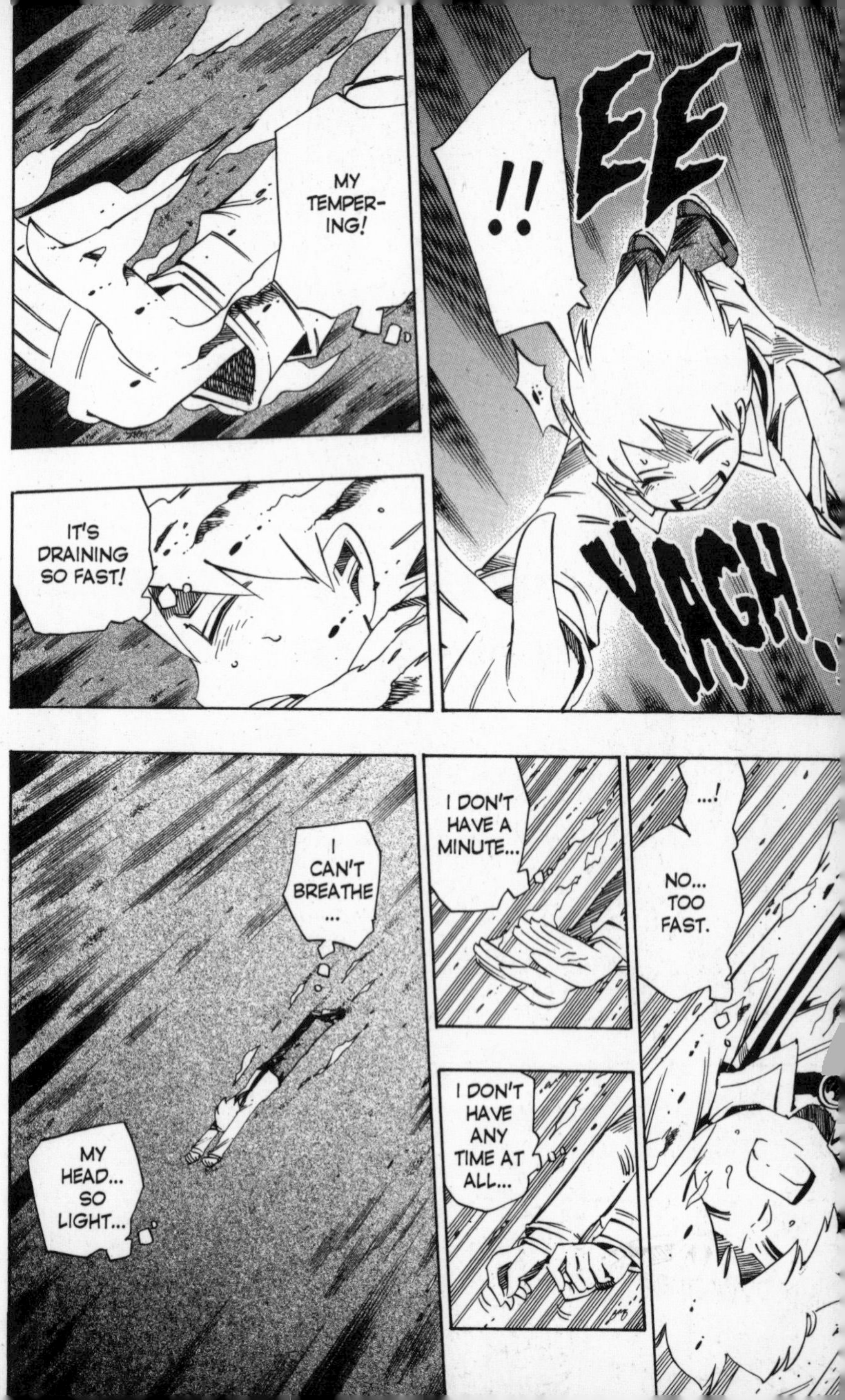
!!
EE
YAGH...
MY TEMPERING!
IT'S DRAINING SO FAST!
...!
NO... TOO FAST.
I DON'T HAVE A MINUTE...
I DON'T HAVE ANY TIME AT ALL...
I CAN'T BREATHE...
MY HEAD... SO LIGHT...

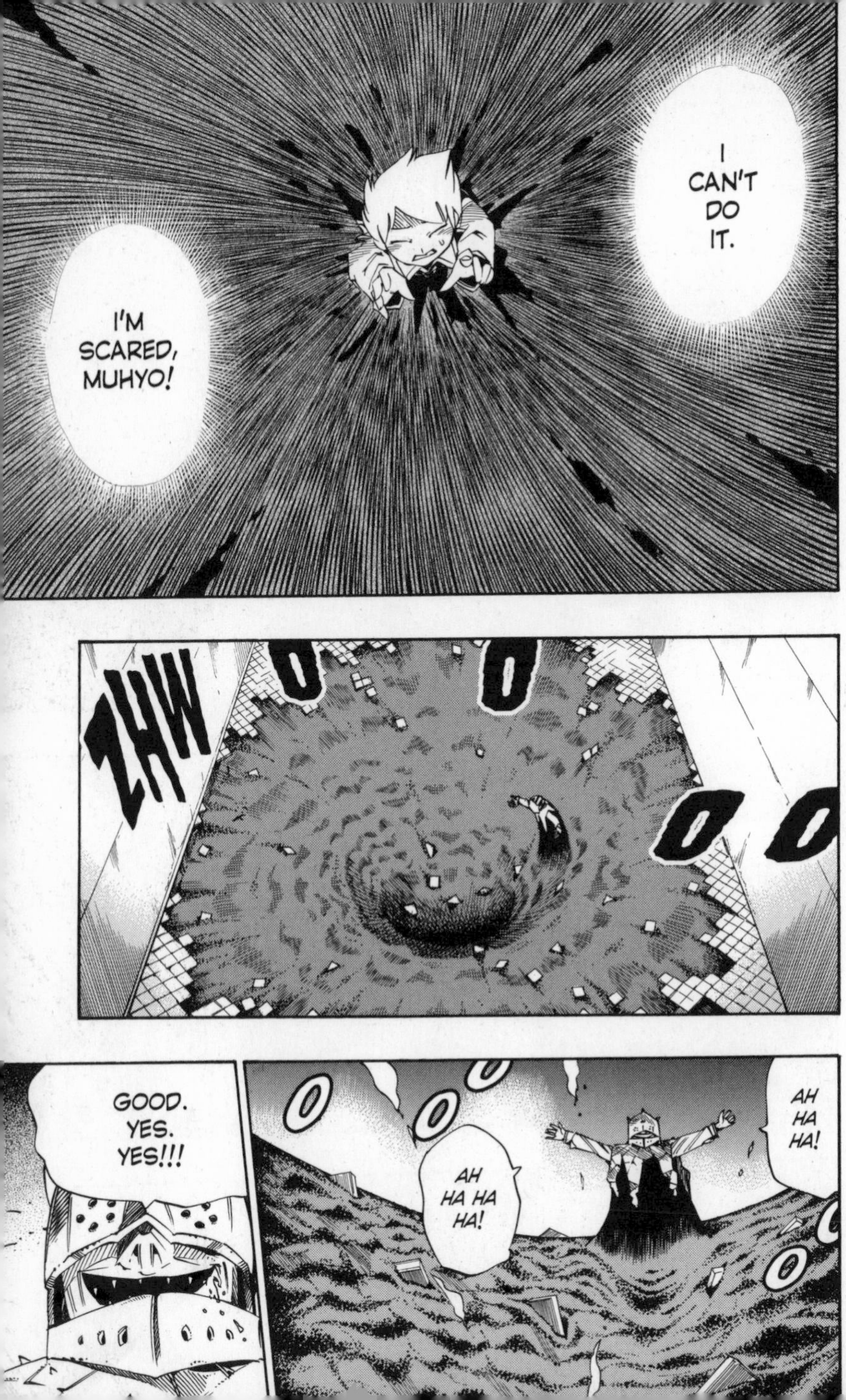
I CAN'T DO IT.
I'M SCARED, MUHYO!
ZHWOOOO
AH HA HA!
AH HA HA HA!
GOOD. YES. YES!!!

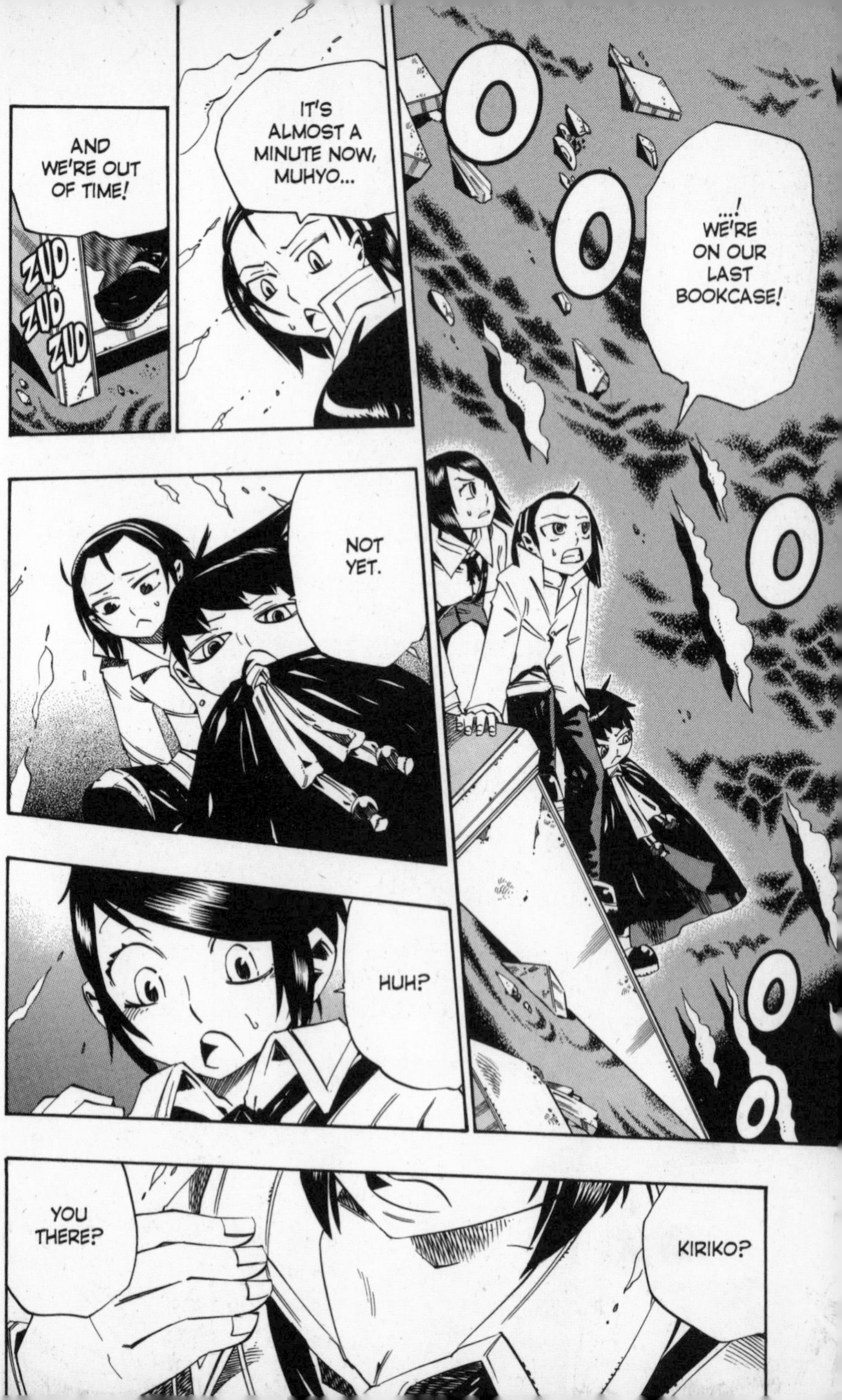
...! WE'RE ON OUR LAST BOOKCASE!
IT'S ALMOST A MINUTE NOW, MUHYO...
AND WE'RE OUT OF TIME!
ZUD ZUD ZUD
NOT YET.
HUH?
KIRIKO?
YOU THERE?

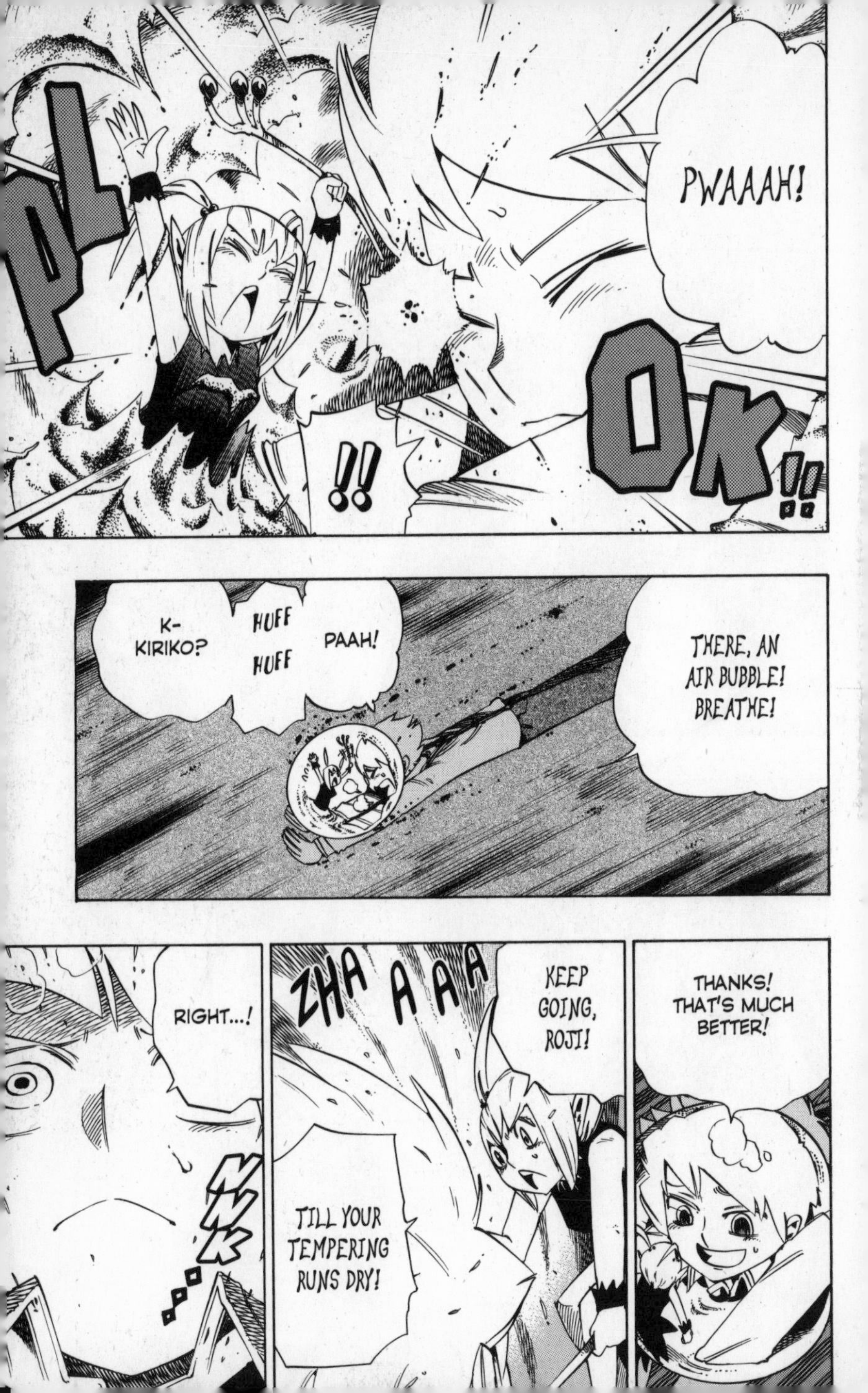
PWAAAH!
PLOK!!
!!
THERE, AN AIR BUBBLE! BREATHE!
PAAH!
HUFF HUFF
K- KIRIKO?
THANKS! THAT'S MUCH BETTER!
KEEP GOING, ROJI!
TILL YOUR TEMPERING RUNS DRY!
ZHA A A A
RIGHT...!
NNK

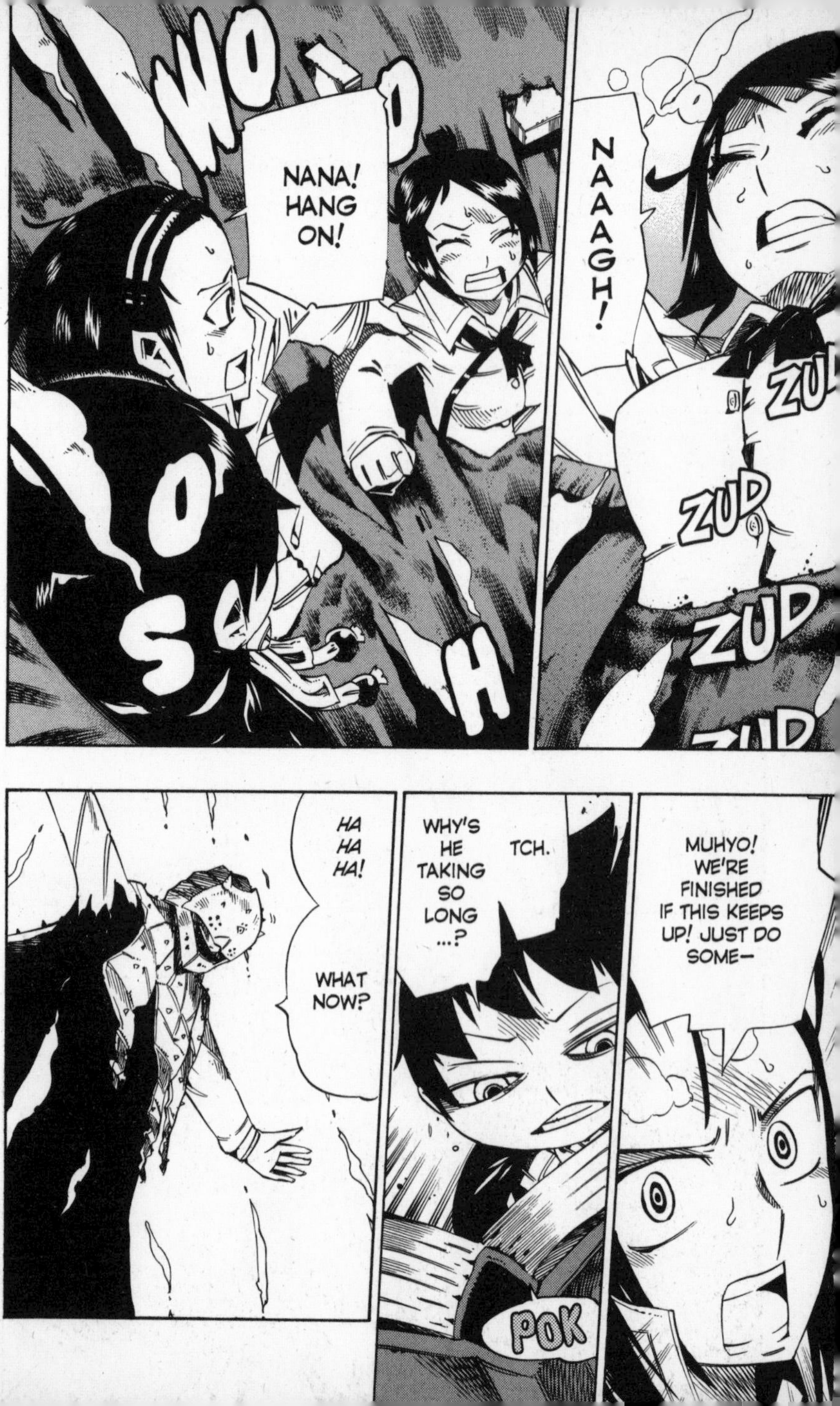
NAAAAGH!
ZUD
ZUD
ZUD
NANA! HANG ON!
MUHYO! WE'RE FINISHED IF THIS KEEPS UP! JUST DO SOME—
POK
TCH.
WHY'S HE TAKING SO LONG ...?
HA HA HA!
WHAT NOW?

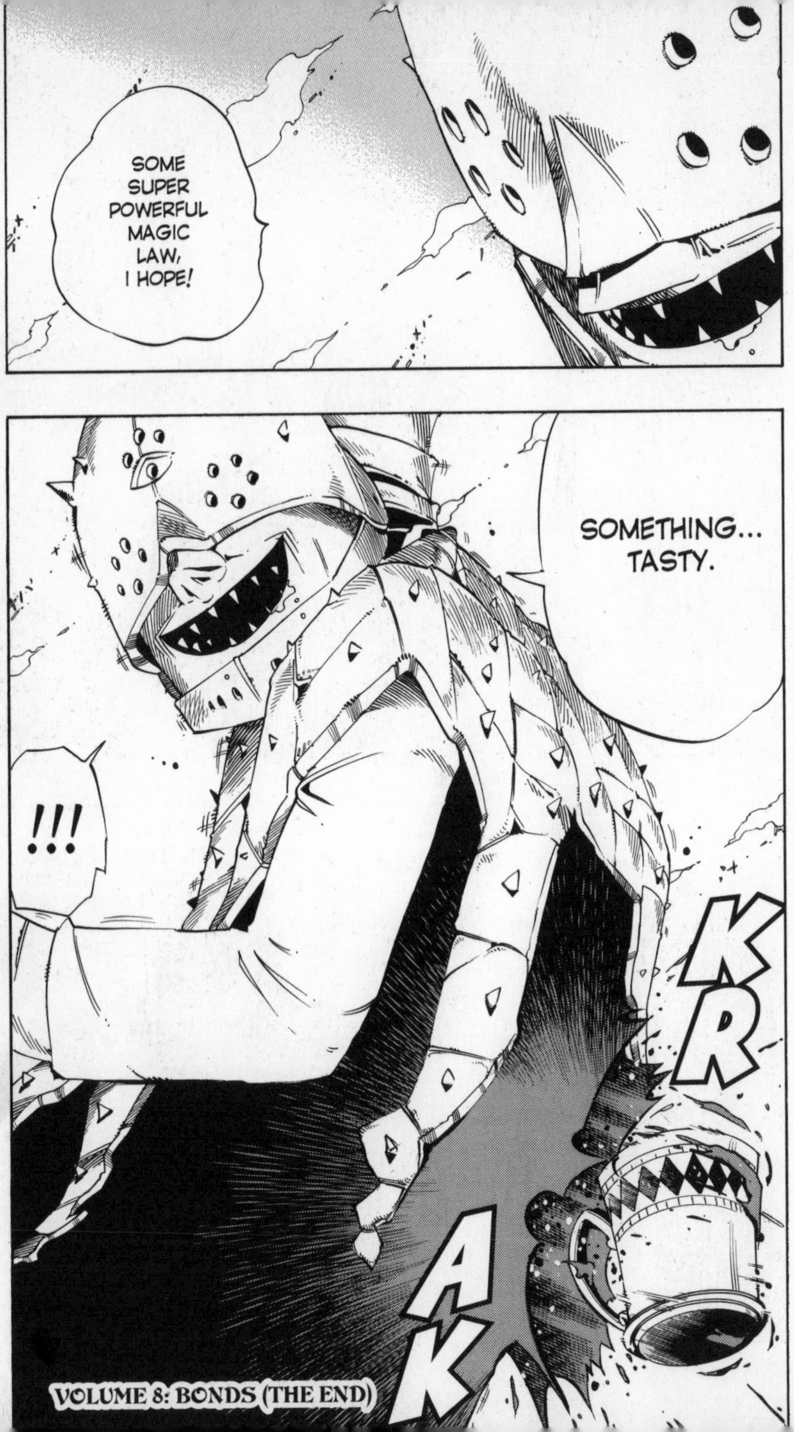
SOME SUPER POWERFUL MAGIC LAW, I HOPE!
SOMETHING... TASTY.
KRAK
!!!
VOLUME 8: BONDS (THE END)

In The Next Volume...

Who is this mysterious girl and what's her business with Roji? One thing's for sure—Ark's up to something sinister!

Available February 2009!

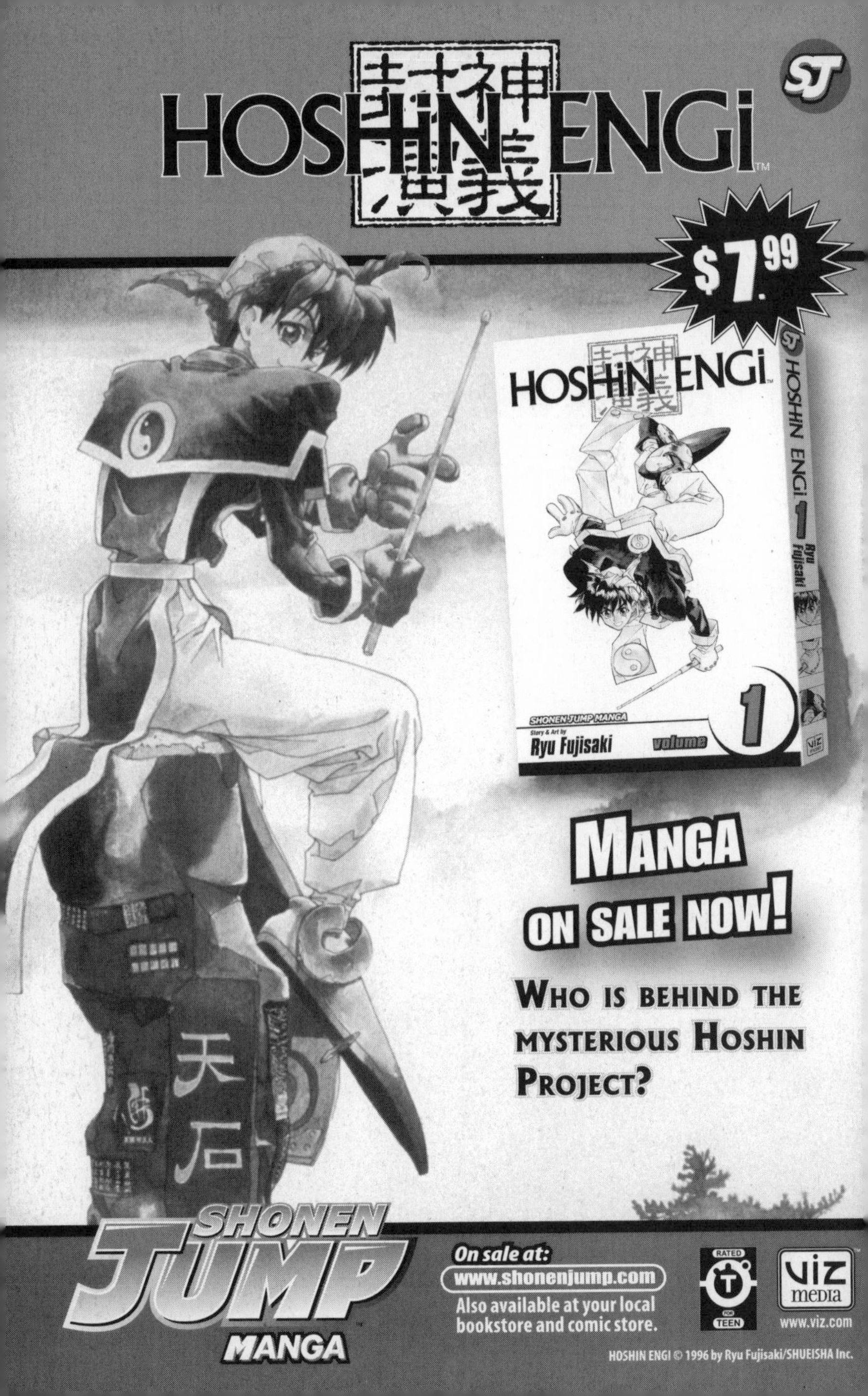
SJ
HOSHiN ENGi™
封神演義
$7.99
SJ
HOSHiN ENGi
HOSHiN ENGi 1
Ryu Fujisaki
SHONEN JUMP MANGA
Story & Art by
Ryu Fujisaki
volume 1
MANGA
ON SALE NOW!
WHO IS BEHIND THE MYSTERIOUS HOSHIN PROJECT?
SHONEN JUMP MANGA
On sale at:
www.shonenjump.com
Also available at your local bookstore and comic store.
RATED T FOR TEEN
VIZ media
www.viz.com
HOSHIN ENGI © 1996 by Ryu Fujisaki/SHUEISHA Inc.

SHONEN JUMP

THE WORLD'S MOST POPULAR MANGA

12 ISSUES FOR ONLY $29.95*

THAT'S 50% OFF THE NEWSSTAND PRICE!

Each issue of SHONEN JUMP contains the coolest manga available in the U.S., anime news, and info on video & card games, toys AND more!

SUBSCRIBE TODAY and Become a Member of the SJ Sub Club!

- **ENJOY** 12 HUGE action-packed issues
- **SAVE** 50% OFF the cover price
- **ACCESS** exclusive areas of www.shonenjump.com
- **RECEIVE** FREE members-only gifts

Available ONLY to Subscribers!